DEMOCRACY IN EXILE

A volume in the series

The United States in the World

Edited by Mark Philip Bradley, David C. Engerman, Amy S. Greenberg, and Paul A. Kramer

A list of titles in this series is available at cornellpress.cornell.edu.

DEMOCRACY IN EXILE

Hans Speier and the Rise of the Defense Intellectual

Daniel Bessner

Cornell University Press
Ithaca and London

First published 2018 by Cornell University Press

Printed in the United States of America

Library of Congress Cataloging-in-Publication Data

Names: Bessner, Daniel, 1984– author.
Title: Democracy in exile : Hans Speier and the rise of the defense intellectual / Daniel Bessner.
Description: Ithaca : Cornell University Press, 2018. | Series: The United States in the world | Includes bibliographical references and index.
Identifiers: LCCN 2017041352 (print) | LCCN 2017043061 (ebook) | ISBN 9781501709395 (pdf) | ISBN 9781501712036 (epub/mobi) | ISBN 9780801453038 | ISBN 9780801453038 (print : alk. paper)
Subjects: LCSH: Speier, Hans. | Sociologists—United States—Biography. | Sociologists—Germany—Biography. | Exiles—Germany—Biography. | National security—United States—History—20th century. | United States—Foreign relations—1945–1989. | United States—Intellectual life—20th century.
Classification: LCC HM479.S (ebook) | LCC HM479.S B47 2018 (print) | DDC 301.092 [B]—dc23
LC record available at https://lccn.loc.gov/2017041352

Cornell University Press strives to use environmentally responsible suppliers and materials to the fullest extent possible in the publishing of its books. Such materials include vegetable-based, low-VOC inks and acid-free papers that are recycled, totally chlorine-free, or partly composed of nonwood fibers. For further information, visit our website at cornellpress.cornell.edu.

To my parents,
Jody and Glen Bessner

A free-floating intelligentsia . . . is not going to show us the way out of the crisis.

—Hans Speier, as recounted by Henry Kellerman, 1990

[Hans Speier was] a scholar who looked modernity in the eye and did not blink.

—Ira Katznelson, 1990

Contents

Preface

This book tells the story of a German-born academic who became one of the early Cold War's most influential American defense intellectuals. It is a story of catastrophe, exile, and success; of rejecting youthful values for more "realistic" alternatives; of a scholar becoming an expert. It is above all a story about how an idea that we currently take for granted—that social scientists ensconced in think tanks and universities should have a voice in foreign policymaking—was institutionalized.

Few historians have heard of Hans Speier (1905–1990). He is at present what I call a "lister"—a person mentioned in lists of midcentury intellectuals (and usually toward the end). Though I cannot be certain exactly why this is the case, I have my suspicions. Speier never wrote a major book and was associated with the RAND Corporation's Social Science Division, which has always been overshadowed by RAND's more prominent Economics Division. Speier was bound to escape the attention of historians interested in examining intellectuals who clearly influenced their fields and disciplines of study. Unlike many in his exile cohort, including Hannah Arendt (his classmate at Heidelberg University), Hans Morgenthau (his realist associate), and Leo Strauss (his colleague at the New School for Social Research and one of his closest friends), until this book Speier had not received a biographical treatment.

Despite his being ignored, Speier stood at the center of—and shaped—some of the twentieth century's most vibrant intellectual and government institutions. He was one of the founding members of the New School's University in Exile in the 1930s; was in charge of the Foreign Broadcast Intelligence Service group that assembled intelligence from Nazi propaganda between 1942 and 1944; was director of the Office of War Information committee that developed policy for U.S. propaganda sent to Germany in 1944–1945; was associate chief of the State Department's Area Division for Occupied Areas in 1946–1947; and was founding head of RAND's Social Science Division from 1948 to 1960. By virtue of these positions, Speier remade what it meant to be an intellectual in the twentieth-century United States.

Today social scientists regularly move between the academy, think tanks, and the government. But this was not always the case. Reconstructing Speier's trajectory illuminates the critical role he played in developing the ideas, culture, networks, and institutions that enable such movements to occur. At the same time, Speier's path captures a pivotal shift in American intellectual history in which hundreds of social scientists, both native and foreign born, left the university and contributed to the creation of an expert-based approach to U.S. foreign relations. To understand the rise of the defense intellectual, we must understand Hans Speier.

A brief note on sources: The RAND Corporation has graciously allowed me to quote extensively from and to cite their materials. However, I would like to highlight that throughout the book, I cite papers written by members of RAND that were given the designation "D." These reports were intended to be preliminary, working papers and not authoritative accounts of the subjects being examined. I expect readers to keep this in mind when I discuss such texts. Moreover, unless otherwise noted, all translations from the German are my own.

Acknowledgments

Hans Speier, the subject of this book, once wrote that "on the whole, I am no friend of intellectual biographers. They write assuming that their intellectual history interests readers as much as themselves. It rarely does, save for St. Augustine or Montaigne or Richard Burton . . . with Jean Jacques Rousseau on the borderline." If this book in any way proves Speier wrong, it is only because I have received the generous support of family members, friends, and colleagues over the years. I am grateful to have the opportunity to now thank them.

This book began as a dissertation undertaken in the Department of History at Duke University, where I worked with a group of historians whose guidance, encouragement, and criticisms informed and strengthened the project from its earliest stages. My *Doktorvater*, Malachi Hacohen, inspired both my subject of choice—an intellectual exile—and my method—intellectual biography—and his influence permeates this entire book. Anyone who knows Malachi is aware that he is a profoundly generous and incisive historian, and it was an honor to work closely with him for many years. At Duke, I was also fortunate to study under Alex Roland and Ed Balleisen, whose perceptive comments repeatedly pushed me in directions that have increased the scope of this book, as well as Dirk Bönker, William Chafe, Klaus Larres, and Martin Miller, who each encouraged me to look more closely at the connections between American and European histories.

Since the autumn of 2014, I have been an assistant professor in the Henry M. Jackson School of International Studies at the University of Washington. The Jackson School is an inspiring place to work, and its members have welcomed me as one of their own. It has been a pleasure to join such a stimulating and caring intellectual community. From my first days here, Reşat Kasaba has been a kind guide who helped make the University of Washington my home. Daniel Chirot, Sara Curran, Kathie Friedman, María Elena García, Christoph Giebel, Don Hellmann, Judy Howard, Sunila Kale, Sabine Lang, Wolf Latsch, Tamara Leonard, Tony Lucero, Joel Migdal, Christian Novetzke, Saadia Pekkanen, Noam Pianko, Ken Pyle, Matthew Sparke, Jim Wellman, and Glennys Young have similarly provided me with thought-provoking conversations, excellent dinners, and a collegial community of scholars. I am also grateful to the Center for Global Studies, the Stroum Center for Jewish Studies, and the Center for West European Studies for connecting me with professors who share my interests. Furthermore, in the autumn of 2016 I was granted the honor of being the inaugural Anne H. H. and Kenneth B. Pyle Assistant Professor in American Foreign Policy, and I thank the University of Washington for offering me this opportunity, the Henry M. Jackson Foundation for creating the professorship, and Lara Iglitzin and Ken and Anne Pyle for their support.

I have also benefited from the feedback of colleagues I met while on two separate postdoctoral fellowships. At Cornell University's Mario Einaudi Center for International Studies, where I spent the 2013–2014 academic year as a Foreign Policy, Security Studies, and Diplomatic History Postdoctoral Fellow, I had the privilege of having Fred Logevall serve as my mentor. As those who know him already appreciate, Fred is not only an excellent scholar but also a compassionate human being, and he made my year at Cornell one of the most exciting and productive of my career. At Cornell, I joined an interdisciplinary community of scholars that included Fritz Bartel, Ray Craib, Matt Evangelista, Durba Ghosh, Molly Geidel, Chen Jian, Jason Kelly, Jonathan Kirshner, Javier Osorio, Judith Reppy, and Barry Strauss, whose insights on manifold topics increased my understanding of both history and international relations.

In addition to Cornell, I spent the 2015–2016 academic year as an International Security and U.S. Foreign Policy Postdoctoral Fellow at Dartmouth

College's John Sloan Dickey Center for International Understanding. At Dartmouth, a number of outstanding scholars offered helpful comments on various parts of this book, including Kate Geoghegan, Mauro Gilli, Alexander Łanoszka, Jennifer Lind, Katy Powers, Daryl Press, Josh Shifrinson, and William Wohlforth. Dartmouth also provided me with the chance to hold a manuscript review session, which was one of the most rewarding experiences of my intellectual career. For this, I must thank James Kloppenberg and Samuel Moyn, who graciously traveled from Harvard to Dartmouth to attend the seminar, as well as Leslie Butler, Vanessa Freije, Udi Greenberg, Ed Miller, Jennie Miller, and Simon Toner, who read and critiqued the entire manuscript.

Many scholars have shaped this book, and I thank Eric Brandom, Elizabeth Cobbs, David Ciepley, Nick Barr Clingan, Josh Derman, Edward J. K. Gitre, Dan Geary, Nicolas Guilhot, Rebecca Herman, Eric Hounshell, Daniel Immerwahr, Martin Jay, Andrew Jewett, Ira Katznelson, Anne Kornhauser, Paul Kramer, Jan Logemann, David Milne, Gregory Mitrovich, Allan Needell, Ken Osgood, Paul Petzschmann, Jefferson Pooley, Joy Rohde, Nicholas Schlosser, Giles Scott-Smith, Alan Sica, Daniel Steinmetz-Jenkins, Noah Strote, Orion Teal, John Toews, Janek Wasserman, David Weinfeld, Stephen Wertheim, and James Wilson for their invaluable comments and suggestions. I must also particularly thank Nils Gilman, Bruce Kuklick, and Cornell University Press's anonymous reviewer for reading the entire book and providing insightful commentaries. Additionally, I am grateful to Christoph Giebel and Naraelle Hohensee for translation assistance as well as Margaret Hogan of the Rockefeller Archive Center, Cara McCormick and Susan Scheiberg of the RAND Corporation, Terri Orguz, Jeanne Swadosh of the New School, and manifold other archivists and librarians for research aid and assistance.

It has been a pleasure working with Cornell University Press over the last several years. Throughout the process of bringing this book to fruition, both David Engerman and Michael McGandy have been extraordinarily helpful and, perhaps most important, extraordinarily patient, answering my questions, addressing my concerns, and offering me much-needed advice. Indeed, they both read the entire manuscript at several points and recommended changes that significantly improved it. It was an honor to work with David and Michael, and I profusely thank them for the help with which they have provided me over the years.

This book could not have been researched and written without the generous financial support of numerous groups and organizations, and

I express my sincere gratitude to the Henry M. Jackson School of International Studies at the University of Washington, the John Sloan Dickey Center for International Understanding at Dartmouth College, the Mario Einaudi Center for International Studies at Cornell University, the Josephine de Kármán Fellowship Trust, the George C. Marshall Foundation, the Society for Historians of American Foreign Relations, the German Historical Institute, and Duke University's Department of History, Kenan Institute for Ethics, Center for Jewish Studies, Center for European Studies, and Graduate School of Arts and Sciences for their pecuniary aid. I further thank the *Journal of the History of the Behavioral Sciences* and the *Bulletin Supplement* of the *Bulletin of the German Historical Institute* for allowing me to reprint as part of chapter 8 some updated and edited portions of "Organizing Complexity: The Hopeful Dreams and Harsh Realities of Interdisciplinary Collaboration at the RAND Corporation in the Early Cold War," *Journal of the History of the Behavioral Sciences* 51, no. 1 (Winter 2015), 31–53, and "Weimar Social Science in Cold War America: The Case of the Political-Military Game," *Bulletin of the German Historical Institute* 54, *Bulletin Supplement* 10 (2014), 91–109.

Writing a book is a solitary endeavor, and I would not have made it through without the encouragement of a strong group of friends, especially Jayadev Athreya, Fahad Bishara, Sam Boyce, Julian Gantt, Radhika Govindrajan, Udi Greenberg, Kate Hall, Paul Johstono, Garnet Kindervater, Jason Leblang, Patrick Martinez, Brandon Melendez and his family, Jennie Miller, James Montalbano, Devin and Andrea Soroko Naar, Izzy Dabiri and Simon Toner, Marc Williams, Brian Wolfson, Hamza Zafer, and Mattia Begali and Corinna Zeltsman.

I have also been very fortunate to have the support of my family. My sisters, Rachel and Deborah, have never let me forget where I came from and still make me laugh more than most. Moreover, I thank my uncle Matt Guldin for remaining a progressive light and my uncle Greg Guldin and aunt M. J. Fung for welcoming me to Seattle with open arms. I have further married into a large and loving family, and I must thank Susan and Pen Caldwell, as well as Matt, Hope, Nicholas, Sophie, and Ethan Freije (I said it was a large family), for providing me with food, shelter, and trips to places I would never go otherwise.

Duke not only provided me with a stellar education; it also introduced me to my partner, Vanessa. She has shaped this book in more ways than I can count—and read it more times than she could count—and has influenced not only how I understand history but also how I understand the world. Vanessa is a true best friend, and I thank her, profoundly, for the last eight years.

This book would not have been possible without the loving support of my parents, Jody and Glen, who encouraged me to go to graduate school instead of becoming a lawyer or pursuing some other, more practical, profession. But more than that, it was my parents who instilled in me a love of history, scholarship, and learning, and it is for this reason that I dedicate this book to them.

DEMOCRACY IN EXILE

Introduction

Democracy, Expertise, and U.S. Foreign Policy

Seven weeks after World War II's outbreak in September 1939, a collection of German exiles at the New School for Social Research in New York City asked Hans Speier, one of their youngest colleagues, to comment on a project proposal regarding Europe's postwar future. Speier accepted the request and quickly set to writing his review. Though pleased to see his fellow émigrés put their knowledge to political use, the thirty-five-year-old was nevertheless disappointed in what he considered their limited vision. "It seems to me," Speier opened his remarks, "that there is a lack of clarity, or at least of understanding, as to what we as a group of social scientists can and should do in the present situation." Speier had devoted much of his short career to rethinking the place of intellectuals in political life. As a social democrat in Weimar Germany, he had argued that intellectuals must educate workers so that the disenfranchised could effect policy change and enjoy the benefits of a newly liberalized state. After being forced into exile when Adolf Hitler assumed the Reich chancellorship in 1933, however, Speier abandoned his Marxism and became convinced that ordinary people from all classes, whose support had paved the Nazis' path to power, could be neither trusted nor educated to make correct political decisions. Instead, he maintained that when democracies confronted existential threats like the Nazis, intellectuals best served the greater good by counseling decision makers directly. Speier therefore insisted to his colleagues that, in 1939, it was the "primary task of the social scientist . . . to give advice to the statesman."[1]

Speier soon followed his own counsel. When the United States entered World War II in 1941, he left the New School to join the wartime government. Then, when the Cold War began in the late 1940s, he became the founding chief of the RAND Corporation's Social Science Division. In these positions, Speier developed policy and advised decision makers without paying attention to public opinion. His experiences witnessing ordinary people vote and fight for Hitler had persuaded him that political extremism could be overcome only if democracy became rule *for* the people, whose interests were determined by expert-influenced elites. With this claim, Speier rejected a central tenet of his original conception of democracy: the idea that the public, enlightened by those in privileged positions, must play an active role, through either referendums or elected representatives, in shaping government policies.

Speier did not easily endorse a jaundiced vision of democracy. Rather, his justification for it relied on a diagnosis of crisis that permitted only the *temporary* suspension of democratic norms. Though during the 1930s and 1940s Speier believed it was acceptable to support projects and programs with which he was uncomfortable, from expert governance to domestic propaganda to mass mobilization, he vowed that when the Nazis were defeated, such measures would no longer be tolerable. Yet the Cold War soon encouraged Speier to return to the framework of crisis he had developed to understand and combat the Nazi threat and to apply this framework in a new context. In particular, the Soviet Union's development of a nuclear bomb in 1949 compelled Speier to diagnose an "unprecedented crisis in world history" that again made it necessary for foreign policy elites to ignore public opinion and adopt emergency measures.[2] Thereafter, the peculiar features of the Cold War—the emergence of a relatively stable bipolar system; the unwillingness of both sides to fight a nuclear war; and the use of measures such as psychological warfare and international development aid that were thought to be effective proxies for military action—changed the implications of Speier's program. In the 1930s, the possibility of a decisive fascist defeat meant that Speier's diagnosed crisis was temporary; in the Cold War, the unlikelihood of a final Soviet defeat made Speier's diagnosed crisis long term. Speier's *moment* of crisis transformed into an *era* of crisis, in which emergency measures became perpetually justified.[3]

As in the interwar period, in the late 1940s Speier placed intellectuals at the center of modern governance and dedicated himself to using knowledge in power's service. He eagerly joined RAND, which made him a "defense intellectual"—a novel social figure who during the Cold War researched, analyzed, and advised decision makers on national security issues while moving between a newly created network of think tanks, government institutions, and academic centers that historians have termed the "military-intellectual complex."[4] Unlike policymakers (who based their authority on elections or their appointment by an elected official), military officers (who based their authority on experience in or knowledge of war), or political operatives (who based their authority on their connections to a political party), defense intellectuals based their authority on training in the social or natural sciences or their deep engagement with scholarly texts. During the Cold War, the appeal to academic knowledge enabled numerous scholars to become influential policy advisers and, in some instances, decision makers themselves. From the end of World War II until today, defense intellectuals have developed and implemented some of the most important U.S. foreign and national security policies, from nuclear strategy to counterinsurgency doctrine.[5]

Speier did as much as anyone to create the community of American defense intellectuals. His position as the chief of RAND's Social Science Division enabled him to direct the research program of the most prominent think tank in the Cold War United States. RAND also provided Speier with access to policymakers, and he quickly emerged as an important consultant on U.S. psychological warfare strategy. He further used RAND's connections to the Ford Foundation to lobby for the establishment of two groups that brought social science research to policymakers' attentions and created networks of social scientists interested in using research to influence policy: the Research Program in International Communication at the Massachusetts Institute of Technology's Center for International Studies and the Center for Advanced Study in the Behavioral Sciences in Stanford, California. By the early 1950s, Speier had become one of the most powerful defense intellectuals in the United States.

Besides permitting Speier to exert influence, RAND—much of whose research was classified—enabled him to fulfill his program, borne from witnessing Weimar's failure, for governing during crises without the input of public opinion.[6] Participating in classified research projects allowed social scientists like Speier, if they so chose, to (mostly) bypass Congress, as well as peer-reviewed academic journals, popular publications, newspapers, television, and other public forums, when offering policy advice.[7] Classified research, in short, made it difficult for the public and its representatives to evaluate, censor, impact, or otherwise hold defense intellectuals accountable for their recommendations. By shaping RAND's Social Science Division, Speier helped institutionalize a system that empowered non-elected experts to influence policy without popular oversight. Although Speier originally considered his participation in and advocacy for such a system discomfiting, he nonetheless insisted that "the loss of the American A-bomb monopoly" required "American leaders [to] consider themselves to be called upon to sacrifice secretly their own cherished values in order to enable their countrymen to live with these values in the future."[8] For the Cold War's duration, the experts would have to rule.

This book argues that to understand the rise of the defense intellectual, historians must examine the ways in which anxieties about democracy's future led thinkers like Hans Speier to reconceive their social role and embrace a logic of crisis that vindicated long-term emergency governance. Historians have tended to emphasize structural reasons for the emergence of the defense intellectual, including the expanding U.S. state; government and military officials' desire for area knowledge as the nation became a superpower and needed to manage its progressively intricate foreign and military relations; the growing complexity of technology; the advent of a more politically, economically, socially, and culturally interconnected globe; and the increased government and foundation funding available to think tanks and universities engaged in defense research. Though essential, these explanations cannot wholly account for why intellectuals decided to join and build the military-intellectual complex. An intellectual biography of Speier shows that fears regarding democracy's weakness in the face of perceived existential threats drove a transatlantic generation of scholars to leave the groves of academe to create institutions that provided them with access to the corridors of power.

Speier's embrace of crisis politics reinforced tendencies toward the establishment of the national security state—of which the military-intellectual complex was a part—evident in the United States between the 1930s and 1950s. Throughout U.S. history, political elites had appealed to crisis to legitimate emergency measures. During the Civil War, Abraham Lincoln suspended habeas corpus, and during World War I, Woodrow Wilson authorized a variety of illegal actions, including the opening of mail and the arrest and deportation of socialists and ethnic minorities. Though severe violations of civil liberties, in both of these cases the end of the crisis eventually resulted in democratic life returning to relative normalcy (even as state power was strengthened). This pattern began to change in the 1930s and 1940s as policymakers encountered the crises of the Great Depression and European fascism and started to expand government authority even more, a process seen in President Franklin Delano Roosevelt's extensive use of executive orders, his bank moratorium, the creation of the National Recovery Administration, and the establishment of wartime agencies such as the Office of War Information and Office of Strategic Services. By the time elites confronted a nuclearized Soviet Union in the late 1940s, many considered the institutionalization of emergency governance legitimate.

Subsequently, decision makers built on the World War II state to create a national security state indefinitely mobilized to fight the Cold War.[9] This novel state formation encouraged secrecy, conformity, and the untrammeled growth of executive power, particularly with regard to making war and foreign policy.[10] Critically, intellectuals like Speier helped undergird the national security state by contributing to the establishment of what Michael Hogan terms a "national security ideology," which he defines in part by the conviction that "the danger of total war [necessitated] a comprehensive program that integrated civilian and military resources and obliterated the line between citizen and soldier, peace and war." This ideology permeated both the elite and popular spheres, convincing Americans that, as Hogan states, "they might even have to compromise some of the blessings of their own liberty, if not liberty itself, in the best interest of peace and freedom worldwide."[11]

The construction of the Cold War as a never-ending crisis—which built on interwar fears explicated by Speier and others—made possible the national security ideology and the state it supported, the institutionalization of which reinforced Americans' general feeling of crisis. Like Speier, throughout the 1950s U.S. political elites invoked the Cold War to justify extraordinary measures that violated broadly acknowledged moral, political, and legal norms. Together, decision makers and intellectuals created, to borrow Mary Dudziak's phrase, "a new logic of governance" premised on persistent crisis.[12] Throughout the twentieth and twenty-first centuries, this logic provided U.S. policymakers with a powerful ideological and rhetorical resource.

Speier's appeal to crisis and his understanding of modern international politics as a Manichean struggle between democracy and totalitarianism was premised on concepts formed and experiences had in Weimar Germany, which suggests that transnational and interwar processes shaped the

United States' logic of governance during the Cold War. Though Speier never articulated an explicit theory of politics, it is possible to look to the work of the fascist legal theorist Carl Schmitt to elucidate his political perspective. Speier published a haltingly approving review of Schmitt's *The Concept of the Political* in Weimar but otherwise did not engage the theorist, whose ideology he found anathema. Nevertheless, an analysis of Speier's political positions reveals that he shared a number of Schmitt's fundamental theoretical premises, the most important of which were the "state of exception" and the "friend-enemy distinction." The similarities between Speier and Schmitt's thought indicate that ideas that contemporary scholars trace to Schmitt were prevalent across the Weimar (and post-Weimar) political spectrum, even among those who, like Speier, rejected Schmitt's authoritarian conclusions.[13]

Speier's use of the state of exception as an organizing concept that justified emergency governance echoed Schmitt's. In *Political Theology*, Schmitt declared that "the exception . . . can at best be characterized as a case of extreme peril, a danger to the existence of the state."[14] For both Schmitt and Speier, the essential question of modern politics concerned whether a polity could ensure "existential self-preservation" during such an exceptional moment, and both agreed that emergency measures could be taken to guarantee that it did.[15] As his framing of twentieth-century politics as an existential struggle implied, Speier also endorsed Schmitt's notion of the friend-enemy distinction, an idea that Schmitt developed in *The Concept of the Political*. Schmitt here asserted that "the specific political distinction to which political actions and motives can be reduced is that between friend and enemy."[16] Speier approved of Schmitt's dualistic definition of politics. He first defined the Nazis as a Schmittian enemy before transferring his anxieties onto the Soviets. Throughout his career, Speier assumed that an existential struggle between friends (the United States, the West, and democrats) and enemies (fascists and communists) defined modern politics. The major differences between Speier and Schmitt were that, first, unlike Schmitt, Speier did not think the friend-enemy distinction was necessarily an ontological fact, even if it reflected the realities of the mid-twentieth century, and second, Speier valued democracy while Schmitt did not. Speier's thought indicates that in the wake of Weimar's collapse, intellectuals politically distant from Schmitt arrived at similar conclusions regarding the weaknesses of liberalism and democratic governance.

The connections between Speier and Schmitt suggest that the liberal-conservative dualism does not accurately reflect the convictions of certain midcentury intellectuals.[17] Though a voter for the Democratic Party and a self-styled social democrat (at least in terms of domestic economic policy), Speier's political commitments were not simply "liberal" or "left," nor did his use of Schmittian ideas make him a "conservative" or a man of the "right." After 1933, Speier was of the opinion that the major battle of the twentieth century "no longer consisted in the economic contrast capitalism-socialism but in the political antinomy terror and persecution versus liberty and democracy."[18] For him, the most important end of political action was to save liberal democracy, and he was willing to use all types of insights to realize this aim.

But Speier *was* convinced that democracy—at the center of which stood the idea that the public should inform policy—was the most just political form, and his labored attempts to justify expert authority reveal the tensions that define governance in a complex post-industrial democracy. On one hand, Speier recognized that policies made without reference to public opinion suffer a democratic deficit. On the other hand, he understood that, as Walter Lippmann argued in the 1920s, most people have neither the time, nor knowledge, nor inclination to consider policy decisions fully.[19] Expertise is therefore a requirement of modern policymaking, which remains the ineluctable tension at the heart of democratic governance in a knowledge-driven society. Speier's appeal to crisis allowed him to resolve the tension between expertise and democracy by (temporarily) privileging the former over the latter.

Yet even on its own terms Speier's solution to this problem was unsatisfactory because it relied on the assumption that the diagnosed crisis would, eventually, end. If it did not, or if it ended only after decades, as happened with the Cold War, Speier was in effect justifying permanent, or at least long-term, emergency governance. Speier, like many in his intellectual generation, never addressed this quandary. Indeed, long-term emergency governance became a particular threat to American democracy after 1945, when the United States emerged as a superpower that involved itself in most world regions. Since this moment, policy elites with a global vision of U.S. power have found it easy to identify potential crises, from a Soviet nuclear assault to an al-Qaeda biological attack, to which they appeal to justify antidemocratic measures from political persecution to spying on their own citizens.[20] Speier never considered the possibility that the logic of crisis could itself become a conceptual resource that decision makers could misemploy or exaggerate, either consciously or unconsciously. However, the history of the postwar United States suggests that it can be, and that democratic rights and practices, while easily abandoned—even with the best and most noble intentions—are less easily recovered.

Speier entered the United States during a period that provided unique opportunities to exiled social scientists interested in using their knowledge in power's service. First, German and American elites shared parallel political, social, and intellectual concerns that made it possible for Speier to assimilate relatively rapidly. Second, the midcentury United States was home to several powerful constituencies, including government officials, military officers, and foundation administrators, who believed social science could improve U.S. foreign and military policy. Speier—and many in his exile cohort—used these groups to enter the halls of American power. Without such American supporters, Speier's program of expert governance would have likely come to naught. With them, he was able to become one of the most influential defense intellectuals in the United States.

Speier's career exemplifies the generational experiences of a transatlantic cohort of scholars who migrated from the academy to the wartime government to the military-intellectual complex in the 1940s and 1950s. In 1940, Speier became co-director of a Rockefeller Foundation–funded project designed to analyze Nazi propaganda in order to learn from and defend against it. The Research Project on Totalitarian Communication in Wartime, as the endeavor was titled, made Speier a nationally renowned propaganda expert. Once World War II necessitated that the American state (whose officials were searching for individuals who knew the German language, culture, and society) open itself to new constituencies it had previously excluded (namely, exiles and Jews), government officials recruited Speier to serve as head of the group that gleaned intelligence from intercepted Nazi materials.[21] After two successful years in this position, in May 1944 Speier moved to the Office of War Information to become chief of its German desk, where he wrote the directives intended to guide U.S. propaganda sent to Germany from the D-Day invasion of June 6 until the autumn of 1945. In January 1946, Speier accepted a post as associate chief of the State Department's Area Division for Occupied Areas, which enabled him to oversee the department's information and education policies in occupied Germany.

By 1947, Speier was frustrated that officials in the field ignored many of his policy directives and he decided to leave government service. He returned to the New School intending to resume his scholarly pursuits but swiftly discovered that writing about foreign relations was not nearly as satisfying as affecting them. Fortunately for him, a new type of organization, the semi-private think tank working primarily on government contracts, was in the process of being formed.[22] Such institutions provided intellectuals like Speier with the opportunity to shape U.S. foreign policy outside government's confines. Moreover, their close, frequently personal, connections to the military, Defense Department, and State Department allowed intellectuals to circumvent the national security bureaucracy and offer advice to decision makers directly. In June 1948, Speier joined the RAND Corporation, the most prominent and well financed of these novel organizations, as chief of its Social Science Division (SSD). Speier's position at RAND made him a founding member of the first generation of defense intellectuals. Though intellectuals had counseled U.S. foreign policymakers for decades before the 1940s, the military-intellectual complex, to which RAND belonged, institutionalized and expanded what previously had been largely ad hoc or temporary associations.[23] It provided permanent and well-funded homes to what Jan-Werner Müller terms, in another context, "in-between figures," who desired to be both "free-thinking intellectual[s] *and* . . . official or unofficial adherent[s] of an organization" with an avowedly political purpose.[24]

RAND quickly became a serious player in U.S. foreign policymaking. As chief of its Social Science Division, Speier was one of the most centrally located and powerful defense intellectuals working outside the government in the United States, and he made the SSD in his image. By virtue of his particular interests, the division became a major center of both psychological warfare research and qualitative analysis. Throughout the Cold War's first decade, SSD research influenced several foreign policies, including psychological warfare strategy in Europe, negotiating tactics at the Korean War armistice talks, and nuclear strategy.[25] Speier's success leading the SSD in the 1950s helped safeguard social scientists' hard-won place at the foreign policymaking table.

The division—along with RAND's Economics Division—also had a significant cultural impact. It demonstrated to a generation of ambitious young social scientists who consulted, interned, or worked for RAND that think tanks provided a home from which one could exert policy influence and, if one was so interested, move to the government. RAND further encouraged social scientists who found career success while working for it to, as Jeremi Suri notes when speaking about Henry Kissinger, "defin[e] American success in the Cold War," and indeed the continuation of the Cold War itself, "as a necessary foundation for personal achievement and belonging."[26] These personal benefits encouraged intellectuals like Speier to be less questioning of

U.S. hegemony and its practices than they otherwise might have been. Furthermore, on the material level, RAND provided the critical economic support that allowed "defense intellectual" to become a viable career path that sometimes ended in government service. Indeed, many social scientists who served in government positions after 1945, including William Kaufmann, Andrew Marshall, Alain Enthoven, Henry Rowen, Condoleezza Rice, James Schlesinger, Francis Fukuyama, and Rose Gottemoeller, consulted or worked for RAND at some point in their careers.

RAND's policy influence led it to become the model Cold War think tank, and it swiftly inspired imitators.[27] In the 1940s, 1950s, and 1960s, intellectual, military, and government elites united to create the Human Resources Research Office (1949), the Human Resources Research Institute (1949), the Foreign Policy Research Institute (1955), the Special Operations Research Office (1956), the Institute for Defense Analyses (1956), the Hudson Institute (1961), and the Center for Strategic and International Studies (1962). These think tanks were joined by research centers affiliated with universities, including Harvard's Russian Research Center (1948), the University of Chicago's Center for the Study of American Foreign Policy (1950), Princeton's Center of International Studies (1951), Columbia's Institute of War and Peace Studies (1951), MIT's Center for International Studies (1952), Johns Hopkins's Washington Center of Foreign Policy Research (1957), and Harvard's Center for International Affairs (1958). Speier's connections to the Ford Foundation, which he gained through RAND, permitted him to shape this process by persuading the foundation to fund both the Research Program in International Communication (1953) at MIT's center and the independent Center for Advanced Study in the Behavioral Sciences (1954).

RAND and similar organizations provided defense intellectuals with access to policymakers and allowed them to impact manifold U.S. foreign policies. Speier's career serves as a case in point. In the early 1950s, Speier was hired by the State Department to participate in MIT's Project TROY, which influenced anti-Soviet psychological strategy; was asked to write a report for State that eventually shaped U.S. psychological warfare policy for East Germany; and was regularly consulted by the Psychological Strategy Board as it developed PSB D-21, "A National Psychological Strategy with Respect to Germany." As Bruce Kuklick highlights, decision makers did not always heed intellectuals' advice and sometimes used think tank and academic research to justify predetermined decisions.[28] Nonetheless, Speier's career shows that in many instances defense intellectuals indeed affected U.S. foreign policy. In the short term, the alliance between defense intellectuals and the government, the military, foundations, and universities enabled thinkers to shape particular U.S. foreign policies. In the long term, this coalition transformed the way U.S. foreign policy was made.

Speier's impact underlines the importance of Atlantic crossings to U.S. history in the 1940s and beyond. He was just one of many émigré social scientists who worked for the government and military-intellectual complex at midcentury, and belonged to a cohort that included Franz Borkenau, Gerhard Colm, Ernst Fraenkel, Carl Friedrich, Olaf Helmer, John Herz, Albert Hirschman, Otto Kirchheimer, Henry Kellerman, Henry Kissinger, Nathan Leites, Karl Loewenstein, Leo Löwenthal, Oskar Morgenstern, Hans Morgenthau, Herbert Marcuse, Franz Neumann, John von Neumann, and dozens of others.[29] Though during the Cold War American-born elites no longer looked to Europe for ideas to the degree they had before World War II, they nevertheless drew on the deep reservoir of exile intellectuals who had immigrated in the 1930s. Taking advantage of the unique opportunities provided by their adopted homeland, the exiles internationalized, one might even say Europeanized, certain aspects of U.S. foreign relations, making themselves influential actors in the drama of the United States' rise to globalism.

In numerous ways, Speier exemplified the exile spirit, and his life illuminates the triumph and tragedy of an elite scarred by fascism and dedicated to saving democracy from the people, for the people. He and several of his émigré contemporaries universalized Weimar's collapse as the potential, perhaps even likely, endpoint for any democracy that confronted an extremist threat. For them, the major reference point of interwar history was not Munich and appeasement but Weimar and democratic collapse. Many of Speier's cohort considered democracy an inherently weak political form that required a robust and at times illiberal defense.[30] Even during the period of postwar American ascendancy, Speier and his European-born colleagues were nervous about democracy's prospects and did all they could to convince American associates that increased power must not lead to complacency. For them, democracy, if not on the verge of collapse, remained always under threat. This embedded pessimism likely explains why neither Speier nor most other German-born exiles became modernization theorists in the 1950s and 1960s; they were simply too cynical to endorse the theory's optimistic notion that democracy could be exported through development aid. If there was an ideology of American exceptionalism evident in Speier's and other exiles' work, it consisted of the negative notion that American democracy—like all democracies—was exceptionally indecisive and feckless when compared with more organized and ruthless fascist and communist regimes.

Yet Speier's trajectory also demonstrates that historians must be careful not to overstate the continuities between exiles' Weimar and American thought. It is true that Speier's writings verify recent claims that many of the Cold War's most critical intellectual frameworks were present in Weimar and the first years of exile.[31] In Speier's case, a commitment to intellectual political engagement, a hatred of communism, and a fear that democracy was weak remained with him from the 1930s onward. The Weimar experience was, undoubtedly, a critical turning point in Speier's and most émigrés' lives. However, changing local, national, and international contexts decisively shaped exiles' thinking, pushing ideas born in the interwar era in unexpected directions.[32] For instance, though Speier continuously insisted that intellectuals were important political actors, in Weimar he argued that they should be educators of the working class, while in the United States he maintained that they should be government advisers or decision makers. Similarly, in Weimar, Speier stressed that democracy implied social, economic, and political equality, while in the United States he insisted that democracy referred primarily to the notion of procedural rights. Both continuity and change characterized Speier's thought, and historians must not overemphasize the former. Weimar was the beginning, not the end, of Speier's and other émigrés' intellectual development.

What did it mean to be an intellectual who wrestled with several of the most profound questions of modern democratic governance in the face of some of the twentieth century's greatest disasters? Speier's biography provides insight into this question by highlighting the disappointment and apprehension that characterized much of his intellectual career. For Speier and many like him, to be a democratic intellectual at midcentury was to be anxious about democracy's future. Speier's trajectory explains how a person who genuinely considered himself a democrat came to endorse a pessimistic theory of politics that supported a culture of classification and secrecy and promoted the institutionalization of expert governance largely impervious to public oversight. The irony of Speier's life was that the trauma of National Socialism's rise compelled him to limit the open society for which he stood in an attempt to defend it. From the 1930s to the 1950s, Speier made one concession after another, to the point that by the early Cold War he had intellectually shorn democracy of one of its major substantive elements: an active public. His path reveals the paradox that democratic practices sometimes were restricted not by those who dismissed them but by those who, like Speier, were invested in them.

But Speier did not arrive at his position for no reason. He was, in fact, correct to see the Nazi victory and consolidation of power as at least the partial result of popular support. However, it was an extreme move to transform this contingent process into a referendum about ordinary people's incapacity for enlightenment. This was ahistorical cynicism born from understandable despair. After all, the American public was mobilized to defeat Hitler, and after World War II the majority of U.S. citizens were anti-Soviet. Moreover, it is a foundational gamble of democracy that citizens might disagree with elite opinion and may support causes that are not considered to be in their own best interests. Intellectuals must deal with this danger not by endeavoring to circumvent, in James Kloppenberg's words, "the unpredictability of the democratic project" but by educating, informing, and debating the public.[33] Otherwise, one forsakes democratic politics in the name of democracy.

Though I disagree with Speier's solutions to the problem of the public, I wish to understand him, not condemn him. While many scholars in the 1990s depicted defense intellectuals as mercenaries motivated mainly by power and prestige, this book contributes to a new historiographical movement that takes a more nuanced and sympathetic, if still critical, view of these figures' motivations and contributions.[34] To denounce Speier without taking his experiences seriously replaces analysis with invective. To avoid repeating what we may currently believe to be his mistakes, we must understand how they came to be.

Approaching Speier from a sympathetic perspective reveals that his thought has much to teach historians and concerned citizens. Most notably, in my opinion Speier was correct to stress that academic expertise is important for modern governance. Bruce Kuklick has incisively noted that Speier's cohort of defense intellectuals "seized on a reality that is hard to dislodge. If we give up on knowledge and thus, to some degree, social science as even a partial guide in human affairs, we leave decisions to habit, authority, or chance. What alternatives do we have to the patient and systematic investigation of phenomena and the exploration of causes and consequences?"[35] Expert advice, in short, must not simply be disregarded. Yet at the same time, since 1945 the history of the United States in the world has repeatedly revealed that experts often support disastrous policies, such as those implemented during the Vietnam War and Iraq War. U.S. foreign policymakers are therefore confronted with a profound dilemma: When should they rely on expert advice? Speier's answer to this question was, in essence, always. He was wrong, but, as a historian, I find myself unable to offer any general guidelines as to when policymakers should heed expert advice and when they ought to shun it. I can only emphasize that there is no easy solution to this problem of modern foreign policymaking and that it remains one that all those concerned with U.S. foreign relations must confront honestly and openly.

This book is titled *Democracy in Exile* for two reasons. Most obviously, the question of democracy and its weaknesses became critical to Speier from his exile onward. His implicit life goal was to save democracy from the type of regime that had forced his emigration. On a more profound level, however, Speier's political program placed traditional notions of democracy in a figurative exile—a suspended state in which democratic norms were neither rejected nor accepted.[36] Several of the twentieth century's major traumas—Weimar's fall, Hitler's rise, World War II, and the introduction of nuclear weaponry into international relations—impelled Speier to exile democracy to a future in which valiant republicans, who had made the necessary moral sacrifices to vanquish their enemies, would be able to live according to their ideals. Tragically, this future was as utopian as the fascist and communist ideologies Speier spent his life combating.

Chapter 1

Masses and Marxism in Weimar Germany

For Hans Speier, crisis defined the Weimar Republic (1918–1933).[1] Though the entirety of interwar Europe suffered profound shocks after the trauma of World War I, Germany's were deeper and longer than most. Between 1918 and 1933, Germans experienced the devastating loss of the war, a punitive Versailles Treaty, popular uprisings, coup attempts against the newly democratic state, foreign occupation of their industrial heartland, hyperinflation and depression, the emergence of extremist political parties of the left and right, presidential dictatorship, and, finally, the rise of Adolf Hitler and the National Socialist German Workers' (Nazi) Party. As he matured, Speier recognized that he was living through an unstable and liminal period in which the assumptions of the past would no longer be relevant in the future. He did not, however, despair at this situation, preferring instead to believe that Weimar's precarity provided a unique opportunity for social democratic intellectuals like himself to reshape society. Hope, rather than anxiety, characterized Speier's early career.

In Weimar's first years, socialist intellectuals had reason to be hopeful. From the ashes of World War I and the *Kaiserreich* arose a constitution that, for the first time in Germany's history, vested sovereignty in the German people. The newly enfranchised "masses"—the term intellectuals and other elites used to describe ordinary Germans—soon thereafter granted the Social Democratic Party of Germany (SPD) pluralities in the federal elections of 1919 and 1920 and victory in the presidential election of 1919.[2] Between 1919 and 1923, the SPD was a critical component of several governing coalitions, which allowed the party to enact policies for which it had long advocated, including welfare reform and the strengthening of labor's rights. The SPD's success persuaded manifold socialist intellectuals that after years of struggle, the revolution Karl Marx had prophesied was at hand.

Political developments, however, quickly dashed socialist dreams. In November 1923, SPD officials withdrew from the parliamentary coalition of which they were a part after their conservative partners enabled the overthrow of Saxony and Thuringia's left-wing governments. As the SPD retreated into political opposition, a crisis of Marxism began to permeate socialist intellectual circles as it became increasingly clear that social democratic governance had not engendered revolutionary socioeconomic transformation and that many economically impoverished Germans had chosen to ally themselves with either the Communist Party of Germany (KPD) or the nationalist right wing, both of which impugned the SPD's parliamentary reformism.[3]

It was during this moment of social democratic uncertainty that Speier matured intellectually. Despite the evident challenges facing the socialist movement, the young Speier was certain he, and others of his generation, could reinvigorate Marxist theory and practice. In particular, Speier insisted that theoretical development and popular education were the keys to social democracy's salvation. If social democratic intellectuals reformed Marxist theory in light of historical experience and dedicated themselves to enlightening Germans in socialism's tenets, Speier argued, both the SPD's and the broader socialist movement's futures would be guaranteed. The young Speier was convinced that the difficulties social democracy faced in the mid-1920s were temporary obstacles that would not prevent socialism's historically preordained realization.

History proved Speier wrong. The mounting electoral successes of the Nazi Party in the late 1920s and early 1930s, which culminated in Adolf Hitler's appointment to the Reich chancellorship in January 1933, eradicated his expectations. For Speier, as for many socialists, the Nazi victory was a profoundly traumatic experience that altered the course of his life. Intellectually, Hitler's triumph had proven false everything in which he had placed his faith. A republic Speier was positive would engender expansive social democratic transformation had instead ended with the victory of radical nationalism and racism. Personally, the new regime forced Speier, who was a socialist married to a Jewish pediatrician, into exile in the United States.

Speier's understanding of the Nazi triumph led him to embrace four ideas that became central to the logic of governance he helped institutionalize in the Cold War United States. First, Weimar's collapse convinced Speier that democracy was a weak political form that could fall prey to radical threats. He became forever wary that extremist political movements of the right and left, no matter how apparently feeble, retained the potential to overthrow democratic governments. Second, Speier attributed Weimar's failure to his own, and by implication other socialist intellectuals', naive conviction that the masses had the capacity to be educated to make wise political decisions. In his exile he held that the Nazi victory demonstrated that mass education was a project doomed to disappoint. Third, the failures of social democratic theory and practice encouraged Speier to reject Marxism as irrelevant, while the KPD's repeated attacks on the SPD and the republic compelled him to diagnose communism as malevolent. Anyone who identified as a Marxist was at best unsophisticated and at worst malicious. Finally, Hitler's rise prompted Speier to redefine his understanding of democracy. Whereas before 1933, democracy had meant for Speier economic, cultural, and political equality, afterward it referred only to an undertheorized notion of procedural equality. Democracy in essence became the vague, negative image of authoritarianism, a concept largely shorn of substantive content.

Despite these shifts in Speier's thought, one theme remained constant in his thinking before and after 1933: in both periods, Speier argued that intellectuals had an essential role to play in modern politics. In his exile, Speier maintained that socialist intellectuals' primary mistake in Weimar had been to focus on educating an uneducable mass constituency. He declared that instead of attempting to enlighten the public, pro-democratic intellectuals must use their knowledge in the service of the American state. In short, the Nazi victory led Speier to conclude that ordinary people were irrational, dogmatic, and manipulable, and that only elites, whether intellectuals or decision makers, could be trusted. This was the first step on a path that ended, across decades and the Atlantic, at the RAND Corporation.

Hans-Heinrich Adolf Ludwig Speier was born in Berlin on February 3, 1905, the only child of Adolf and Anna, a white-collar worker and housewife. As an adult, Speier remembered his father as a free thinker who was nonetheless "Prussian" when it came to discipline, and recalled that his mother was a gentle woman. Throughout his youth, his parents were ill; Anna had

Figure 1. Speier as a teenager with his parents, Adolf and Anna, ca. early 1920s, *photo courtesy of Sybil Speier Barten*

multiple sclerosis while Adolf suffered from Parkinson's disease. Despite the comfortable existence Adolf's position as director of the Berlin office of the New York Insurance Company provided the Speiers, Anna's and Adolf's infirmities made Hans's childhood a difficult one. From a young age, Speier felt responsible for his parents' well-being, which provided him with a profound sense of self-reliance.[4]

Adolf and Anna were conservative Lutherans who endorsed the nationalistic politics shared by many middle-class Protestants. As an adolescent, Speier rejected his parents' political and religious values, a decision likely informed by his position as caretaker. He asserted his agnosticism and, at the age of fifteen, refused to receive the Lutheran confirmation blessing. Speier's most rebellious act, however, was his declaration of allegiance to the Weimar Republic and its socialist movement. During the Wilhelmine era (1890–1918), the majority of German Protestants were dedicated imperialists and nationalists. After the republic's creation, conservative Lutherans like Adolf and Anna critiqued democracy as a liberal betrayal of the German *Volk* request, Samuel Paul Altmann, an economist, directed Speier's committee and his field in sociology, though Mannheim was the one who actually read and passed Speier's dissertation. In addition to Altmann, the conservative historian Willy Andreas, the liberal philosopher Karl Jaspers, and Lederer oversaw Speier's other fields—a politically ecumenical collection of scholars that reflected Speier's innate ability to get along with people who shared different political opinions. Although Mannheim could not direct Speier's dissertation, Speier nevertheless became a founding member of the Mannheim Circle, a group of young left-wing intellectuals that congregated around the scholar and included several individuals who would become well known in the future, such as Norbert Elias, Werner Falk, Hans Gerth, Ruth Neuberg, and Svend Riemer. As Speier remembered, between 1926 and 1928 he "attended all [of Mannheim's] seminars and lecture courses and saw him at his house quite often." Until the end of his life, Speier proudly referred to himself as Mannheim's first doctoral student.[9]

Speier's decision to become a sociologist, however, likely was motivated by more than his admiration for Mannheim. Throughout the Weimar era, the discipline of sociology, and especially the subfield of the sociology of knowledge, was identified with liberal governance and practical, pro-democratic political action. Sociology's progressive reputation, for instance, led figures like Konrad Haenisch, Prussia's socialist minister of culture, and Carl Becker, his liberal successor, to make sociology a central discipline in their educational reform efforts. Mannheim in particular maintained that sociological education was by definition a political act, and his work galvanized pro-democratic intellectuals throughout Germany. As we will see below, Mannheim's sociology of knowledge endowed intellectuals with the crucial duty of guiding Weimar's pluralistic politics, which probably appealed to a young intellectual like Speier who sought to make his mark on the world. Moreover, as Speier recalled, in Weimar "sociology was not necessarily regarded as a specialized discipline, but as a science concerned with the structural and historical problems of society as a whole," which surely stoked the wide-ranging and ambitious Speier's interests.[10]

When Speier enrolled at Heidelberg in 1926, German academia was undergoing a period of social and economic instability. The high inflation of the early 1920s had caused intellectuals' savings to disappear and decreased their real purchasing power. Academics had already experienced a loss of social prestige caused by educational democratization and the rise of a business elite whose status was premised on wealth as opposed to knowledge. The political emergence of the newly sovereign masses also posed a significant challenge to academics' traditional authority. Whereas in the late nineteenth century intellectuals were one of Germany's most respected social groups, to which ordinary people and elites alike looked for spiritual and political guidance, by the 1920s this was no longer the case.[11]

These socioeconomic and status transitions engendered a crisis of *Bildung*, the dominant educational ideal of German academia in the nineteenth and early twentieth centuries. *Bildung*, a term that does not translate well into English, referred to a process of cultivating oneself through, first, extensive reading in classical texts and, second, conducting original research in a *Wissenschaft* (science). Before 1918, not only scholars but also state officials and other elites appealed to *Bildung* to justify their authority. As the conditions of German academia and society changed after the war, however, the discursive coalition that had defended *Bildung* throughout the Wilhelmine era disintegrated. Socialist and liberal academics, who had critiqued traditional *Bildung* as elitist and out of step with modern times, quickly recognized that the collapse of the pro-*Bildung* coalition provided them with an opportunity to redefine *Bildung* in more progressive directions.[12]

The relationship between knowledge and power had occupied German academics long before the Weimar Republic. On one hand, some professors advocated for intellectuals to take a direct role in politics; before 1918, for instance, sixty-two professors had served in the Reichstag. On the other hand, most intellectuals maintained that *Geist* (spirit, mind) and politics must be kept separate, and argued that the creation of *Kultur* was intellectuals' highest purpose (though these professors also maintained that superior *Kultur* would naturally inform and improve politics). But the crisis of *Bildung* demanded a rethinking of the connection between knowledge and power. Max Weber, Germany's most famous and influential liberal sociologist—as Speier recalled in 1971, "Max Weber *was* German sociology"—was the one to initiate this project.[13]

Toward the end of World War I, Weber gave a lecture titled "Science as a Vocation" that inaugurated years of debate surrounding German intellectuals' political function. In his lecture, which was delivered before a student group at the University of Munich, Weber encouraged professors to adopt a neutral perspective in their teaching that "serve[d] the students with his knowledge and scientific experience and [did] not . . . imprint upon them his personal political views." An intellectual, Weber argued, should imbue students with "methods of thinking, the tools and the training for thought," and not his or her own political opinions. Properly accomplished, such

Figure 2. Speier with his wife, Lisa, on their honeymoon in Murano, Italy, 1928, *photo courtesy of Sybil Speier Barten*

at an auspicious moment for the party and the movement. Over the course of the mid-1920s, Germany experienced economic growth that allowed for the implementation of expansive social welfare programs. Moreover, in the federal election of May 1928—the same month Speier earned his PhD—the SPD received around 30 percent of the popular vote and won a plurality of seats in the Reichstag. To govern the republic, the SPD allied with the liberal German Democratic Party (DDP), the liberal German People's Party (DVP), and the Catholic German Center Party (Center) in a so-called great coalition. In addition, the SPD controlled the governments of many municipalities, had a large communications network that published 202 daily newspapers, and boasted a party membership over 937,000. It was, by far, the most powerful individual party in the republic.[22]

Nonetheless, the SPD's national success heightened internal party disputes. The reemergence of the great coalition—a similar group had governed earlier in Weimar's history—brought the party's strategic disagreements into the open. While SPD centrists and those on the right were happy to rebuild the great coalition, those on the party's left maintained that they would support a coalition government only if the SPD joined it on favorable terms. When it became clear that the party's centrist executive committee would not exact significant concessions from its bourgeois allies, many leftists rejected the coalition and insisted that the party stand in political opposition.[23]

Speier's first published writings reflected his left-wing conviction that the only viable socialist politics was a politics dedicated to satisfying the proletariat's particular interests. In his dissertation, "The Philosophy of History of Ferdinand Lassalle," which he published in 1929 in two parts in the *Archiv für Sozialwissenschaft und Sozialpolitik*, Germany's most prestigious social science journal, Speier pilloried Lassalle—a contemporary and critic of Marx—for failing to recognize that capitalist society was defined by the struggle between classes. In so doing, Speier implicitly criticized the conciliatory politics of the SPD's center and right, some members of which proudly referred to themselves as "Lassalleans." Throughout his dissertation, Speier lambasted Lassalle, and hence the Lassalleans, for the fact that his "politics lacks . . . the class character which Marxism claims for all politics." According to the young Speier, in capitalist society a socialist politics premised on cross-class appeal instead of class conflict was doomed to fail.[24]

Speier's critique of Lassalle highlighted his commitment to a class-based politics that was distrustful of socialist-bourgeois alliances. But unlike many of his fellow left-wing socialists, Speier did not simply encourage the SPD to reject its partners in the great coalition; the people had spoken, and if the party wanted to govern, it needed to develop a way to engage with German liberals, albeit on the party's own proletarian terms. The question that remained for Speier concerned how the SPD would convince its coalition partners that the party's socialist view of the world was the correct one. The way to do so, Speier averred in the late 1920s, was to enlighten liberal intellectuals—the brains of the DDP, DVP, and Center—by demonstrating that their individualistic ideology did not conform to contemporary reality and was in fact a nineteenth-century atavism.

In Speier's 1929 "Toward a Sociology of the Bourgeois Intelligentsia in Germany," which appeared in *Die Gesellschaft*, the SPD's leading theoretical journal, Speier attacked *Bildung*, which he considered to be the source of liberal intellectuals' blinkered, pro-capitalist understanding of the world. In this piece, Speier argued that a lack of interest in politics characterized the liberal intelligentsia's "current state of consciousness" and implied, as he asserted elsewhere, that this disinterest emerged from the inability of "the culturally critical bourgeois intelligentsia [to] systematically confront the economic realities [of modern capitalism], as Marxism does." Speier attributed this inability to liberal intellectuals' commitment to traditional *Bildung*, which he declared was a notion steeped in a nineteenth-century individualism that was designed to create unpolitical scholars dedicated to developing their own personal selves at the expense of the collective. This individualism, Speier maintained, contributed to contemporary liberal intellectuals' rationalization of the status quo.[25]

Speier further explained that while traditional *Bildung* was not particularly damaging in a nineteenth-century world defined by muted social antagonisms, in the post–World War I era, in which the "mechanizing and rationalizing forces of capitalism had changed the face of the times into a grimace, [making] a mockery of humanity," individualistic *Bildung* actively harmed society by preventing liberal intellectuals from seeing capitalism for the vicious system that it was. As Speier clarified in a piece published in *Die Gesellschaft* in 1930, "the concept of *Bildung* . . . is not that of our times" because "this educational ideal was destroyed . . . by capitalism." Speier thus avowed that *Bildung* must be reformed to emphasize collectivism over individualism. Furthermore, liberal intellectuals needed to recognize that "as capitalism progressed . . . the unity of economic and ethical liberalism was undermined and the true legacy of liberalism was taken up by the socialism of the working class." If they accepted this claim, Speier concluded, liberal intellectuals could contribute to historical progress by creating cultural products that enlightened the masses about the proletariat's degraded social position, stimulated collective political action, and, he indicated, brought the SPD's coalition partners over to the socialist side.[26]

Unsurprisingly, liberals did not heed Speier's advice, and from the spring of 1928 until the spring of 1930 Speier viewed the SPD's alliance with Weimar's liberal and bourgeois parties as the primary obstacle to socialist reform. However, the ascendance of the Catholic Center's Heinrich Brüning to the Reich chancellorship in March 1930, the advent of the conservative Brüning's presidential dictatorship, the increasing popular appeal of communism and Nazism, and, most important, the retreat of the SPD into permanent opposition compelled Speier to shift his critiques from liberal intellectuals to social democrats and their support for a Marxist theory that Speier insisted must be transformed if the socialist movement was to remain effective. In so doing, Speier began to move away from both political and theoretical socialism.

Speier expressed his initial dissatisfaction with Marxist theory and SPD politics in "Sociology or Ideology?," a review of Mannheim's *Ideology and Utopia* that was published in *Die Gesellschaft* in April 1930. The review appeared one month after internal SPD disagreements over funding an unemployment insurance program led to the fall of the great coalition and the rise of the Center's Heinrich Brüning to the chancellorship. With Brüning's appointment, the SPD became an opposition party, which provided Speier with a propitious opportunity to educate socialist intellectuals by highlighting the problems with Marxist theory that he believed had led them to underestimate their own centrality to the movement (which, he affirmed, had inadvertently stifled social democratic transformation). Though Speier retained some hope that the party could meet Brüning's right-wing challenge, even at this early stage in Weimar's collapse he displayed significant pessimism regarding the future of the socialist movement and Marxist theory. Speier remained, however, firmly committed to the notion that intellectuals were of critical importance to socialist party politics.

Speier began the review by rejecting what he took to be Mannheim's nonpartisan understanding of the free-floating intelligentsia, asserting that "every class possesses its own intelligentsia to represent its interests and its will." In Speier's opinion, what made intellectuals unique was not their disconnection from the socioeconomic structure, as Mannheim declared, but rather their natural "*ideological flexibility*." This flexibility, Speier maintained, enabled "intellectuals, within limits, to *choose* the ideology of one class or another" (which explains why Speier earlier proclaimed that socialists could encourage liberal intellectuals to support the proletariat). Unlike ordinary people, intellectuals had "the important ability to cross over from one class to another ideologically . . . without thereby leaving the intelligentsia." By making this claim, Speier justified how someone who emerged from the middle class, such as himself, could nevertheless represent workers' interests. Speier's statements, though, also reflected an innate elitism, declaring as they did that intellectuals thought at a more sophisticated level than ordinary people.[27]

Speier further derided Mannheim for positing that intellectuals' social purpose was to develop a synthetic view of society. According to Speier, "the demand for synthesis invariably implies a call for cessation or even a denial" of the "struggles to either preserve or overturn an economic system and hence a way of life," that is to say, class conflict. "If this demand were universally met," he asserted, "the wheel of history would come to a halt. If it were partially met, e.g., only by the intelligentsia, this intelligentsia would withdraw from the social struggle. The result would be a strengthening of a non-political attitude, in which *contemplation* is achieved at the price of an ivory-tower existence." Speier instead avowed that intellectuals should participate in politics as partisans and, because he was a socialist, implied that the best way they could do so was to contribute to the effort to push capitalism in a social democratic direction.[28]

Unfortunately, Speier explained, socialist party officials incorrectly assumed "that the intelligentsia's class interest naturally gravitates toward socialism" and adopted a passive attitude toward intellectuals' participation in the movement. Speier believed that this posture "represents a capitulation of theory to reality as long as large segments of the intelligentsia consciously ignore [the proletariat's] class interest, or even provide ideological ammunition for the opponents of the proletariat." In Speier's opinion, socialist officials' assumption that intellectuals would support them reflected a critical theoretical mistake, namely, the erroneous application of "*the concept of class to the intelligentsia*." Simply put, socialists "attempt to group blue-collar workers and those who perform mental labor as *workers* in *one* class" despite the fact that this did not accurately represent reality. According to Speier, "the intelligentsia is *not a class*" because "it lacks what unites people into a class: a position in the process of commodity production which can be clearly set down in theoretical economics." Instead, intellectuals could choose the class to which they wanted to belong. When they considered intellectuals to be mere workers, Speier warned, "Marxists ignore differences that—far from being peripheral—are constitutive of a social stratum."[29]

believed that the beginning of the "democratization of the economy" was, in fact, the final success for which they had hoped, which led them to lose their zeal for reform. To correct this misunderstanding, Speier insisted that intellectuals assume positions of leadership within the socialist movement and help workers see, first, that the struggle for socialism was not yet complete and, second, that the only way forward consisted in navigating a moderate path between communists of the extreme left and socialists of the right. As Speier stated, a responsible socialist intellectual "fights against the utopians of the left, who see the striving for partial success as a betrayal of the revolutionary goal [and] he fights against the reformists of the right, who see political success as something ultimate and inflexible."[33]

Speier's program begged a question: How exactly should a socialist intellectual work to engender the correct proletarian consciousness? Speier declared that in the era of mass politics, a socialist needed to "use his powers where they work best: as a journalist, a scientist, a politician, through educational work, or within the [workers'] organization." To what did Speier think he should dedicate himself? Influenced by Mannheim's educationist vision of political change (though turning it in a socialist direction), Speier decided to abandon his earlier reticence about becoming an educator to accept a position as a lecturer at the Deutsche Hochschule für Politik (German College for Politics), a college dedicated to workers' education. Speier hoped to use his position at the Hochschule to convince workers of the wisdom of his vision of social democracy. Ironically, after getting to know workers at the college, he became convinced that they could not be educated effectively.[34]

For Speier, as for most German academics, the late Weimar period was one of economic precarity, and he was forced to work several jobs. Besides working at Hilferding's Berlin office, Speier served as a writer, editor, and manager at the Ullstein Publishing House, which was his introduction to the administrative labor he undertook throughout his career in the United States. He also began a renewed assistantship with Emil Lederer, who had moved from Heidelberg to the University of Berlin. Under Lederer, Speier served as an editor of the *Archiv für Sozialwissenschaft und Sozialpolitik*, which made him a gatekeeper for late Weimar social science. In his free time, Speier gave lectures to young SPD members and volunteered at both the party's labor education office and Berlin's social service organization. The most important position Speier accepted in terms of his intellectual and professional development, though, was a lectureship in political sociology at the Hochschule für Politik, where he for the first time came into extensive contact with members of Berlin's working classes. Contrary to his expectations, Speier was not impressed with what he saw.[35]

Speier taught at the Hochschule from November 1931 until the spring of 1933, when the Nazis seized the college and dismissed him. Founded in 1920 with the intellectual support of Max Weber and other pro-democratic elites, the Hochschule was designed to educate ordinary Germans in the politics and mores of democracy. It offered evening classes for all genders and allowed students who had never taken the *Abitur* to enroll, reconfiguring *Bildung* for the masses. Philosophically, the institution's founders sought to move beyond the *Staatswissenschaften* (sciences of state, sciences of public administration), which were designed to train civil servants, to initiate a program of political education for democracy. The similarities between the goals of Mannheim's pedagogy and the Hochschule no doubt eased Speier's transition into the college. The historian Ernst Jäckh, who served as the school's director, also rejected *völkisch* nationalism and the communist left, and did not allow adherents of either to teach at the school. Thus, until Hitler's rise to power, the Hochschule served as an institutional home for pro-democratic intellectuals—one-quarter of the faculty were social democrats—many of whom later immigrated to the United States, including Werner Falk, Hajo Holborn, Franz Neumann, Sigmund Neumann, and Hans Simons. It was one of the most vibrant intellectual spaces in Weimar Germany, and its faculty later transformed American, and West German, intellectual life.[36]

The Hochschule was one of a number of new institutions, including the Institute of Social Research and the Academy for Labor, both in Frankfurt, and the Institute for Social and State Sciences, housed at the University of Heidelberg, which provided an institutional base for left-wing and liberal intellectuals interested in influencing public policy. The Hochschule in particular served as a proto–think tank whose faculty desired to advise government officials in light of cutting-edge social scientific research, and its identity and function foreshadowed that of the RAND Corporation and other organizations of the U.S. military-intellectual complex for which Speier and other members of the Hochschule's faculty worked in exile. As Sigmund Neumann, a colleague of Speier's at the Hochschule and a future émigré, declared in 1931, the college "dedicated itself to the task of putting together the building blocks of a political science in order to create the basis for insightful state practice." Moreover, like the think tanks and research institutions that emerged in the Cold War United States, the Hochschule received substantial government funding and presented itself as committed to "nonpartisanship" (*Überparteilichkeit*) and "objective" political analysis. In short, the Hochschule provided an institutional model for later U.S. think tanks and introduced Speier and several future exiles to the notion that their knowledge could be used to inform policymaking.[37]

The Hochschule marketed itself as an institution concerned with public policy and empirical social research and in so doing attracted substantial American aid, notably from the Rockefeller Foundation and Carnegie Corporation. U.S. funding encouraged the college's social scientists to familiarize themselves with at least some of the norms and structures of American academia, which inadvertently helped them prepare for their lives in the United States. Most important, the Hochschule's associations with Rockefeller and Carnegie built bridges between the college's faculty, foundation administrators, and American academics, which proved useful once the Nazis gained power and forced pro-democratic intellectuals into exile. In 1933 and after, approximately half of the Hochschule's faculty fled Germany for the United States, often with the aid of foundations.[38]

The Hochschule had two focuses, foreign policy and domestic policy. The liberal Jäckh was himself a foreign policy expert, which allowed the members of the left-leaning sociological faculty, who were primarily interested in domestic policy, to express their socialism easily. As a social democrat focused on bringing the SPD to power through workers' education, Speier found the most appealing aspect of the Hochschule to be its reformulation of traditional *Bildung*, which he had earlier condemned for its individualism. He was excited, as he remembered years later, that the school's worker-students could "prove through political activity that [they] had life experience, [and] this life experience was regarded as the equivalent of *Bildung*. This was an entirely new principle."[39]

In the months before he joined the Hochschule in November 1931, Speier continued the intellectual transformation earlier begun with his critique of Marxist theory by attacking the SPD's quiescence in the face of Brüning's de facto dictatorship. After the Nazis' September 1930 electoral breakthrough, the SPD leadership adopted a "policy of toleration" toward Brüning, in which the party provided the chancellor's government with, in the words of Donna Harsch, "passive support," so as to ensure the Nazis did not become more powerful. Though they were not happy about it, many socialists of the right and center, as well as a number of the moderate left, agreed with the party leadership that protecting democracy necessitated tolerating Brüning's abrogation of democratic norms, at least for a time. However, those on the party's left who still endorsed a class-based politics, such as Speier, vehemently condemned the toleration policy as collaborationism, maintaining that the SPD needed to focus on increasing its working-class support in order to build a constituency able to challenge the German right.[40]

While Speier would not countenance any toleration of Brüning, he desired to understand the SPD's betrayal. In his March 1931 "The Proletariat's Embourgeoisement?," which appeared in the *Magazin der Wirtschaft*, a mainstream journal of economics, Speier explained the toleration policy with reference to the sundering of the connection between the SPD's leadership and its natural working-class constituency. Though increasingly fearful for the republic, Speier continued to endorse socialist class politics, identifying the "embourgeoisement" of the SPD as the cause of the party's weak opposition to Brüning. However, at the same time, he also began to express his concern that workers themselves might not be up to the task of establishing a social democratic world.

Speier was not naive, and in "The Proletariat's Embourgeoisement?" he recognized that the "demiurge of democratic politics is the principle of the majority." In other words, he understood that if the SPD was to enact positive change, it needed to convince "masses of voters," especially liberal middle-class voters, to support its cause. Yet, Speier noted, this structural incentive created two problems. As middle-class voters entered the party, they diluted socialist principles, engendering internal party battles that prevented concerted socialist action. Speier further claimed that a cross-class party, which he believed the SPD had become, required the creation of a large bureaucracy, whose "fat cats" (*Bonzen*) depended on the perpetuation of class barriers to retain their jobs. He thus argued that the logic of large party bureaucracies created a system in which there were few incentives for SPD leaders to pursue reform. For these reasons, the SPD tolerated Brüning.[41]

But why did the party's working-class members accept the toleration policy? Speier attempted to answer this question in "The Proletariat's Embourgeoisement?" and in the process for the first time expressed his personal disillusionment with workers themselves. This was an important shift that would soon result in his disavowal of political and theoretical socialism. In the essay, Speier accused the SPD's working-class constituency of embracing the "mass luxury industry, kitsch films, kitsch novels," and other bourgeois cultural products. Speier attributed workers' interest in bourgeois culture- and related disinterest in class politics to two factors. First, he argued that because their jobs did not allow them to have a wide sociocultural purview, workers could not produce their own cultural products and looked to popular art for intellectual satiation. Second, following Max Weber, he maintained that "the (universal human) desire to strive for prestige" (*Geltungsstreben*) compelled workers to ape the bourgeoisie. This latter claim was a critical intellectual move, as it indicated that Speier blamed not only capitalism but also an unchanging—and unchangeable—human nature for the proletariat's false consciousness.[42]

Speier ended "The Proletariat's Embourgeoisement?" pessimistically, quoting the socialist pastor Günther Dehn's declaration that most people are "totally disinterested in politics. . . . There are many young men and women whose thinking is entirely privatized. One has no other wish than to go one's way with the quiet hope to reach somehow somewhere a moderately secure petit bourgeois position, from which one can observe life around one with indifference." Speier concluded that, tragically, people's longing for bourgeois comforts and social prestige encouraged the party to defend the status quo and, he indicated, accept the toleration policy. The young Speier, who in 1928 had been so certain of socialism's ultimate success, was in the wake of the Nazis' electoral victory and Brüning's presidential dictatorship becoming a cynical realist.[43]

Political events that occurred over the course of late 1931 and 1932 deepened Speier's pessimism about social democracy's future. First, far right leaders established a coalition called the "Harzburg Front" that was dedicated to overthrowing the republic. Second, the Nazis did extraordinarily well in the provincial elections of late 1931. Third, the SPD's reaction to the Harzburg Front and the Nazi victories, which included the creation of a largely ineffective paramilitary "Iron Front," did little to stem the fascist tide. Fourth, in the March 1932 presidential election Hitler came in second to the SPD-supported Paul von Hindenburg, who defeated Hitler in the run-off election in April. These events demoralized Speier and many within the SPD, who began to worry that the republic was on the verge of collapse.[44]

Speier expressed his growing political cynicism and anxiety about Weimar's future in a cautiously admiring review of Carl Schmitt's *The Concept of the Political* that he published in the Institute of Social Research's *Zeitschrift für Sozialforschung* in 1932. In *The Concept of the Political*, Schmitt argued that "the concept of politics is governed by the 'ultimate' difference" between "friend" and "enemy." Speier embraced Schmitt's Manichean worldview, asserting that the friend-enemy distinction emerged from "the best sociological lineage" and had been articulated by several of the greatest sociological minds, including "Saint-Simon, Comte, Marx, and others." Speier thus affirmed that the friend-enemy distinction, which implicitly derided parliamentary compromise, accurately reflected modern politics. In 1932, he believed this dichotomy explained the relationship between social democrats and political extremists. Seventeen years later, he would use the friend-enemy framework to understand the U.S.-Soviet rivalry.[45]

The *Preussenschlag* accelerated Speier's disenchantment with SPD politics and Marxist theory. In July 1932, Franz von Papen, who had replaced Brüning as chancellor in June, initiated a coup in which he illegally deposed the SPD-led government of Prussia. In an interview given late in his life, Speier recalled his reaction to the von Papen coup:

> In [one of Speier's classes at the Hochschule] a student stood up and said: "Do you know"—he was a Nazi—"Do you know that the Prussian government is finished?" And I said, "No, I didn't know that. Tell me about it:" Then he told me about the Papen-Putsch, and I thought that indeed the lights would go out in the next few minutes because a general strike [called by the SPD] seemed inevitable, if what he said was true. The workers had struck against the Kapp-Putsch [a conservative putsch that occurred in Berlin in March 1920] and now it was a matter of the survival of the social democratic government in Prussia!

But the party, and its working-class constituency, did not strike, which to Speier demonstrated its incapacity to govern and Marxist theory's inability to support a viable political movement. Moreover, after working at the Hochschule for almost a year, Speier had come to learn that many workers, such as his Nazi student, were antagonistic to social democracy. These were the final straws in the years-long process of Speier's disillusionment with political and theoretical socialism. After the SPD failed to defend itself against von Papen's coup, Speier attempted to persuade socialists, whom he still believed had noble political instincts, to jettison their theoretical commitments and embrace democracy, as opposed to social democracy, as the primary idea worth defending in this moment of political crisis.[46]

In his September 1932 "The Proletariat and Its Critics," which appeared in *Die neue Rundschau*, a literary magazine, Speier carefully elucidated the ways in which Marxist theory had failed to predict reality. The theory of class consciousness, Speier argued, assumed that workers' economic position would stimulate them to develop a unified, pro–social democratic ideology. However, Speier acidly declared: "The facts are the following. The proletariat has no unified class consciousness, neither the German proletariat nor any other in all of the late-capitalist countries. The idea of international [proletarian] unity is fully absurd. Thus Marxist doctrine is contradicted by an authority, which, in spite of its bourgeois prejudices, Marx repeatedly called as a witness: history." Even in the midst of the Great Depression, a socioeconomic collapse that should have made it easy for the working class to assert itself politically, one "finds a proletariat, which, weakened through internal battles, is concentrating its powers on repelling the reactionary right" instead of achieving its own goals. In Marxist terms, though the depression engendered the objective conditions for a social democratic transformation, the subjective conditions, such as a unified working-class consciousness, were not present and, in Speier's opinion, might never be. Speier averred that socialists needed to recognize that "if Karl Marx was the greatest critic of the proletariat, the history of the proletariat is the only objectively qualified critic of Marx." The struggle for social democracy, in other words, was unlikely to be won anytime soon, and intellectuals needed to focus first and foremost on defending the democratic structures of the Weimar Republic. Speier therefore asserted that "the intellectual history of socialism in Germany in its essence is about the Marxist assimilation of democratic ideas, while the social history of the proletariat in its essence is about an attempt—not to, say, overthrow the bourgeois system—but to secure rights for itself within it, to escape from misery, to break the privileges of education, in a word, to become stake-holding citizens." Speier's reading of recent socialist history in light of the working classes' inaction in the face of von Papen's coup led him to conclude that workers had never truly wanted to achieve economic transformation but merely desired to join the bourgeois society from which they were excluded. Without an interested proletariat, Speier indicated, social democracy was a chimera.[47]

At the end of "The Proletariat and Its Critics," Speier developed a nonsocialist but still proletarian political program that he hoped would make use of what he considered to be many, if not all, workers' noble instincts. In particular, he stressed that the proletariat's historical mission was not to overcome capitalism but to defend against extremist nationalism, fascism, and communism. As he said, the proletariat's "goal is not actually to overthrow an order, for capitalism is not worthy of this title, but simply to do away with economic, societal, and moral anarchy. Herein lies the cultural mission of the proletariat: to protect the world from barbarism." On the eve of Hitler's triumph, Speier transformed the working classes' mission from a Marxist to an anti-extremist one.[48]

On January 30, 1933, three months after "The Proletariat and Its Critics" appeared, Speier's worst fears were realized when Hindenburg appointed

Hitler chancellor. The Nazis quickly restructured Germany and created a single-party state with a coordinated civil society. In addition to numerous violations of German citizens' rights, Hitler banned the SPD, arrested socialist politicians, and forbade prominent socialist intellectuals, including Speier's former adviser Emil Lederer, from teaching at German universities. As Hitler dismantled the socialist movement and the Weimar Republic, Speier looked on, helpless.

The trauma of Hitler's victory and the easy success of the Nazis' *Gleichschaltung* (coordination) program compelled Speier to publicly disavow the basic premises of Marxist theory and embrace a Weberian understanding of German society. In "Remarks toward an Understanding of the Social Structure," which was written in the spring of 1933 and appeared in the last issue of the *Archiv für Sozialwissenschaft und Sozialpolitik* published before the Nazis shuttered it, Speier broke with Marx and embraced Weber, moving from an economistic to a psychological interpretation of history. This was an important move for Speier; in the milieux within which he wrote, Weber, he recalled, "was generally regarded as the real antagonist of Marx," and embracing his sociology was understood as a rejection of Marxist social science.

In this essay, Speier argued that the two basic categories of Marxist theory, "proletariat" and "capitalist," were nineteenth-century atavisms that emphasized the economic at the expense of the psychological. Building on his earlier discussions of social status—recall that in 1931 he had castigated workers for imitating bourgeois norms—Speier declared that to understand modern social structures sociologists required a new theoretical system based on the concept of prestige (*Geltung*). As he said, "if it were possible to deepen and to broaden our understanding of the essence, the formation, the distribution, and the historical transformation of social prestige, then it would be possible to construct an elastic sociological system of concepts, which would allow a differentiated and subject-appropriate assessment of social structure with reference to the types of prestige that prevail and what social units they bring about." Speier thus contended that the economistic interpretation of society and history that socialists championed was faulty. Evident here was a dual disappointment: first, with Marxist theory's failure to predict reality and, second, with workers themselves, whose desire for bourgeois status provided the historical-empirical refutation of Marxist theory.[49]

Theory and experience combined to convince Speier that salvation was not to be found in the working classes. After Hitler's ascension to the chancellorship, Speier stated in no uncertain terms that the "great majority [of impoverished workers] did not belong to the Social Democracy, were even hostile to it, and refused to draw from their economic position those conclusions which the Marxian theorists expected." His personal experiences further emboldened his rejection of workers. Since the outbreak of the depression, a "culture of radicalism," to use Pamela Swett's phrase, had swept through Berlin's proletarian neighborhoods. Working-class members of the fascist right and communist left repeatedly fought each other in public, and often very violent, street battles. Speier, who lived in Mariendorf, a town within the Tempelhof district that abutted the Kreuzberg and Neukölln districts, which were centers of Weimar-era working class political violence, likely witnessed and certainly knew about the street disturbances. Moreover, he occasionally attended Nazi rallies for research purposes and was no doubt frightened by the fervor Hitler engendered in his audience, many of whom were workers. Berlin's destabilizing violence and workers' support for the Nazis led Speier to conclude that the working class would never become a force for progressive change.[50]

Speier's conversations with workers themselves also compelled him to determine that manifold people were simply apolitical. When conducting research for a seminar on unemployment at the Hochschule, for example, Speier met with dozens of workers and their families, where he encountered many people who were "Nazis today, who tomorrow became communists, or who were communists yesterday and had today become Nazis. This depended partly on chance, [partly on] where there was more beer or where there was more noise. I had the feeling that [there] was not a very big difference" between worker support for the Nazis and for the communists. Without a politically conscious working class, Speier's socialism had no object to focus on, and he discarded the ideology completely.[51]

By the autumn of 1933, Speier had abandoned socialist theory and politics. Furthermore, he began to distrust ordinary people writ large, an opinion expressed in his 1933 monograph *White-Collar Workers in German Society. White-Collar Workers* was intended to be Speier's *Habilitationsschrift*—which, in Eric Weitz's phrasing, was "the second thesis required for acceptance into [German] faculties"—and was scheduled to appear in the Ferdinand Enke Press's series *Sociological Inquiries*, which was edited by Sigmund Neumann, Albert Salomon, and Alfred von Martin. Once Hitler assumed power, however, the Nazis dismissed these editors and replaced them with Theodor Geiger and Andreas Walther, the latter a Nazi who refused to publish Speier's clearly antifascist tract. *White-Collar Workers* remained unpublished until 1977, when the historian Jürgen Kocka persuaded the Vandenhoeck and Ruprecht Press to release a revised version as *White-Collar Workers before National Socialism*. The closest we have to Speier's original *Habilitationsschrift* is a 1939 Works Progress Administration translation of the book's slightly revised first four chapters, titled *The Salaried Employee in German Society*.[52]

In the book, which was heavily influenced by Weber, Speier attributed significant responsibility to white-collar workers for the Nazis' rise: "When the middle classes were impoverished [after World War I], they tried to discover the authors of their misery. They prepared the way for a political counter-revolution by actively supporting those political leaders who were striving to undo an unwanted change [e.g., the political ascent of the SPD, the weakening of the German army, or general political chaos], ascribing it to 'guilty' politicians and demanding their punishment." White-collar workers, Speier continued, blamed German labor for their socioeconomic woes and therefore had no interest in allying themselves with blue-collar workers. This indicated that although white-collar workers were economically proletarian—that is to say, they occupied a similar economic position as blue-collar workers—their conception "of the social hierarchy was determined by the values and notions" of their social betters and not their economic position, as Marxist theory would have it. In this, white-collar workers mirrored Germany's blue-collar workers, who "had created a society of [their] own in [their] clubs and organizations and . . . this society was, in part, nothing more than a society of proletarians aspiring to be petits bourgeois." According to Speier, ordinary Germans, both white collar and blue collar, were most concerned with raising their social status. They could not be trusted to be agents of progressive change, nor could they be trusted to support pro-democratic political movements.[53]

By his September 1933 exile, Speier had lost faith in the SPD, Marxist theory, the proletariat, and ordinary people as a whole. For the remainder of his life, he considered most of humanity to be fickle, ignorant, and incapable of enlightenment. The crisis of Weimar democracy had ended in the nightmarish collapse of parliamentary governance and the advent of a fascist society. The worst had come true. In exile, Speier would use this trauma as an inspiration, dedicating himself to ensuring that intellectuals did all they could to prevent another Weimar.

Chapter 2

The Social Role of the Intellectual Exile

Exile engendered a variety of reactions among the thousands of intellectuals forced to flee Nazi Germany. Some émigrés descended into despair, others into political reaction, while a number viewed exile as an opportunity to combat the regime that had forced their emigration. Speier belonged to this third group. In the United States, he reframed the project he had initiated in Weimar. As in Germany, Speier asserted the political importance of intellectuals. However, he now argued that intellectuals must sever all ties to political parties and offer advice to U.S. policymakers directly, regardless of decision makers' political affiliation. His conviction that intellectuals best served the greater good as nonpartisan advisers became a critical component of the vision of the defense intellectual he institutionalized in the early Cold War.

Speier immigrated into circumstances that cultivated the development of his activist program of intellectual exile. First, he moved to New York City, "the most European of American cities," as Thomas Bender has shown.[1] New York was especially hospitable to Berliners like Speier, who found traces of their old lives in the five boroughs' densely populated concrete geography.[2] Moreover, the New York of the 1930s was home to a diverse intelligentsia that accepted the émigrés as equals.[3] Second, Speier entered the United States under the sponsorship of Emil Lederer, whose patronage provided him with stable employment at the New School for Social Research's "University in Exile." Serendipitously, the New School's cosmopolitan ideology complemented Speier's, which facilitated his transition to U.S. academia.[4] Third, American social scientists' fascination with the sociology of knowledge eased Speier's intellectual assimilation into the U.S. scholarly community. As Karl Mannheim's first graduate student, Speier served as a symbolic representative of progressive German sociology, a status that enabled him to engender interest in his work among prominent scholars, most notably Louis Wirth of the University of Chicago, who praised Speier to American colleagues. Finally, the United States of 1933 was politically hospitable to a former social democrat like Speier. President Franklin Delano Roosevelt's first one hundred days in office were defined by a number of activities, including the establishment of the Federal Emergency Relief Administration and the Tennessee Valley Authority, which suggested that the new president was willing to experiment with innovative institutional, economic, social, and political arrangements. For all of these reasons, Speier was able to happily embrace the United States as his new home.

Figure 3. Speier with Carl Mayer *(left)* and unidentified man at a garden party held by the philanthropist Hiram Halle, one of the early funders of the University in Exile, ca. 1936–1937, *photo courtesy of the New School*

Speier's easy immigration allowed him to avoid what Edward Said referred to as the "essential sadness" of "the unhealable rift forced between a human being and a native place, between the self and its true home," which has characterized exile for so many people throughout history.[5] For the entirety of his career in the United States, Speier retained a profound loyalty to the nation that had saved him and his family. Even when U.S. officials violated the principles for which the nation supposedly stood, Speier never questioned America's fundamental goodness. Such devotion, perhaps, helps explain why Speier remained silent in the face of McCarthyism, the U.S.-backed coups in Guatemala and Iran, and, most dramatically, the Vietnam War. The United States protected Speier and his family, and for this he was eternally grateful.

Despite Speier's quick assimilation, in the first years of his exile he primarily socialized with fellow émigrés. The exile world of 1930s New York was remarkably small. Émigrés regularly debated with each other, read each other's scholarship, and attended each other's talks. Though the émigrés argued about manifold topics, one of the most controversial—and personally sensitive—concerned the social role of the intellectual exile. Discussions about this theme were sites in which émigrés grappled with their pasts in Germany and their present and future places in American society. Speier was an active participant in these debates, and it was in dialogue with Max Horkheimer, the director of the Institute of Social Research, that he initiated a process of Americanization characterized by his shedding of German concerns and embrace of the U.S. state. In so doing, Speier began to separate himself from his German colleagues and adopt a self-consciously American identity.

In addition to the exiles, New York City was home to another small community of intellectuals who would exert profound influence on U.S. thought and culture in the 1930s and beyond: the "New York Intellectuals."[6] Speier had no relationship with this group, which is somewhat surprising, as he and the New York Intellectuals participated in overlapping social circles, and several, including the philosopher Sidney Hook, were connected to the New School. This cohort's absence from Speier's life may be best explained by its politics. Unlike Speier, in the early 1930s most of the New York Intellectuals retained their Marxist faith, even as they adopted an anti-Stalinist position. For Speier, who had left his Marxism in Germany, there was little reason to engage intellectually with people he could have only perceived as naive Americans unfamiliar with, or unwilling to admit, Marxism's ineradicable problems. Ironically given their distance in the 1930s, the trajectories of several New York Intellectuals mirrored Speier's. Like Speier, numerous members of this cohort began their careers by attempting to reform Marxism before adopting a jaundiced view of workers and Marxist theory. The interwar rise of fascism and Stalinism led the New York Intellectuals to find themselves in 1945 where Speier found himself in 1933.

Instead of the New York Intellectuals, Speier developed relationships with three young social scientists associated with the University of Chicago. Gabriel Almond, Harold Lasswell, and Edward Shils, like Louis Wirth, were interested in the German sociology of knowledge and considered Speier an important representative of that tradition.[7] Each was also dedicated to using social science to improve U.S. policy and was skeptical about ordinary people's political rationality. The concerns and beliefs of Almond, Lasswell, and Shils thus mirrored Speier's, and by the late 1930s he had begun friendships with all three. Within this group, Speier had a unique epistemological authority as the only one to witness Hitler's rise—and the masses' support for it—firsthand. His physical presence served as a constant reminder to his American colleagues of what could happen when fascism succeeded.

The interwar connections that developed between Speier, Almond, Lasswell, and Shils proved critical to the composition of the military-intellectual complex and highlight the importance of prewar relationships to postwar intellectual history. Over the course of midcentury, as Speier and the Chicago social scientists became respected members of the first generation of defense intellectuals, they provided each other—and those who thought like them—with ideological support, employment, publication opportunities, and access to government decision makers. Ideologically, they created a new intellectual consciousness that promoted scholarly engagement with the state, distrust of ordinary people, and fear of "totalitarianism," a catch-all term that analogized the Nazi and Soviet regimes. Practically, they established an intellectual elite and nongovernmental institutions defined by a particular set of ideas and interests. In the early Cold War, those who did not have access to this (or a similar) network, or who disagreed with the assumptions about international and domestic politics that undergirded it, had few means by which to make their voices heard in the corridors of power.

Speier felt comfortable in his exile because Alvin Johnson and the New School for Social Research provided him with a stable home whose cosmopolitan perspective complemented his own. Johnson, who served as head of the New School from 1922 until 1946, subscribed to a social vision that considered intellectuals members of an international "republic of letters" who produced knowledge disconnected from any national context. This idea was accepted, and indeed embraced, by the intellectuals who comprised the University in Exile. The majority of these émigrés were the inheritors of a Central European Jewish intellectual tradition that denied the importance of particularistic ethnic associations in favor of a secular, cosmopolitan, and universalistic intellectual identity. Though not Jewish himself, Speier matured intellectually under the tutelage of two Jews, Karl Mannheim and Emil Lederer, who imbued him with a respect for the imagined republic of letters. The cosmopolitan affinities shared by Johnson and Speier help explain why the latter felt safe enough in his new home to assimilate into the U.S. intellectual community and develop an activist political program.[8]

The New School was founded in 1919 by a group of well-known progressive intellectuals and philanthropists that included Charles Beard, John Dewey, Thorstein Veblen, and Felix Frankfurter, to protest Columbia University president Nicholas Murray Butler's stifling of antiwar criticism during World War I. The New School was established as a self-conscious bastion of academic freedom, partially modeled on German *Volkshochschulen* dedicated to adult and worker education. It was one of numerous American institutions, including the Rand School of Social Science, Brookwood Labor College, and the Workers' School of the Amalgamated Clothing Workers, as well as German institutions, such as the Hochschule für Politik and the Institute of Social Research, which were intended to unite social science research with workers' interests.[9]

Johnson, the central figure behind the University in Exile's creation, was one of the New School's founders. He was born and raised in Nebraska, the son of Danish immigrants. Johnson served in the U.S. Army during the War of 1898, and at war's end he matriculated as a graduate student in economics at Columbia. There he studied under Franklin Giddings and Edwin Seligman, the latter a Jew of German descent who had studied in Germany under Karl Knies and Gustav Schmoller. Seligman was particularly influential on Johnson, and the relationship between the two mirrored the one Speier had with Lederer. Like Lederer, Seligman served as a government consultant and attempted to promote liberal goals, such as the establishment of a progressive income tax. He provided a model to Johnson of what the career of an activist intellectual looked like.[10]

Through Johnson, the image of the intellectual embodied by Seligman influenced Speier. In Germany, Speier had connected the intellectual to the socialist movement. In the United States, however, he would increasingly advocate for intellectuals to become expert consultants to the U.S.

government or to join the government itself, a transformation that indicated Johnson and Seligman's impact. Seligman's vision of intellectual political engagement centered on participation in state institutions, not partisan political action of the type Speier had earlier advocated. Seligman believed that the intellectual needed to be isolated from public opinion and party politics in order to contribute effectively to progressive social change by advising the nation's elite directly. Johnson endorsed this view—as he said, the intellectual should never "apply all their resources, guns or clubs or propaganda, to the support of party dogma and party purposes"—and repeatedly urged New School scholars to work for government agencies as opposed to partisan organizations. The intellectual, in Johnson and Seligman's—and later, Speier's—vision, was to serve as power's guide.[11]

Johnson received his PhD in economics in 1902. He worked in academia until 1915, when Herbert Croly, a co-founder of the progressive *New Republic*, invited him to join the magazine as an assistant editor. Croly had read and been impressed with Johnson's essay "The Soul of Capitalism," which asserted that "toleration and its counterpart, personal liberty, . . . are the first constituents of the soul of capitalism." Johnson accepted Croly's offer, hoping, as he remembered in his memoir, to "get nearer to the mature lay public that the economist would have to reach if his ideas were ever to mesh with political realities." Through the *New Republic*, Johnson became involved with the New York intellectual circle that founded the New School and eventually accepted a position as one of the college's first faculty members. In 1922, Johnson became the New School's director, which altered the school's trajectory. Over the next twelve years, he improved the New School's finances and built its reputation as a leader in arts education. Nevertheless, Johnson was unable to secure the funds or faculty necessary to pursue a significant research program, and the school established itself primarily as an institute of adult education. Until the University in Exile's founding, social research, ironically given the college's official name, was not a New School focus.[12]

Transatlantic connections forged in the 1920s were the seeds of the University in Exile's germination. Johnson was fluent in German and had since the beginning of his career been interested in German scholarship. In 1924, he and Bernard Baruch, the financier and statesman, traveled to Germany to study the postwar hyperinflation. On this trip, Johnson made Lederer's acquaintance, and the two maintained an epistolary friendship throughout the 1920s. In 1927, Johnson accepted Seligman's offer to serve as associate editor of a Rockefeller Foundation–funded English-language encyclopedia modeled on the *Handwörterbuch der Staatswissenschaften* (Dictionary of the

Sciences of State) titled the *Encyclopaedia of the Social Sciences*. Foundation officials, Seligman, and Johnson envisioned the *Encyclopaedia* as a cosmopolitan project that would incorporate entries from social scientists around the world. Having little inside knowledge of German academia, Johnson asked Lederer to recommend scholars to contribute to the *Encyclopaedia*. Lederer thus brought some of his colleagues to Johnson's attention years before the University in Exile was even a consideration. By the mid-1930s, several members of the University in Exile, including Speier, Lederer, Gerhard Colm, Fritz Lehmann, and Jacob Marschak, had written entries for the *Encyclopaedia*.[13]

As he watched the rise of National Socialism from abroad, Johnson began to recognize that if Hitler triumphed, many left-wing and Jewish German academics would be expelled from their country and would require a home in exile. Soon after Hitler became chancellor in January 1933 and started to forbid his political enemies to teach, Johnson decided "to create a situation in which the displaced German scholars would be able to keep alive the traditions and methods that had been the glory of their universities." Johnson hoped that such a "University in Exile," as he dubbed his venture, would serve "as a liaison between American university culture and the pre-Nazi German university culture" he greatly respected, bringing the best of progressive German social science to bear on U.S. thought. An intellectual migration, Johnson further anticipated, not only would reinvigorate U.S. social science generally but also would transform the New School into both a premier research organization and a symbol of international scientific cosmopolitanism.[14]

Lederer was centrally involved in the University in Exile's creation. In early 1933, Lederer fled Germany for London, where Johnson approached him about his plans "to get ten or a dozen [German professors] to the U.S., to set up a German university in exile." Lederer quickly accepted Johnson's request to become a founding member of this group, turning down a position at the University of Manchester to move to New York. According to Speier, Lederer "was impressed by Johnson's pragmatic liberalism and considered work at a new free university, which in the prevailing circumstances could become a political symbol, to be more worthwhile than joining a well-established institution." Lederer committed himself to doing what he could to fight the Nazis from his exile.[15]

Throughout the spring and summer of 1933, Johnson worked to raise funds for his project. By the summer, he had collected tens of thousands of dollars from the philanthropist Hiram Halle and individual donors. In June, the University in Exile received a provisional charter from the Board of Regents of New York State and was thereafter able to offer classes. To win American intellectual support for his venture, Johnson drafted a letter signed by several hundred social scientists supporting the University in Exile's founding. In its first year, he also established an Advisory Committee that consisted of prominent Americans who, according to Johnson, believed "in freedom of thought and teaching"; this group included Dewey, Frankfurter, Seligman, Oliver Wendell Holmes, Robert Hutchins, Robert MacIver, and George A. Plimpton. The University in Exile thus enjoyed the imprimatur of several of the nation's most influential intellectuals, which eased the émigrés' academic assimilation.[16]

In the summer of 1933, Johnson and Lederer asked Speier to serve as a liaison between the University in Exile and the scholars the two wanted to recruit to their endeavor. Johnson and Lederer believed that Speier, as a talented, young, and, importantly, non-Jewish intellectual, could safely carry the New School's contracts from England to Germany. The opportunity to join the University in Exile arrived at a fortuitous moment for Speier. In April, the Reich Ministry of Public Enlightenment and Propaganda had seized the Hochschule and fired him and other left-wing colleagues. However, because his wife, Lisa, was pregnant, Speier felt he could not immediately leave Germany. Nonetheless, once Lisa's Judaism led to her dismissal from her position as a pediatrician in Berlin's welfare office, the Speiers swiftly realized there was no future for them in their birth nation. When Speier received Lederer's invitation in July, he began to prepare to emigrate.

Throughout July and August, Speier traveled between London and Berlin carrying contracts to the University in Exile's founding members. Upon completing his duties, on September 15 he moved to New York, with his family, which now included a baby daughter named Sybil, following in October. Speier's exile had begun. German academics were technically nonquota immigrants but in practice could obtain U.S. visas only if they had guaranteed employment and had worked as professors for at least two years before their immigration. Though Speier did not have quite this amount of teaching experience, Johnson's assurance that he had a position was enough to enable him and his family to immigrate successfully. His early arrival in America made Speier one of the first of the approximately two thousand German intellectuals who escaped there between 1933 and 1939.[17]

Johnson, Lederer, and Speier recruited ten academics to found the University in Exile: Karl Brandt (agricultural economics), Gerhard Colm (economics), Arthur Feiler (economics), Eduard Heimann (economics), Erich von Hornbostel (sociology of music), Herman Kantorowicz (law), Lederer (economics), Speier (sociology), Max Wertheimer (Gestalt psychology), and Frieda von Wunderlich (social policy). Johnson recruited these scholars because each, as he stated, "supported the democratic government under the Weimar constitution." Additionally, most were associates of Lederer, were empirically oriented social scientists, and were social democrats or held social democratic sympathies that mirrored Johnson's—though to colleagues Johnson insisted that "no member of the [University in Exile] is a Marxist as the term is understood in America." The University in Exile's founders hailed primarily from three institutions: the Hochschule für Politik, the University of Frankfurt, and the Kiel Institute for World Economics. Most important for Johnson, the majority of the founders were intellectuals concerned with using social science to reach progressive ends through government work. As he admiringly reported in 1935 to the New School's trustees, "the German social scientist stands nearer to the political and administrative life of the country [than American scholars], participating in expert commissions and in national and city governmental bodies." Johnson's positive attitude toward bridging the gap between academia and the government proved critical to Speier, who was granted several leaves of absence from the New School to join the wartime administration during World War II. With the faculty and funding in place, the University in Exile—which was renamed the Graduate Faculty of Political and Social Science because the New York State Department of Education would not allow an institution with only a single faculty to call itself a "university"—opened its doors in October 1933.[18]

Johnson made significant efforts to generate a sense of community among the Graduate Faculty and to popularize its research among American audiences. He convened a weekly, public General Seminar in which faculty members discussed their research and its relationship to contemporary problems and which eventually resulted in two edited collections, *Political and Economic Democracy* and *War in Our Time* (the latter edited by Speier and the economist Alfred Kähler). He also started the journal *Social Research* to offer a collective forum for the Graduate Faculty's scholarship and pressured the faculty to publish in it—in English—regularly. Speier, in fact, served as the first editor of *Social Research*, building on his experience as editor of the *Archiv für Sozialpolitik und Sozialwissenschaft*. Throughout the 1930s, a number of social scientists who later became prominent, including Gabriel Almond, Lewis Coser, C. Wright Mills, Charles H. Page, and Edward Shils, encountered European scholarship through the journal or through meeting with members of the Graduate Faculty. Owing to Johnson's efforts, by World War II the Graduate Faculty was recognized as one of the most important collections of exiled European scholars in the United States, if not the world.[19]

Institutional and cultural affinities eased Speier's transition to the United States. Like the Hochschule, the New School was part of a transatlantic trend in which left-wing reformers established colleges of higher education that sought to politicize and educate a working-class constituency. Though Speier was no longer dedicated to this project, he was nonetheless familiar with the norms and culture of such institutions. Moreover, both the New School and the Hochschule faculty committed themselves to using social science to solve problems of public policy, a goal to which Speier remained devoted. The cultural and physical setting of New York City also encouraged Speier's acculturation. The city was home to an ethnically diverse intelligentsia that admired European intellectual and scientific achievements and provided the exiles with intellectual stimulation if they sought it. Additionally, New York was especially welcoming to Berliners like Speier, who found traces of their old lives in the city's geography, diversity, and cosmopolitanism.[20]

Speier's assimilation was further fostered by the fact that he and Johnson shared a cosmopolitan vision of intellectual life. Since the early twentieth century, left-wing American intellectuals cognizant of an increasingly globalized world had committed themselves to cosmopolitan values. Johnson himself endorsed a specific intellectual strand influenced by the philosopher John Dewey, which sought to incorporate European scientific, social, and cultural traditions into a reinvigorated "international nationalism"—an American nationalism informed by non-American cultures—that would undergird a cosmopolitan U.S. future. In the 1930s, the exiles became integral to Johnson's project. For their part, the German émigrés, including the philo-Semitic Speier, were the heirs of a complementary post-emancipation German-Jewish commitment to cosmopolitanism that considered it an ideological means through which Jewish intellectuals could supersede their ethnic identity, embrace secular culture, and escape anti-Semitism. Although Speier was not a Jew, through Mannheim and Lederer he became a member of Weimar's secular community of progressive Jewish intellectuals and imbibed the cosmopolitan vision of this group. These ideological affinities help explain the ease with which Speier assimilated into the Graduate Faculty.[21]

In the Graduate Faculty's first course catalog, Johnson used the language of international scientific cosmopolitanism to explain why the University in Exile was "an institution long overdue in the modern world":

> Whatever may be the condition of the other departments of life, scholarship is international. A scientific discovery achieved in the laboratories of Paris or Berlin, Helsingfors or Tokio [*sic*], becomes immediately the property of American scholars, the foundation upon which further discoveries of practical utility or intellectual advance may be based. It follows that every modern nation should have institutions to offer temporary or permanent hospitality to scholars who have been deprived of the opportunity of functioning by the political requirements, real or imaginary, of any country. The hundreds of able scholars who have been displaced from the German universities represent a priceless resource of all civilization which is in danger of sterilization.

"Scholarship," Johnson later declared, "never has been bound to a particular environment. European scholars can function in exile. In exile they can contribute to the lands that give them shelter a vast number of ideas that in the end are bound to make for the enrichment of thought, the strengthening of the intellectualism upon which peace and good order ultimately depend." In this way, Johnson asserted that the exiles he saved would benefit not only the New School but also the United States, and the world, as a whole.[22]

Speier endorsed a similar cosmopolitan vision in his 1937 essay "The Social Conditions of the Intellectual Exile":

> The intellectuals as a group may cut across the boundaries of local, national, religious divisions. Every intellectual worker discovers this unity when he experiences the essential endogamy of his group, when he recognizes a fellow worker as a fellow intellectual rather than as a member of a different nation or race, class, party or locality. This is the natural recognition of what intellectuals have in common, ignoring any unlike qualities they may have. The community of intellectuals is ultimately based on reason, the supreme and common property of man, or, if you prefer, on the value of truth. It is therefore universal and capable of social representation by any two persons who communicate with each other in order to say something true.

The intellectual, Speier avowed, "owes his supreme loyalties to the community of the spirit," not to particularistic identities. Moreover, echoing Johnson's argument that the exiles would aid the United States, Speier maintained that in situations where "sympathy governs the relations" between an expelled scholar and her or his adopted homeland, the intellectual had the duty to contribute "his small share to the culture of his new country." For both Johnson and Speier, the cosmopolitan intellectual exile should dedicate himself or herself to strengthening the United States, which, they implied, was the current bearer of the universalistic values cherished by scholars.[23]

As Speier's statements indicate, ideological affinities united him and Johnson. Most important, both endorsed the idea that there was a "republic of letters" to which intellectuals belonged and through which they could contribute to the betterment of the United States, which Speier and Johnson assumed was the representative of Western civilization. Speier and Johnson were thus devoted to the same meta-intellectual project, which provided a common sense of mission between the two that enabled Speier, and indeed many of his colleagues, to view exile as a moment of opportunity, so that by 1986 he could honestly report to the sociologist Volker Meja that his experience revealed that "not every emigrant was 'damaged,' as [the exile philosopher Theodor] Adorno thought." Indeed, Speier quickly adapted to his new homeland. Though he initially found the United States "overwhelmingly new," and though at first Germany "made itself felt in almost every [one of his] thought[s]," within a year of his September 1933 immigration Speier had learned English and had begun to embrace American life. The security he felt at the New School provided Speier with the opportunity to look beyond the University in Exile to establish connections with social scientists working at other universities, which proved critical to his future success.[24]

Throughout his career, Speier was surprised to find that American academics were fascinated with the "German-Jewish intellectual ghetto" that was the New School. In the 1930s, he took advantage of U.S. scholars' attentions to make his reputation as an authority on Karl Mannheim's sociology of knowledge, which had aroused interest among U.S. social scientists, particularly sociologists and political scientists interested in sociology. American sociologists' eager reception of Mannheim, and subsequently Speier, reflected a discipline in flux. The Great Depression had engendered a crisis of legitimacy among sociologists. Their failure to provide effective solutions for the economic downturn led elite and ordinary Americans alike to disregard sociologists, despite the strides the discipline had made in the American imagination over the course of the 1920s as a result of sociologists' participation in various government groups, including the Chicago Commission on Race

Relations, the Department of Agriculture's Division of Farm Population and Rural Life, and Herbert Hoover's President's Research Committee on Social Trends. Moreover, the depression had forced universities and private foundations to contract. As a result, fewer graduate students pursued PhD's in sociology, membership in the American Sociological Society declined, and the private funding that had been available to sociologists in the 1920s dissipated, all of which threatened future research. To add insult to injury, the government appeared far more interested in recruiting economists, political scientists, and lawyers into its ranks than sociologists, which provoked concerns about irrelevance throughout the discipline.[25]

For these reasons, sociologists began to fear they were losing their hard-won place within both the disciplinary pantheon and American public life. Sociologists' anxieties resulted in several structural and intellectual changes within the discipline. Most dramatically, a group of scholars came together to wrest control of the discipline from the University of Chicago sociologists who had dominated it after World War I, running successful campaigns for offices in the American Sociological Society and founding the *American Sociological Review* as an alternative to the Chicago-published *American Journal of Sociology*. Furthermore, disciplinary chaos engendered epistemological heterogeneity. The natural scientific approach, which was defined by methodological positivism and which came to dominate academic sociology after 1945, was during the interwar era just one of many legitimate methods. In addition to scientistic methodologies, scholars considered grand theory, ethnography, statistical surveys, historical sociology, and other approaches valid. This disciplinary turmoil and lack of a methodological consensus encouraged sociologists to search for inspiration in European sociology, which eventually led some to the sociology of knowledge.[26]

What did American sociologists seek in the sociology of knowledge? A number of respected scholars argued that the sociology of knowledge would open new vistas of research that, they implied, would bolster the discipline's intellectual legitimacy, increasing its attenuated academic and public prestige. For instance, Talcott Parsons, who had studied with Speier at Heidelberg and who was by the 1930s a professor at Harvard, praised "*Wissenssoziologie* [sociology of knowledge] as a most fruitful field of sociological investigation" because it correctly revealed "that the explanation of why given theories have arisen and spread at given times and places and in given social classes is to be sought to a large extent in various aspects of the social milieu." Likewise, Louis Wirth, an influential sociologist at the University of Chicago, lauded the sociology of knowledge for demonstrating "that thought, besides being a proper subject matter for logic and psychology, becomes fully comprehensible only if it is viewed sociologically." For Parsons and Wirth, the sociology of knowledge provided empirical access to the social origins of human thought, an accomplishment that could only increase sociology's intellectual status.[27]

Wirth's patronage was especially crucial to Speier's intellectual assimilation. Wirth was a German immigrant who had met and been impressed with Mannheim in 1932. After meeting Mannheim, Wirth began offering a course on German sociology and received funding to pursue research on the subject. He was thus primed to be interested in an exile like Speier. Speier and Wirth began their relationship in 1935, when Wirth asked Speier to serve as a mentor to his student Gabriel Almond, who was in New York on a Social Science Research Council (SSRC) fellowship, and Speier asked Wirth for suggestions regarding publishing his *Habilitationsschrift* on white-collar workers. Upon reading Speier's work, Wirth began praising him to colleagues as "one of the outstanding younger scholars in the recently developed field of the sociology of knowledge." Though Wirth declared that he was impressed with Speier's "empirical grounding" and his "rather striking work in the field of theory," the lack of specifics in his discussions of Speier's scholarship indicated that Speier was important to Wirth less because of his own research and more because he was a symbol, a representative of Mannheim and the German sociology of knowledge in America.[28]

To promote the sociology of knowledge, in 1935 and 1936 Wirth invited Speier to deliver lectures at both the American Sociological Society's annual meeting and the University of Chicago. Wirth's endorsement provided Speier with the intellectual clout he required to be accepted as a rising figure in the field and an outstanding representative of German sociology. In the 1930s, Speier's articles and reviews appeared in the discipline's two major journals, the *American Journal of Sociology* and the *American Sociological Review*, and numerous institutions of higher education, including Brooklyn College, courted him for a permanent position. He also published the major review of the English translation of Mannheim's *Ideology and Utopia*—which Wirth invited him to write—in the *American Journal of Sociology*.[29]

In addition to Wirth, Harold Lasswell, a Chicago political scientist interested in sociology, expressed admiration for and popularized Speier's scholarship, inviting him to speak at a Chicago seminar. Indeed, Speier listed Lasswell and Wirth, along with Alvin Johnson and Robert MacIver, the Columbia sociologist, as professional references when he applied for a grant from the Rockefeller Foundation. In his private recommendation to the foundation, Lasswell went so far as to refer to Speier as "one of the most distinguished sociologists of his generation" who "belongs to that small group of men capable of balancing rich theoretical perspectives with rigorous technical work on detail." Wirth, for his part, averred in his recommendation that he had "the highest regard for [Speier] as a gentleman and as a scholar" and considered him "a man of wide and deep learning, imagination, and insight." The two professors, though, said little that was specific to Speier's work, which underlined that for them Speier was important as a symbol more than as a scholar.[30]

The younger generation of social scientists who would shape their fields after World War II also admired Speier for his indigenous connections to German sociology. As discussed above, Gabriel Almond, a Chicago graduate student in political science who spent a year in New York on an SSRC fellowship, "sought out [at Wirth's suggestion] Hans Speier . . . for what he could tell me of Max Weber, who had become my scholarly hero." Almond took classes at the New School, where Speier served as his "mentor," and Speier even introduced Almond to his future wife, Maria Dorothea Kaufmann, a German émigré. Edward Shils, a Chicago PhD student in sociology and, with Wirth, the translator of Mannheim's *Ideology and Utopia*, also became friends with Speier, writing him in 1934 to see his unpublished *Habilitationsschrift*. Speier's position as Mannheim's protégé particularly attracted Shils, who was then "an exhilarated devotee of Mannheim." As Shils remembered at the end of his life, "the fact that [Speier] had written his dissertation at Heidelberg under Mannheim's inspiration and supervision . . . brought us closer together." Moreover, Robert Merton, a PhD student in sociology at Harvard, was inspired by Mannheim and the German sociology of knowledge because of Speier. For these young intellectuals, Speier represented a sociological tradition that they for a time maintained could reinvigorate U.S. social science. Though by 1937 Speier had turned against Mannheim, critiquing the latter for what he considered to be the sociology of knowledge's relativistic implications, U.S. social scientists continued to champion him. Wirth, Lasswell, Almond, Shils, and Merton wanted to be associated with Speier not because of his own scholarship but because he provided them with a link to Mannheim specifically, German sociology generally, and, at the broadest level, a progressive German intellectual tradition they profoundly respected.[31]

The ambitious Speier was himself quite interested in increasing his status among U.S. social scientists, a fact demonstrated by a 1938 letter to Shils in which Speier asked whether his editorial position at *Social Research* "adds to the academic status of [his] otherwise insignificant personality." Speier was cognizant of his symbolic importance and shrewdly presented himself as a native interpreter of the sociology of knowledge and a bridge between European and American thought. In a 1934 review of Oswald Spengler's *The Hour of Decision*, for example, Speier stated that he

> should like to call attention to the book of a writer whose similarity to Spengler has not been emphasized by Spengler's critics: Nikolay Danilevsky's *Russia and Europe*. A direct influence of Danilevsky on Spengler is improbable and comparatively uninteresting. I mention the book in this connection by way of illustrating the general theory that similar political aims often lead various writers of the same period to use similar methodologies, to order their material from similar points of view, and to formulate much the same concepts. The investigation of such interrelationships has been accorded particular attention by the discipline known in Germany as sociology of understanding [another term for the sociology of knowledge].

In addition, Speier regularly gave lectures on the sociology of knowledge and associated himself with Mannheim even as their intellectual paths diverged. In doing all of this, Speier subtly proclaimed himself an indispensable translator of the sociology of knowledge for American audiences.[32]

Throughout the 1930s, the content of Speier's work was less important for U.S. social scientists than his ability to serve as a symbol that linked two distinct Western intellectual traditions. This is not to imply that Speier's writings were never cited for content; they were. But to explain U.S. social scientists' embrace of him, one cannot point to Speier's scholarship, which was well received but not revolutionary. Rather than his work, it was Speier's position as a representative of the German sociology of knowledge—which appeared to have the potential to open up new areas of research—that explains why American scholars supported him.[33]

Speier's smooth transition into American academia encouraged him to view exile as a moment of opportunity, and he spent the mid-1930s attempting to convince fellow émigrés that they should abandon previous disagreements and cooperate to defend the freedoms Hitler denied them by working with the U.S. government. In the process, Speier singled out the philosopher Max Horkheimer, the director of the Institute of Social Research, for criticism. Though Speier lambasted the institute's reconstructed Marxism and embrace of psychoanalysis, it was primarily Horkheimer's approach to politics and exile that rankled him. For Horkheimer, the Nazi victory made clear that in the current historical moment the forces of reaction had triumphed over the forces of progressivism, and therefore the best an intellectual could do was develop a critique of the present society. Speier firmly rejected this perspective and what he understood to be its concomitant assumption that intellectual exiles should remain aloof from the concerns of their adopted homeland. In response to Horkheimer, he elaborated his own activist program of intellectual exile.

Founded in 1923 and affiliated with the University of Frankfurt, the Institute of Social Research was one of the first Marxist organizations connected with a German university. In 1930, Horkheimer ascended to the institute's directorship and reshaped it in his image. He gathered a circle around him that consisted of the economist Friedrich Pollock, the psychoanalyst Erich Fromm, the philosopher Herbert Marcuse, and the sociologist Leo Löwenthal. These individuals, along with the philosopher Theodor Adorno, who officially joined the institute in 1938, and the philosopher Walter Benjamin, who was loosely associated with the group, are today collectively known as the Frankfurt School and have become famous for their development of what they called a critical theory of society. For many scholars, the members of the Frankfurt School, along with Hannah Arendt and Leo Strauss, are the paradigmatic representatives of the émigré generation.

Horkheimer and most of his circle escaped Germany soon after Hitler seized power. They initially fled to Geneva before moving to New York City in the summer of 1934, where the institute became affiliated with Columbia. Over the course of the 1930s, the Frankfurt School developed a negative social theory defined by dialectical critique. Inspired by the proletariat's inability or unwillingness to transform German society during Weimar, Horkheimer and his colleagues sought to reinvigorate Marxism through the incorporation of psychoanalysis and a critique of culture. This melding, they hoped, would provide Marxists with the requisite tools to analyze the relationship between ideology and material reality, which they believed orthodox Marxist theory, with its base-superstructure model, downplayed. Moreover, they maintained that their critiques of capitalism would preserve the hope for a future emancipated society. Horkheimer, who served as the institute's guiding light, dubbed this approach critical theory.[34]

Speier was personally and professionally connected to the Frankfurt School. In Weimar, he and institute members had moved within the same left-wing intellectual circles. Speier regularly saw institute members at social gatherings, and for years he sent them copies of his publications and even met with them when some returned to Europe after World War II. He had further reviewed Carl Schmitt's *The Concept of the Political* for the institute's *Zeitschrift für Sozialforschung* at the request of Löwenthal, his friend and the editor of the *Zeitschrift*'s book review section. However, Speier decidedly did not respect or like Horkheimer. As he remembered, he regarded Horkheimer as "an orthodox, fairly uninteresting philosopher who did not know very much about macro-sociology." Indeed, the personal and professional connections Speier had to the institute did not prevent him from articulating a profound critique of its American debut, the 1936 *Studien über Autorität und Familie*, in *Social Research*.[35]

At the most obvious level, Speier's critique centered on the Frankfurt School's use of psychoanalysis, which he had long rejected due to its "unhistorical implications." In the review, he asserted that the results of the institute's research project on German workers, which relied on the psychoanalytical interpretation of questionnaires, were "somewhat meagre," and with a sweeping methodological condemnation averred that psychoanalytical "concepts perhaps do not deserve the attention which they arrest." As Speier said late in the piece, "the reviewer has been doubtful as to the value of Freudian psychology for an analysis of social phenomena. He must confess that the performance of Erich Fromm [the institute's primary psychoanalyst] has not removed his doubts."[36]

Speier also offered a subtle critique of the Frankfurt School's Marxism. In the midst of the review's final paragraph, in which he recommended that the institute examine the relationship between religious ideas and authority, Speier affirmed that "in this connection it will certainly have to be noticed that the bearing of Protestantism on the authoritarian structure of the family cannot be understood in terms of the changing social and economic order." The reference to Protestantism was a nod to Max Weber's famous *The Protestant Ethic and the Spirit of Capitalism*, an allusion that highlighted Speier's preference for Weber's emphasis on ideology and psychology over what he considered to be the Frankfurt School's Marxist economism. While Speier was correct to detect an economistic core to the *Studien*, which partially sought to explain the erosion of the father's familial authority with reference to socioeconomic transformations, he must have known that his ascription of a vulgar Marxist philosophy to the Frankfurt School was not only an exaggeration—in myriad essays, Horkheimer and his colleagues examined cultural phenomena as more than reflections of the economic base—but likely would have negative implications for the institute in the anti-Marxist U.S. intellectual community. Though its effects are hard to measure, for decades after the review's publication, members of the Frankfurt School pointed to it as a major reason their work was not accepted in the United States before World War II.[37]

More significantly, Speier's review expressed disapproval of Horkheimer's approach to exile. For most of the 1930s, Horkheimer viewed the institute as the embodiment of an endangered German-Marxist-Humanist intellectual tradition and remained steadfast in his commitment to maintaining its German-European character. Although most members of the Frankfurt School lived in the United States, Horkheimer, as Speier later haughtily recalled, published the *Zeitschrift* in German with the Parisian publisher Félix Alcan and criticized other exiles for writing in English. Moreover, the institute's members, unlike Speier and many of his New School colleagues, regularly traveled to Europe, where the institute retained offices, at least for a time, in Geneva, Paris, and London. Though they were physically in the United States, Horkheimer and his cohorts' hearts remained on the Continent, which discouraged their intellectual acculturation—a fact that Speier found distasteful.[38]

During their first years in exile, Horkheimer and his circle made little effort to assimilate their scholarship to U.S. norms. The Frankfurt School's writings were famously characterized by an arcane and difficult style that made them very trying for nonspecialists to understand, especially Americans who had little grounding in European social theory and philosophy. While the Frankfurt School's members justified their style by maintaining that their opacity prevented the commodification of their texts, it nonetheless worked against their assimilation. Furthermore, in the mid-1930s most of the school's members rejected Anglo-American empiricism and positivism and rarely interacted with American colleagues outside of Columbia. The institute's substantial endowment also enabled its members to pursue research without the aid of U.S. funding agencies, which meant there were few incentives for them to incorporate U.S. methods into their writings. Until financial difficulties in the late 1930s forced them to reconsider their voluntary segregation, Horkheimer and his fellow institute members lived in a state of "splendid isolation."[39]

Speier considered Horkheimer's insularity an insult to émigrés like himself who used their exile to join the U.S. intellectual community, and as such he condemned Horkheimer's approach to exile in his review of the *Studien*. Though he praised the institute for examining why relationships of authority changed over time, he nevertheless argued that "the [institute's] answer that the family is important in this respect is not so alien to American sociology as the terminology of the German scholars might sometimes suggest." By referring to members of the Frankfurt School as "German scholars" and by highlighting their obscure jargon, Speier implicitly set them apart, both intellectually and ideologically, from potential American colleagues. In so doing, he signaled to U.S. scholars that exiles like himself and the rest of the Graduate Faculty were willing to assimilate U.S. scholarship into their own work whereas the Frankfurt School was not. To underline further the institute's narrow-mindedness, Speier concluded his review with the recommendation that future institute studies "draw upon well established results of sociological and historical research," which suggested that the Frankfurt School was ignorant of such presumably American scholarship. At the same time that Speier presented himself as a bridge uniting European and American social science, he offered Horkheimer and his associates as examples of exiles who consciously separated themselves from U.S. scholars, providing a reason for these academics to ignore the institute's work.[40]

Horkheimer despised Speier's review. At a party thrown by Emil Lederer in 1937, Horkheimer, as Speier recalled, "reprimand[ed] me furiously in public," declaring that "I was not only wrong, I [also] had betrayed the solidarity on which refugees from the Third Reich had to depend." Speier, in contrast, considered his critical comments balanced and expressed shock at Horkheimer's outburst, attributing Horkheimer's response to his inability to "tolerate criticism like many men in positions of authority," his "lac[k] [of] a sense of humor," or his suspicion that Speier had "sinister designs against his Institute." Horkheimer was, in fact, sensitive to the slights, both real and perceived, of others; for example, he forever refused to associate with the cultural critic Siegfried Kracauer because of a supposedly insulting comment Kracauer made in the 1920s. Despite Speier's claims and Horkheimer's sensitivity, however, Horkheimer was correct to identify Speier's review as a serious remonstrance of the Frankfurt School's scholarship and approach to exile that had the potential to prevent U.S. academics from taking the institute's work seriously. Indeed, Speier later admitted that he "had been offended by what appeared to [him] as [the Frankfurt School's] arrogant treatment of [unemployed] Americans" and expressed his anger in his review.[41]

Speier's and Horkheimer's divergent approaches to exile emerged from a profound disagreement regarding the intellectual exile's relationship to modern politics. Where Horkheimer rejected practical politics in the current historical moment—as Herbert Marcuse remembered in an interview with Jürgen Habermas, in the 1930s it "was strictly forbidden [by Horkheimer]" for members of the Frankfurt School to engage in political activity—Speier argued that intellectual exiles must participate in the political life of their adopted country. In fact, Speier and Horkheimer had much in common, and at first glance there was no reason to believe that the two would not have been friendly with each other. Both entered academia over their fathers' protests, rejected vulgar positivism, were influenced by critical social science, emphasized culture and ideology's importance to history, and argued that salvation was not to be found in the working classes. However, the different political-intellectual projects each pursued in exile engendered decades-long tensions between the two, which can be seen in anecdotes from Speier's later life. For example, in a 1952 report to his superiors at the RAND Corporation, Speier referenced the *Studien*, initially calling it "a very ambitious and interesting book" before crossing out "interesting." Similarly, in 1954 Speier responded to a former German military officer who "thought highly of Horkheimer" and the institute's work by stating that he himself was "not impressed" by the institute and insisting that the officer "is undoubtedly not in a position to judge [Horkheimer's] scientific competence." Finally, in a 1977 letter to Edward Shils, Speier simply commented that save for the political scientists Otto Kirchheimer and Franz Neumann, "I do not think much of the Horkheimer group." These petty remarks reflected a dislike of Horkheimer difficult to attribute to the Frankfurt School's use of psychoanalysis alone. Instead, the source of the Speier-Horkheimer feud may be found in their conflicting views regarding the intellectual exile's social role.[42]

Horkheimer had long rejected practical political engagement. In Weimar, he and his colleagues considered political compromise an insalubrious act that necessarily weakened revolutionary potential and for that reason refused to associate with the reformist Social Democratic Party of Germany. During the republic's final years, when the possibility of socialist transformation appeared utopian, Horkheimer began to argue that in the era of monopoly capitalism and fascism, radical action was possible only in the realm of ideas, which made any political engagement anathema. Horkheimer retained this conviction after Hitler's victory in 1933. As he declared in his 1937 essay "Traditional and Critical Theory," critical theory's aim "is not simply to eliminate one or other abuse, for it regards such abuses as necessarily connected with the way in which the [capitalist] social structure is organized. Although it itself emerges from the social structure, its purpose is not, either in its conscious intention or in its objective significance, the better functioning of any element in the structure. On the contrary, it is suspicious of the very categories of better, useful, appropriate, productive, and valuable, as these are understood in the present [capitalist] order." Horkheimer simply refused to participate in an "organism [i.e., capitalist society] which lacks reason."[43]

Independence, not only from political parties but also from the government, was for Horkheimer a virtue, and in the Frankfurt School's first years in the United States he prohibited institute members from participating in politics—a decision no doubt emboldened by his wish to avoid the attentions of anti-German, anti-Semitic, and antileftist Americans. His disenchantment with and distrust of practical politics led Horkheimer to argue that, at least in the contemporary moment, the social role of the intellectual exile consisted exclusively in posing a fundamental critique of reality that preserved and established possibilities for future action. As he said in "Traditional and Critical Theory," "in a historical period like the present true theory is more critical than affirmative," providing "an image of the [more just] future . . . when the course of events seems to be leading far away from such a future and seems to justify every reaction except belief in fulfillment." For Horkheimer, "continued theoretical effort, in the interest of a rationally organized future society," was the only means to keep alive "the hope of radically improving human existence," which must pass for action in a world dominated by capitalism. Speier's program of engaging with power, described in detail below, was therefore abhorrent to Horkheimer.[44]

Horkheimer expressed his disappointment with intellectual exiles like Speier who embraced the United States in his 1939 essay "The Jews in Europe." Horkheimer began this piece by angrily deriding "the refugee intellectuals" for rejecting Marxism and accepting the hegemonic capitalist American ideology. This was dangerous, Horkheimer asserted, because fascism emerged from capitalism:

> No one can demand that, in the very countries that have granted them asylum, the émigrés put a mirror to the world [i.e., the capitalist world] that has created fascism. But whoever is not willing to talk about capitalism should also keep quiet about fascism. The English [i.e., American] hosts today fare better than Frederick the Great did with the acid-tongued Voltaire. . . . The intellectuals have not abandoned hope that somewhere the reformation of Western capitalism will proceed more mildly than in Germany and that well-recommended foreigners will have a future after all. But the totalitarian order differs from its bourgeois predecessor only in that it has lost its inhibitions. . . . Fascism is that truth of modern society which has been realized by the [anticapitalist] theory from the beginning.

commitment to Marxism and critical theory, he implied, was an example of such provinciality.[49]

Speier concluded his speech by proposing an activist exile as the ideal one:

> It is more gratifying to speak of the responses [to exile] which spring from the right use that the intellectual immigrant may learn to make of his freedom. Experience matures judgment. Familiarity with new facts and new ways of looking at them increases apprehension and circumspection. In a sense every immigrant passes through a second period of youth with its blunders and invigorating hopes, its dangers and slow achievements. To his profit, he learns by experience and participation. Where sympathy governs the relations, he may contribute, as is expected of him, his small share to the culture of his new country.

Speier thus decisively scorned Horkheimer's resigned project and offered action as the solution to the existential problems exile raised. The fact that Horkheimer kept a copy of this speech in his archives for decades may indicate that Speier had indeed struck a nerve with the institute's director.[50]

Of course, other differences besides a divergent approach to exile divided Speier from Horkheimer and the Frankfurt School. Unlike the New School, which was plagued by financial troubles, the institute's endowment enabled its members to live in relative comfort, at least in the mid-1930s. This likely increased tensions between Horkheimer and Speier, who recalled that "almost every month, or in any case at the end of each semester, one did not know [whether the Graduate Faculty] continues or not." Speier and the institute members also had different social origins. Most of the Frankfurt School was Jewish, and the majority hailed from privileged backgrounds. Though Speier was embedded in the largely Jewish exile community, his Protestant middle-class origins may have strained his relationship with the Frankfurt School. For instance, the sociologist Paul Massing, an associate of the institute, reported that his non-Jewish background had separated him from his colleagues. Certainly, Speier's background provided him with advantages unavailable to the institute's members. In particular, his Protestantism made it easier for him to assimilate into the majority Anglo-Saxon community of American intellectuals than the Jews of the Frankfurt School, who were understandably reticent about acculturating into a group that retained anti-Semitic prejudices.[51]

Professional rivalries further contributed to intra-exile conflicts. The New School and Institute of Social Research quickly emerged as the two most prominent institutions housing exiles in the United States. Tensions naturally arose when both sought research funds from U.S. organizations after the institute's finances dwindled in the late 1930s and early 1940s because of poor real estate investments. Such rivalry would sometimes be expressed in personal attacks. For example, in the midst of discussing whether, for financial reasons, the Frankfurt School's project on anti-Semitism should be undertaken in cooperation with the New School, Franz Neumann, who joined the institute in 1936, called Max Ascoli, the New School's dean, "a pompous idiot of unsurpassable vanity" and referred to Speier as "a wily, very bright and technically [*formal*] extremely clever scoundrel." Despite these various strains, however, the rancor between Speier and Horkheimer, which reflected more general disagreements that divided the New School and Frankfurt School, cannot be explained solely with reference to personal, methodological, or financial conflicts. It was in their approach to politics and intellectual exile that Horkheimer and Speier fundamentally differed, and it is in this disparity that a significant, if not the only, source of their public and lasting acrimony may be found.[52]

A profound impatience characterized Speier's scholarship between his exile in 1933 and his cofounding of the Research Project on Totalitarian Communication in 1940. During this period, he attempted to shed what he considered to be Weimar's legacy of placing philosophy and discussion above politics and action. He thus spent very little time endeavoring to provide a philosophical grounding for democracy's superiority vis-à-vis fascism and communism. Whereas John Dewey and other American-born intellectuals engaged in philosophical gymnastics throughout the 1930s to justify democracy's superiority, Speier simply accepted the latter as the most just political form. Even though the Weberian notion of "the ethics of commitment" (*Gesinnungsethik*), which proclaimed that political commitments and values emerged ex nihilo, provided Speier with a theoretical resource to undergird his dedication to democracy, he never invoked it. Speier did not feel the need to explain his commitment to democracy. The trauma of Weimar had demonstrated to him that in moments of crisis, philosophy distracted more than it illuminated. For Speier, actions mattered more than words.[53]

But what types of actions should an intellectual émigré pursue? Throughout his exile, Speier never argued—as he had in Germany—that intellectuals should associate with political parties; Weimar had convinced him that the realities of contemporary politics made it impossible for intellectuals to assert themselves within partisan movements. As he said:

> In our age the means of criticism of culture are more abundant than ever before. With the collapse of Christian thought the competition and struggles of those secularized *Weltanschauungen* [worldviews] in terms of which the various interests in society seek to justify themselves have multiplied the forms which criticism may take, while at the same time the democratic leveling of culture has been conducive to the greatest perversion of criticism. Anyone who has a command of words can set up as a critic. The necessary phrases are cheap; the necessary arguments are available almost for the asking. All there is to be said against trade-unionism and socialism can be found in chamber of commerce pamphlets. The crimes of the upper classes are common knowledge of every socialistic agitator. . . . The effeteness of liberal individualism is known to almost every fascist. The opponent of revolution is not called on to read Burke or de Tocqueville or Goethe, for mediocre conservatives have stuffed their coffers with small change minted from the gold of these writers.

Speier argued that in the modern era intellectuals could not function effectively as members of partisan movements because in the popular consciousness the line separating them from the masses had disappeared. There had been a "democratic leveling of the intellectual *bellum omnium contra omnes* [war of all against all] [that] has tended to arouse distrust of the critics of culture" because "their trade has become altogether too easy." In short, ordinary people were under the incorrect impression that their capacities were equal to intellectuals' and no longer looked to the latter for guidance.[54]

Speier thus avowed that intellectuals should not associate with political parties. But he had posited an active exile as the moral duty of the émigrés, which implied participation in U.S. politics. In what way did he think an intellectual exile should partake in American life? Speier answered this question in 1939 by simply declaring that "it is the primary task of the social scientist . . . to give advice to the statesman (who may take or leave the advice)." Speier, then, endorsed Max Weber's notion that an intellectual's political function was to present several courses of action and their potential outcomes to a policymaker, who, having accepted responsibility (*Verantwortung*) for his or her decision, could heed or ignore the intellectual's counsel.[55]

Throughout his U.S. career, Speier displayed little reticence about using his knowledge in the service of the American state. His trust in the state reflected the lingering influence of the German *Staatswissenschaften* (sciences of state, sciences of public administration) on his thought. In the Wilhelmine era, a significant segment of the German professoriate maintained that intellectuals' research must be geared toward the production of instrumental knowledge to be used by the state. Following G. W. F. Hegel, these German academics argued that the state represented citizens' collective interests and stood above political parties, which represented only particularistic interests. In the wake of Weimar's collapse, Speier's jaundiced view of ordinary people and their indifference to intellectuals compelled him to embrace the German notion that the state was the body most capable of transcending partisan interests and acting on behalf of the entire nation (and indeed, Western civilization). Therefore, working with or for the U.S. state—which, after all, had saved them—was the proper means by which émigré social scientists could fulfill their duty to make proper use of their exile. Because it complemented the muscular, national security–centered liberalism that became increasingly prominent among American elites in the 1940s, Speier's statism would continuously aid his future career.[56]

All this makes clear that Speier had no qualms about bringing value judgments into social science. Though deeply influenced by Weber, Speier nonetheless rejected his notion that social science must be value free. As he wrote Edward Shils in the late 1930s, "I am afraid that the great Max Weber made a very great mistake by barring value judgments from science. This is the major fault I find in his theory. . . . To my mind there is literally *nothing* more misleading in the social sciences than the sacred doctrine that we must never valuate." For Speier, "the consciously subjective attitude of the scholar was decisive"; that is to say, social science was meaningful only to the degree that it was informed by one's particular value commitments, as it was these commitments that provided the individual intellectual with motivation and guidance in both the world and scholarship. In Speier's opinion, social research absent value commitments was not only directionless but pointless, and he was determined to operationalize his dedication to democracy.[57]

World War II provided Speier with the opportunity to realize his activist vision of intellectual exile. After Japan attacked the United States at Pearl Harbor in December 1941, he became one of the first of thousands of social scientists—dozens of whom were German exiles, including a number of intellectuals associated with the New School and Institute of Social Research—to leave academic employment for a position in the wartime government. Speier could do so because he spent the 1930s becoming a nationally recognized expert on propaganda, an instrument he believed the United States would need to use in the coming war against Hitler. Speier's justification for propaganda, which he considered an antidemocratic tool, emerged from his participation in the famous debate between Walter Lippmann and John Dewey over the ability of public opinion to serve as a bellwether for decision makers in a democracy. In this debate, Speier ultimately sided with Lippmann, who argued that public opinion could not be used as a policy guide. From this position, Speier rationalized the democratic use of totalitarian methods like propaganda and in so doing embodied a broader shift in U.S. intellectual culture. In an era in which the United States was besieged by totalitarian threats, Speier, Lippmann, and other so-called democratic realists asserted that "not the economics of preparedness nor the propaganda of national honor nor the regimentation of labor will remain an exclusive concern of dictatorship." To defend democracy in an epoch of war, Speier and many of his colleagues affirmed, the United States needed to become more authoritarian.[58]

Chapter 3

Public Opinion, Propaganda, and Democracy in Crisis

Speier's eyes were fixed on Europe throughout the 1930s, and what he observed was profoundly disheartening. Fascism was ascendant in Germany and Italy while Spain descended into a civil war eventually won by right-wing Nationalists. To Speier and his colleagues at the New School, it was clear the United States would soon be forced to confront a European right fixated on destroying democracy not only on the Continent but throughout the world as well. Years before World War II erupted, Speier prepared himself for battle.

The mid to late 1930s were the most important years in Speier's intellectual development. It was during this period that, in his understanding, the struggle for democracy transformed from a domestic to an international fight. In a subtle intellectual shift, Speier began to assume that the collapse of the Weimar Republic reflected not merely the historically contingent weakness of interwar German democracy but the universal weakness of democracy as a political form. He came to believe that democracy was prone to falling prey not only to internal threats, as happened in Weimar, but also to external threats, as appeared to be occurring in Europe and, perhaps in the future, in the United States as well. Speier thus maintained that the intellectual exile, who had the deep knowledge of German politics, culture, and society required to combat the Nazis, must use his or her skills in the service of the American state. This was, in some ways, a safe position for an émigré like Speier to adopt. By locating threats to democracy outside the United States—however accurate—Speier was able to avoid critiquing economic and social problems internal to America and to offer himself as a model immigrant. Moreover, by presenting himself as an expert on Germany, he was able to market himself effectively to American foundation and government officials who also desired to defeat Hitler.

Speier's focus on the coming war compelled him to abandon political and sociological theory. After his exile, he composed only two essays on these subjects: a half-hearted attempt to justify a procedural theory of democracy and an abandoned effort to develop his own system for the sociology of knowledge.[1] It was practical politics that interested him now. The best—and only overt—expression of the political convictions that animated Speier after 1933 was found in an essay he wrote about Emil Lederer in the late 1970s. In this piece, Speier explicated what he took to be Lederer's political ideology:

> [After Hitler,] Lederer placed in opposition to [Nazi Germany and the Soviet Union, the two totalitarian states] no longer the economic-organizational idea of socialism but the political idea of democratic freedom. He did not cease to advocate measures of economic planning in order to preserve what capitalism had accomplished and to accomplish what capitalism could not undertake[,] . . . but the decisive point of his libertarian humanism after 1933 no longer consisted in the economic contrast capitalism-socialism but in the political antinomy terror and persecution versus liberty and democracy.[2]

This was, in essence, Speier's political philosophy, and with it came a tragic perspective. As Arthur Vidich, a sociologist at the New School who became friends with Speier late in the latter's life, put it, "Speier's world view was guided by a rejection of the Enlightenment conceptions of progress, utopianism and human perfectibility." For Speier, as for many in his generation of exiles, the "sanguine idea of humankind's inevitable march into a radiant future," to use Vidich's phrasing, was a chimera that needed be abandoned, or democracy itself would fall prey to its enemies.[3] The best an intellectual could do was to defend the progress Western civilization had already made by ensuring that extremist forces of the right and left did not overrun America and Europe.

Speier's analysis of Weimar's collapse had led him to conclude that German intellectuals' obsession with social theory, as opposed to practical knowledge, was a major cause of their inaction in the face of Hitler. To avoid repeating this mistake, he dedicated his research to exploring the theory and practice of propaganda, which he maintained would be a critical tool in the coming war with Hitler. Why propaganda? Speier, like many democratic intellectuals in both the interwar United States and Western Europe, avowed that the failure of German democracy had raised a critical, albeit uncomfortable, question: What do you do if you cannot trust ordinary people to make wise political decisions? Propaganda provided a simple, and powerful, answer to this query: you manipulate them. With the financial support of the Rockefeller Foundation, in 1940 he and Ernst Kris, a New School colleague, initiated a study of Nazi propaganda for the purpose of learning from and defending against it. Speier's research made him a well-known expert on German propaganda, which, after World War II's outbreak, fostered his entrance into government service.

But Speier's interest in propaganda forced him to confront a moral problem: How could he justify the use of propaganda, which he argued was "an infringement of the basic intellectual rights of man"?[4] To do so, Speier appealed to two arguments. First, he accepted Walter Lippmann's "democratic realist" claim that ordinary people were too ignorant and disinterested to make astute political choices and therefore elites had the right and duty to manipulate them, at least during moments of crisis. Second, he embraced the pragmatic assertion that to defeat the Nazis, democrats needed to adopt their methods. As Speier insisted in 1945, one reason Weimar had failed was because democrats had refused "to prevent [the republic's] enemies from abusing democratic rights and institutions for the destruction of this democracy."[5] This reading of Weimar's collapse led Speier to declare that in extraordinary times, democrats must limit democratic practices and norms to ensure that democracy survived.[6] For the greater good, he averred, U.S. elites, who were more knowledgeable and intelligent than ordinary Americans, must use propaganda to manipulate those who declined to recognize the existential threat posed by Hitler.

Though he justified the democratic use of propaganda, Speier remained uncomfortable with it. To limit the scope of his claims, Speier held that U.S. elites would need to employ propaganda only during moments of crisis. While the character of modern war made it necessary for democracies to use the tools of totalitarian regimes to defeat them, Speier argued that when the crisis ended, these tools must be swiftly abandoned. Indeed, Speier distinguished between democracies and autocracies with reference to the latter's institutionalization of antidemocratic means of social control. Institutionalization implied permanence, and the lack of an American version of Joseph Goebbels's Ministry of Public Enlightenment and Propaganda suggested to Speier that democratic governments did not, as he and Kris asserted in a grant proposal the two co-wrote, "aim at subjugating the individual and at controlling men permanently."[7] For this reason, he trusted that his plan to temporarily suspend democratic practices was feasible.

By World War II's eruption, Speier promoted a new type of democratic consciousness premised on the idea that during moments of crisis, elites must limit democracy in order to save it. This notion became a critical component of the early Cold War intellectual consensus endorsed by the majority of the first generation of defense intellectuals. Speier's arguments, however, were rife with problems. Most important, they created an intellectual space within which he and other elites could legitimately employ antidemocratic means whenever they diagnosed a crisis. In the 1930s, Speier assumed that Western democracy's confrontation with fascism was a unique occurrence that would soon be resolved in the former's favor. But in the era of the Cold War, which was defined by a long-term struggle with a nuclear-armed Soviet Union, elites could easily use the logic of crisis to rationalize and institutionalize antidemocratic means and methods of governance, which is precisely what they did.

Speier's concern with democratic governance was assimilated easily into a major American debate that emerged after World War I regarding propaganda's apparent ability to manipulate ordinary people's thought and actions. In the early 1920s, propaganda's alleged effectiveness, which American intellectuals believed was demonstrated by both the United Kingdom's successful effort to persuade the United States to enter the war and the emergence of mass-based advertising, challenged traditional liberal assumptions about citizens' innate capacity to develop informed opinions and serve as policymakers' guides. As such, two liberal intellectuals, the philosopher John Dewey and the journalist Walter Lippmann, initiated a discussion about the relationship between propaganda, public opinion, and democratic governance that permeated intellectual circles throughout the interwar era. Dewey and Lippmann agreed that propaganda, disseminated through modern communication technologies, could manipulate public opinion to serve elite interests. The two disagreed, however, as to what this meant for democratic theory.[8]

Dewey and Lippmann offered divergent solutions to the problem of public opinion. On one hand, Dewey and other "democratic optimists" asserted that programs of public enlightenment could create informed civic communities able to overcome propaganda's manipulations and exert a positive influence on public policy. On the other hand, Lippmann and his democratic realist supporters argued that the realities of modern social existence prevented the establishment of a public able to guide decision makers. Instead of educating the public, Lippmann declared that experts needed to help statesmen make political decisions. Moreover, Lippmann affirmed, citizens' rational disinterest in governance made it ethical for political officials and experts to use propaganda to direct public opinion—especially during crises. The Lippmann-Dewey debate addressed issues with which the exiles were concerned and provided a framework that facilitated German-American intellectual encounters. In fact, participating in the debate helped Speier shape his own inchoate ideas about the public into a democratic theory that echoed Lippmann's.

Lippmann provided democratic realism with its theoretical foundations. In his *Public Opinion* (1922) and *The Phantom Public* (1925), he declared that communications technologies and the complexities of social life had led each modern person to live in a mental "pseudo-environment," "a representation of the environment which is in lesser or greater degree made by man himself" and which did not reflect objective reality. Lippmann further maintained that "stereotypes," which were "the stored up images, the preconceptions, and prejudices which interpret," and in some sense distorted, the facts individuals could access, prevented people from seeing the world as it really was. In Lippmann's opinion, because the individual citizen did not, indeed could not, have direct knowledge of factual information, she or he had neither the ability nor opportunity to obtain, as traditional democratic theorists assumed, "a knowledge of the world beyond their reach." This guaranteed that ordinary people could not be "omnicompetent," able to choose wisely between multifaceted policy alternatives. For these reasons, Lippmann concluded that the public could not be relied on to guide policy.[9]

Lippmann, however, was also worried that policymakers were themselves prone to make decisions without sufficient factual information. To solve this problem, he proposed that experts or social scientists—whose knowledge of the scientific method allowed them to see beyond their pseudo-environments and stereotypes—assume positions in "an independent, expert organization" connected to the government. Lippmann hoped that members of this group would be able to make "the unseen facts intelligible to those who have to make the decisions." Like Dewey and other liberals, Lippmann endorsed the establishment of a scientific elite. Unlike Dewey, though, Lippmann downplayed the traditional liberal faith in public education and called for a system in which elites enlightened other elites.[10]

For Lippmann, the democratic public did not even exist. It was, as his 1925 book's title proclaimed, a "phantom," an incoherent and inarticulate mass. Lippmann affirmed that most citizens had little interest in participating in practical governance and were satisfied with their lives as long as their political representatives "produc[ed] a certain minimum of health, of decent housing, of material necessities, of education, of freedom, of pleasures, of beauty." If ordinary people's needs were being met, Lippmann averred, it was ethical for elites to use propaganda to "manufacture consent" among them. He therefore embraced a procedural democratic theory within which citizens' primary political function was to vote in elections to determine who ruled them. In Lippmann's opinion, "the problems that vex democracy seem to be unmanageable by [the] democratic methods" that Americans had championed since the eighteenth century. The United States, he argued, needed to develop an elitist system of governance that reflected a more realistic view of ordinary people's rather limited capabilities.[11]

Dewey firmly rejected Lippmann's pessimistic conclusions in two book reviews he wrote for the *New Republic* and in *The Public and Its Problems* (1927). In these pieces, Dewey argued that ordinary people desired to partake in governance and that the public's participation in politics was a defining feature of democracy. Any political system or theory that ignored these facts, he avowed, was undemocratic, untenable, and doomed to fail. Though Dewey accepted Lippmann's claim that there were presently no democratic "publics" able to speak on their own behalf, he focused his energies on examining the conditions that would enable such groups to arise. Unlike Lippmann, Dewey did not trust "that the policies of the experts are in the main both wise and benevolent, that is, framed to conserve the genuine interests of society." Instead, he asserted that "in the absence of an articulate voice on the part of the masses, the best do not and cannot remain the best, the wise cease to be wise. It is impossible for high-brows to secure a monopoly of such knowledge as must be used for the regulation of common affairs." For Dewey, modern democracy needed to rely on both experts and publics.[12]

In Dewey's proposed vision, experts would teach ordinary Americans to approach life scientifically and would use mass communication technologies to "mak[e] known the facts upon which [policies] depend." Dewey insisted that these actions would improve the "methods and conditions of debate, discussion and persuasion" in American society and, when combined with citizens' participation in the collective experiences of democratic rituals, would help publics become conscious of themselves. With experts' aid, such knowledgeable and conscious publics would have "the ability to judge . . . the bearing of the knowledge supplied by others upon common concerns," which would enable them to combat propaganda and assert themselves on the political stage. Like Lippmann, Dewey recognized the importance of experts and new media technologies to modern social life; unlike Lippmann, he hoped to use these to enlighten, not manage, ordinary people.[13]

Lippmann and Dewey agreed that mass communication techniques shaped the way American citizens viewed the world, though they disagreed as to the use to which such techniques should be put. For Lippmann, elites should use propaganda to force ordinary people to follow their lead; for Dewey, elites should use mass communication technologies to enlighten ordinary people and make them aware that they had a stake in democratic governance. As the Lippmann-Dewey debate suggests, in the interwar years discussions about propaganda became sites for American—and, as we shall see, European—intellectuals to explore the relationships among democracy, public opinion, expertise, and mass communication. It was through his participation in these debates that Speier developed his own procedural democratic theory.[14]

Speier's interest in propaganda emerged naturally from his training in the sociology of knowledge. As Louis Wirth pointed out in his introduction to the translation of Karl Mannheim's *Ideology and Utopia*, "the sociology of knowledge, by virtue of its concern with the role of knowledge and ideas in the maintenance or change of the social order, is bound to devote considerable attention to the agencies or devices [such as propaganda] through which ideas are diffused and the degree of freedom of inquiry and expression that prevails." Moreover, Wirth noted, "an adequate understanding" of propaganda would "contribute to a more precise conception of the role of ideas in political and social movements and of the value of knowledge as an instrument in controlling social reality." Propaganda was an obvious topic of inquiry for Speier to choose as he committed himself to transforming academic concerns into practical ones.[15]

Experiences in Germany also encouraged Speier to study propaganda. As in the United States, in Germany World War I had highlighted propaganda's importance to modern governance. During the war, the Wilhelmine government made propaganda an integral element of its strategic planning and consistently monitored public opinion. After the war, propaganda became a preoccupation of both government officials and intellectuals as individuals across the political spectrum attributed the German defeat to the Second Reich's failure to use propaganda to maintain citizens' and soldiers' morale. In Weimar, media studies and propaganda analysis quickly emerged as popular subjects of investigation, and political parties decisively incorporated propaganda into their campaigns and programs.[16]

The Social Democratic Party of Germany, to which Speier belonged, had a robust history of employing propaganda that dated back to the nineteenth century. Throughout Weimar's last years (1929–1933), the period in which Speier was most politically active, the party engaged in extensive propaganda campaigns designed to combat those of the Nazis and communists, and party officials regularly asserted that propaganda was central to their political future. For instance, in Prussia, Speier's home state, the socialist interior minister Albert Grzesinski argued that those who supported the republic must use "positive propaganda" "to educate the people in democratic thought and action." Unlike the propaganda of their political enemies, however, socialist propaganda was didactic and, in retrospect, ineffective. It was designed, in the words of the Reich's socialist interior minister Carl Severing, "to shift politics away from the activities of the vocal chords towards the functions of the head." Unfortunately for the SPD, most Germans found such propaganda boring.[17]

Hitler's appointment to the chancellorship in January 1933 and the subsequent *Gleichschaltung* process, both of which were bolstered by Joseph Goebbels's propaganda machine, demonstrated to socialists and former socialists like Speier that propaganda was an undeniably effective tool of modern governance that democrats ignored at their own peril. Looking back on Weimar in the early 1940s, for example, Speier argued that "the main weapons" the Nazis used to seize power "were not made of steel" but rather were made of experiential propaganda: "Nazi skill in [the late 1920s and early 1930s] consisted, to a large extent, in attracting popular attention by organizing mass meetings and parades, and by filling the streets with men who wore uniforms without belonging to any armed force. After the Nazi party succeeded in gaining power the professional pride of the propagandists was strengthened." Weimar's collapse had underlined propaganda's importance to Speier. Once in the United States, he initiated a years-long investigation of the subject that culminated in his joining the Foreign Broadcast Intelligence

Service as the head of the section that analyzed Nazi propaganda in order to learn from and defend against it.[18]

However, in his first year in exile, Speier was unwilling to endorse a tool he still associated with fascism. For this reason, in his first article on propaganda, appropriately titled "On Propaganda" (1934), Speier embraced Dewey's position that propaganda was anathema to democracy. In this piece, Speier argued that "if historical experience has taught that public opinion is not always so reasonable as it appeared in the original conception, one conclusion is that the methods of obtaining a more reasonable one, be they educational, journalistic or political, must be improved; this is the conclusion which is drawn by those who respect man." In contrast, Speier continued, "those who hold man's reason cheap" asserted "that public opinion is worth just so much as can be achieved with it." Such people—and Speier here implicitly referred not only to fascists but also to democratic realists like Lippmann—"deprive [man] first of the opportunity and finally of the courage to use [reason]." In the process, these individuals contributed to "the destruction of democratic morals including public opinion" and gave succor to the enemies of democracy.[19]

Speier went so far as to distinguish democracies from autocracies with reference to the ways in which each regime type viewed and institutionalized—or did not institutionalize—propaganda. Though he admitted that democratic governments occasionally used propaganda, he nevertheless claimed that "in democracy . . . propaganda passes for an infringement of the basic intellectual rights of man. . . . Under dictatorship, however, propaganda is legitimate." Speier declared that unlike in a democracy, in a dictatorship "one establishes ministries for [propaganda] and thus officially proclaims cynicism as permanent." According to Speier, it was the dictatorial state's happy endorsement, institutionalization, and widespread and repeated use of propaganda that changed the implications of its use:

> While in democracies [propaganda] merely makes the stream of public opinion turbid, in dictatorships it obstructs the sources of that stream: criticism, reason and the love of one's country which is blind without the political responsibility of the citizen. Public opinion disappears. . . . The fascist propagandists proclaim that which is a private vice in democracy to be the fundamental virtue of the state. They not only reduce reason to silence but also deny its right to existence, to which history testifies. They create myths, convert fictitious forces into real ones, and cultivate the taste of the crowd

for illogical action instead of restraining it. They necessarily lower the intellectual level of the people.[20]

Despite these assertions, though, the intellectual roots of Speier's embrace of both democratic realism and propaganda were already present in "On Propaganda." First, at the same time that he recommended that democrats use "educational, journalistic or political" methods to improve public opinion, Speier suggested that democratic propagandists could ethically restrain "the taste of the crowd for illogical action." This indicated that elites retained the right to limit the public's influence if they deemed it necessary. Second, Speier agreed with Lippmann that in modern society "the social reality of many facts is established through belief and not through personal experience and knowledge," which he confessed allowed propaganda to present a significant "danger . . . to democratic culture." Finally, Speier's German experiences led him to doubt that "in the complexity of modern life education can diminish the power of the propagandist to spread lies successfully," though in 1934 he remained willing to try. These three ideas—that elites could legitimately restrict the public's influence, that propaganda was effective due to modern social realities, and that mass education was likely a utopian fantasy—undergirded Speier's later rejection of Dewey.[21]

Between 1934 and 1938, events in Germany and the United States compelled Speier to endorse democratic realism and, subsequently, propaganda. In 1934, Speier could still hope that Hitler would fail; by 1938, it was obvious Hitler's triumph would last. The German people had made clear that they would express little opposition to the dismissal of political and racial undesirables from academic and other professional positions and would offer no outcry over the draconian Nuremberg Laws and other racist Nazi restrictions. Meanwhile, during these years the popularity of various U.S. anti-interventionist movements, coupled with Congress's passage of three Neutrality Acts, demonstrated to Speier that the American people were by no means willing to fight Nazism, a manifestly existential threat. As a result, Speier accepted Lippmann's antipublic views.

Speier fully embraced democratic realism in his 1938 review of Grete de Francesco's *Die Macht des Charlatans* (The Power of the Charlatan). In this review, Speier asserted the identity of political "charlatans," of which "present dictators" were a modern example, and the public a charlatan ruled:

> The boldness of the exploiter has its counterpart in the insecurity of the exploited, and the disappointment of the victims, which is eventually inevitable,

> causes the constant insecurity of the charlatan himself. . . . It is this insecurity which, to my mind, not only increases the boldness of the charlatan but also constitutes the ultimate affinity between him and his prey. As long as his followers are not yet disillusioned they create the atmosphere in which trickeries prosper, and by producing the legends which increase the charlatan's fame they become efficient agents of his propaganda. Thus it may perhaps be said that the public of the charlatan consists of passive charlatans.

Speier thus posited that a reciprocal relationship characterized the link between a dictator and his public; each relied on the other. As he declared in an earlier essay, "the very existence of authority presupposes a certain freedom of choice on the part of the subject" who decided to bow to that authority, and Speier fully blamed the German people, even though they were manipulated by propaganda, for Hitler's successes. Speier's pessimism regarding ordinary Germans explains his embrace of the term "totalitarian" during this period. "Totalitarian" implied not only the analogizing of the Nazi and Soviet regimes but also a political theory that insisted that the masses were the ones upon whom such regimes relied. For Speier, "Hitler is the political leader of a modern, subversive, mass movement" who must be understood as a "plebiscitarian mass leader." According to him, Hitler's victory occurred because of mass enfranchisement, not in spite of it.[22]

But Speier's review was most important for transforming his historically contingent critique of Germans' support for Hitler into a universal referendum on ordinary people's capacity for enlightenment. In the piece, Speier rejected the very notion that reason was a tool that could be used to educate the masses. He boldly declared that "the belief that the unfortunate inclination to fall for [the charlatan] can be destroyed by means of enlightened reason [was] ultimately traceable to non-belief." Those who, like Dewey, argued otherwise misunderstood "the relation between reason and belief," which was that the latter did not depend on the former, especially when one was speaking about ordinary people. Echoing Lippmann's elitist political theory, Speier avowed that the only people "'immune' [to charlatans] are realists [i.e., intellectuals like himself] . . . and they alone, by their example, may furnish the effective attack against the charlatan." As he had since the 1920s, Speier placed intellectuals in a critical political position. In the struggle against fascism, they, and not the public, were the ones able to create the ideological and rhetorical weapons that must undergird democracy's defense.[23]

Speier's democratic realism led him to affirm a procedural democratic theory premised on voting that excluded notions of economic and social democracy popular among socialists in Weimar and liberals in America. In a 1936 essay titled "Social Stratification," he proclaimed that throughout history, "democratic political institutions have coexisted with many kinds of social superiority, differences of rank and forms of discrimination." "Equality in democracy," he continued, "is not the same as the particular equality that exists in a classless society." Rather, Speier professed that "the specific equality which resides in democracy is an equality of *political* rights." Once certain political rights, namely the right to vote, were secure, Speier maintained that democratic equality was achieved, and the elites chosen to govern a democracy could therefore make any decisions they wanted regardless of public opinion. Though it was shorn of much substantive content, by enabling him to still consider himself a democrat while endorsing methods and processes that guaranteed his preferred goals were achieved, Speier's procedural democratic theory fulfilled an important psychological need.[24]

Permeating Speier's discussions of democracy was his Weimar-engendered fear of political partisanship, which was an anxiety that defined his politics and shaped his justifications for propaganda. As Max Ascoli, a philosopher exiled from Italy who worked at the New School, wrote in 1944, "although politically minded, [Speier] is not what may be called a political partisan. His only fundamental hatred is against the Nazis and his greatest devotion is to American ideals." Propaganda became for Speier a critical tool of social control, a means to tame potentially violent partisan commitments. From his exile onward, he maintained that ensuring stability and consensus through state management of an irrational public was critical to democracy's survival.[25]

Speier's studies of modern war in the late 1930s and early 1940s further vindicated his embrace of propaganda. His inquiries into modern war began from the premise that contemporary war was uniquely "total" in character. "Total war," he argued, "has three distinct traits: 1. a particularly close interdependence between the armed forces and the productive forces of the nation, which necessitates large scale governmental planning; 2. the extension of siege warfare enveloping the nation as a whole in both offensive and defensive actions; and 3. a general vilification of the enemy nation." Unlike wars before World War I, total wars were "waged by the whole of society rather than by the armed forces alone," which made "the old distinction between combatants and non-combatants" "obsolete." Crucially for his acceptance of propaganda, Speier maintained that total war was necessarily totalitarian war, in the sense that totalitarian regimes were the ones most ready to fight and win total wars. Whereas "in nontotalitarian societies [destructive energies] are submerged and held in check," in totalitarian regimes they were given "official and almost unctuous institutionalization" and were strengthened by "political beliefs so dear to the belligerents that they arouse a crusading spirit." In short, totalitarian regimes had an advantage in modern war of which democracies must be cognizant.[26]

The only way to overcome this advantage, Speier argued, was for democracies to adopt totalitarian methods, even if these methods violated democratic norms. In his opinion, "the character of a major war under modern social, economic and technological conditions approaches the totalitarian type regardless of the political organization of society. Democracies are not free to choose a 'limited war' if their adversaries wage a 'total war.'" For this reason, "democracies in modern wars will have to adopt dictatorial devices of political organization, at least for a time." As Speier and Alfred Kähler wrote in the introduction to the New School's volume *War in Our Time*, "the techniques of preparedness as they are being developed in the dictatorial countries today indicate at least the direction into which democracies will be forced to move when war comes." In particular, they concluded that neither "the economics of preparedness nor the propaganda of national honor nor the regimentation of labor will remain an exclusive concern of dictatorship. They are of the substance of modern war." In arguing this, Speier accepted the critiques of antiwar activists who, in the publisher Henry Luce's words, offered a "fearful forecast . . . that some form of dictatorship is required to fight a modern war." Though Speier did not go so far as to advocate dictatorship explicitly, he understood the antidemocratic implications of his argument but nevertheless believed the historical moment necessitated such sacrifices.[27]

Propaganda was the primary totalitarian tool that Speier advocated for democracies to adopt. This position faced significant resistance from American liberals like Dewey, who considered propaganda a tool unbecoming of democracy. Speier attempted to overcome the liberal critique of propaganda by appealing to its pragmatic utility, arguing that the realities of total war made domestic propaganda necessary to keep morale high and ensure that civilians provided supplies to soldiers without interruption. In total war, Speier affirmed, "the morale of the nation itself becomes of decisive *military* importance." Because propaganda was "a concomitant, or rather an integral element, of modern war as such," democracies needed to embrace its use lest they fall prey to the Nazis.[28]

Speier condemned liberals who maintained that democracies must fight wars more justly than their enemies. This had been the social democrats' mistake in Weimar, and Speier would do everything he could to guarantee it did not recur. "Since man does not live in a utopia of liberal extraction," he insisted, it was the tragic reality that during moments of crisis such as the present "life and death struggle against Fascism," democrats "do what they would not have to do in a perfect world." Though Speier admitted that propaganda was morally abhorrent—he variously referred to its practice as "the odious vocation of handling human attitudes" and "the ungentlemanly method of warfare"—he nonetheless maintained that liberals' antipropaganda moralism represented a "fallacy of misplaced righteousness." Liberal moralism, Speier feared, allowed evil people to govern: "In the depths of his heart a liberal cannot but conscientiously object to politics in general, since politics involves illiberal coercion and double-crossing. Men without a conscience have thus been given a chance to rule, and they have seized upon it, using nothing but coercion and fraud and extending their sway beyond national boundaries by the same means that brought them to power." "Many liberals," Speier further claimed, "have difficulty in recognizing the illiberal rule of violence and war in politics. . . . Liberals like to beautify history by substituting for the struggle between the might of right and the might of wrong, the alternative between might and right. And for some noble and impolitic reason they are convinced that their own right must always conquer the might of the others. Incidentally, this is what Fascist intellectuals have in mind when they speak of the decadence of democracies." Speier argued that liberals must adopt a realistic understanding of the world and recognize that the threat posed by Nazi Germany made it necessary for them to make moral compromises essential to defending democracy.[29]

However, Speier's need to justify and morally condemn propaganda demonstrated that he embraced it only reluctantly. Throughout his writings, Speier used time-limiting phrases to indicate that democracies would not need to employ propaganda permanently. For example, he asserted that democratic propaganda differed from totalitarian propaganda because "in a democracy [propaganda] does not aim at subjugating the individual and at controlling men permanently." Elsewhere, Speier maintained that democracies will be forced to use propaganda, "at least for a time," which implied that when the crisis abated they would abandon it. These time-limiting phrases revealed that Speier believed it was acceptable to use antidemocratic methods only in a moment of crisis, or during what he and a colleague termed, using the language of Carl Schmitt, "the emergency situation." Once the emergency situation ended—that is to say, once the Nazis were defeated—Speier indicated that the United States would be able to reinstitute normal democratic practices.[30]

Speier and his exile colleagues had since 1933 argued that the United States and Nazi Germany were bound to fight each other (hence the ironic title of the New School's 1938 volume, *War in Our Time*, published in the wake of the Munich Agreement and Neville Chamberlain's declaration that he had secured "peace for our time"). Once World War II erupted in 1939, Speier quickly set about making himself useful to U.S. policymakers. With Ernst Kris, an Austrian psychoanalyst and art historian who emigrated from Vienna to London in 1938 before joining the New School in 1940, he initiated the Research Project on Totalitarian Communication in Wartime. In London, Kris had been the director of a British Broadcasting Corporation (BBC) research unit that produced weekly analyses of German propaganda broadcasts for government use. When he arrived at the New School, Kris, as he reported, "discussed with [Speier] problems of methodology [i.e., how to study propaganda] and of procedure [and he] got so much inspiration from him that a closer collaboration was envisaged." Kris informed Speier that he had access to the BBC's Daily Digest of Foreign Broadcasts, which translated classified Nazi propaganda materials, and asked him if he would be interested in working on a research project that would analyze these materials in order to develop methods of propaganda content analysis that would be of theoretical and practical utility. Speier quickly agreed to collaborate with Kris, believing that the United States would learn how to fight a total war only by studying the Nazis, who were masters of it.[31]

Speier and Kris recognized that their project required pecuniary resources that the New School, which remained under financial stress, could not provide. Consequently, Kris spent several months engendering interest in the project among the administrators of the Rockefeller Foundation, a New York–based foundation that was one of the wealthiest in the United States. Owing to the influence of John Marshall, the associate director of its Humanities Division, the Rockefeller Foundation emerged in the 1930s as the most important private funder of communications research. The foundation had also since 1924 subsidized German social science as a means to support German democracy and had financed both the Hochschule für Politik and the

University in Exile. For these reasons, Speier and Kris assumed the foundation would be fascinated by their work, and in the wake of Kris's lobbying efforts they submitted an application to Marshall asking for support for a research project on Nazi propaganda.[32]

In their proposal, Speier and Kris presented their project as "a contribution of science to defense" designed to contribute to both practice and theory. At this stage in their careers, the two presented themselves as defense *intellectuals*, interested not only in affecting the world but also in learning about it. As they said, the project had two primary benefits:

> The first is of practical importance. If the analysis based on field work succeeds in establishing a pattern or model of the action of the propagandist and of his plan, this may eventually be of practical importance; one may be able to predict to some extent, as with the hurricane, what the next onslaught will be. There is some evidence that such attempts may be successful. The second concerns a field which is of considerable theoretical importance; only those who are near in time have a certain chance of evaluating the reaction to propaganda. The question of how far estimates of this kind are practicable in this field is controversial. There is, however, some evidence that in certain limited fields the study of reaction to propaganda may be attempted not without some success.

Speier and Kris further asserted that because "German broadcasting activity . . . is the one which is best organized and whose control functions most smoothly," it provided a model that "may enable us to assess the potential value and the potential limitations of broadcasting as a medium of national and international communications," which would be critical for both U.S. practice and theory should the nation join the Allied war effort.[33]

Upon receiving the grant application, an intrigued Marshall asked several prominent social scientists, including Harold Lasswell and Louis Wirth, to evaluate Speier and Kris. In his reply to Marshall, Lasswell referred to Kris as "a valuable person who can be readily integrated into the [foundation's] total program on communications research" and praised Speier's scholarship for "combining exact methods of collecting data with the type of comparative historical analysis" on which the proposed project would depend. Wirth, for his part, informed Marshall that Speier was "a man of wide and deep learning, imagination, and insight" who "would no doubt bring a critical mind to bear upon such a problem as totalitarian communication in war time." The relationships that Speier had developed earlier in the 1930s were thus critical to ensuring the Rockefeller Foundation trusted him to co-direct a significant research project.[34]

Marshall was impressed with these recommendations and was himself attracted to the project's potential, as foundation meeting minutes reported, to "provide for training in the methods of analysis developed by Dr. Kris" in his earlier BBC studies. In March 1941, the foundation granted Speier and Kris $15,960 for what was now officially titled the Research Project on Totalitarian Communication in Wartime. Marshall was particularly happy to fund two exiles, as he believed "Central Europeans" were "representative of a broad humanistic tradition which might well enrich humanistic study in the United States." Speier and Kris were also fully supported in their endeavor by Alvin Johnson, the New School's president, who granted them free time to work on it.[35]

In their grant application, Speier and Kris had emphasized their interest in contributing to propaganda theory. However, when they actually began their research, practical exigencies compelled them to ignore theory and, as they stated in the Research Project's 1942 progress report, focus on "develop[ing] *experimental techniques* which might be of use to the work of Government agencies engaging in similar research." The two émigrés emphasized that for three reasons their research was "of immediate practical use." First, it enabled U.S. propaganda analysts to anticipate Nazi propaganda and create their own materials to defend against it. Second, by learning the strengths and weaknesses of Nazi propaganda, U.S. propagandists could make their own materials more effective. Finally, Speier and Kris maintained that analyzing Nazi propaganda's transformations over time would allow them to gather intelligence about Nazi strategy, tactics, and morale.[36]

Despite their faith in the project's utility, Speier and Kris understood that there were few obvious reasons for government officials to incorporate social scientific research into the policymaking process. To assert their epistemological, and hence policy, authority, the two endeavored to establish the scientific and objective character of their work. To do so, Speier and Kris attempted to work within the quantitative paradigm preferred by the Rockefeller Foundation while also using the types of qualitative methods each favored in his own scholarship. The two hoped their method of analysis would create "a reasonable relation between qualitative judgment and judgment based on quantifiable data" that would be respected by the foundation and adopted by government agencies.[37]

The Nazi communications Speier and Kris initially analyzed were news bulletins, and the inductive method established to study them became the project's model. A Speier-Kris propaganda content analysis proceeded as follows. First, an analyst would read a news bulletin and infer "the predominant subject matter and the intention with which the item is being presented" by the propagandist to the public. Second, the analyst would check the subject he or she identified against "a library index system" divided into numerous standard categories, such as "'aircraft versus aircraft,' or 'aircraft versus immobile objects.'" Third, when enough subjects were known, the analyst would ascertain propaganda patterns. Finally, once these were established, the analyst would hypothesize a reason for the patterns. For instance: "In March of 1940 a great number of items deal with shipping losses sustained by the neutrals, the introduction of rationing in neutral countries and other similar items[;] the cluster around neutrals tends clearly to show that the main line of German policy in broadcasts to Germany was to establish the picture of the neutral powers oppressed by Britain—and thus we may say gradually to prepare the way for the invasion of Denmark and Norway in defense of the interests of these countries." A Speier-Kris analyst also inferred a broadcast's theme (e.g., "Britain oppressed the neutrals"), intent (e.g., the desire to impress the German people with British cruelty), presentation (e.g., whether an item was presented as fact), and nature (e.g., whether an item was meant to convey news, arouse the listener's emotions, predict the future, etc.). Several of these were then coded and graphed to allow for visual representation of patterns, frequency, and change over time.[38]

Notwithstanding their attempt to scientize content analysis, after the release of the project's first two reports in December 1941 and January 1942, respectively, Speier and Kris admitted—likely in response to critiques from foundation and government officials—that their "procedure seems to allow for a considerable subjectivity in interpretation." Though they personally had humanistic inclinations, the two émigrés, who were convinced that any influence they would have would depend on the perceived objectivity of their conclusions, were unwilling to abandon their scientistic pretensions. Going forward, Speier and Kris tried to guarantee "a high degree of constancy in interpretation" in their work by introducing the concept of the "idea." The two characterized an idea as follows: "An announcement on the New British Broadcasting Station [a Nazi-controlled radio station] states that they 'are in a position to deny the rumor that reservations have been made on the clipper for the Royal Family'. Another announcement of the same station says that 'Churchill and other members of the Cabinet have transferred their fortunes to America'. These two statements . . . are in fact two versions of one and the same 'idea': the leaders will desert the British people at the moment of their greatest distress." To ensure the intersubjectivity of their conclusions, Speier and Kris had analysts place ideas within what they termed a "construct." A construct was an analyst-created "system of categories" that included classifications such as "the nature of society and government in Britain," which, once developed, was unalterable. As Speier and Kris reported (using language that revealed their scientistic aspirations):

> The construct is supposed to be a "model," the use of which should permit us to study the propagandistic manipulation of the content. It is comparable to a set of mathematical formulae which give a precise description of a concrete object where concrete values are substituted for the abstract relations. While the analyst is relatively free in devising the category scheme, he is closely bound in his interpretation of the concrete material once the construct is established. This, then, accounts for the consistency and the high degree of reliability of the interpretation.

Speier and Kris deployed technical-sounding language to demonstrate to foundation and government officials that their conclusions were scientific and hence objective, which was the major claim on which their (potential) authority rested.[39]

Speier and Kris's gambit worked. From the project's beginning, the two successfully generated interest in their research among government officials. In December 1941, Speier and Kris sent the project's first report to the Office of the Coordinator of Information (COI) (the precursor to the Office of Strategic Services [OSS] and Office of War Information [OWI]); Harold Lasswell's Experimental Division for the Study of War Time Communications at the Library of Congress; the State, War, and Justice Departments; the Military Intelligence Division of the General Staff; and the Foreign Broadcast Monitoring Service. Several agencies responded positively to their research. The COI's Edward Y. Hartshorne, a sociologist who had studied in Heidelberg and written a dissertation on German universities under Nazism, considered the report "very illuminating" and asked Speier and Kris to "keep us supplied with the remaining portions of your analyses as they appear." Moreover, in a letter to John Marshall, the COI's Robert Tryon, head of its Psychology Division, related that "it is our feeling that of all the work we have seen, that being done in the Totalitarian Research Project is by far the best." The report's seemingly scientific character was particularly appealing to policymakers. As Goodwin Watson, the chief broadcast analyst of the Foreign Broadcast Monitoring Service, informed Marshall, he was especially impressed with "the insight, care and objectivity" of the project's research.[40]

Academics and foundation officials also admired the Research Project for its scientific character. The psychologist Hadley Cantril, who was then part of the Rockefeller-funded Radio Research Project, praised Speier and Kris for their work, asserting in a letter to the latter that "I know your generalizations are based on an enormous amount of data, [and thus] I tend to take them much more seriously than I would if I read them in other contexts." In a report to Marshall, Lasswell respectfully affirmed that the project was "making some progress toward the development of sufficiently objective procedures to reduce the area of mere guess-work" inherent in propaganda analysis. Marshall himself was deeply impressed with Speier and Kris's "first-rate project" and was particularly "struck by the intellectual quality of the work, which seems . . . admirably balanced between empirical inquiry and theoretical conceptualization." Indeed, in April 1942 the foundation granted the project an additional $19,740.

When it was completed in 1944, the Research Project on Totalitarian Communication in Wartime had produced seven reports and numerous articles, all of which culminated in the book *German Radio Propaganda*, which became a foundational text of propaganda content analysis. However, by the time the Research Project received more funds in 1942, Speier had left the New School to join the Federal Communications Commission's (FCC) Foreign Broadcast Monitoring Service (FBMS), which was the government agency responsible for propaganda analysis. After years of writing that intellectuals needed to use their knowledge in the service of the state, Speier was finally given the opportunity to put his ideas into practice.[41]

The FBMS (whose name changed to the Foreign Broadcast Intelligence Service, or FBIS, in July 1942) began formal operations in 1941. The division emerged from a late 1940 meeting between Cordell Hull, the secretary of state, and Franklin Delano Roosevelt, in which Hull suggested that the government create a unit to monitor foreign propaganda aimed at the United States. The president agreed, and on February 25, 1941, he allocated $150,000 from his emergency fund to found the FBMS, which opened the next day. Very quickly, the division became the major center for open-source intelligence—intelligence gathered from publicly available materials—within the government.[42]

Since its inception, the FBIS (this acronym used hereafter) had connections to the Rockefeller Foundation, which facilitated Speier's entrance into the organization. Institutionally, it had absorbed the Rockefeller-funded Princeton Shortwave Listening Center, whose director, Harold Graves, became the FBIS's senior administrative officer. When Graves received Speier and Kris's reports, he forwarded them to his superiors while encouraging the two to send more as they appeared. Speier had himself been communicating with the service since November 1941, when the University of Chicago political scientist Sebastian de Grazia informed Lloyd Free, a Princeton professor who had become the FBIS's director, of the Research Project's work. Free, who was interested in recruiting PhD's to the FBIS's Analysis Division (AD), was intrigued by Speier. On reading the project's reports, Free and Goodwin Watson, a former professor of social psychology at Columbia and the current head of the AD, came away impressed with their sophistication. Watson subsequently asked Speier and Kris if they could discuss "problems of common interest," and in January 1942 he traveled to New York from Washington, D.C., to visit the project for a day. After his visit, Watson informed Marshall that in his opinion, the project represented "the most important contribution now being made anywhere to the analysis of propaganda" and asked him if he would be upset if Speier were invited to join the FBIS.[43]

After receiving Marshall's blessing in mid-February 1942, Watson offered Speier a position as senior political analyst and head of the AD's Central European Section. Watson implored Speier to accept the job, asserting that "we believe that the research that you have done now needs to be harnessed in the service of our Government at war. In peacetime, with less urgency, one might prefer the freer academic approach. Now there is so much at stake that we feel justified in urging you to give up other activities and enlist your trained abilities in this service." Though moved by Watson's message, Speier was initially reluctant to join the division, fearing, as Marshall related, "that the work to which he would be assigned there would be necessarily routine in nature, thus preventing him from bringing to bear the wider competence in analysis of German propaganda which he knows himself to possess." Nevertheless, Speier eventually concluded that despite his misgivings, it was his moral duty to use the "talents that I have for a war purpose," and no other government agency had expressed interest in him. At the end of the month, he accepted Watson's offer.[44]

Alvin Johnson was worried that Speier would never return to the New School and was therefore unenthusiastic about granting him leave to join the FBIS. Yet, as Marshall reported, Speier was able to persuade Johnson to assent to his decision "by pointing out how unwise it would be for [Speier] as a German refugee to decline a government appointment, on the ground that it might seem to involve a question of his loyalty." Speier was correct to be concerned about questions of loyalty. Though he had received U.S. citizenship in the spring of 1940, the Federal Bureau of Investigation continued to entertain, as Speier conveyed to his colleague Kurt Riezler, "suspicions of [Speier] having been a dangerously subversive character" because he had published on Marx and "was not a Jew and yet left Germany in 1933," which implied—to the FBI, at least—that he was a communist. Adding to the FBI's apprehension was the fact that in 1940 a disgruntled former student erroneously told the bureau that Speier and four of the Graduate Faculty "were anti-English and strong national socialists" who had established "an espionage system" at the New School. These accusations forced Speier to begin work at the AD in March without a security clearance. Despite these difficulties, however, Speier was happy he enlisted in the FBIS. Weeks after joining the division, he informed Riezler that contrary to his original expectations, his "job promises to be quite interesting. . . . Many of the people in the [analysis] section I know personally, and quite a few of them are highly qualified men." Finally, after the FBI cleared Speier in May, he became a full-fledged member of the AD.[45]

Speier was one of several New School faculty who entered government service during and after World War II. Max Ascoli (Office of the Coordinator of Inter-American Affairs), Gerhard Colm (Bureau of the Budget), and Hans Simons (Office of the Military Government–United States) also left New York for Washington or Germany. As this suggests, by the early 1940s many American elites accepted exiles as part of their increasingly ethnically and religiously diverse community. This was due largely to practical exigencies. According to H. Stuart Hughes, the young historian who throughout the war worked in the Research and Analysis Branch of the Office of Strategic Services with several exiles, after Pearl Harbor "an expert knowledge of central Europe had overnight become a precious commodity." Because the New School was the major center of German intellectual exiles in America, officials frequently looked to the University in Exile for information on Nazi Germany. As Claus-Dieter Krohn has noted, "many members of the faculty contributed to the 'war effort' by being involved in over twenty-five government and army committees and projects." The New School's influence on policy further extended beyond the impact of faculty members; by 1945, over two hundred students who had studied or worked at the University in Exile had joined the government, including several of Speier's assistants from the Research Project.[46]

Nonetheless, there were limits on Americans' embrace of the exiles. Though they accepted Speier, the FBIS's administrators did not welcome many other émigrés, which underlined the liminal position the exiles occupied in wartime Washington. On one hand, the government required émigrés' unique knowledge and respected them as researchers. On the other hand, traditional anxieties about foreign encroachment on the United States continued to influence how native-born Americans viewed Europeans. In May 1943, for example, Watson, at Speier's request, submitted to former Bennington College president Robert Leigh, who had replaced Lloyd Free as FBIS director, a list of potential recruits to Speier's Central European Section. The list included the émigrés John Herz, Sigmund Neumann, Hans Simons, and Arnold Wolfers. Upon reading the list, Leigh informed Watson that it "does not seem to me the right direction in which to go" because he wanted to bring only "scholar[s] trained in American Universities" to the FBIS. "As a matter of personnel policy," Leigh insisted, "we should get a person of American training to associate with the German group which represents the excellent training of the German universities which, however, is different in its viewpoints from that produced on the American soil." Leigh did not specify how German training differed from American, implying simply that the former was somehow alien and to be distrusted. In his response to Leigh, Watson agreed that "if Hans Speier stays, we may want to look for someone of American background and training." In the end, the FBIS hired none of the recommended exiles. Even when they achieved remarkable success in the United States, to many American elites there remained something foreign, perhaps even "Jewish," about the exiles as a group.[47]

Speier's entrance into the wartime government was his initiation into a cohort of young social scientists that would build the military-intellectual complex during the Cold War. In addition to Speier, all of his colleagues from the University of Chicago, including Gabriel Almond, Harold Lasswell, and Edward Shils, worked for the government during the war. As one observer noted in 1944, "the scholarly mobilization which has been going on since the beginning of the war has brought to government service and particularly to Washington probably the greatest aggregation of social scientists which has ever been assembled in one place." After the war, the psychiatrist Alexander Leighton would boast that social science "played a part in the selection of men and women for particular jobs, in the maintenance of morale both in the armed forces and at home, in the prevention and treatment of neuropsychiatric disorders, in propaganda analysis, in selling war bonds, in studies of the social and psychological make-up of the enemy, in training military government personnel for dealing with many kinds of people from Germany to the Pacific islands, and in numerous other operations." World War II was the first time that the government asked social scientists, as a collective, to use their knowledge for policymaking purposes. This experience with the wartime state would transform the production and co-production of U.S. policy and social science.[48]

Speier directed the Central European Section of the Foreign Broadcast Intelligence Service's Analysis Division. In this position, he was responsible for the analysis of all broadcasts and printed materials gathered by the United States that originated in Germany. Speier and his employees explored the content and tone of Nazi propaganda, war reports, and, of special interest to Speier's superiors, leaders' speeches, all in the hope that doing so would reveal Nazi strategies, policies, and objectives in a variety of fields, from propaganda to military action. Determining these, FBIS analysts anticipated, would enable them to predict German behavior and take steps to neutralize or alter it. Each week, Speier's Central European Section produced a "Weekly Survey," which, along with a briefer "Weekly Review," was sent to the State Department, Army, Navy, Office of Strategic Services, and various other government departments. In addition to producing these reports, the AD regularly received requests from other agencies to gather information and intelligence related to particular issues.[49]

Speier had several specific duties as a senior political analyst. He attempted to predict future Nazi policies; suggested themes for U.S. counterpropaganda; and served as a liaison between the FBIS, State Department, and military. His work, Speier recalled, was exhausting. Daily office life was frenetic as he and his analysts scrambled to listen to, read, and analyze an enormous amount of Nazi propaganda, which was gleaned primarily from British listening stations and printed materials smuggled through Portugal. At the FBIS, Speier remembered, "we were all always dead tired."[50]

The frantic pace of Speier's work stripped the scientistic tendencies from the content analysis method he and Kris had earlier developed for the Research Project on Totalitarian Communication in Wartime. As the political scientist Alexander George, who worked with Speier at the AD, wrote after the war in a book that examined the Central European Section's output, Speier and his subordinates found it "often *difficult*, sometimes *imprudent*, and sometimes *unnecessary* to utilize systematic quantitative procedures" in their work. The war required the FBIS "to turn out concrete results of immediate value" to policymakers, and there was no time to place propaganda "ideas" in larger "constructs." For this reason, George noted, "the content analysis performed by the [AD] was in many respects a creative, intuitive process without a systematic basis or doctrine." Central European Section analysts developed what George termed an "implicit methodology" defined by the attempt "to identify the intermediate events linking [propaganda] content to [an] elite behavior (or situational factor)." This method relied on "sophisticated and detailed knowledge of the [Nazi] political elite, its political and propaganda behavior, and the specialized political vocabulary which it employs"—that is to say, qualitative area knowledge. Speier's experience at the FBIS convinced him that knowledge relevant to policy emerged more from qualitative than quantitative approaches, and from the war onward he largely abandoned the latter.[51]

Central European Section analysts were remarkably successful in making accurate inferences about Nazi motivations and actions. George's postwar book, which compared a sample of the section's deductions with materials gathered from Germany, demonstrated that approximately 81 percent of the former were correct. Speier was himself an excellent propaganda analyst whose reputation quickly spread throughout the FBIS and other government agencies, including the Office of War Information, to which he would later move. One example suffices to demonstrate Speier's reliance on qualitative analysis as well as his astonishing ability to forecast Nazi behavior.[52]

On October 29, 1943, Speier produced a report that predicted the contents of Hitler's forthcoming speech commemorating the twentieth anniversary of the failed November 8, 1923, Beer Hall Putsch in Munich. Speier's intensive study of Nazi propaganda and Hitler's public addresses enabled him to identify relevant patterns that proved critical to foreseeing what Hitler would say in his speech. First, he noted that "all Hitler speeches follow a certain pattern which is more or less appropriate for the occasion of the speech," and the annual Beer Hall address always focused on party history. Second, Speier maintained that "all Hitler speeches are in a way summaries of Nazi propaganda" that reaffirmed previously publicized themes and predictions. Finally, he declared that Hitler spoke in generalities when the Nazis lost battles and in specificities when they won, so his speech would be affected by the events immediately preceding it. Speier's analysis, as George put it in his book, thus "rested to a considerable extent on the intuitive skill and judgment" of someone "who had become expert in the ways of Nazi propaganda and political behavior."[53]

Speier correctly foretold that Hitler would speak for less than an hour; devote half of his speech to Nazi party history, focusing on its prewar history; avoid referencing Frederick the Great; stress the need for Germans to persevere and remain loyal, determined, and fanatical; highlight the Italian situation (Benito Mussolini had been deposed in July), criticizing General Pietro Badoglio and King Victor Emmanuel III more than Winston Churchill or Franklin Delano Roosevelt; emphasize that Germany's suffering was similar to other nations', particularly Italy's; say that Germany, by virtue of its conquests in 1941 and 1942, could weather retreats; refuse to predict whether the Germans would regain lost territory on the Soviet front; assert that Germany's position was better than at the beginning of the war; highlight British air war guilt, arguing that any actions taken against women and children were indefensible; declare that the war was forced on Germany; ignore the U-boat campaign but assert that the enemy could not navigate the Mediterranean; use quasi-mystical terms and also mention God; degrade German defeatists more than Churchill or Roosevelt; avoid threatening Britain and America, except to mention air force retaliation; disregard the concept of German hegemony; offer sweeping and vague references to victory, stressing the importance of nonmaterial factors to success; and make traditional anti-Semitic claims. All told, an astounding seventeen of Speier's twenty-five (68 percent) predictions were correct.[54]

Before Hitler delivered the speech, Speier handed his analysis to an Office of War Information contact who brought it to the attention of Representative Joseph Martin (R-MA) and Senator Alexander Wiley (R-WI). Martin and Wiley then delivered a radio address, as Watson reported to Leigh, "to discount in advance any propaganda advantage Hitler might gain through his speech." Watson pointed out that the two congressmen took "most of the content of their remarks . . . directly" from Speier's memorandum, which made them appear prescient once Hitler gave the address. Reports of this incident, and Speier's role in it, quickly spread throughout the FBIS and OWI, enhancing his status in both organizations.[55]

Speier generally impressed his superiors beyond this particular event. Watson praised his "extraordinarily good job of analysis" and "uncanny memory," which enabled Speier "either to remember or to dig out of his files precedents or comparisons for a given propaganda line." He further declared that there was "nobody in the United States whom I would willingly trade for him." A staff report similarly commended Speier's "top-notch performance." Indeed, Speier's reputation was so great that the OWI endeavored to poach him in July 1943. When Leigh learned of Speier's refusal to join the OWI, he informed him that he was "very happy for our sake that you are remaining on the job to carry along continuously and with greater influence the analyses of the German radio propaganda. I seldom have the opportunity to tell you how frequently I hear of the splendid work you are doing and the value you are to people in other agencies." It was because of efforts like Speier's that during and after World War II American foreign policy elites accepted social scientists into their fold.[56]

Speier and his colleagues' various successes, however, did not prevent the evisceration of the FBIS's Analysis Division, which in 1943–1944 fell prey to congressional attacks against the Federal Communications Commission. The saga began in November 1941, when Martin Dies (D-TX), an anti–New Deal congressman who considered the FCC to be Franklin Roosevelt's mouthpiece, accused Goodwin Watson, the AD's director, of harboring communist sympathies. For the next year and a half, Dies worked tirelessly to orchestrate the firing of Watson and William E. Dodd Jr., another FBIS employee. In May 1943, Dies succeeded in convincing the House of Representatives to add a section to the Urgent Deficiency Appropriations Act that denied Watson and Dodd payment, which soon resulted in their dismissal. While Dies's crusade accomplished little of substance, it nonetheless placed the FCC in a defensive position.[57]

Eugene Cox (D-GA) was another congressman who during the war attacked the FCC. Cox focused his attentions on the commission once it began investigating him for corruption in late 1942. In January 1943, Cox persuaded the House to create a Special Committee to Investigate the FCC, and in a brazen display of insouciance Cox's colleagues appointed him the committee's chairman. To combat Cox's selection for this position, the FCC released information about his illegal activities, which forced him to resign his chairmanship. Nevertheless, Cox's replacement, Clarence Lea (D-CA), continued the congressman's spurious witch hunt.

During Lea's investigations, Congress defunded the already weakened FCC, which made it impossible for the commission to continue its work unaffected. A January 1945 article written by Robert Leigh, the FBIS's director, described in detail the process by which the FCC was financially disemboweled:

> When we had submitted our estimates [for fiscal year 1944–1945] to the Budget Bureau we had asked for practically no increases. The Bureau,

> always intelligent and severe in its review of estimates, had sent us down to Congress with our estimates sustained. The House Appropriations Committee gave us a full hearing. If one reads the record one searches in vain for a basis for any reduction [in funds] at all. . . . [Nonetheless,] the [Appropriations] Committee's report . . . recommended a straight 25 per cent cut in [the FCC's] whole appropriation. The House passed the measure without a record vote and with almost no debate. FCC asked for a hearing before the Senate Appropriations Committee to restore the cuts, an unusual proceeding. The request was granted, and the . . . Commission [received] a full hearing of a day and a half. At its end there was again the illusory feeling that there could be no cut because there was no evidence in the record to sustain it. But ten days later, [the chair of the Senate Appropriations Committee] reported out the bill with a further reduction of $500,000. Members of his own committee put up a fight against the cut on the floor of the Senate, and an amendment to restore the full appropriation to my own service [the FBIS] lost by only four votes. But the job was done.

Neither the House nor the Senate publicly revealed why it had taken such drastic action. According to Leigh, though, "the real purpose [of the cuts] was clear to the congressmen themselves when one discussed it with them in their offices. It was not a *fiscal* cut, it was a *punitive* cut." To prove his point, Leigh related that one congressman privately told him that "it was a punitive cut. [The FCC] has been defiant of Congress for a long time. . . . Now [the] chickens have come home to roost."[58]

In response to the new budget limitations, the FBIS drastically reduced the AD. The FBIS focused on cutting the AD because, in the words of Joseph Roop, who worked at the FBIS during the war and later wrote a history of it, "information brought out during the Cox Committee hearings indicated that [government agencies] could do without analysis better than other FBIS services." Moreover, Watson, the subject of Dies's investigation, had been the AD's director, and it probably appeared prudent to the FCC's leaders to exenterate the division with which he was associated. The budget cuts in effect ended the AD's European analysis. As Theodore Newcomb, who became administrative head of the AD after Watson's firing, described, between 1943 and early 1944 the Central European Section's German desk "lost every one of our experienced analysts except Dr. Speier." By early April 1944, only "four inexperienced assistants" aided Speier, and soon thereafter the AD stopped producing its weekly analyses of European propaganda.[59]

In late May, Speier, frustrated with the AD's decline, moved to the OWI. There he became head of the German desk, which made him responsible for producing the directives that guided OWI propaganda sent to Germany. It was at the OWI that Speier fully realized the intellectual program he had developed over the course of the 1930s. No longer was he a scholar or an analyst disconnected from the decision-making process. Instead, he was a policymaker, in charge of propaganda dispatched by the world's most powerful nation to the country that had forced his exile. Speier finally would have his revenge on the Nazis.

Chapter 4

Psychological Warfare in Theory and Practice

By the time Speier joined the Office of War Information in May 1944, World War II's tide had turned in the Allies' favor. Finally, after years of planning, the United States and United Kingdom were set to begin their ground invasion of Western Europe. In Italy, Allied armies advanced toward Rome, which they would seize in early June; in Eastern Europe, the Red Army continued to retake territory lost during the German invasion of 1941. Meanwhile, Allied bombers regularly assailed Germany and its territories while Allied ships and submarines dominated the Atlantic and Europe's seas. The Axis, most Western observers concluded, was hurtling toward defeat.

Speier's position as head of the OWI's German desk allowed him to contribute to Hitler's downfall. In this post, he was personally responsible for developing the directives that guided the work of the thousands of writers, artists, and broadcasters who created the propaganda the OWI sent to Germany. Speier was eager to accept this duty. While at the Foreign Broadcast Intelligence Service, he had criticized OWI propaganda as "uninspired and uninspiring, unexciting and producing nothing but sleepiness."[1] Speier had spent years studying Nazi propaganda and was confident he could use what he learned to improve the U.S. psychological warfare effort. As chief of the German desk, Speier devoted himself to reinvigorating what he considered to be the OWI's lackluster propaganda program by implementing lessons learned from the Nazis. In so doing, he followed his own advice from the 1930s concerning the need for democrats to study totalitarian methods to defeat those who would destroy democracy.

Speier's OWI work may be divided into six phases. The first began with the D-Day invasion of June 6, 1944, and ended with the attempted assassination of Hitler on July 20. During this period, Speier stressed the power of the Allies' military force in order to compel German soldiers to surrender. The failed July 20 assassination plot initiated the propaganda war's second phase, which lasted until mid-September. Over the course of these two months, Speier constructed a fictitious struggle between a "peace movement" composed of anti-Hitler plotters and a silent majority of Germans, and an "annihilation party" composed of die-hard Nazis. When it became clear by mid-September that no broad anti-Nazi movement was emergent in Germany, Speier inaugurated the propaganda war's third phase, in which he focused on discussing the salutary benefits of the future occupation.

The Battle of the Bulge's eruption in mid-December instigated the propaganda war's fourth phase. For about two months, Speier argued that regardless of the German counteroffensive's initial successes, the Allies' overwhelming power guaranteed they would win the war. By February 1945, the Allies had repulsed the Germans in Western Europe and were on the path to ultimate victory. Speier thereafter commenced the propaganda war's fifth phase, which lasted from February until the war's end in May. Throughout these months, Speier discussed the U.S. occupation of Germany in detail. His directives also underwent a tonal shift characterized by the expression of deep anger with the German people for supporting Hitler. As the Allies advanced on Germany from the east and west, Speier began to assert, openly and furiously, that without ordinary Germans' backing, Hitler could not have ruled. For this reason, he avowed that all Germans were responsible for Nazi crimes. Speier inaugurated the sixth and final phase of his OWI work after Germany unconditionally surrendered on May 7. From May until the autumn of 1945, he focused on "winning the peace" by ensuring that the OWI's propaganda did all it could to prevent Germans from embracing ideas similar to those that had doomed the Weimar Republic.[2]

Speier's impact on the OWI's propaganda directives highlights the Europeanization of U.S. foreign policy during and after World War II. Speier used his unique and, in the minds of his superiors, "outstanding experience and comprehensive knowledge of the political, economic, social, and cultural background of the German people" in his directives.[3] For example, in a December 1944 directive he declared that OWI propaganda must make clear that the Allies intended to reinstate a *Rechtsstaat*—a reference to liberal German legal theory—that would stand in stark contrast to capricious Nazi governance.[4] Moreover, after the war his belief that Weimar's collapse had been at least partially caused by nationalist legends led him to insist that OWI propaganda attempt to prevent the creation of a "stab in the back myth" similar to the one that had weakened German democracy after World War I.[5] Though a naturalized American citizen, some part of Speier remained a German determined to avenge the Weimar Republic and resurrect the democratic project Hitler had strangled in the crib. Nevertheless, when the Allied victory enabled Speier to return to Germany in October 1945, his encounter with his former homeland compelled him to reject his German heritage and to identify, explicitly and forcefully, as an American. Poignantly, Speier's homecoming made him feel less German than he ever had before.

Speier was one of thousands of social scientists who became decision makers, analysts, or researchers in the United States' war administration. Together, these intellectuals realized the activist vision that Speier had championed since the mid-1930s. Most important, the sojourns of so many scholars to Washington, D.C., laid the ideological and social foundations of the Cold War–era military-intellectual complex. Ideologically, after their World War II experiences most scholars were convinced that, first, government support did not inevitably distort scientific analysis; second, that classification and secrecy were necessary parts of making foreign policy; third, that interdisciplinary, team-based research could solve pressing policy problems; fourth, that there was a place for them within the foreign policy establishment; and finally, that social science could, in Harold Lasswell's words, "(1) clarify goals, (2) clarify alternatives, and (3) provide needed knowledge" to policymakers.[6] Socially, the personal relationships formed during the war proved crucial to the military-intellectual complex's composition. For instance, Leo Rosten, Speier's OWI colleague, brought Speier to the RAND Corporation. Speier, for his part, recruited several wartime colleagues to the organization, including W. Phillips Davison, Alexander George, Paul Kecskemeti, and Nathan Leites. The war also solidified relationships that Speier had formed in the 1930s. For example, throughout his time at the FBIS and OWI he frequently collaborated with Gabriel Almond, who headed the OWI's Enemy Information Section; Lasswell, who directed the Library of

Congress's Experimental Division for the Study of War Time Communications; and Edward Shils, who worked for the Supreme Headquarters, Allied Expeditionary Force's Psychological Warfare Division. After the war, Speier continued to work with each of these scholars in various capacities. In short, World War II was the crucible in which the defense intellectual was forged.

The United States began to build its propaganda program several months before the Pearl Harbor attack of December 7, 1941. On July 11, Franklin Delano Roosevelt authorized the creation of the Office of the Coordinator of Information to organize and implement a U.S. propaganda effort for the coming war. Roosevelt appointed William Donovan, a Republican lawyer, the head of the COI, and Robert Sherwood, a pro–New Deal playwright and White House speechwriter, the director of its Foreign Information Service (FIS), which was responsible for producing propaganda sent abroad. Roosevelt located the FIS in New York City—the only East Coast metropolis with communications facilities able to broadcast radio to Europe—and the remainder of the COI in Washington, D.C.[7]

Sherwood shaped the FIS in his image. He primarily hired New Dealers who agreed with his belief that U.S. propagandists should embrace a "strategy of truth," in which civilians used "overt" or white propaganda—that is to say, American-produced propaganda that was attributed to the United States—to publicize the nation's moral, social, cultural, economic, and political superiority. Sherwood averred that because the United States was so obviously superior to Nazi Germany, all American propagandists needed to do to win ideological adherents abroad was to present the (selected and censored) "truth" of the nation to foreign audiences.

Sherwood's opinions permeated the FIS and distinguished it from the rest of the Donovan-led COI. In contrast to Sherwood, Donovan rejected the idea that propaganda should try to change foreigners' beliefs. He instead argued that only "covert" or black propaganda—that is to say, American-produced propaganda that was not attributed to the United States—that concentrated on supporting military operations was effective during wartime. These differing opinions resulted in intra-organizational tensions that Roosevelt resolved on June 13, 1942, when he dissolved the COI. In its stead, Roosevelt created the Office of War Information, which absorbed the FIS and concentrated its efforts on white propaganda. At the same time, the president installed Donovan as the director of the newly established Office of Strategic Services, which was made responsible for black propaganda and other covert activities.[8]

Roosevelt appointed Elmer Davis, a popular radio commentator, the OWI's director, while Sherwood retained control of the FIS, whose name was changed to the Overseas Branch (OB). Tensions between the two were quick to emerge. Though both Davis and Sherwood endorsed the strategy of truth, they disagreed as to propaganda's function. Sherwood continued to affirm that propaganda should attempt to change foreign audiences' ideological preferences. Davis, who embraced increasingly prominent social scientific theories that doubted propaganda's ability to transform individuals' core beliefs, scorned Sherwood's opinion. Like Donovan, Davis wanted to use foreign-directed propaganda to support military operations. As he declared in 1943, "we in O.W.I. . . . know that the war is going to be won primarily by fighting," and thus the best U.S. propaganda could do was "pave the way for [military] operations and make their success easier." Another major disagreement that distinguished Sherwood from Davis concerned propaganda's policy role. Whereas Sherwood desired to use propaganda to shape U.S. foreign policy—he assumed that if propaganda said something, policymakers would be forced to follow it—Davis maintained that propaganda must reflect and amplify, not influence, policy.[9]

These differences resulted in conflicts that in early 1944 led Davis to reorganize the OB and replace the New York–based Sherwood with a cohort of leaders based in Washington, D.C. Davis stood at the apex of this new hierarchy, followed by the journalist Edward Barrett, who served as the OB's executive director. Davis also established three "areas" within the OB that he charged with developing propaganda directives for specific world regions. He persuaded Wallace Carroll, a journalist who had headed the OWI's London office, to direct Area One, which was responsible for creating the directives for propaganda sent to Western and Central Europe, the Iberian Peninsula, Scandinavia, Italy, the Balkans, North Africa, and Turkey. Carroll, like the others whom Davis appointed to managerial positions in the restructured OB, agreed with Davis that propaganda should reflect and sell U.S. foreign policy, not make it; be truthful; and support military operations.[10]

When Carroll began his work, he inherited a staff of only fifteen and immediately started hiring more people. Carroll was particularly interested in recruiting experts on Germany, because, as he recalled in his postwar memoir, he personally lacked the "considerable knowledge of Germany" required to produce effective propaganda guidances. One of the first places he looked for new recruits was Speier's Foreign Broadcast Intelligence Service, which was the only organization historically eager to share intelligence with the OWI. By this point in the war, Speier had developed a considerable reputation for his extensive knowledge of Nazi propaganda. Moreover, as an émigré, he had an epistemological authority that few Americans could challenge. Thus, in late March 1944 Carroll asked Speier to serve as the chief of Area One's German desk. Speier accepted Carroll's offer, which made him, according to his job description, "responsible for the policy control and appropriateness of the productive output in all media to Germany, Austria, and Switzerland; [responsible for supervising] the evaluation of intelligence material on these countries that comes from OWI outposts and other government agencies; [and responsible for supervising and assisting] the regional specialists for these countries."[11]

The FBIS's Analysis Division, for which Speier worked, had collaborated with the OWI for years, which facilitated Speier's transition to the OB. From the time the United States entered the war, Goodwin Watson, the head of the AD, had provided the OWI with analysis and recommendations; in the autumn of 1942, Robert Leigh, the FBIS's director, had established weekly meetings between the AD and its OWI counterpart; in April 1943, the AD and the OB's Bureau of Research and Analysis had reached an agreement whereby the OWI would use the AD for analyzing radio broadcasts; and finally, in May 1943, the AD had moved to the OWI's headquarters in the Social Security Building. Speier thus had extensive contact with the OWI, and in early 1944, when Congress began to cut the FBIS's budget, he had started to eye moving to the OB.[12]

OFFICE OF WAR INFORMATION
WASHINGTON, D. C.
This is to certify that: Hans Speier (Name of Bearer)
whose signature, photograph, and fingerprints appear on this card is an authorized representative of the Office of War Information, and that information verified to the satisfaction of this organization has been presented that he is a citizen of and loyal to the United States.
Director.
(Signature of Bearer)
COUNTERSIGNED (Signature of Security Officer) (Deputy)
[INVALID WITHOUT EMBOSSED SEAL OF OWI]
DISTINGUISHING CHARACTERISTICS
Color eyes Blue Color hair Brown
Weight 155 lbs. Height 5 ft. 8½ in.
Race W Date of birth 2/3/1905
Date issued September 5, 1945
VOID AFTER September 5, 1946
FORM NO. OWI 11
FINGERPRINTS RIGHT HAND
THUMB

Figure 4. Speier's Office of War Information identification badge, 1945–1946, *photo courtesy of the New School*

Upon officially joining the OB on May 22, Speier became the most important member of Area One after Carroll. As Carroll remembered after the war:

> It was Speier who quickly established his pre-eminence in the arts of propaganda among the old members of the staff as well as the new. Germany was his native land, and he had been a student and political writer there before Hitler seized power. . . . Since the outbreak of the war, he had devoted most of his time to the study of propaganda. He was the co-author of *German Radio Propaganda*, the classic work on the techniques of Goebbels, and he knew as much about German propaganda methods as anyone working on the side of the Allies. This alone would have made him useful to us, but he had something which was much more valuable—sound political sense and a talent for originating propaganda ideas. Around Speier we built our planning team for Germany.

After years of analyzing propaganda campaigns, Speier began to orchestrate them.[13]

Beginning in December 1944, Speier served not only as chief of the German desk but also as propaganda policy adviser to Edward Barrett, the OB's executive director. According to his job description, in this capacity Speier regularly attended OWI policy planning meetings "as chief policy adviser on German matters." Speier's position also took him outside the OWI, where he served as a member of the German Propaganda Policy Committee, which was, his job description reported, "an inter-government agency group which includes representatives from the State and War Departments and other government agencies, the function of which is to plan the propaganda phases of the military occupation of Germany." This responsibility provided Speier with access to State Department officials, with whom he built friendly relationships that helped him become the acting chief of State's Division for Occupied Areas in 1946–1947.[14]

Speier's understanding of wartime propaganda's purpose mirrored Davis's and Carroll's exactly, which encouraged the latter two to entrust him with primary responsibility for creating the directives that guided OWI propaganda sent to Germany. Speier agreed with the OWI's leaders that propaganda should support military operations and avoid attempting to change a target population's ideological inclinations. For example, in a 1944 essay he and Margaret Otis, a colleague from the FBIS, argued that Nazi psychological warfare revealed that "the function of propaganda to the enemy in total war" was "*to realize the aim of war—which is victory—without acts of physical violence or with less expenditure of physical violence than would otherwise be necessary.*" In short, Speier asserted that propaganda should not try to change people's beliefs—which could take a very long time—but must instead concentrate on ending the war as quickly and peacefully as possible.[15]

Indeed, Speier's study of Nazi propaganda provided the theoretical foundations upon which he constructed his own propaganda directives. Based on their analyses of the Nazis, in their article Speier and Otis elucidated the five actions that effective propaganda compelled the enemy soldier or civilian to take. First, it provoked "the enemy's surrender without fighting"; second, it tricked the enemy into fighting "the wrong opponent," such as his or her fellow soldier; third, it persuaded the enemy to trust the propagandist's side and not her or his own; fourth, it convinced the enemy that he or she should concentrate on preserving his or her personal safety instead of fighting the war; and finally, it induced panic, which prevented the enemy from fighting effectively. Speier and Otis further argued that Nazi propaganda demonstrated that there were five universal tactics that propagandists from all countries fighting a total war should deploy if they hoped to aid military operations:

> 1. They *may attack the enemy's confidence in victory* by pointing out that the odds are against him; because he is weak or has failed, while the propagandist's side is strong or has had success. 2. Similarly, propagandists may point out that the enemy is socially divided or that the propagandist's side is really united with that of the propagandee. 3. They *may attack the enemy's conviction of the right to victory* by telling him that he is guilty of all sorts of immorality, whereas the propagandist's side shines in the glory of a just cause and is generally angelic. 4. They *may confuse the enemy's understanding of the complex world he lives in*, in particular by presenting certain groups and leaders on his own side as his real enemies, i.e., as internal enemies or exploiters. Correspondingly, propagandists may make every effort to present their own side, the external enemy, as a partner, real friend or protector who is going to treat his misled foe with consideration. 5. Finally, propagandists may depoliticize their audience not by confusing the roles of enemy and friend, but by presenting non-political values and loyalties as more important than the political ones.

These tactics permeated Speier's directives throughout the war.[16]

Speier also shared Davis and Carroll's conviction that propagandists had no right to shape U.S. foreign policy. As he wrote in his 1945 essay "War

Aims and Political Warfare," the propagandist's function was to "inform the world about the policy of the country for which they speak" and, in certain instances, "interpret this policy" for "people who are not experts on foreign policy." These interpretations, though, "have to stay within narrow limits and are, as a matter of routine, subject to clearance by policymaking agencies." Propagandists' subservience to policymakers was not only acceptable, Speier averred, but wise, as "propagandists are usually inclined toward short-range considerations" while policymakers must consider "enduring interests, future conditions and long-range objectives." "Statesmen," Speier unequivocally argued, "not propagandists, must make policy."[17]

Finally, Speier approved Davis and Carroll's contention that propaganda was an ancillary weapon during wartime. Before and during the war, Speier maintained that propaganda's "power is limited. . . . Only when morale is already shaken may hostile propaganda succeed in dealing a decisive blow" to the enemy by inducing surrender, sabotage, or confusion. "A victorious nation," he professed, "cannot be defeated by slogans; an army whose food supply functions satisfactorily will not be demoralized by the however often repeated statement that it is starving; civilians who suffer from air attacks cannot very long be fooled by pronunciamentos that there is no reason to fear them." Because "the propagandist deals in words and ceremonies within a framework [war] dominated by action and blood," "propaganda campaigns are neither so important nor so final as military campaigns." Speier, Carroll, and Davis all agreed that propaganda could have an impact at the margins, but they rejected hopes that it could serve as a primary weapon of war. Nonetheless, they were each devoted to using the skills they had to contribute to the Allies' victory and worked tirelessly to aid the war effort in any way they could.[18]

The OWI of 1944–1945 was divided between propaganda policymakers like Speier and Carroll, who were based in Washington, D.C., and propaganda "operators," who worked in regional offices and actually created the radio programs, pamphlets, and other materials sent abroad. The primary problem for policymakers was how to control the content of operators' propaganda. To do so, they used written directives, which had a variety of functions: they specified the themes and subject matter that policymakers wanted operators to emphasize; suggested particular phrasings operators should use in their materials; and explained the logic behind certain themes. The two most important types of OWI directive were the weekly central directive, which provided general guidelines for the OB's propaganda, and the weekly regional directive, which provided more granular instructions for propaganda sent to individual countries. Occasionally, OWI policymakers also released special directives that addressed particular or time-sensitive issues.[19]

Area One's section of the central directive was composed in the following manner. Each Saturday, Carroll met with Speier and other members of Area One to read and discuss news and intelligence reports produced by the OWI or other groups, such as the OSS or the State, War, and Navy Departments. After these deliberations, Carroll drafted a report detailing the themes that he, Speier, and their colleagues wanted operators to highlight in their propaganda. When writing this initial draft, Carroll collaborated closely with Speier, whom he later affirmed was "an ace" and "the decisive man" in the OWI's European propaganda effort. To ensure compliance with their instructions, once they had a draft Carroll and Speier sometimes traveled to New York—where most of Area One's operators were based—to discuss the directive and, if necessary, make changes. Carroll then took this refigured draft to his superiors, who approved it and placed it in the central directive.[20]

On Tuesdays, the OWI's leaders presented the central directive to an interdepartmental Overseas Planning Board, which was responsible for endorsing it before it was diffused throughout the OWI. Davis presided over the Overseas Planning Board, whose other official members included, but were not limited to, Barrett, Carroll, and Speier; ranking members of the OWI's New York office; and officials from the State Department and the Joint Chiefs of Staff. In addition, representatives of the OSS, the Coordinator of Inter-American Affairs (which controlled U.S. propaganda sent to Latin America), and the British Political Warfare Mission regularly joined meetings in advisory capacities. Once the board approved the central directive, the OWI's leaders transmitted it to operators.[21]

Regional directives were the other major document that OWI policymakers used in their effort to control operators' propaganda. According to Charles A. H. Thomson, who worked at the OWI with Speier, by the war's end the more detailed regional directives emerged as "the [OWI's] chief means of formal coordination with current military and diplomatic operations." Speier was responsible for producing the regional directives for propaganda sent to Germany, and for two reasons he exerted primary control over their creation. First, as described above, Speier shared most of Davis and Carroll's strategic and tactical opinions about propaganda, so they were inclined to grant him the freedom to write directives as he wished. Second, Speier had spent years establishing his reputation as a propaganda expert and was quickly able to convince Davis and Carroll that he did not require close supervision.[22]

Several other individuals were prominent members of the OB's German desk and aided Speier in the development of his propaganda directives. Douglas Miller, the former commercial attaché to the U.S. embassy in Berlin who had previously occupied Speier's job, remained after the OWI's 1944 reorganization to help. Erich Rinner, an exile and former parliamentary secretary of the Social Democratic Party of Germany, was another important member of the group. Speier also worked closely with several members of the OWI's New York office, including the sociologists Paul Kecskemeti and Nathan Leites, both European exiles whom Speier would later bring to RAND. Finally, Speier collaborated with others within the OWI, including the psychologist Leonard Doob, the journalist and scholar Hans Mayer, and the playwright Sam Spewack, as well as some outside it, such as the psychologist Hadley Cantril and the economist Winfield William Riefler. Despite these individuals' help, however, Speier was the main figure behind the OWI's anti-German propaganda effort. For this reason, for the remainder of this chapter I quote all the directives that dealt with Germany as if they reflected Speier's voice. This is not to minimize the contributions others made to the OWI's anti-German propaganda. Rather, it is to stress that of all the OWI's policymakers, Speier exerted the most significant influence on the organization's directives for Germany.[23]

Unlike most of the OWI's propaganda directives, Speier's German directives were not guided by the strategy of truth. While Carroll endorsed this strategy for the propaganda sent to the majority of countries for which he was responsible, he and Speier decided that it was inappropriate for their anti-German propaganda effort. Recapitulating arguments Speier had made in the 1930s, the two propagandists asserted that the extreme nature of the Nazi menace made it unwise for anti-German propaganda to be defined by, to use Carroll's phrasing, "the free communication of facts." Instead, as Carroll wrote after the war, he and Speier "felt free to employ any device, any *ruse de guerre*, which would speed the collapse of Germany and save Allied lives." In the struggle against fascism, ends justified means. The emergency situation, Speier and Carroll maintained, required a sacrifice of values for the greater good.[24]

The first phase of Speier's propaganda war against Nazi Germany began with the June 6, 1944, Allied invasion of Normandy and ended with the failed July 20 assassination attempt against Hitler. During these six weeks,

Speier developed a campaign in which he endeavored to "creat[e] a state of mind [in] the German people which is favorable to surrender." To do so, his directives urged the OWI's operators to stress the Allies' "overwhelming force" in order to engender "piecemeal surrender of German soldiers singly or in groups." Speier instructed his subordinates to use all examples of Allied superiority, from technology to men to materiel, to suggest that the Germans could not possibly withstand the Allies' onslaught. "Surrender," he urged his operators to assert, was "the normal and honorable thing to do in [the] face of hopeless odds."[25]

Other mini-campaigns intended to promote surrender permeated Speier's directives at the same time that he emphasized overwhelming force. To divide the Germans from their political leaders, he asked operators to lambast high-ranking Nazis, especially Hitler, for "know[ing] very well that the war is lost and that their game is up" but continuing the war regardless. Though Speier wanted his operators to admit that German soldiers had displayed "bravery and stubbornness," he also wanted them to underline that "the failures of Nazi leadership" made it necessary, even patriotic, for "outnumbered, outmaneuvered, [and] overpowered" troops to capitulate. Throughout June and the first half of July, Speier did all he could to induce Germans to surrender.[26]

Speier inaugurated the second phase of his propaganda war on July 20, when a group of disaffected German military officers tried and failed to assassinate Hitler at his East Prussian headquarters. Speier was positively giddy over this plot, which he excitedly referred to as "the biggest propaganda break of the war." While he believed that "the Nazi regime probably will be able to overcome the present crisis," he nonetheless maintained that the botched assassination attempt provided salient proof that a number of Germany's elite understood that the war was lost and were willing to do whatever it took to end it immediately. "Never before," Speier crowed, "had German officers made an attempt on the life of the Supreme War Lord and chief of state to whom they had taken an oath of loyalty. Their action can only signify the beginning of the end, with the children of the Nazi revolution devouring each other."[27]

In the aftermath of July 20, Speier developed a propaganda campaign that insisted that the assassination plot reflected "a clash between [a] growing peace movement (Friedensbewegung) [present in Germany] and [an] annihilation party (Vernichtungspartei)" of devoted Nazis, which "has arisen as a result of Germany's hopeless military position." Speier wanted his operators to make clear to Germans that both the peace and annihilation parties recognized that the war was lost. The only difference between them was that "the 'peace movement' wants to end the war now and to surrender in order not to turn Germany into a battlefield, whereas the 'annihilation party' wants to prolong the war until all of Germany is destroyed." If Germans desired to save their country from the Nazis, Speier beseeched his operators to imply, they needed to work with and for the peace movement.[28]

Speier subsequently focused on convincing Germans that it was safe to join the peace movement. He wanted OWI propaganda to suggest "that the peace movement reaches into all walks of life: it comprises not only military men but also civilians; it is not confined to a handful of 'reactionaries,' but cuts through all classes of the population." In this way, Speier hoped operators would present the peace movement as a mass movement analogous to, and presumably as powerful as, the Nazi Party. For the entirety of August and the first half of September, Speier continued to urge his subordinates to emphasize to Germans "that the crisis persists" and that the peace movement "is essentially intact."[29]

However, by mid-September it was clear, as Carroll later wrote, "that the conspiracy [against Hitler] had failed to obtain mass support." Speier thus slowly eliminated discussions of the peace movement from his propaganda directives. By this point in the war, Allied troops had liberated Paris, Lyon, Brussels, and Luxembourg and appeared on the inevitable march toward Berlin. On September 12, General Dwight D. Eisenhower, the supreme commander of the Allied forces in Europe, officially announced that the Battle of Germany, the war's final struggle, was imminent. In response to Eisenhower's statement, OWI propaganda, as Carroll reported after the war, "swiftly made" "the transition . . . to the Battle of Germany."[30] Specifically, Speier returned to attempting to induce German surrender.

During this third phase of his propaganda war, Speier began to discuss in earnest the Allied occupation of Germany. Initially, a November directive from outside the OWI forbade Speier from promising the Germans anything about the occupation. Nevertheless, on December 4, Speier was granted freedom to maneuver when the Psychological Warfare Division, the Anglo-American agency that oversaw propaganda in the European Theater of Operations, released thirteen statements that described the coming occupation in some detail. By finally providing a blueprint for the occupation, these statements enabled Speier to tell Germans what the war's end meant for them—essentially, peace and democracy—which, he hoped, would prompt their surrender.

Throughout this period, Speier used his propaganda directives to promote the completion of projects that had collapsed with Weimar. For example, he instructed operators to emphasize that the Allies were committed to the "restoration of [a German] Rechtsstaat," in which the law respected civil liberties and constrained the arbitrary use of power. Though he acknowledged that "the Military Government of Germany will be firm and strict," Speier wanted his operators to affirm that "it will also be just. . . . It will be guided by the dictates of humanity, justice and civilized standards which will take the place of Nazi brutality, terror and barbarism." Speier thus asserted that the Allies would reestablish the Weimar *Rechtsstaat* that Hitler and his cronies had destroyed.[31]

Speier further believed that with the war's end in sight, he could persuade ordinary Germans to sabotage the Nazis. He exhorted operators "to insist that after the occupation of Germany only those Germans will be regarded as true opponents to the Nazis who have proved during the war that they actively contributed to the downfall of the regime." "Anti-Nazi Germans," Speier wanted his operators to make clear, "must act now" by refusing to mobilize in local military units, by contributing to work slowdowns, and by aiding persecuted minorities and foreign workers.[32]

The Battle of the Bulge of 1944–1945 dashed Speier's hopes that World War II would soon be over and initiated the fourth phase of his propaganda war. On December 16, the Germans launched a massive assault on the Allied front lines in Western Europe. In response to the initially successful attack, Speier and the rest of the OB, as Carroll recalled, "floundered about, changing our line from day to day," unable to decide on a propaganda theme that would mitigate the boost to German morale engendered by the Wehrmacht's advances. Finally, on December 26, Speier, in discussion with Carroll and others, released a flurry of memos that instructed the OWI's operators as to how they should address the counteroffensive. By this point, the Allies had stopped the Germans and had started to reinforce besieged troops. Though Speier and his colleagues concluded "that the German counter-offensive will not fulfill the high expectations which German propaganda has expressed" for it, they remained concerned that the attack would bolster "German morale in consequence of the demonstrated ability of the German armies in the west to seize the initiative for a limited period of time." For this reason, they decided to initiate "an all-out propaganda campaign to show our audiences that, 1. Germany has been weakened. 2. Futile and irreplaceable sacrifices in men and material have been made in a desperate sortie in order to relieve Germany's hopeless situation. 3. In consequence of the military failure of the offensive both German civilians and the German armed forces are worse off than ever. 4. The offensive played into the hands of Eisenhower's strategy which is to dispose of as many Germans as possible west of the Rhine." Throughout January 1945, Speier instructed operators to frame the offensive's failure as the "inevitable" result of the Allies' overwhelming force as well as Nazi confusion, demoralization, and military weakness.[33]

By mid-February, when the fifth phase of Speier's propaganda war began, the western Allies had repulsed the Germans, and the Red Army had taken Warsaw. The war, it was clear to all observers, would soon be over. Moreover, Franklin Delano Roosevelt, Winston Churchill, and Joseph Stalin had met at the Yalta Conference and had reached several agreements regarding postwar Germany. The Big Three had announced that Germany would be divided into four occupation zones, would be demilitarized and denazified, and would pay reparations. To prepare the Germans for the war's conclusion, Speier focused OWI propaganda "on making the Germans realize that the military and political development in the final phase of the war has reached its climax: in the military field by the merging of the fighting on the various fronts into one great battle, in the political field by the decisions of the Crimea [Yalta] Conference." Most important, the Yalta declaration provided Speier with more material regarding the occupation. As he had done before the Battle of the Bulge, he started to use his directives to address the future occupation at length.[34]

On March 21, Davis and Carroll left the United States for Europe to observe propaganda operations on the ground and to plan postwar information efforts. Carroll no doubt continued to shape anti-German propaganda policy via cable instructions, but given that he does not discuss OWI propaganda at all from this period in his memoir, it is likely that in his absence he exerted less control over it than previously. It is perhaps for this reason that an angrier tone entered the OWI's anti-German propaganda directives, as Speier was now free to express his disgust at the actions taken by the country that had forced his exile.

For the first time, Speier was able to comment on war crimes in his directives. Carroll had earlier banned discussions of Nazi atrocities in OWI propaganda because he believed, as he clarified in his memoir, that "the indiscriminate reporting of atrocity stories to Germany threatened to make the Germans fight even more desperately behind their Nazi leaders by giving them the impression that the allies had a heavy score to settle with them." Davis, for his part, was concerned that describing Nazi brutality, which was so horrible as to be unbelievable, would persuade Germans that OWI propaganda was disingenuous and not to be trusted. With

Carroll and Davis in Europe, however, Speier used the OWI's propaganda directives to ensure the Germans understood that the Allies considered them morally responsible for the war crimes committed by the regime they had embraced.[35]

Speier asserted that operators must "make the Germans aware of Germany's responsibility for the war and of German war crimes." This, he argued, was a historical burden propagandists needed to accept with aplomb: "What we now say about the facts coming to light from the Nazi concentration camps will contribute to fixing the image of Nazism and of Nazi pre-war and war practices which will go down in history. In treating this subject, therefore, we are not conducting psychological warfare; we are speaking for the record." Speier wanted OWI propaganda to emphasize that although Germans were not personally liable for Nazi atrocities, "the German people" were "responsible as a political unit for acting under, and supporting, the authority of the Nazi regime." By accepting the rule of Hitler, whom Speier referred to as "the enemy of western civilization and its Christian-humanitarian foundation as well as the enemy of all religion and the ideals of political and economic freedom which arose at the time of the American and French Revolutions," the Germans had rebuffed the Enlightenment, a crime of world-historical importance. For this, they would have to pay.[36]

After Hitler committed suicide in his underground bunker in Berlin on the evening of April 30, 1945, Speier redoubled his efforts to induce feelings of guilt and responsibility in ordinary Germans. He stressed that operators must "avoid giving the impression that Hitler was the inevitable product of his time and circumstances." Instead, OWI propaganda should underline that "large masses of the German people" "in all walks of life . . . willingly followed and supported Hitler." Nazi crimes, Speier contended, did not emerge ex nihilo but rather were the result of conscious political choices for which ordinary Germans were culpable. Because Germans "gave enthusiastic support to Hitler's schemes of aggression and enslavement," he averred in no uncertain terms, they "share responsibility for these schemes and their disastrous final outcome." Speier wanted to guarantee that his former countrymen recognized that not only the Nazis, but also the entire German people, needed to answer for World War II and the Holocaust.[37]

In the early morning of Thursday, May 7, in Rheims, France, General Alfred Jodl unconditionally surrendered to Eisenhower on behalf of the German government. The war in Europe was over. "With V-E Day," Speier happily declared in the first regional directive written after the armistice, "our psychological warfare to Germany has ended." In the final analysis, how effective were Speier's efforts? Three factors make it difficult to answer this question definitively. First, the OWI was one of several organizations, including the OSS, the Psychological Warfare Division, the British Ministry of Information, and the BBC's European Service, that sent propaganda to Germany, and isolating the particular effects of one of these organizations' propaganda is impossible. Second, Speier produced directives, not propaganda. Operators interpreted directives, which regularly led to a transformation in meaning between a theoretical directive and actual propaganda. Moreover, as a former OWI official noted after the war, "you could lead an operator to a directive, but you could not make him implement it." Despite attempts to monitor operators' output, they sometimes ignored directives, either because they disagreed with them, because they did not have the necessary materials to implement a particular theme, or because they found them too long, too complicated, or too disconnected from the dynamic situation on the ground. In addition, the fact that the OWI's German policy was made in Washington but implemented in New York worked against harmonization. Finally, the OWI did not have final authority over what propaganda was actually broadcast to or distributed in the European Theater of Operations. Since Roosevelt's issuance of Executive Order 9312 on March 9, 1943, military officers could veto any propaganda materials intended for their areas of operation, which was a courtesy the OWI extended to diplomats as well. If an officer or diplomat in Europe disapproved of OWI propaganda, he could simply not circulate it. Combined, these realities make it difficult to determine the degree to which Speier's directives influenced, or did not influence, the war in Europe.[38]

In general, the scant information available regarding Western propaganda's effects on German morale remains inconclusive. For example, studies on German soldiers' morale conducted in the war's aftermath determined "that the ideology of the 'average' German soldier remained singularly steadfast" throughout the fighting and changed only as a result of "reverses in the fortunes of battle and the deterioration of the conditions of life at the front," not propaganda. However, these studies were primarily based on interviews with and questionnaires filled out by prisoners of war, which, the social scientists who conducted them admitted, "left much to be desired from the standpoint of scientific rigor." Some more recent analysis, in fact, argues that propaganda did exert an impact on German behavior. For instance, in April 1944 the Nazis imposed the death penalty on those found consuming Allied propaganda, and in June the German High Command created a special unit to combat Western propaganda's effects. Furthermore, the Germans repeatedly tried to jam Allied radio broadcasts. These actions suggest that the German leadership, at least, believed Allied propaganda could shape German morale, though its actual influence will likely never be known.[39]

The focus of OWI propaganda shifted immediately upon the cessation of hostilities. As Speier affirmed on May 11, 1945, "our future operations will be directed towards the aim of winning the peace." The ghosts of Weimar haunted this sixth and final phase of Speier's propaganda war. His major fear was that, as occurred in Germany after World War I, "the [true] record of the war" would "slip into oblivion" and be replaced with falsehoods. Since December 1944, Speier had asserted that OWI propaganda must be dedicated to preserving the history of the war while "preventing the rise of another 'stab in the back' legend and thus . . . preventing another war." OWI propaganda, he argued,

> must emphasize that Germany would have lost this war (as she lost the last one), even if she had been led by more competent men. There is a definite possibility that we will encounter the germs of two different "stab in the back" doctrines. Die-hard Nazis will try to persuade the Germans that Germany lost the war, because she was betrayed by generals (by certain parts of the home front, by her allies, etc.). By the same token, other Germans will think that Germany might have won the war if she had had different political leaders who had not amateurishly interfered with the operations of her military experts.

To counter such myths, Speier instructed operators to "tell the story of the war in such a way that every German becomes convinced that Germany would have lost the war under any circumstances, regardless of the quality and wisdom of her leadership, that any similar venture in the future would be equally futile and that it would end in a similar disaster." When World War II concluded, Speier remained concerned that Germans would learn the wrong lessons from it. "There will be strong and contradictory tendencies in Germany," he warned operators,

> 1. to sweep aside any discussion of Nazism as a thing of the past; 2. to "turn over a new leaf" and ignore the war; 3. to feel and act as if world history has just begun with Allied authorities assuming power in Germany; 4. to "forget" about politics and to concentrate on the immediate requirements of survival and adjustment; 5. to develop nostalgic feelings for the "heroic"

> past of Nazism; 6. to blame the Nazi leadership for the loss of the war and thus to exempt German militarism and all others who supported the Nazi regime from their share of responsibility; 7. to blame military leaders for the loss of the war and thus to exempt all others from their responsibility; 8. to attribute all present and future hardships of the Germans to the measures and the presence of the occupying powers; 9. to become utterly cynical about politics and life in general; 10. to regard the war in Europe as unfinished in view of the still unsolved problems in Europe.

If Allied propagandists failed to preserve the war's true memory, Speier worried, the history of Weimar would repeat itself.[40]

For this reason, Speier made the "war guilt" of ordinary Germans a major theme of OWI propaganda throughout the summer and autumn of 1945. Speier commanded the OWI's operators "to shatter the belief . . . that other governments and nations rather than the German government and the German nation were responsible for the outbreak of this war." OWI propaganda, he avowed, must "stress that this war was unnecessary and could have been avoided had it not been for the fact that the German people allowed itself to be represented by the Nazi regime and that the people tolerated and actively supported that regime and its aggressive policies." Though the Nazis admittedly ruled with terror, "the authority of the Nazi regime rested upon the active support of the 'masses of the German people,' the 'majority of the Germans.'" Speier wanted ordinary Germans to accept that without their backing Hitler would have been unable to commit the crimes that he did. This, he hoped, would convince Germans both that their authoritarian political instincts were the source of their misery and that the only viable way forward was to embrace Allied governance and, eventually, democracy.[41]

Speier's postwar focus on demilitarization, as opposed to denazification, further reflected anxieties borne from Weimar's collapse. Since the 1930s, Speier had argued that Nazism, with its emphasis on war and conquest, was attractive to Germans precisely because "in modern Germany the soldier enjoys conspicuous honor." After the war, he suggested that Germans were less racist than militarist and argued that preventing Nazism's reemergence depended upon eradicating German militarism. To do so, Speier instructed operators to highlight that "the German armed forces have been decisively defeated on the battlefield," which he insisted would reduce the military's prestige and "achieve our ultimate objective of destroying German militarism."[42]

Speier's desire to right Weimar wrongs also emerged in his discussion of the actions German democrats would have to take to guarantee the future viability of German democracy. In his propaganda directives, Speier argued that Weimar had failed for two primary reasons. First, the republic had been defined by "the inability of German democracy to prevent its enemies from abusing democratic rights and institutions for the destruction of this democracy." Speier declared that going forward, German democrats must accept that democracy survived only when they employed illiberal means to protect it from existential threats; it was thus legitimate, for instance, for Germans to ban the Nazi Party. Second, Speier claimed that Weimar democrats had been unable "to grasp the importance of agreement on fundamental issues, the role of compromise in democratic procedures, and the role and responsibilities of the minority." In the 1920s and 1930s, Speier clarified, too many democrats had considered the "willingness to accept compromises with the purpose of furthering common democratic interests . . . a betrayal of party aims and party principles. Disagreement between democratic parties was carried to a point where sight was lost of the common interest of these parties in defending German democracy against its totalitarian enemies." Speier avowed that a politics of compromise and consensus must replace the overheated partisan politics of Weimar. If it did not, he feared that internecine fighting would again destroy German democracy.[43]

After the war, Speier used his position as chief of the OB's German desk to attempt to prevent the conditions he believed had doomed the Weimar Republic from recurring. In exploiting the capacities of the U.S. government for this purpose, Speier contributed to the Europeanization of U.S. information policy. During and after World War II, Speier and the American-born leaders of the OWI developed a symbiotic relationship. On one hand, Carroll and Davis relied on Speier's skill and knowledge of Nazi propaganda and German society; on the other hand, Speier relied on Carroll and Davis's patronage, trust, and goodwill. Together, Speier, Carroll, and Davis made the OWI's German directives into transnational documents that reflected both American and European concerns.

On August 31, 1945, the recently installed President Harry S. Truman signed Executive Order 9608, which transferred the OB to the State Department's Interim International Information Service. The OB remained organizationally coherent in the move, which allowed Speier to continue his work uninterrupted through October. That month, he was dispatched to Europe in order to "counsel those who are concerned with information activities with respect to Germany." Speier had not returned to Germany since his emigration in 1933, and his first letters home reveal the distance that had grown between him, his nation of origin, and former colleagues who had refused to leave.[44]

Speier, like many visitors to Germany immediately after the war, was profoundly struck by the nation's total devastation. As he wrote his wife Lisa, "the first impression in Berlin, which overpowers you and makes your heart beat faster, is that anything human among these indescribable ruins must exist in an unknown form. There remains nothing human about it. The water is polluted, it smells of corpses, you see the most extraordinary shapes of ruins and more ruins and still more ruins: houses, streets, districts in ruins. All people in civilian clothes among these mountains of ruins appear merely to deepen the nightmare. Seeing them you almost *hope* that they are not human." The abattoir horrified Speier, provoking within him the corporeal response of a rapidly beating heart. His emotive description, written in confidence to his wife, vividly expressed his sensory encounter with war's inhumanity. Indeed, Speier was so disturbed by the wreckage that he did not want to associate it with human action or human misery, declaring that he hoped the civilians he encountered were "not human" and hence not responsible for, or victims of, the war. But as Speier would soon find out, the people he

Figure 5. Speier in Berlin at Tempelhof Airport with unidentified colleagues, autumn of 1945, *photo courtesy of Sybil Speier Barten*

encountered in postwar Germany were all too human; the war's end was hardly the "zero hour" for which many Germans wished.[45]

Though he pitied civilians for having to endure such suffering, Speier found, much to his chagrin, that even in the wake of the Nazi terror, many Germans remained "affected by the totalitarian way of thinking." For example, when Speier moderated a discussion after a screening of the exile Billy Wilder's film *Die Todesmühlen (The Death Mills)*, which documented Nazi crimes against humanity, he discovered that many of the Germans who had watched the film thought in militarist, nationalist, and hierarchical terms. Similarly, Speier met a young couple in Berlin who "retain certain reactionary attitudes: they have contempt for the common people, and they plead for an American information policy using Nazi methods of not allowing any freedom of expression." To Speier, incidents like these demonstrated that he had little in common with Germans who had lived under the Nazis.[46]

This feeling was strengthened by a meeting Speier had with Karl Jaspers, the existentialist philosopher who at the University of Heidelberg had overseen Speier's minor PhD field in philosophy. Speier met Jaspers at his home in Heidelberg as the latter was composing his book *Die Schuldfrage* (The question of guilt; later translated as *The Question of German Guilt*). Unsurprisingly given Jaspers's current project, he and Speier discussed German war guilt at length. During this conversation, Jaspers asserted that "there is collective liability (*Haftung*) [among the Germans], but there never can be collective guilt (*Schuld*) of a whole nation." In other words, Jaspers maintained that Germans may have been criminally liable for Nazi crimes, but they were not morally guilty of them. Speier was shocked by Jaspers's claim and was taken aback that his former teacher "did not speak about what the Germans—as distinguished from the Nazis—had done; that is to say, he did not dwell on what they had done or left undone to make it possible for criminals to prosper and command respect or at least enjoy impunity." Moreover, in Speier's opinion the very act of staying in Germany after 1933 represented a moral failure. "As far as Jaspers himself is concerned," Speier wrote to Lisa, "I would have liked to ask him, 'One does not expect a philosopher to join a conspiracy against tyranny, but why did you not leave Germany in 1933? Any university in any country of your choice would have extended a welcome to you, and *your* exile would have been a symbol of resistance.' Again, even men like Jaspers—who probably were among the best Germans we left behind us in 1933, or at least the most thoughtful ones—appear not to have realized what the Germans did to Europe. Instead, they concentrate on what

Figure 6. U.S. occupation troops in Heidelberg, Germany, 1945, *photo courtesy of Sybil Speier Barten*

the Nazis have done to Germany." These statements reveal the gulf that had arisen between Speier and those who had remained in his native land.[47]

Throughout his trip, Speier maintained the air of an ethnographer who observed a foreign population, "the Germans," to which he no longer belonged. He never affected the tone of someone who, after twelve years in exile, had finally returned home. Germany had become for Speier an alien land, its people—even former mentors like Jaspers—foreigners with whom he no longer shared a connection. To Speier, both ordinary and elite Germans had lost all moral sense. Not only did they retain fascist beliefs or deny their responsibility for Nazi crimes; they also appeared disinterested in the fate of those whom the Nazis had forced into exile. Speier was dismayed, for instance, that Jaspers "never asked what had happened to me in the United States. In fact, none of the Germans I met has asked this question." Speier was convinced that Germans wanted to pretend that the previous twelve years had never happened, and he refused to associate himself with such a morally obtuse population.[48]

Speier explicitly embraced his American identity during a visit with Dolf Sternberger, a friend from Heidelberg who had remained in Germany. Sternberger edited a magazine, *Die Wandlung* (The transformation), and was interested in exploring, as Speier reported, "the relation between Germans who stayed and Germans who left" in a future issue. Sternberger asked Speier, who had intimate knowledge of this subject, to propose suggestions about how best to address it. Speier could only reply "that this was [Sternberger's] magazine and that I was but an intensely interested *American observer.*" Whereas during the war, Speier was figuratively a German in an American uniform, his postwar encounters with Germans forced him to recognize how American he had become. It was this shift in identity, and Speier's subsequent and total identification with the U.S. state, that enabled him to become one of the architects of the military-intellectual complex and the national security state it supported.[49]

Chapter 5

The Making of a Defense Intellectual

Speier emerged from World War II a self-identified American. For three years, he had worked closely with native-born elites who were as dedicated as he was to defeating the Nazis. For all the mistakes they had made during the war, U.S. leaders had proven to Speier that they were able to defend Western civilization during a moment of crisis. Moreover, these same elites had entrusted him, an émigré academic, with significant responsibility for the U.S. propaganda effort against Germany. Speier was intensely grateful for the opportunities with which the United States had provided him, and by 1946 he no longer considered himself to be living in exile.

For Speier, the immediate postwar period was one of transition. The project to which he had dedicated himself since 1933, the military defeat of Nazism, was completed. All that remained was to eradicate the ideas that had allowed Nazism to triumph. Speier therefore accepted an offer to become associate chief of the State Department's Area Division for Occupied Areas (ADO). In this position, he was responsible for developing the State Department's information and education policies in occupied Germany.

Speier evinced no qualms about forcing democracy on the German people. The Germans had shown time and again that they were unable to establish democracy of their own volition, and Speier thought it entirely appropriate to use U.S. power to impose a liberal democratic regime on the ruins of the Nazi state. Yet at the same time, Speier maintained that German democracy would survive only if ordinary Germans accepted it as legitimate. Weimar had demonstrated to Speier that democracy was not only about institutions but also about citizens' states of mind. As head of the ADO, he confronted a practical problem: How was he to ensure Germans embraced democracy? Speier insisted that the best way to do so was for Germans to experience democratic life firsthand. That is to say, Speier *did not* promote the manipulation of the German people through propaganda. In 1946–1947, he abided by his earlier claim that after the Nazis' downfall, democratic life, defined by intellectual freedom and open debate, would return to normal (or, in the case of Germany, as normal as life under a foreign imposed regime could be).

Speier's unwillingness to engage in the psychological manipulation of the German people suggests that after World War II he did not seamlessly transfer his existential anxieties about Nazi Germany onto the Soviet Union. In fact, Speier's writings between 1945 and 1949 indicated that he considered the Soviet Union a normal, albeit aggressive, international actor—in other words, he did not consider the Soviets an existential threat that required U.S. elites to adopt emergency measures to overcome them. This changed, however, once Speier learned in September 1949 that the Soviets had successfully detonated an atomic bomb. The shock of the Soviet bomb and the fear that a nuclear war between the two superpowers could eradicate not only democracy but humanity itself encouraged Speier to diagnose a new crisis of international politics analogous to the one he had identified in the 1930s. The Soviets became for Speier what the Nazis had earlier been for him: an enemy of geopolitical order, Western civilization, and, ultimately, humankind. Speier's relatively late embrace of the idea that the U.S.-Soviet struggle was an existential one—a notion one might term the early Cold War's logic of crisis—implies that the Cold War was, as much as anything, a state of mind. Just as "the Cold War . . . had not one but many endings," to use Odd Arne Westad's apt phrasing, so too did it have not one but many beginnings, which differed according to each individual's subjective experiences and worldview.[1]

Speier's new diagnosis of crisis led him to advocate for a return to the state of exception that for him had defined politics after Weimar. As he had in the 1930s, Speier argued that elites should ignore public opinion whenever they deemed it necessary. He again exiled democratic practices to a postcrisis future, declaring that, as with the Nazis, when the Soviets were defeated democratic life would return to normal. Nonetheless, a critical structural difference between the pre- and postwar periods transformed the implications of Speier's argument. Whereas before the advent of nuclear weapons, it was possible for the United States to defeat an existential enemy such as the Nazis decisively, once the Soviets acquired the atomic bomb, it was unlikely the United States and Soviet Union would fight a conclusive war. Simply put—and as history would demonstrate—neither American nor Soviet leaders were willing to risk eradicating humanity by engaging in nuclear war. However, the very threat of nuclear annihilation necessitated that the United States remain forever vigilant. For these reasons, Speier's *moment* of crisis transformed into an *era* of crisis, in which the state of exception was perpetually normalized.

In Speier's opinion, the Soviet bomb made it urgent for intellectuals to retain their newly won seat at the foreign policymaking table. The negative results that would come as a result of poor Cold War foreign policymaking were even more dire than they had been before and during World War II, and Speier averred that decision makers must ignore the (ignorant, capricious, and short-sighted) public and listen to the (knowledgeable, dependable, and prescient) intellectuals. To guarantee that U.S. elites had access to experts, Speier dedicated himself to constructing new types of national security research institutions that existed outside the traditional structures of the U.S. state. The most important of these was the Air Force–funded RAND Corporation, which in 1948 Speier joined as the founding chief of its Social Science Division. In its first years, when RAND relied almost exclusively on Air Force contracts, the SSD had few connections to Congress and, owing to the extensive classification of national security information, little public accountability. For Speier, RAND represented the culmination of a decades-old project to insulate experts from public opinion and to furnish a home for intellectuals dedicated to using their knowledge in the state's service. As the most important think tank of the early Cold War, RAND, as one historian recently noted, "helped reify the secrecy that became so essential a component of national security in the decades after World War II" and provided the institutional model that allowed "defense intellectual" to become a viable career path.[2]

Speier's position at RAND made him one of the most powerful defense intellectuals in the Cold War United States. RAND stood at the center of an emerging network of think tanks, university centers, and government institutions that would coalesce into the military-intellectual complex over the course of the 1950s and early 1960s. In addition to RAND, think tanks that were established during this period included the Foreign Policy Research

Institute (1955), the Hudson Institute (1961), and the Center for Strategic and International Studies (1962). None of these organizations, however, was as influential as RAND, whose analysts had unique access to decision makers in the U.S. government and military. Through formal briefings, informal get-togethers, quarterly and staff reports, and traditional academic publications and conference presentations, Speier and his colleagues shaped U.S. foreign policy. Furthermore, RAND's access to Air Force capital enabled Speier to become an important patron who provided old friends and colleagues who shared his worldview, such as Gabriel Almond, Alexander George, Paul Kecskemeti, Harold Lasswell, Nathan Leites, and Edward Shils, with employment or research support that helped solidify networks whose seeds had been planted years earlier.

RAND's location outside the heavily Protestant structures of the U.S. state allowed it to have a diversifying effect on the foreign policy establishment. While the State Department, the traditional center of U.S. foreign policymaking, primarily employed Anglo-Saxon male elites who had attended a small number of boarding schools and Ivy League universities, RAND provided new constituencies, including exiles (Speier, Kecskemeti, Leites), Jews (Bernard Brodie, Herman Kahn, Albert Wohlstetter), and—in rarer instances—women (Elsa Bernaut, Jean Hungerford, Roberta Wohlstetter), with privileged access to decision makers.[3] These individuals often hailed from working-class and immigrant backgrounds and, without novel organizations like RAND, would have likely been unable to achieve the influence they did. In short, RAND and similar institutions contributed to a process that ultimately changed the composition of the U.S. foreign policy establishment.

At RAND, Speier became a vocal proponent of global U.S. hegemony. For Speier, and indeed, for many in the first generation of defense intellectuals, the United States had proven with its victory in World War II that it was the future of Western civilization. Though Speier sometimes couched his support for U.S. hegemony in nostrums regarding the benefits of democracy for the world's peoples, he mainly supported it because he assumed that U.S. global leadership was the only means by which to ensure that the Enlightenment ideals he cherished would survive in a hostile world. Speier thus transformed the defense and promotion of democracy, which in the interwar period he had implicitly framed as limited to the United States and Western Europe, from a North Atlantic to a global project. In this way, he, and others like him, provided intellectual succor to U.S. imperialism. Throughout the Cold War, Speier's anxieties about democracy's future led him to ignore the obvious tensions, even confusions, in his thought, specifically the irony that

Figure 7. Speier, autumn of 1950, *photo courtesy of Sybil Speier Barten*

he desired to limit the open society at home in order to guarantee its (eventual) domestic survival and (eventual) spread abroad. He never considered that restricting democracy or encouraging hegemony could have unforeseen, deleterious, and long-term consequences in both the United States and the world.

Before his trip to Germany in the autumn of 1945, Speier intended, as he wrote Sigmund Neumann, his old friend from the Hochschule für Politik, "to be out of the government service by the end of [the] year." Bureaucratic frustrations and endless work hours had eliminated his enthusiasm for life in Washington. However, a chance encounter with William Benton, the assistant secretary of state for public and cultural relations, changed Speier's mind. Speier met Benton in November in Bad Homburg, Germany, at the headquarters of the Information Control Division (ICD) of the Office of Military Government, United States (OMGUS), which was the group responsible for implementing U.S. media policy in the German occupation zone. Poor weather had delayed Benton's flight out of Bad Homburg, and General Robert McClure, the ICD's chief, asked Speier to entertain the bored official. In their hours-long conversation, Speier greatly impressed Benton with his knowledge of German affairs.[4]

Benton subsequently had a cable sent to Washington singing Speier's praises: "Speier has made a great impression here. One Army officer known to Benton said that he is the best man OWI ever sent to Germany and has the best grasp and most knowledge and understanding of any man ever sent over by US. Benton queries whether Speier shouldn't be kept here in Germany in a top key role, if he can be persuaded, as the kind of staff man absolutely essential to the top civilian authority State is now seeking to send over here." Upon receiving this cable, the State Department authorized Benton to give Speier a job. Speier, however, rejected Benton's ensuing offer of a policy planning position. The assistant secretary countered with a proposal for Speier to become the acting deputy chief of the Washington, D.C.–based Area Division for Occupied Areas. Speier accepted this offer because, as he later wrote, he believed "its close connection between matters of policy and operations" would allow him to control policy implementation more efficaciously than he was able to at the OWI. With the New School's blessing, from January 1, 1946, onward, Speier served as the effective head of the ADO, as his boss, Henry P. Leverich, was, according to Speier, an alcoholic often unable to fulfill his duties.[5]

The ADO was part of the Office of International Information and Cultural Affairs (OIC) and was charged with developing the State Department's information and education policies in all U.S. occupation zones. Unfortunately, despite Speier's high expectations for his job, he swiftly learned that when it came to Germany, "the good people in the War Department [who controlled OMGUS, which managed the German occupation] and the good people in the State Department do not cooperate as closely" as he would have liked. Namely, the ICD and the Education and Religious Affairs Branch of OMGUS, which was responsible for formal education policy in occupied

Germany, regularly ignored State's directives and developed their own policies on the ground. Furthermore, the occupation's byzantine organization prevented Speier from exerting a significant influence on how policy was implemented. According to a State Department article, the department's "instructions to the American commanders in Europe are sent through War Department channels," and such instructions were often lost or disregarded. At the same time, Benton, who theoretically could have served as the ADO's champion, was consumed, as the OWI veteran Charles A. H. Thomson reported, with "keeping [the OIC's] program alive in the face of indifference, misunderstanding, or hostility within the Department of State, elsewhere in the executive branch, and in the Congress." Finally, General Lucius Clay, who directed OMGUS, distrusted civilian advice and often ignored it. Speier quickly discovered, as he informed Bryn Hovde, the president of the New School, that "it is not pleasant to work in . . . circumstances" where he was frequently overlooked.[6]

Speier's problems with OMGUS began immediately after he assumed his position. In February 1946, Speier and Leverich traveled to Germany to investigate the possibility of broadcasting U.S. propaganda to Soviet-dominated Eastern Europe. The two determined that a radio relay station based in Munich would permit the United States to beam propaganda behind the Iron Curtain and suggested to Clay that he build such a station. Speier remembered in 1981 that Clay, who was then committed to maintaining positive relations with the Soviet Union, "objected strongly" to this recommendation because he believed it would "be a violation of the quadripartite principle of collaboration" that was then governing the occupation. Moreover, after delivering his pronouncement, Clay, as Speier recalled, "remarked bluntly that Americans of German birth [like Speier] were poorly qualified to appreciate American interests." This insult deeply bothered Speier, who vividly remembered it almost forty years later. Indeed, his disagreement with Clay was merely the first in a series of conflicts he had with War Department officials that permanently soured his taste for government work.[7]

Speier's interest in government service was further attenuated by the fact that, as he wrote his wife Lisa in March 1946, he found it "difficult to maintain that we are working toward the 'reeducation' of the Germans . . . or are making progress in a definite direction." Speier was correct to doubt reeducation's progress. In its first two years, the effort received little support from OMGUS officials, who were most concerned with economic reconstruction and feeding, clothing, and housing the Germans. This worried Speier, who feared that as in Weimar, democrats had surrendered in the battle for the

German mind, which could easily embrace communism or Nazism, before the struggle had truly begun.[8]

Speier elucidated his disappointment with the U.S. reeducation effort in his May 1946 memorandum "Immediate and Future Responsibilities of the Department of State for the Reeducation of Germany." In this piece, Speier beseeched OMGUS officials to make reeducation "an integral part of a comprehensive program for the rehabilitation of the Germans." For Speier, cultural, educational, and informational reconstruction was as critical to German democracy's future as political and economic reconstruction. In particular, Speier asserted that Germans would accept democracy only if they experienced life under it firsthand, free of the autocratic constraints that had defined the Nazi period. For this reason, he criticized OMGUS's information policy for forbidding Germans from "say[ing] anything in public which could be regarded as fostering dissent among the occupying powers." Though this policy might make governing Germany easier in the short term, Speier warned, in the medium and long terms it "may actually foster doubt among intelligent Germans that the American belief in freedom of information is wholly sincere." If Germans determined that the stated American desire to transform Germany into a functioning democracy was disingenuous, Speier worried they would turn toward communism or Nazism.[9]

Speier thus urged OMGUS officials "to increase freedom of information and expression in the American zone [of occupation]," which he hoped would establish the conditions for the emergence of a robust German public opinion. This was an ironic platform for Speier to champion, as for years he had insisted that public opinion was volatile and foolish. Speier never addressed this tension in his thought, and one can only speculate as to the reasons for his democratic optimism in the immediate postwar period. Perhaps Speier thought that some form of public opinion was a sine qua non of democracy. Moreover, Germany was totally destroyed, and the war had delegitimized the nationalist, militarist, and fascist ideology to which Germans had expressed allegiance for twelve years. It is possible Speier believed that in such a "zero hour," Americans could change minds in ways that were impossible under normal conditions. Finally, Speier might have viewed his time at the ADO as the moment to fulfill his decades-old dream of liberalizing Germany and was therefore willing to take a leap of intellectual faith.[10]

In the end, none of Speier's recommendations was implemented. The ghastly winter of 1946–1947 forced OMGUS officials to persist in downplaying cultural reconstruction in favor of material concerns. Most troubling for

Speier, Clay continued to ban Germans from establishing printing presses associated with political parties. In Speier's opinion, this restriction severely inhibited the possibility of German democratization, and in 1946 he tried to persuade Clay to license party presses. His failure to do so helped convince Speier that he could play no positive role in the occupation.[11]

One of U.S. officials' major takeaways from the pre-occupation planning effort was that the political polarization of the Weimar press had been a major cause of the republic's downfall. Thus, throughout 1945–1946 OMGUS was determined, as Charles A. H. Thomson noted, "to apply to German newspapers American traditions of a nongovernment nonparty press." Speier considered this policy absurd, especially in light of the fact that OMGUS had begun to license German political parties in the summer of 1945. In an attempt to reconcile the inconsistencies between OMGUS's information and political policies, in November 1946 Speier submitted a memorandum to Clay in which he recommended that OMGUS license party presses. Though he had had his disagreements with the military governor, Speier nonetheless expected Clay to endorse his suggestion.[12]

Speier was shocked to learn that Clay rejected his proposal, and disgusted when he discovered the general's reasons for doing so. As Speier recounted in a January 1947 memo, Clay stated that he spurned Speier's recommendation because he "had 'the hunch' that this policy was premature and that he was playing his 'hunch' against [Speier's] advice." When the War Department asked Clay to expand on his remarks, the military governor, in Speier's opinion, provided "reasons [for rejecting Speier's suggestion] which were either invalidated in the discussion of the ADO draft [i.e., Speier's original proposal] . . . or were spurious in character." These included claims that, first, a poll of Germans in the British zone indicated that there was no interest in party presses and, second, that the "policy would create difficulties in [OMGUS's] reallocating newsprint." Speier reasonably argued that U.S. policy should not "be derived from preferences of Germans in the British Zone" while reminding the readers of his memo that "OMGUS has continuously reallocated newsprint for the last fifteen months, since the total newsprint supply remained constant, while the number of licensed papers was greatly increased." Despite his protests, however, Speier's superiors, including Secretary of State James F. Byrnes and Assistant Secretary for Occupied Areas John H. Hilldring, decided, in Byrnes's words, to "'give a chance to General Clay' to establish a nonpartisan press." With no support from the State Department, Speier withdrew his original memo. Nevertheless, this experience enraged him. As he wrote

William T. Stone, the OIC's director, the entire episode was for Speier "an illuminating illustration of the difficulties the Department sometimes faces in its activities regarding Germany."[13]

The other major incident that compelled Speier to leave government service was his failure to receive OMGUS support to publish the expressionist author Fritz von Unruh's *Der nie Verlor* (translated as "The End Is Not Yet"). Speier read a draft of the book sometime in 1945, and in early 1946 he asked Douglas Waples, the chief of the ICD's publications control division, to locate a German publisher for it. Waples sent the manuscript to several publishers, all of which rejected the book, which for Waples meant that the matter was settled. Speier, though, was furious at this outcome and angrily informed Waples that:

> some of the readers [who reviewed *Der nie Verlor* for the publishers] were personally known to me, and none of them could I regard as really competent to judge Unruh's novel. . . . You will understand that I got quite impatient when I read the comment of some German nobodys [*sic*] that the book is "journalistic," has no form, his material for a novel indicates that Unruh did not live in Germany under the Nazis, charged him with inaccuracies, although only stupidity could assume that he intended to write a "realistic" novel. It is, of course, true that I, like all the other admirers of Unruh's novel, am wrong and that your German readers are right, but you won't blame me for doubting that. . . . I cannot help feeling that the impossibility of publishing this book at once in Germany where, if you permit me to say so, a lot of less important books appear, is a minor indictment of our cultural policies in Germany.

Speier refused to abandon *Der nie Verlor*, and in October he sent Waples and Hans Wallenberg, the émigré editor of the American-sponsored newspaper *Die Neue Zeitung*, a copy of a celebratory book about von Unruh. Though Wallenberg subsequently published a positive piece on the author, Waples still refused to force German publishers to release *Der nie Verlor*. Finally, after a year of trying to locate a publisher, in February 1947 Speier reluctantly relinquished the manuscript.[14]

Speier emerged from the ADO convinced he could not control policy implementation from Washington, and his frustration with government service led him to assail the entire reeducation effort in an unpublished 1947 essay titled "'Reeducation'—The U.S. Policy." In this piece, Speier argued that reeducation was failing for three primary reasons. First, OMGUS had too much authority vis-à-vis Washington, while the State Department was too weak to assert itself over the War Department. Second, OMGUS—that is to say, Clay—"disparag[ed]" reeducation. Finally, U.S. officials were too conservative to promote "comprehensive social planning not only of the political institutions, but also of the non-political institutions," such as media and religious organizations, "which bear upon the formation of political attitudes." Recent German history, Speier averred, was repeating itself; just as in Weimar, Germans had access to democratic institutions like political parties but did not embrace democratic ideals.[15]

In mid-1947, Speier's irritation with government work, which had already contributed to a case of acute appendicitis, prompted him to reject an offer to transfer to OMGUS. Instead, he prepared to return to the New School. As he wrote Arnold Brecht, his colleague on the Graduate Faculty, in August:

> Needless to say, I am glad to return to the faculty, because I have missed academic work for more than five years. . . . Last week I received an offer from the Office of Military Government in Berlin to join their staff for two years as coordinator of all information media in the American Zone,—a rather attractive offer in many respects. . . . But I turned the offer down, hoping that I was not too foolish. The point is that by this time I have grown tired of governmental frustrations, and I know the people and the conditions in Berlin too well not to expect more and different kinds of frustrations. So, for a while at least, I shall try to cope with the frustrations of an intellectual.

Yet Speier's experiences had engendered within him a taste for influence that scholarship alone could not satiate. As he remembered in a late-in-life interview, he "was very aware of the fact that I had been connected to real life only since I had left the New School." In a 1946 letter to Speier, Alexander George, his future RAND colleague, expressed well many of the problems the first generation of defense intellectuals had with government service, as well as these scholars' simultaneous attraction to power: "With the government one should learn never to accept any assurances or promises of any sort; it specializes in bad faith with its employees. It raises to a position of power the petty, warped characters, misfits, who can't do anything else so they turn to 'administration' (with few exceptions); they really take out their accumulated discontent with mankind. Ah well, Hans, you have had enough experience of your own. What I really wanted to write you about was the following: We are in need of people for intelligence jobs in the [European] theater [of Operations]." In his first two sentences George condemned the government, while in the final one he asked Speier to help recruit analysts. For intellectuals like Speier and George, the war both impelled a desire for influence and instilled a hatred of government inefficiencies. What they—and many of their colleagues—required was a new type of organization that would allow them to shape foreign policy while avoiding governmental frustrations, an institution that would provide them with direct access to military and political decision makers. What they needed, in short, was an organization like the RAND Corporation.[16]

In September 1947, Speier returned to the New School. By the time he arrived in New York, however, he had already had several disagreements with colleagues that tainted his opinion of the Graduate Faculty. Whereas before his entrance into government service, Speier and his fellow exiles were united in their struggle against Hitler, after the Nazis' defeat there was little that bound them together save for a common national origin whose importance had diminished over time. For Speier, the esprit de corps that had characterized life at the New School in the 1930s was lost during the war, never to return.

Speier's first conflict with his colleagues concerned the Institute of World Affairs, a research center the New School founded in 1943 in order to bring the Graduate Faculty's scholarship to bear on postwar international relations. In the autumn of 1943, the sociologist Albert Salomon, Speier's erstwhile associate from the Hochschule für Politik, asked Speier to serve on the institute's council. Speier informed Salomon that he "would be glad to cooperate if the faculty thinks I could be useful, but that I should like to have some information about the functions of the Council, the amount of work and the responsibilities of Council members etc., before accepting definitely." By early 1944, Speier had received no response regarding the council's duties from Salomon, from faculty dean Hans Staudinger, or from institute director Adolph Löwe, which greatly angered him. Furthermore, when Speier learned that joining the council would force Salomon to resign from it, he told Staudinger that he believed he was being "used as a pawn in ridiculous faculty politics" and, for this reason, did "not want to be a member of the Council." As Speier wrote Löwe in February, his "associations with the World Institute has [*sic*] been a series of baffling disappointments."[17]

Upon learning of Speier's unhappiness, Löwe tried to assuage his anger and again asked him to serve on the council. Speier, though, was having none of it. In his reply to Löwe, he testily declared: "I have been of the opinion that the information policy [of the institute] has been handled badly; from my own experiences in administration (which are far from equaling yours) I know how great the temptation is to follow a policy of 'persuading others by establishing facts.' This is often more efficient than democratic methods and almost always time saving. I have opposed this policy throughout my life and shall continue to do so with every means at my disposal, because I don't think it works in the long run and because I dislike it for personal reasons." In this way, Speier presented himself as being more democratic, in a sense more American, than his German colleague. While the conflict was eventually resolved—Speier never served on the council—the whole incident, as he told Kurt Riezler, "made a *very* unfavorable impression on" him.[18]

Speier was also disappointed with the methodological direction in which the New School's sociology program was headed. During World War II, Speier's encounters with American-trained social scientists at the Foreign Broadcast Intelligence Service and Office of War Information had demonstrated to him, as he informed Staudinger in early 1944, that "after this war" any major sociology program would need to offer courses "in descriptive sociology, social statistics and similar subjects." Speier worried that the New School's sociology course offerings were "*relatively* heavy on the theoretical, historical, and philosophical sides and *relatively* light on the side of empirical research of social conditions and of instruction in research techniques." Staudinger, though, told Speier that he could do nothing to rectify this situation because the New School did "not have the financial bases" to hire someone "in the field of quantitating Sociology." Speier was unmoved by Staudinger's excuse and remained dissatisfied with the New School's sociology program. For instance, in 1946–1947 he divulged to Leo Strauss, who was then a fellow member of the Graduate Faculty, that he thought Salomon's course offerings on topics such as "Epicureanism" "will make the whole faculty [look] a little ridiculous." Speier was clearly anxious that his wartime cohort would disdain the New School's intellectual agenda.[19]

More petty disagreements further harmed Speier's relationship with the Graduate Faculty. For example, Speier became upset when he read a memo in which Salomon characterized him as nothing more than a propaganda specialist. Upon reading this, Speier dispatched a letter to Salomon to let him know he "was a little sad" to discover that "one is pigeonholed when one leaves for Washington, and one's closest colleagues disregard ten years of teaching in Social Stratification, the Sociology of War, Social Theory, History of Sociology etc." Given that Salomon's memo was public, it was unlikely he intended to insult Speier. Nonetheless, Speier chose to read Salomon's remarks as an affront, which revealed his sensitivity and, ultimately, feelings of disconnection from the Graduate Faculty.[20]

All of these events made Speier resent his colleagues well before he returned to the New School. As he wrote Riezler in February 1944, Speier believed that "things have changed a great deal [in the Graduate Faculty] since I have left, and the atmosphere of freedom has been replaced by strangely autocratic ways." He ruefully reported that he "fe[lt] for the first time that it may be good for me to stay in Washington." Whereas in the 1930s, Speier and his fellow exiles had shared a common sense of mission and had been united by a common experience, such connections had diminished by World War II's end. The war, which had allowed Speier and several of his émigré colleagues to achieve prominent positions in the government, also attenuated the personal and professional bonds that had united the Graduate Faculty in the first years of exile.[21]

Beyond his disputes with the Graduate Faculty, when he returned to academia Speier recalled that he found "the activity at the New School [to be too] removed from political life" to interest him. As he remembered, "the year when I went back to the New School was a disappointment for me. I felt that I was a fish out of water. Once you work for the government, and you have first, very good contacts and very good, responsible work to do, this struck me as—almost provincial by comparison. So I didn't like it very much anymore." Speier's course offerings for the 1947–1948 academic year, which included classes such as "Public Opinion and Propaganda," "International Tensions," and "Propaganda Analysis," testified to his overwhelming concern with practical affairs. While the Graduate Faculty graciously eased Speier's reentry into university life, allowing him to serve as a State Department consultant, be free of most committee obligations, and travel to Germany when he pleased, he almost immediately began searching for an exit. Luckily for Speier, he discovered one in the RAND Corporation, whose Conference of Social Scientists he attended in mid-September 1947.[22]

General Henry "Hap" Arnold, the commander of the Army Air Forces (AAF) during World War II, developed the idea for the RAND Corporation. By the war's end, Arnold was convinced that the rise of intercontinental airpower made it necessary for the United States to have access to, as he testified before Congress, "the most advanced types of weapons" at the outbreak of a future war. For this reason, Arnold wanted to ensure that the AAF retained its connections to the civilian scientists who had joined the service during the war. Yet Arnold was certain that few civilians would voluntarily remain in uniform after demobilization, and he also feared that universities, to which most scientists would return, would be unwilling to oversee classified weapons research. He therefore decided to establish a private-sector research group that would employ civilians working exclusively on AAF contracts. To aid in this effort, Arnold turned to the Douglas Aircraft Company, one of the nation's largest aircraft manufacturers.[23]

In 1944, the AAF had collaborated with Arthur Raymond, Douglas Aircraft's chief engineer, and Frank Collbohm, Raymond's assistant, on a project regarding the B-29 bomber and had been very impressed with the results of this partnership. At Arnold's request, in the summer of 1945 Raymond and Collbohm, who shared Arnold's conviction that postwar U.S. national security depended on scientific expertise, persuaded Donald Douglas that his company should serve as the home to Arnold's envisioned research group. On October 1, Arnold granted $10 million to the new venture, which was dubbed Project RAND, an acronym for "research and development." Once Collbohm agreed to serve as the project's first director, on March 2, 1946, RAND and the Air Force signed a contract officially initiating it.[24]

Project RAND originally operated out of the Douglas Aircraft offices in Santa Monica, California. However, the project quickly grew too large for the company and, in March 1947, moved to its own headquarters in downtown Santa Monica. By this time, tensions had arisen between RAND and Douglas Aircraft. On one hand, RAND's leaders believed their relationship with the company was more a liability than a benefit: it made it difficult to cooperate with other aircraft manufacturers, whose data RAND analysts required for research, and it also made it challenging to recruit academics, many of whom refused to work for a private business. On the other hand, Donald Douglas was convinced that his company had lost a contract bid to build C-47 transports for the Air Force because the service's officers felt that it was necessary to demonstrate that they did not play favorites with any particular manufacturer. Thus, in November 1947, RAND and Douglas mutually agreed to sever ties. With the aid of H. Rowan Gaither Jr., a wealthy San Francisco lawyer who became the first head of RAND's Board of Trustees, on May 10, 1948, Collbohm incorporated the RAND Corporation as a nonprofit in California. Though the newly independent RAND had separated from Douglas Aircraft, the (also newly independent) Air Force remained the corporation's primary client.[25]

RAND initially employed engineers, physicists, and mathematicians. From mid-1946 onward, however, several important members of the organization sought to incorporate the social sciences into its research program.

John D. Williams, the mathematician who directed RAND's Evaluation of Military Worth Section, was especially critical in this regard. As presentation notes for an early RAND meeting explained, Williams's section pursued two broad questions: "(a) What constitutes military worth [i.e., the value—however defined—of a given military operation], and (b) How may it be measured." In a memorandum from June 1946, Williams insisted to Collbohm that to discover the worth of any military operation, RAND required the assistance of specialists in "military history and strategy; economics; . . . psychology; etc." Later that summer, Williams, as he reported in an internal company memorandum, began to consider organizing a large symposium of social scientists that would serve as both a forum to discuss "the concept of military worth and its ramifications" and an audition for RAND.[26]

After Williams received Collbohm and the AAF's blessing to recruit social scientists, in December 1946 he held a small conference to discuss the contributions such intellectuals could make to RAND's research program. Williams invited the mathematicians Warren Weaver and Samuel Wilks, the statistician Frederick Mosteller, and the philosopher and mathematician (and exile) Olaf Helmer to this conclave. Throughout the meeting, Weaver and Helmer stressed the importance of social science to RAND's mission. Weaver argued that analysts could understand war only if they examined issues such as the economy and enemy morale, while Helmer affirmed that the U.S. government and Air Force required "recommendations . . . concerning the conduct of our foreign policy during peacetime, in particular as far as the timing and the kind of economic, political and psychological pressure are concerned." Social science, Weaver and Helmer asserted, was critical to RAND's success.[27]

Weaver and Helmer's enthusiasm convinced Williams that RAND needed to hire social scientists. Thus, over the course of 1946–1947, Williams and Collbohm started to organize two new sections devoted to social science research: an Economics Division and a Social Science Division (the latter of which would employ specialists in every social science except economics), whose chiefs would be recruited from Williams's envisioned symposium. Williams, however, personally knew few scholars in these fields. He therefore turned to the political scientist Leo Rosten, the philosopher Abraham Kaplan, and Helmer—who all happened to be native-born Europeans—for help in composing a list of social scientists to invite to the symposium. Although no documentary evidence remains from these discussions, it is likely that Rosten, who worked with Speier at the OWI, and Helmer, who taught at the New School in 1936 and, according to the émigré philosopher Nicholas Rescher, "saw [hiring exiles to RAND] as a mode of mutual aid to fellow refugees," proposed that Speier receive an invitation.[28]

To ensure that Speier and other invitees attended his symposium, in the spring and summer of 1947 Williams traveled to the East Coast, where most were located, to confer with them. When Speier and Williams met, the former asked the latter about tenure at RAND. As Speier remembered, Williams responded to this inquiry by claiming that "anybody who is worried about tenure isn't good enough to come to RAND" because "the point is that the people we have are of such high quality that we have trouble keeping them." Speier found Williams's reply "very impressive" and indicative of the high quality of RAND's research staff. After consulting with his former State Department colleagues to confirm that RAND was "a legitimate baby," Speier decided to attend the so-called Conference of Social Scientists, which was held in New York City from September 14 to 19.[29]

A number of prominent social scientists, several of whom were friends with Speier, attended RAND's conference. In addition to Speier, attendees included the anthropologist Ruth Benedict (the only woman invited), the library scientist Bernard Berelson, the political scientist Bernard Brodie, the political scientist William T. R. Fox, the political scientist Pendleton Herring, the economist Charles Hitch, the art historian Ernst Kris, the political scientist Harold Lasswell, the psychologist Donald Marquis, the political scientist Franz Neumann, the sociologist Samuel Stouffer, and the economist Jacob Viner. Most of these scholars had worked for the wartime administration and were familiar with the frustrations one experienced in government service, which likely made many wary about associating with an organization that functioned as an Air Force research unit. To assuage these fears, Collbohm inaugurated the conference by highlighting RAND's operational independence. He insisted that "the RAND Project is for the purpose of advising the military what to do, and therefore the military cannot tell RAND what to do, but must confine itself to telling RAND what others are doing." If the assembled scholars desired to influence policy without suffering bureaucratic indignities, Collbohm argued, RAND was the only place to do so. Such a message resonated with Speier, and no doubt with other attendees as well.[30]

Warren Weaver delivered the conference plenary. In his speech, the mathematician presented RAND as the sole civilian organization to recognize the new realities of post–World War II policymaking. The war, Weaver averred, had eliminated the traditional boundary between civilian and military. For the first time in U.S. history, "the military has come to realize . . .

that they have to accept and want to accept a type of partnership with civilians . . . such as they have not been interested in accepting in the past." Most important, Weaver continued, military officers "want us [intellectuals] in the back room with them" to plan and develop strategy. Scholars finally had a seat at the decision-making table, and Weaver maintained that RAND was the only independent group able to provide the gathered social scientists with access to this table.[31]

As they prepared the conference, RAND's leaders were anxious that academics would consider working closely with the Air Force during peacetime a militaristic betrayal of intellectual values. Weaver addressed this apprehension directly and in the process provided a powerful justification for intellectual-military collaboration. Weaver avowed that affiliating with the military during peacetime was, paradoxically, profoundly antimilitaristic: "There is a real danger in becoming so concerned with the hardware weapons that one gradually loses interest in the more constructive possibility of avoiding war. It is inevitable that the military are particularly subject to this risk. This makes it all the more important that civilians also be concerned with defense. I think it is our duty as citizens to be so concerned. I think it is an intellectual and moral duty of very considerable dimensions." Weaver's argument struck a chord with Speier. For example, in an early RAND working paper Speier claimed that one of the major duties of his Social Science Division was to guarantee that "military strategy [was not] determined solely by military capabilities." Speier, like other exiles with a tragic, "realist" perspective, including Henry Kissinger and Hans Morgenthau, considered war a fact of human existence. For him, RAND was an institution that could constrain military action, ensuring that the United States fought fewer, less destructive, and more humane wars than it otherwise would. Speier—similar to many defense intellectuals—considered himself to be, if not a man of peace, at least a man of less war.[32]

After Collbohm and Weaver's introductory remarks, the conference attendees broke up into smaller groups that examined and criticized a series of potential RAND research projects that each had submitted before the symposium. Excitement and a sense of possibility characterized the proceedings. Most of the attendees were veterans of the wartime government and believed there was little they could not accomplish if given access to policymakers, time, and capital. The small groups analyzed a litany of imaginative project proposals, including a study on hypnotizing Soviet citizens to act as sleeper agents, an exploration of the relationship between Russian folklore and Soviet strategy, and an examination of whether handwriting analysis could reveal foreign leaders' intentions. In the halcyon years after World War II, social scientists considered every topic, no matter how "wild," to use Speier's phrase, worthy of inquiry.[33]

The primary reason RAND's leaders had organized the Conference of Social Scientists was to hire directors for its nascent Social Science and Economics Divisions. When the conference ended, Collbohm and Williams met with several consultants, including Leo Rosten, to determine whom they should recruit to RAND. Though Speier did not speak much during the symposium, Rosten, as he revealed in an interview that in 1969 was released as a RAND working paper, insisted that Speier was the man to lead the Social Science Division. Williams initially doubted Rosten's suggestion because he believed, as Rosten remembered, that Speier was too "quiet to be the head of a division." Rosten countered that while it was true Speier was quiet, "Hans is systematic, he's German, he's Germanic, he's well-trained, and he comes out of a tradition that's very valid, and he's particularly interested in military psychology, and has done work on it." No archival materials record why Collbohm and Williams eventually heeded Rosten's proposition and asked Speier to direct the Social Science Division. However, Rosten's last comment, which underlined Speier's psychological expertise, indicated a probable reason: the government and military's intense postwar interest in psychological warfare.[34]

In the late 1940s, U.S. policymakers desired to avoid a third world war but also aspired to destabilize the Soviet Union and its satellites. To reconcile these potentially conflicting interests, decision makers placed their hopes in psychological warfare, which many considered an effective means to attack the Soviet bloc that was nonetheless unlikely to provoke a military response. In 1947–1948, the National Security Council authorized several resolutions that endorsed psychological warfare, including NSC-4, NSC-4A, NSC-10/2, and NSC-20/4. For its part, the Air Force recognized that psychological warfare was of increasing importance to policymakers and, as Speier noted in a 1950 working paper, "requested RAND to devote adequate attention" to the subject. The widespread concern with psychological warfare probably convinced Collbohm and Williams that RAND required experts in the field. Speier, one of the nation's most experienced psychological warfare professionals, was thus a natural choice to direct the Social Science Division.[35]

Speier remembered that he left the Conference of Social Scientists with "the feeling these are persons with imagination, these are persons who are dedicated to their work, and they are doing important work." Nevertheless, he also recalled that he "was very much bothered by the fact that [RAND] was working for Douglas Aircraft." After his recent government experiences, Speier had no desire "to explain to somebody who doesn't know anything about intellectual work . . . [for example] a businessman or administrator or so, why I am doing what I am doing." He was further unwilling to relocate his family from Washington, D.C., to Santa Monica. When, upon receiving RAND's offer, Speier informed Collbohm of his concerns, he discovered that the organization was in the process of separating from Douglas Aircraft and moreover would allow him to headquarter half of the Social Science Division in Washington. In light of this new information, he happily joined RAND.[36]

In retrospect, Speier's decision to join RAND appears to be an obvious one: given his interests, why would he spurn a think tank with strong connections to decision makers? At the time, however, there was no guarantee RAND would survive, and Speier's move to the organization was a substantial risk. As Collbohm later stated, those who first joined the think tank "came to RAND when it had no assets and a substantial debt. The vast majority left positions of tenure and security in academic institutions and industry. They had to gamble upon a reasonable continuity at RAND in the face of a major contract [with the Air Force] which can be cancelled without cause at any time." Speier must have been very attracted to RAND to take such a gamble. Indeed, in many ways RAND was the exact type of organization for which he had long advocated. First, the fact that RAND research could be classified provided a legitimate means to make policy free of the public's input. Second, RAND allowed Speier to bring his knowledge to decision makers' attentions without bureaucratic interference. Third, the organization was characterized by youth, excitement, and imagination. Finally, RAND was nonpartisan and dedicated to working with whatever administration was in power, which fulfilled one of Speier's long-standing goals.[37]

In June 1948, Speier officially became the Social Science Division's founding chief. Collbohm, Speier remembered, granted him "complete freedom with respect to the personnel [whom he hired] . . . and with respect to the work to be pursued by the division. Nothing, not a line of the suggestions that I made was changed by RAND, by the top management." When hiring for his division, Speier "favored people whom [he] knew well" and used his position to dole out patronage to friends and colleagues, in effect creating a network of intellectuals that would form an important part of the nascent military-intellectual complex. Scholars whom Speier personally brought to RAND included W. Phillips Davison, Alexander George, Herbert Goldhamer, Joseph Goldsen, Jean Hungerford, Victor Hunt, Paul Kecskemeti, Nathan Leites, Walter Rudlin, and Eric Willenz. Some of the consultants he funded included Bernard Berelson, William T. R. Fox, Arkady Gurland, John Herz, Irving Janis, Henry Kellerman, Harold Lasswell, Paul Lazarsfeld, Margaret Mead, Philip Mosely, Franz Neumann, Ithiel de Sola Pool, and Edward Shils. Many of these intellectuals had positive experiences with RAND, which provided the emergent military-intellectual complex with much-needed legitimacy. As Shils told Speier shortly after first visiting the organization in the summer of 1948, RAND "made an extremely favorable impression on [him]," and he went so far as to compare its atmosphere to the one he had found at Oxford University's All Souls College. Experiences like Shils's helped spread positive information about RAND throughout academia, which aided in creating a constituency of intellectuals who believed they could, as Shils put it, pursue "political and sociological studies [that] have some relevance to policy while maintaining the best possible intellectual level."[38]

Speier's hiring practices highlighted the fluidity of disciplinary boundaries within RAND. In the SSD, disciplinary training mattered far less than one's ability to have what Speier's erstwhile mentor Karl Mannheim termed a "total perspective." Speier was interested in hiring someone to his division only if, as he wrote in 1948 when describing the type of person best suited to understand international relations, he or she was "a specialist with a non-specialist's state of mind," able "to bring knowledge from fields other than his own to bear upon the understanding of the international matter he studies." Though Speier wanted those whom he recruited to be trained in a particular discipline, he affirmed in a 1950 working paper that it was most important for RAND analysts to "share a common interest in the study of man, his behavior, his motivations and aspirations, the way he plans and organizes his life and the ways he acts with or against others." For Speier, an intellectual was an intellectual first and a sociologist, psychologist, or anthropologist second.[39]

The SSD was well funded and received approximately 8 percent of RAND's total budget. This enabled Speier to freely explore his curiosities, especially psychological warfare and elite studies. Following Speier's personal preference, the division's research was decidedly qualitative. For example, Speier's SSD developed a sociological theory of psychological warfare, analyzed elite behavior in the Soviet Union, and funded a study of Soviet culture directed by Margaret Mead at the American Museum of Natural

History. Nonetheless, Speier did not totally ignore quantitative social science and also supported "a general survey of measurement techniques in the social sciences" conducted by Samuel Stouffer at Harvard's Laboratory of Social Relations. A number of the SSD's studies attracted interest among government and military officials. In addition to the Air Force, in RAND's first years Speier and his colleagues consulted for or worked with the Army, Defense Department, State Department, Psychological Strategy Board, Research and Development Board, and Central Intelligence Agency.[40]

Speier was fiercely devoted to RAND's mission of bringing scientific knowledge to bear on U.S. foreign policymaking. His loyalty to RAND emerged clearly in a letter he sent to Edward Shils in December 1953 explaining the reasons why he turned down the offer of a deanship in the University of Chicago's Social Science Division. Though Speier recognized that holding an administrative position at Chicago would have made him one of the most powerful social scientists in the United States, he nevertheless believed he had a duty to use his knowledge in the service of the American state. As he informed Shils:

> The opportunities to do some scientific work of political usefulness are greater at RAND than at any other place I know of. The country is in great peril, and while no single individual in our field of interest can do much to avert the dangers we face, the chance of doing *something* is good at RAND as long as our group [George, Goldhamer, Leites, etc.] remains intact. It may become more difficult in the future to work against the obstacles erected by the zealots of our time and against the anti-intellectualism that is spreading [i.e., McCarthyism]. More and more people withdraw for these reasons, but things are bound to get worse, if the bridgeheads of serious effort are abandoned. . . . I do not belittle the importance of Chicago as an educational institution, and I feel honored having been asked to join the faculty. I am of the opinion, however, that it will be easier to find somebody else for Chicago than it would be to replace me at RAND.

For Speier, it was the intellectual's duty, even in the face of adversity and, sometimes, outright contempt, to defend the United States in an era of crisis. He was convinced no other task could ever be as important.[41]

It was at RAND that Speier and his colleagues "learned secrecy," to borrow Janet Farrell Brodie's evocative phrase. The rise of the military-intellectual complex was accompanied by the emergence of a culture of secrecy that permeated the institutions of the national security state.

Defense intellectuals working at RAND became active participants in this culture, producing secret reports based on classified information and attending secret conferences where discussions were off the record. In many instances, not only the public but also members of Congress were unaware of the goings-on of the budding defense elite to which RAND analysts belonged.[42]

RAND took secrecy very seriously and established daedal procedures to ensure that neither the public nor America's enemies gained access to the classified information contained within its corridors. In its very first year as an independent corporation, an unidentified government official who had visited RAND underlined the organization's focus on security, and the tense atmosphere this focus engendered, in a letter to Speier's fellow exiles Otto Kirchheimer and Herbert Marcuse, who were then working for the State Department: "The building itself [RAND's building] looks like a former medical building: clean, white, aseptic, and streamlined. . . . Policemen guard entrance and exit. . . . The visitor . . . receives a badge to be fastened to one's lapel or belt which is an exact replica of the old OSS badge. . . . The total impression of facilities is that of a clean, quiet, smooth, and highly sterilized outfit. One hesitates to drop one's [cigarette] ashes on the floor." As time went on, RAND's security procedures became increasingly elaborate. Based on interviews with former RAND employees, Janet Farrell Brodie recently described the process by which a RAND analyst gained access to and returned classified documents in the mid-1950s: "Employees who were allowed access to top-secret materials checked them out from the top-secret control office after providing a signature in multiple places including the pink form affixed to the front of the document—a form containing the names of everyone permitted access. All top-secret documents had to be hand carried back to the top-secret control office by the person who had signed them out and then one of the top-secret control officers hand carried it to the next person on the approved list." Bureaucratic rituals such as these had several functions. On the most basic level, they highlighted to RAND analysts that the materials to which they had access must never be leaked. More important, they helped cohere defense intellectuals into a distinct community with its own norms and rules. The elaborate practices RAND developed to protect classified information emphasized to the organization's analysts that it was illegal to discuss significant portions of their work with family, friends, or academic colleagues. If Speier wanted to chat about his research, he could do so only with fellow defense intellectuals who had the proper security clearances, which created a barrier between him and all those who were not similarly vetted. The émigré sociologist Paul Lazarsfeld, who spent time at RAND in 1950, described this barrier well:

> During the summer, a lot of visiting consultants, of whom I am one, are invited [to RAND]. These consultants are in another building [separate from the main RAND building] called quite generally the Isolation Ward. . . . [The people who work there] are waiting for clearance to the main building—which sometimes takes many months. (Consultants are not cleared because they would be gone before the FBI had finished the inquiry.) The really interesting point, however, is the effect of this situation on social relations between the two buildings. You have to realize that in the main building there are such old standbys like Phil Selznick and Herb Goldhamer. But when we get together there is the strangest kind of overlapping between academic and security hierarchy. They would like to get advice but they don't quite know what they are entitled to talk about. I am curious about their work, but don't want to embarrass them with questions. So there is always a slight strain in the air.

These types of distinctions forced defense intellectuals to establish networks of trust that closely connected them. As Speier's lifelong correspondence with Alexander George, Herbert Goldhamer, and Joseph Goldsen demonstrated, many defense intellectuals developed lasting friendships. To some degree, defense intellectuals' relationships with one another were as intimate as an individual's relationship with a life partner. While Speier almost certainly did not discuss work secrets with his wife, there were, as Collbohm remembered in the 1980s, "no secrets within RAND."[43]

Access to secrets also formed an important component of defense intellectuals' self-perception. RAND witnessed the emergence of a prestige economy premised on security clearances, in which one's level of clearance was considered a proxy for one's status within the organization. For example, decades after Speier retired from RAND, he reported proudly to an interviewer that unlike many of his colleagues, he had "clearance for research on nuclear developments," which, he noted, "was especially difficult to receive" and which indicated that he occupied "a relatively leading position at RAND." For an exile like Speier, obtaining nuclear clearance must have felt like a confirmation that he both belonged to the U.S. political community and was accepted as a trustworthy member of its defense elite. This imprimatur no doubt increased his identification with the U.S. state and its ancillary institutions.[44]

One might have expected RAND's obsession with secrecy to have troubled Speier. For him and many other exiles, intellectual freedom—the freedom to engage in the open exchange of ideas—was a defining characteristic of democracies that distinguished them from autocracies. As Speier's mentor Emil Lederer declared in no uncertain terms in 1935, "intellectual freedom is the basis of personal freedom." Why, then, did Speier feel comfortable joining and building RAND, an organization that—at least before it diversified its research program in the 1960s—used secrecy to prevent the free exchange of ideas? To answer this question, we must turn to Speier's postwar diagnosis of an international crisis that he believed was analogous to the one he had identified in the 1930s.[45]

Though Speier had abhorred communism since the 1920s, he did not consider the Cold War an *existential* struggle until the Soviet Union acquired nuclear weaponry in 1949. Rather, after World War II Speier initially viewed the Soviet Union as an aggressive but normal competitor in the eternal struggle for international power. He did not think, in short, that it was an enemy as dangerous as Nazi Germany. However, once Speier learned in September 1949 that the Soviets had detonated an atomic bomb—and therefore could theoretically eradicate humanity—he re-embraced the logic of crisis that he had used to understand international relations in the 1930s and began to assert that the Soviets were an existential threat akin to the Nazis.

Speier's postwar diagnosis of crisis compelled him to reexamine the problem of policymaking in a democracy, which he had ignored since World War II's outbreak. As in the 1930s, Speier avowed that public opinion could not serve as a guide for decision makers. Unlike in the 1930s, however, Speier insisted that the novel realities of postwar international relations made it necessary for elites to ignore public opinion not only for a limited time but for the foreseeable future. The struggle against the Soviet Union differed from the struggle against Nazi Germany, Speier implied, because it was a conflict in which the United States was unlikely to defeat its enemy decisively; neither the Americans nor Soviets would risk a third, nuclear, war. Thus, the Cold War necessitated perpetual mobilization and vigilance, in which responsible elites, headquartered at organizations like RAND, ignored democratic norms in order to guarantee that the United States survived a long-term battle with an unscrupulous enemy. With this argument, Speier transformed his earlier, time-limited *moment* of crisis into an indefinite *era* of crisis, in which previously extraordinary measures became permanently normalized.

Speier premised his understanding of international relations on the assumption, as he affirmed in his 1945 essay "War Aims in Political Warfare," that it was natural for states to attempt "to gain a relative advantage within the balance [of power]." Even if a state went to war with the United States to do so, Speier asserted, as long as it did not seek to establish a new geopolitical order, its "status . . . as an enemy is a temporary one." In the immediate postwar period, Speier insisted that the Soviet Union was an ambitious but nevertheless ordinary state, which, as any state would, was trying to increase its relative power position. Though he admitted in his 1948 article "The Future of German Nationalism" that the United States and Soviet Union had "conflicting military, economic, and ideological interests," Speier nonetheless maintained that both nations were members of the same international society, which is to say that they operated according to the same rules and norms. Speier even empathized with the Soviet search for security. In "The Future of German Nationalism," for example, he noted that it was understandable for "the Soviet Union [to] look on a Germany integrated into western Europe with as little favor as the Western powers would look on a disarmed Germany in the Russian orbit." Because he considered the Soviet Union a normal international actor, between 1945 and 1949 Speier advised U.S. officials to "make every effort that can be made without sacrifice of principle to reduce the rivalry between the East and West in Germany," which was the Cold War's primary battlefield.[46]

Several events that occurred between 1947 and 1949, however, encouraged Speier to slowly embrace a more negative image of the Soviet Union. During these three years, Joseph Stalin ended the democratic interludes in Hungary and Czechoslovakia, where, with Soviet aid, local communist parties seized control of the state. Meanwhile, throughout Eastern Europe, Stalinization, which was characterized by forced agricultural collectivization and the stifling of political dissent, became official Soviet policy. Most important for the German-focused Speier, on June 24, 1948, the Soviets imposed a blockade on West Berlin to protest the creation of the Anglo-American Bizone, the implementation of the Marshall Plan, the founding of the Bank deutscher Länder, and the institution of the deutsche mark. Stalin blocked all land and water routes to West Berlin and cut off its electricity. In response, the Western Allies, under American leadership, initiated the Berlin Airlift, which brought millions of tons of supplies to the city's residents between June 1948 and May 1949. To Speier, Stalin's actions, particularly the blockade, revealed that the dictator was unwilling to negotiate with the United States in good faith. Speier's judgment that the Soviet Union was a normal geopolitical actor began to attenuate.[47]

In the midst of the airlift, Speier asserted in a memorandum titled "Soviet View of Diplomacy" that "the very structure of Marxist thought with its division of the human world into exploiters and exploited, engaged throughout history in conflict and struggle," ensured that "the Soviet approach to world politics is 'military' in fact and language." "Regardless of whether peace or war prevails at a given time," Speier claimed, "the division of the world into Soviet states and non-Soviet states implies that the policy makers of the non-Soviet states are *enemies*. They can never be 'partners'. Negotiating with them means negotiating with an enemy. Being allies with them means being temporarily allied with an enemy. All these peaceful international relations are not *essentially* different from war-like relations; they differ from war merely in 'the form of action', as Lenin puts it." By arguing that Marxism-Leninism necessarily poisoned the Soviet view of the West, Speier started to define the Soviet Union as a permanent enemy of the United States. Whereas earlier he had sympathized with the Soviet search for security, Stalinization and the Berlin Blockade suggested to Speier that Soviet leaders might not consider the contemporary international order legitimate. If the Soviet Union was truly a power intent on revolutionizing international relations by defining peacetime as wartime, Speier indicated, it was a state that all Americans must fear. Nevertheless, as late as April 1949 Speier remained reluctant to remove the Soviet Union from international society completely. For example, he informed RAND analysts that for the time being their studies must "attempt to consider both ourselves and the Russians 'normal.'"[48]

The Soviet procurement of nuclear weapons, which most Americans learned about in September 1949, finally led Speier to proclaim that the Soviet Union was an existential enemy of democracy analogous to Nazi Germany. In a series of essays, speeches, and notes written in 1949 and the early 1950s, Speier deployed the language of crisis he had used in the interwar period. For instance, Speier maintained that "the loss of the American A-bomb monopoly" "signifies not only a crisis in American foreign relations but, given Soviet-American world rivalry, an unprecedented crisis in world history. . . . The loss of this monopoly means that peace and Western civilization are in jeopardy." Speier further asserted that as a general rule, "the foreign policies of the Western coalition . . . cannot be derived from wishes, patriotic or humane, from satisfaction with purges among the Soviet elite, from admiration for workers rioting against Communist regimes; nor can [they] be adjusted with impunity to the tactics of domestic party struggles. In the interest of survival, [they] must be based on the best estimates of

Soviet capabilities and on an unemotional prognosis of Soviet political and military intentions." Because in Speier's opinion there was no indication of "a dilution of doctrinaire [i.e., Marxist-Leninist] fanaticism in the Soviet Union," he insisted that U.S. decision makers should indefinitely assume that the Soviets were dedicated to the capitalist West's destruction and should thus be ready to fight a war at a moment's notice.[49]

Speier avowed that the seriousness of the postwar crisis necessitated a reevaluation of conventional democratic thinking about war and politics. As he had in the earlier struggle against fascism, Speier urged U.S. policymakers to accept that the Cold War required them to employ "means of policy and warfare that are not traditional," such as domestic propaganda campaigns designed "to guard against weaknesses [of] morale on the home front." Though he admitted that such "subversive measures in times of peace are profoundly repugnant to the American people and conflict with its moral and religious heritage shared by its leaders," Speier nevertheless affirmed "that a point has been reached in world history where some American leaders should consider themselves to be called upon to sacrifice secretly their own cherished values in order to enable their countrymen to live with these values in the future." The perspective that it was legitimate for elites to manipulate ordinary people as long as they deemed it necessary was shared by several of Speier's fellow defense intellectuals, including Gabriel Almond, George Kennan, Harold Lasswell, Daniel Lerner, Walt Rostow, and Edward Shils. To each of these individuals, "modern man," as Speier stressed in 1946, was defined by "the lowering of intellectual and moral standards" and during a period of crisis could not be trusted to make wise political decisions absent elite coercion.[50]

Speier elucidated his antipublic argument in his 1950 essay "Historical Development of Public Opinion," which appeared in the *American Journal of Sociology*. In this piece, Speier claimed that recent history, from the League of Nations' collapse to the advent of the Cold War, had demonstrated that "the liberal faith in the moralization of foreign . . . affairs by means of [popular] enlightenment" was misplaced. Simply put, "the hope that public opinion will be able to solve the problems of international policy" would never be fulfilled. Speier thus beseeched decision makers to admit that "the belief in the perfectibility of man"—that is to say, the belief that reason could enlighten ordinary people—was a chimera that must be abandoned if Western democracy was to overcome the Soviet threat. Instead of placing their faith in the public, foreign policy elites must accept the tragic truth that "those who carry political responsibility are obliged to peer into the uncertain future and to care as best they can for the others who have no such responsibilities," even if doing so betrayed the values for which they stood.[51]

For Speier, domestic propaganda campaigns, which became increasingly prominent over the course of the 1950s, were an important means to encourage the public to endorse elites' foreign policy views. However, in the era of the Cold War, Speier was disinclined to take any risks with the future of Western civilization, and he was not convinced that propaganda was always effective. How, then, could he *guarantee* that elites—especially intellectuals—were the primary drivers of U.S. foreign policy? To do so, Speier dedicated himself to building national security research institutions that had little democratic accountability. RAND, of course, was one such institution. RAND analysts were neither elected nor appointed, but were hired and given access to decision makers on the basis of their scientific expertise. Their research, if they so decided, could be classified and made inaccessible to the majority of the public and even members of Congress. Though elected officials could theoretically sanction RAND analysts, in practice this rarely occurred. To a significant degree, RAND and other organizations of the military-intellectual complex—including MIT's Center for International Studies, with which Speier was also involved—comprised a shadow state free from traditional forms of democratic accountability. What happened in RAND stayed in RAND, and there was little an ordinary citizen could do to change that fact.[52]

But Speier's turn to institution building reflected more than a simple change in tactical preferences; it also indicated a shift in the way he conceptualized international relations. Whereas in the 1930s Speier believed he had identified a temporary crisis, in 1949 and beyond he considered the crisis of geopolitics permanent, or at least long term. The fact that both the United States and Soviet Union could wield nuclear weapons that had the capacity to eradicate humanity suggested to Speier that atomic bombs would rarely, if ever, be deployed and would instead mainly be used as blackmail. At the same time, Speier was convinced, as he asserted in a 1949 working paper he co-wrote with Nathan Leites, that the Politburo endorsed "the axiom that the outer world is always going to the limits of its capacity and interests in its always present . . . intent to annihilate the Soviet regime." In other words, the threat of a nuclear holocaust made it unlikely that the United States and Soviet Union would engage in a decisive war, while the Politburo's paranoia made it unlikely that Cold War tensions would decrease. For these reasons, Speier concluded that crisis was the status quo condition of postwar international relations. To manage this historically unique situation, he helped build institutions like RAND, which he hoped would become enduring features of the U.S. foreign policymaking landscape. RAND and its brethren, in essence, provided a lasting and reliable solution to the problem of public opinion, which for Speier was the central issue of democratic politics during an era of international crisis.[53]

By the early 1950s, Speier had firmly committed himself to what one might term the early Cold War's logic of crisis. In this framework, the Soviet Union was an existential threat devoted to the United States' defeat that was nevertheless unlikely to begin an atomic war. However, the very threat of nuclear war made it necessary for decision makers to recognize three important realities: first, that the United States must be put on an indefinite war footing; second, that abrogating traditional democratic norms was legitimate in the struggle against Soviet communism; and third, that elites, not the public, must make foreign policy. The majority of defense intellectuals endorsed this, or a similar, logic.

With these arguments, Speier completed his journey from German social democrat to American cold warrior. He was completely comfortable working for RAND, an organization that had significant influence but little public accountability. For Speier, democratic foreign policy was not by the people, of the people, and for the people, but was for the people, by the intellectual, who had finally assumed his or her proper place within the (shadow) American state. Over the course of the 1950s, Speier would blossom into a quintessential defense intellectual, a new social type that would shape U.S. foreign policy throughout the Cold War.

Chapter 6

The Adviser

The Soviet detonation of an atomic bomb in 1949 was just one of several events that persuaded defense intellectuals and decision makers alike that communism was an existential threat to democracy. In addition to the detonation, Stalinization in Eastern Europe and the Berlin Blockade of 1948–1949 suggested that the Soviet Union intended to adopt a hostile posture vis-à-vis the United States and its allies. Furthermore, in the autumn of 1949 Mao Zedong's communists seized power in China. To many foreign policy elites, it seemed that the United States was losing the war against communism before it had even truly begun.

To stem the tide of communist expansionism, in the early 1950s decision makers in the Truman and Eisenhower administrations embraced a policy of "rollback" designed to push the Soviets out of Eastern Europe. With memories of appeasement fresh in their minds, policymakers were convinced that the only way to defeat an existential enemy bent on democracy's destruction was to go on the offensive. Officials, though, were determined to roll back the Soviets not with physical violence but with psychological warfare, a means that attracted them for several reasons. First, decision makers insisted that psychological warfare was unlikely to provoke a third world war. Second, policymakers believed that the Cold War was, to a large degree, an ideological struggle between liberal democratic capitalism and totalitarian communism that could be prosecuted with psychological operations. Third, they considered "paranoid" communist leaders mentally weak and perfect targets for psychological warfare. Finally, psychological warfare had proven effective at preventing communist parties from winning elections in postwar France and Italy, and many officials concluded that it might very well be used for more aggressive purposes.[1]

Despite policymakers' interest in psychological warfare, however, officials were worried that they lacked the scientific and area knowledge needed to plan successful psychological campaigns. Therefore, when developing the United States' psychological strategy, decision makers often turned to outside consultants for advice. Social scientists formed an integral part of the expert cohort of psychological warfare consultants. During World War II, social scientists had occupied leading positions in the Office of War Information, Office of Strategic Services, and other government bodies responsible for psychological warfare; even after the war, many continued to devote themselves to the subject. It was thus natural for policymakers to ask social scientists for guidance on how the United States should psychologically destabilize the Soviet Union and its satellites. Speier, who in the early 1950s was a nationally renowned psychological warfare expert, emerged as one of the most influential consultants on the subject.

Speier's experiences in Weimar had convinced him that when facing a totalitarian threat, democrats needed to take the offensive, and he ardently supported rollback. Between 1950 and 1953, Speier helped convince decision makers that the time was ripe for the United States to psychologically attack the Soviet Union and its hold on the Eastern Bloc, particularly the German Democratic Republic (GDR, East Germany). By providing policymakers with advice they deemed useful—and which echoed their own opinions—Speier solidified intellectuals' recently won seat at the foreign policymaking table. Moreover, by arguing that decision makers could legitimately violate the sovereignty of foreign nations, he contributed to the construction of an "ideology of intervention" defined by the belief that the United States had the right and duty to intervene abroad when, where, and how it saw fit. Speier's advocacy for intervention reflected broader trends evident in U.S. foreign policy throughout the early 1950s. Besides the rollback strategy, during this period policymakers evinced a commitment to intervention in the Korean War and the overthrow of democratically elected governments in Iran and Guatemala.

Speier's career reveals that nongovernmental advisers could shape U.S. foreign policy in the early Cold War.[2] Although not a statesman, nor the author of pivotal documents like George Kennan's Long Telegram, Speier was nevertheless able to appeal to two different types of expertise to exert influence. On one hand, and similar to many defense intellectuals, he asserted his authority by referencing his academic training. On the other hand, Speier's unique identity as a German exile who had witnessed Nazism's rise allowed him to point to his personal confrontation with totalitarianism to affirm his distinctive capacity to contribute to anti-Soviet and anti–East German psychological strategy. As a European exile, Speier possessed an authority that native-born Americans could not replicate.

Dozens of other émigrés besides Speier navigated the military-intellectual complex in the early Cold War. In addition to individuals who later reached the heights of power, such as Zbigniew Brzezinski and Henry Kissinger, the group of intellectual exiles who influenced U.S. foreign policy in the 1950s and 1960s included Ernst Fraenkel, Otto Kirchheimer, Karl Loewenstein, Leo Löwenthal, and Hans Morgenthau. While the extant archival record rarely reveals why the largely Anglo-Saxon and Protestant foreign policy establishment welcomed a cohort of mostly Jewish Europeans into its fold, it is probable that, as in Speier's case, an important reason it did so was because the émigrés had observed totalitarianism firsthand. Furthermore, the exiles had access to useful area knowledge and exhibited a continental, "realist" sensibility that U.S. elites respected. These factors enabled the émigrés to join the cohort of U.S.-born Jews and Catholics who after World War II diversified traditionally Anglo-Saxon and Protestant bastions, including academia, Wall Street, and the government.[3]

Though for a time Speier informed the course of U.S. psychological warfare directed against the Soviet Union and GDR, it is important not to overstate his influence. Like the majority of defense intellectuals, Speier was an adviser who did not manipulate the levers of policy directly. Advising was a unique, and uniquely limited, way to shape foreign policy. Speier did not make decisions, nor did he have permanent access to policymakers. He exerted his influence in an ad hoc manner that ultimately relied on decision makers' largesse. Government officials could heed Speier's advice when they agreed with him and ignore it when they did not. Likewise, Speier's ability to affect foreign policy was dependent on officials' interest in using psychological warfare to engender rollback. When this interest waned after the failure of the East German uprising of June 1953, so did Speier's influence.

Speier spent the first years of the Cold War attempting to reform the U.S. psychological warfare effort. In particular, he hoped to convince policymakers and propagandists that the "strategy of truth," which was the reigning psychological warfare strategy in the 1940s and early 1950s, was based on faulty principles. According to the strategy of truth's advocates, once foreign peoples learned the "truth" about the United States—which usually referred to a highly idealized vision of the benefits ordinary people supposedly enjoyed under liberal democratic capitalism—they would naturally support U.S. interests. Speier rejected this claim, asserting that the strategy of truth had two major problems. First, he argued that it ignored the real interests that divided nations, which could not simply be overcome with propaganda. Second, and more important, he affirmed that it incorrectly assumed that ordinary people had the capacity for reasoned analysis. In the early Cold War, Speier devoted himself to persuading decision makers to adopt a new psychological strategy whose primary targets were elites, not masses, and whose primary tactic was deception, not reason.[4]

Speier had set himself a difficult task. Throughout the postwar period, the strategy of truth permeated U.S. information policy and psychological warfare strategy. Policymakers first institutionalized the strategy in the Fulbright Act of 1946, which funded international educational exchanges, and the U.S. Information and Educational Exchange Act of 1948, which provided support for overseas information programs. In March 1950, William Benton, Speier's former boss at the State Department and since 1949 a Democratic senator from Connecticut, testified before Congress that the United States would win "the struggle for the minds and loyalties of mankind" only if it commenced a "world-wide Marshall plan in the field of ideas" that countered Soviet propaganda's lies with American truth. One month later, President Harry Truman announced a worldwide "Campaign of Truth," which he premised on the notion that spreading the "plain, simple, unvarnished truth" about the United States was the key to victory in the Cold War.[5]

Speier considered U.S. elites' endorsement of the strategy of truth a reflection of liberal idealism's continued deleterious hold on the American mind. As he stated in his 1948 essay "The Future of Psychological Warfare," which was published in *Public Opinion Quarterly*, the leading theoretical journal of psychological strategy, the strategy of truth presumed "that [the] dissemination of knowledge and news enables man to reason rightly and that anyone who reasons rightly will necessarily act rightly." But, Speier declared in his 1950 article "Historical Development of Public Opinion," "the overwhelming experiences of the twentieth century" had revealed that ordinary people were fundamentally irrational. For this reason, Speier averred, any propaganda strategy that relied on a public's capacity for enlightenment was doomed to fail.[6]

To counter the strategy of truth's dominance, in the early 1950s Speier developed an elite-focused psychological warfare strategy whose major tactic was deception. Though dozens of intellectuals created their own peculiar psychological warfare strategies during this period, unlike most scholars Speier was in a position to actually affect policy. By this point, he was one of the United States' foremost experts on psychological warfare and retained connections to the government that dated back to World War II. Moreover, his position as head of RAND's Social Science Division provided an imprimatur that enhanced his already impressive résumé. Consequently, decision makers, particularly those in the State Department and High Commission for Occupied Germany (HICOG) (which regulated governance in the newly established Federal Republic of Germany), frequently asked Speier for advice.

Speier's elite strategy of psychological warfare had origins dating back to the 1930s and 1940s, when a number of European émigrés engaged in a debate surrounding the nature of totalitarian society. While Speier did not participate directly in this discussion, he was influenced by two scholars, the sociologist Franz Borkenau and the economist Friedrich Pollock, who did. In various books and essays, Borkenau and Pollock maintained that a relatively small cohort of political elites were the primary power holders in totalitarian regimes like Nazi Germany and the Soviet Union. Speier was intrigued with this claim and in the late 1940s asked members of his Social Science Division to investigate it; when they did, they determined that it was correct. Speier thus had two reasons to focus his psychological warfare strategy on elites: first, because ordinary people were incapable of enlightenment, and second, because in the Soviet Union only elites made political decisions. Speier and the rest of the SSD's staff subsequently dedicated themselves to discovering, as a 1948 report from the division's Conference on Elite Studies stated, the "weak spots, cleavages, and susceptibilities in . . . enemy leadership groups" that psychological warfare could exploit.[7]

Speier elucidated his elite strategy of psychological warfare in his 1951 RAND report *Psychological Warfare Reconsidered*, which he wrote during the autumn of 1950 in the wake of the Campaign of Truth's announcement. In this piece, Speier argued that all types of societies were divided into four primary groups: the political elite (who governed); the military elite (who controlled the nation's military); the working population (civilians); and the fighting population (soldiers). Speier further subdivided the political elite into two groups: central decision makers (who "determine the policy of the nation as a whole") and auxiliary personnel (who advised policymakers and implemented their decisions). He did the same for the military elite, which he declared was made up of a central contingent of military officers who determined a nation's strategy and who were supported by an auxiliary staff that advised them and implemented their decisions. Finally, Speier subdivided the working and fighting populations into "persons of high skill"—the top strata of whom were the "key personnel" (elite professionals such as scientists, intellectuals, military experts, administrators, and engineers) without whom a society could not function—and "persons of low skill," that is to say, the masses of ordinary people and low-ranking soldiers.[8]

Speier asserted that given what social scientists knew about the masses' irrationality and the centralized nature of power in totalitarian societies, the numerically small political elite, military elite, and key personnel were the only relevant targets of anti-Soviet psychological warfare. Specifically, Speier insisted that U.S. psychological warfare should attack the bonds of trust that united these Soviet elites. This would be an easy task, he contended, because Soviet elites were "insecurity elite[s]" who already distrusted one another. The central decision makers of the political elite were distrustful of their superiors because they—especially Stalin—"either promoted or . . . demoted [them], and when [central decision makers] are demoted the chance is [they] will be killed." Meanwhile, the auxiliary personnel of the political elite, the central contingent of military officers, the auxiliary personnel of the military elite, and, implicitly, the key personnel were distrustful of the central decision makers of the political elite because "they are always suspected [by the central decision makers] of being potential counterelites" and were therefore constantly in danger of being murdered or disappeared.[9]

Speier thus averred that intra-elite distrust was a weak spot that anti-Soviet psychological warfare must exploit. He encouraged policymakers to heighten this distrust through false intelligence leaks, the provision of misinformation, and similar methods. If U.S. psychological warfare could trick Soviet elites into being more suspicious of each other than they already were, Speier concluded, it would harm their ability to make effective decisions, which would destabilize the Soviet Union and, ultimately, its hold on the Eastern Bloc. Furthermore, Speier recommended that U.S. decision makers develop means to attenuate the key personnel's "will to work and obey" the political and military elite because "substitutes for key personnel are difficult to find [and] also because malfunctioning members in this group affect the operations of many others."[10]

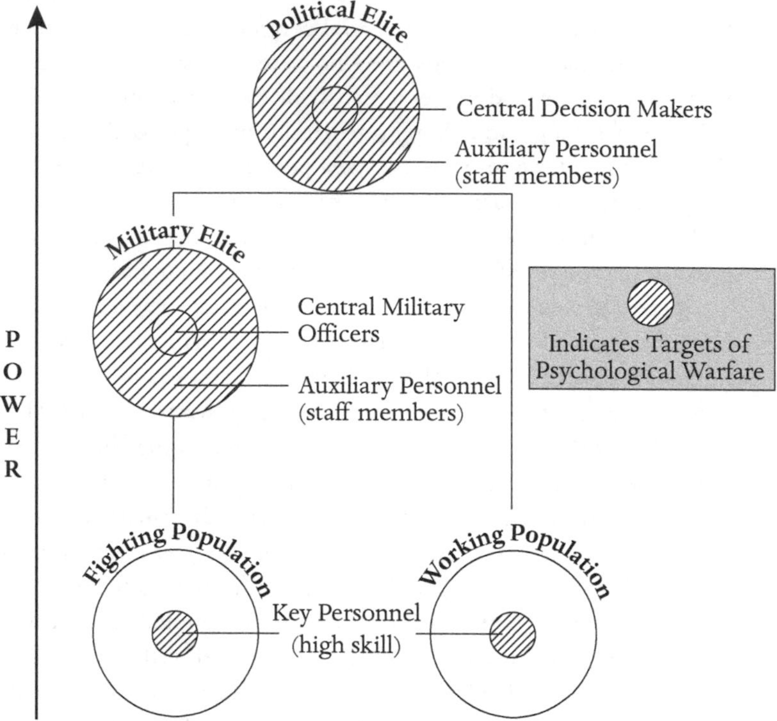

Figure 8. This image is a graphic representation of Speier's theory of totalitarian-directed psychological warfare

Speier's elite-focused psychological warfare strategy firmly rejected any attempt to persuade the Soviet masses to switch their allegiance from their homeland to the United States. "Truth," in this case, would set no one free. Indeed, Speier was just one of many psychological warfare experts who, over the course of the 1950s, spurned mass propaganda campaigns. In addition to Speier, W. Phillips Davison, Leonard Doob, George Kennan, Paul Lazarsfeld, Daniel Lerner, Saul Padover, and Ithiel de Sola Pool expressed their support for an elite strategy of psychological warfare. Happily for these intellectuals, at the same moment the Campaign of Truth launched, government decision makers began to explore the ways in which psychological warfare could "undermine the Kremlin," to borrow Gregory Mitrovich's phrase. This shift in strategic thinking would bring Speier into the corridors of power, where he became, in one colonel's words, the "willing friend and adviser to many staff officers in the Pentagon and the State Department."[11]

Speier directly influenced anti-Soviet psychological strategy through his participation in Project TROY, the first major collaboration between social scientists and the government after World War II. TROY's origins are found in an early 1950 meeting between Harry Truman and David Sarnoff, the chairman of the Radio Corporation of America, in which Sarnoff criticized the U.S. psychological warfare effort and recommended that a group of experts review and reform it. Truman asked Dean Acheson, his secretary of state, to investigate Sarnoff's remarks, at which point Acheson told James Webb, his undersecretary of state, to undertake Sarnoff's suggested reassessment. Webb, for his part, instructed Edward Barrett, Speier's former boss at the Office of War Information and since February 1950 the assistant secretary of state for public affairs, to direct the review. Barrett, who agreed with Sarnoff that the U.S. psychological warfare effort had significant problems, embraced his assignment with aplomb.[12]

Barrett's review got off the ground in the summer of 1950, when he and Webb began to explore the possibility of holding a symposium at the Massachusetts Institute of Technology to which they would invite the nation's top psychological warfare experts to devote several months of uninterrupted time to reenvisioning U.S. psychological strategy. MIT was a natural place to hold such a meeting. During World War II, the institute had profited enormously from government contract work and continued to do so in the early Cold War, undertaking the Air Force's Project LEXINGTON in 1948 and the Navy's Project HARTWELL in 1950. After these positive experiences with the military, the institute's administrators were eager to expand their list of government patrons. Therefore, in July 1950, James Killian, MIT's president, and John Burchard, MIT's dean of humanities and social studies, agreed to oversee Barrett and Webb's envisioned symposium. The State Department dubbed its collaboration with MIT Project TROY, after the wooden horse the Greeks used to infiltrate that ancient city.[13]

TROY ran from October 1950 until January 1951. Just over one-third of the project's twenty-two permanent members were social scientists. In addition to Speier, who was among the first social scientists invited to participate in the meeting, the TROY group included Alex Bavelas (psychologist, MIT), Jerome

Bruner (psychologist, Harvard), Clyde Kluckhohn (anthropologist, Harvard), Donald Marquis (psychologist, Michigan), Max Millikan (economist, MIT), Elting Morison (historian, Maryland), and Robert Wolff (historian, Harvard). Besides these social scientists, TROY's membership comprised physicists, electrical engineers, a city planner, a physiologist, and a geographer. Of all these individuals, Speier was the most experienced in psychological warfare, had the strongest connections to State Department officials, and was most familiar with the conditions in Europe. It is therefore likely that he assumed a leading role in TROY's discussions, although no conference proceedings were recorded to confirm or deny this supposition.[14]

TROY began on October 23 with five days of briefings by government and military officials (Speier was the only project member to also give a presentation). At the end of this week, TROY's participants moved to Lexington, Massachusetts, where, except for intermittent briefings, they worked uninterrupted for the remainder of the autumn. (At the government's request, Speier spent October, November, and early December in Germany but almost certainly rejoined the TROY sessions when he returned to the United States.) In Lexington, TROY's members were divided into interdisciplinary groups that created outlines of the difficulties the United States might face when prosecuting an anticommunist psychological war. After creating these outlines, the entire group reconvened to criticize them and determine which issues the final TROY report should emphasize. When this was decided, the group was again broken up into interdisciplinary "working parties" that wrote individual memos addressing particular problems the group had identified as important. These were then "examined, discussed and amended by the whole group" before being collated into a draft report. Finally, an editorial committee revised the report, which was reviewed and approved by the entire group. Because the process was collaborative, the final, anonymous TROY report made clear that its "conclusions and recommendations . . . are unanimously those of the group."[15]

Despite the TROY report's anonymity, the similarities between its recommendations concerning anti-Soviet psychological warfare and those offered by Speier in *Psychological Warfare Reconsidered* suggest that he was a primary author of the report's section on this topic. Most fundamentally, the report endorsed Speier's elite theory of totalitarianism, asserting that "control of [Soviet] power is, today, concentrated in the hands of a little group of Soviet leaders." But, more significantly, the report also emphasized the importance of disrupting the bonds of trust that united Soviet elites. "There appear to be several ways," the report maintained, "in which [Soviet elites'] confidence in themselves and in each other may be undermined to such an extent that the control they exert over their country may be seriously impaired." As Speier did, the report urged U.S. propagandists to "*stimulate mutual distrust*" among Soviet elites by spreading misinformation. Moreover, in another echo of *Psychological Warfare Reconsidered*, the report avowed that "the principal targets" of U.S. psychological warfare should be the Soviet Union's key personnel, "the intelligentsia, skilled workers, bureaucrats . . . [and] personnel of the mechanized armed forces" upon whom "the regime relies" to govern.[16]

Even before TROY's sessions ended, State Department officials declared it a success. In late December, Howland Sargeant, the deputy assistant secretary of state for public affairs, proclaimed that TROY demonstrated that independent experts "are able to attack problems for which our own staffs are unable to free themselves" and "can approach problems without Departmental inhibitions both as to the customary way of doing things and our relations with other parts of the Government." State Department officials' praise for TROY continued after they received its main report in February 1951 and its annexes in March. For example, Barrett professed that the report "blazed important new paths . . . in helping to solve the major problems we face"; W. Park Armstrong admired the report "as an extremely useful document"; J. Robert Schaetzel referred to the report as "really quite an extraordinary piece of work" and celebrated the section on the Soviet Union as "one of the most thoughtful and penetrating treatments of this subject [he had] seen recently"; and Robert Hooker commended the report's "very high order of technical competence, political sophistication, and common sense."[17]

As a State Department document from August 1951 affirmed, the TROY report was the "principal research undertaken [by the department] with reference to [the psychological] penetration of the Iron Curtain," and its recommendations quickly began to permeate State's policy documents. For instance, an April analysis of the Soviet Union's "psychological vulnerabilities" sent to department propagandists repeated the TROY report's (and Speier's) claim that distrust characterized the interpersonal relations of Soviet elites:

> There is every indication that within the Soviet Party-Burocracy [*sic*] there is jealousy of the position and privileges of superiors, resentment of toadies and bootlickers who gain undeserved advancement, resentment of others for their unwillingness to take responsibility, a sense of insecurity owing to the necessity of finding a scapegoat for everything that goes wrong, frustration

at the continual lying that one is forced to do, a sense of shame at the hypocracy [*sic*] necessary to disassociate oneself from a person on the way out, and continual fear of intra-office spying, compromising oneself, making a mistake, and of the "slow way down" courtesy of the party or the fast way out courtesy of the MGB [Ministry for State Security].

In a further demonstration of TROY's (and Speier's) impact, this analysis also suggested that U.S. propaganda target the Soviet Union's key personnel, including factory managers, engineers, and the intelligentsia.[18]

By early 1952, the TROY report's (and Speier's) opinion that the Soviet Union was an elite-run society had become State Department dogma. As Charles Bohlen noted in March of that year, one of the "fundamental features of the Soviet system which [was] generally uncontested by all analyses" was "that the Soviet system . . . is a totalitarian state . . . where the power of decision rests entirely in the hands of a small group of men." Barrett likewise avowed in 1953 that in totalitarian regimes like the Soviet Union "successful opposition is impossible unless there is a division in the ruling group," and for this reason psychological warfare must focus on "the possibilities of [provoking] divisions within the élite."[19]

The TROY report also influenced November 1952's PSB D-31, "A Strategic Concept for a National Psychological Program," which was released by the Psychological Strategy Board, an interdepartmental psychological warfare planning group established as the result of a TROY recommendation. As TROY and Speier did, PSB D-31 asserted that "inherent suspicion and lack of mutual trust and confidence" characterized the relationships communist elites had with one another. The report therefore insisted that to weaken the Eastern Bloc, propagandists must attempt "to increase this suspicion . . . to the point of systematic removal or elimination of personnel [working] in important and effective positions" in the Soviet Union and its satellites. "The communist reservoir of able and experienced personnel," PSB D-31 averred, "is not unlimited, and individuals of demonstrated power and effectiveness would [thus] be excellent targets" of psychological warfare. In essence, PSB D-31 repeated TROY and Speier's arguments that communist elites were critical targets for U.S. psychological warfare and that engendering distrust among these elites was a vital means to destabilize the Eastern Bloc.[20]

It is likely that in the early 1950s the TROY report served as a key planning paper for anti-Soviet psychological warfare campaigns. However, it is impossible to know for certain, because the majority of documents concerning these operations remain classified. At the very least, the report affected the ways in which U.S. officials understood anti-Soviet psychological strategy by convincing them of three claims that can be partially traced to Speier: first, that the Soviet Union was an elite-run society; second, that the Soviet elite was insecure and distrustful; and finally, that this distrust was a weak spot that psychological warfare must exploit.[21]

Expert conclaves such as Project TROY were just one way for a defense intellectual like Speier to influence U.S. foreign policy; serving as a consultant was another, and it was through this latter method that Speier shaped the U.S. psychological warfare effort directed against the German Democratic Republic. Speier's anti-GDR psychological strategy differed from his anti-Soviet strategy in one crucial respect: because he believed that the structures and culture of a totalitarian society were not yet solidified in East Germany, he concluded that some form of broad-based resistance to the GDR's ruling elite was possible. Consequently, between 1950 and 1953 Speier argued that U.S. policymakers should dedicate themselves to encouraging a mass resistance within the GDR.

In late 1950, Shepard Stone, the director of the High Commission for Occupied Germany's Office of Public Affairs, asked Speier and Wallace Carroll, Speier's former OWI superior, to travel to Germany to produce a report that would offer recommendations for improving the local U.S. psychological warfare effort. Earlier that year, HICOG officials had determined that the United States would retain its power position in Europe only if they prosecuted a psychological offensive designed to roll back the Soviet Union from the GDR. In February 1950, John J. McCloy, the U.S. high commissioner for occupied Germany, established the Political and Economic Projects Committee (PEPCO) to coordinate a more aggressive anti-GDR psychological warfare campaign. Though PEPCO initiated a psychological offensive, by the end of the year officials like Stone felt it lacked direction and required the help of outside consultants. Moreover, in the autumn of 1950 the Soviet Union had made clear that it wanted Germany to unify and demilitarize, which engendered anxieties in U.S. officials who desired to retain the nation's division and incorporate a potentially rearmed Federal Republic into the Western sphere of influence. In the words of Christian Ostermann, the Soviets' behavior revealed "the need for a more coordinated and effective psychological warfare effort in Germany." HICOG officials thus turned to Speier and Carroll, two renowned and experienced experts on anti-German psychological warfare, for advice.[22]

Speier and Carroll traveled to Germany in late October and remained there until early December. Because Carroll could not speak German, Speier was responsible for interviewing German journalists, broadcasters, and publishers; German government and intelligence officials; and Germans who lived in the GDR. What Speier learned in these meetings both pleased and disappointed him. On one hand, Speier found, as he stated in a report he wrote immediately upon returning to the United States, that "in the Soviet zone [i.e., the GDR] . . . the overwhelming majority of the population is opposed to the present regime." On the other hand, though, he discovered that young East Germans, who "have no memory of democratic life," increasingly embraced communism.[23]

Speier and Carroll also met with manifold high-ranking American officials, including McCloy, the chiefs of all HICOG divisions, the staff of PEPCO, the editors of numerous U.S. occupation publications, and the staff of the Radio in the American Sector (RIAS), which broadcast U.S. propaganda to the GDR. Speier was happy to learn that unlike the Office of Military Government of 1946–1947, the High Commission of 1950 was a well-organized machine that retained both local support and the capacity to carry out complex psychological operations. He particularly admired PEPCO, which, he approvingly reported, "has worked out an impressive plan [for the psychological offensive already under way] in which its expectations about Soviet actions, U.S. moves, alternative courses of action, timetables, and so on, are set forth in detail." Furthermore, Speier found his "visit to RIAS a moving experience" that highlighted the skill and dedication of its staff.[24]

Speier's trip to Germany convinced him that conditions on the ground—especially widespread East German discontent with the Soviet Union and the ruling Socialist Unity Party (SED) and the presence of skilled and dedicated U.S. officials—provided the United States with the opportunity to stimulate an anticommunist revolution. However, Speier also claimed that policymakers must do so quickly, before young East Germans became the nation's governing elite and transformed the GDR into a rigidly totalitarian society. This opinion shaped "Psychological Warfare in Germany," the report Speier and Carroll submitted to the State Department and HICOG in December 1950. In the report, the two declared that "we have in Eastern Germany all the elements of a resistance movement which can be turned into a potent instrument against the occupiers and their henchmen," as well as "an efficient [U.S.] propaganda instrument which reaches the population far behind our opponents' lines." But the report also warned that "the Soviet hold on youth in the Soviet zone is bound to increase." For this reason, "Psychological Warfare in Germany" urged HICOG officials to immediately "shed the vestiges of our defensive mentality and combine the powerful means at our disposal in a great psychological warfare offensive" that had as its "ultimate aim . . . getting [the Soviet Union] out of Germany." This idea—that the United States had only a limited time to use psychological warfare to push the Soviet Union out of the GDR—permeated U.S. strategic thinking for the next two and a half years.[25]

In their report, Speier and Carroll proposed that HICOG initiate a propaganda campaign they dubbed "Operation Exit," which would keep the "hope and courage of the opposition in the Soviet zone . . . alive, while organizational and other preparatory steps for intensified resistance are being taken." The two consultants offered several recommendations for propaganda themes they insisted would have particular resonance among East Germans. The most influential of these was a theme they termed "Return to Europe," which was premised on the Orientalizing notion that the Soviet Union was not truly a European nation but rather embodied a non-European—implicitly Asian—civilization that was innately hostile to the West and its values. U.S. propagandists, Speier and Carroll stated, must make clear to East Germans that "the Soviets *hate* and *fear* Europe" and that any anti-Soviet resistance "work[s] for the *Return to Europe* of the Soviet Zone." "Return to Europe," in short, rehabilitated German culture as part of Western civilization as it simultaneously "othered" the Soviet Union and tacitly claimed that no stable peace could be reached with a power that had so little in common with the United States and Western Europe. It was a theme that portended a permanent Cold War.[26]

As Christian Ostermann has noted, "Psychological Warfare in Germany" "struck HICOG like a thunderbolt." The report could hardly have arrived at a more auspicious moment. Though the Truman administration wanted to "increase the spirit of resistance to Communism in the [Iron] Curtain Countries," as the minutes from a December 1950 PEPCO meeting professed, HICOG officials were not sure how to do so. They thus enthusiastically seized on the recommendations in "Psychological Warfare in Germany." According to Shepard Stone, within weeks of receiving the report, HICOG's Office of Public Affairs was "working along the lines [Speier and Carroll] proposed." Similarly, PEPCO and other government groups embraced the report "as a distinct contribution to plans for psychological warfare in Germany" and considered it "a valuable tactical guide."[27]

Speier and Carroll's suggestion that "Return to Europe" become a major U.S. propaganda theme proved particularly influential. On May 8, 1951, the

State Department sent a special guidance to its propagandists, titled "The Concept of Europe," which presented "Return to Europe" as a "positive" idea that should augment, and perhaps even replace, the "main propaganda concept [then being used in Eastern Europe, which stressed the importance] of building situations of strength and seeking the containment of Communism and of the Soviet Union." In language that mirrored the Orientalist discourse of "Psychological Warfare in Germany," "The Concept of Europe" averred that speaking in terms of "Europe" would clarify to all those living in the Eastern Bloc that "the European nations [were bound] together [by a] . . . Graeco-Roman, Hebrew-Christian tradition" that formed "a common heritage" distinct from the Asiatic and communist culture promoted by the Soviet Union. This, the guidance argued, would give "the people in the satellite countries . . . new courage to stiffen their resistance to Communist domination and retard thereby the Sovietization of their minds, especially the minds of their youth."[28]

In July, Henry Ramsey, a foreign service officer then working for HICOG, produced a report in which he insisted "that the 'Return to Europe' concept should play an integral part" in the U.S. effort to roll back the Soviet Union. Ramsey affirmed that the theme would underline to audiences that the United States continued to favor the assimilation of Eastern Europe into the Western sphere of influence, which would "counteract a growing belief [behind the Iron Curtain] that the Soviet occupation is permanent [and] that the West has written-off the East." Ramsey further claimed that "such an infusion of hope would confer added strength and courage among the [Soviet] Orbit's resistance potential" and would engender "an awareness and a certainty that the captive populations can contribute to their own freedom and to the achievement of a great European ideal by passive resistance and, when the time comes, by active resistance to the Soviet concept of empire."[29]

HICOG and the State Department endorsed Ramsey's report. Soon after it was released, Edmond Taylor, a consultant to HICOG's Office of Public Affairs, revised his "Interim Plan for Intensified Psychological Warfare in Germany" in order to stress that the "Return to Europe" theme provided "a general framework for specific appeals or instructions to intensify resistance [in the GDR] and . . . a means for promoting a broad sense of solidarity [among East Germans] not merely with West Germans but with all the West." Likewise, in their November Airgram 1622, State Department officials declared that they were "in substantial agreement with the treatment [for 'Return to Europe'] outlined" in Ramsey's and Taylor's reports.

However, developing the "Return to Europe" theme was not the only way in which Speier informed the U.S. psychological warfare effort directed against the GDR. His ideas also shaped PSB D-21, the "National Psychological Strategy with Respect to Germany," which was the planning document that inaugurated an aggressive psychological warfare offensive that helped inspire the failed East German uprising of June 1953.[30]

Over the course of 1951, officials in the Truman administration progressively expressed their desire to prosecute a psychological offensive that would push the Soviet Union out of Eastern Europe once and for all. Policymakers argued that if the United States could destabilize the Soviets' hold on the Eastern Bloc—particularly the GDR—Stalin and his cronies would be deprived of the revenue, labor, and raw materials they needed to fight the Cold War. In October, Truman approved NSC-10/5, which authorized "the intensification of covert operations" designed to "place the maximum strain on the Soviet structure of power, including the relationships between the USSR [and] its satellites." NSC 10/5 further demanded that the United States "develop underground resistance [movements] and facilitate covert and guerilla operations in strategic areas to the maximum practicable extent." With these instructions, the stage was set for the initiation of an anti-GDR psychological offensive whose goal was to stimulate a widespread resistance movement against the Soviet Union and SED. [31]

At the request of CIA director Walter Bedell Smith, in December 1951 the Psychological Strategy Board (PSB) commenced an effort to develop a strategy for Germany that accounted for the stipulations contained in NSC-10/5. To devise this strategy, the PSB formed an ad hoc panel dubbed "Panel F." The panel, which consisted of officials from the PSB, State and Defense Departments, CIA, and Mutual Security Agency, met repeatedly throughout 1952 and eventually released PSB D-21, the "National Psychological Strategy with Respect to Germany," in October. As Raymond Allen, the director of the PSB, observed, the panel was "notable for the extensive use it . . . made of outside consultants." Specifically, Panel F sought the advice of Speier and Carroll, as well as W. Phillips Davison (sociology, RAND), Henry Kissinger (political science, Harvard), Stefan Possony (economics, Georgetown), and Walt Rostow (economic history, MIT), among others. These thinkers, especially Speier, profoundly shaped PSD D-21.[32]

Before Speier even met with Panel F, his ideas were familiar to its members. In October 1951, the PSB had condensed Speier's RAND report *Psychological Warfare Reconsidered* into an easily digestible "Technique Guidance" it distributed throughout the government. Moreover, Speier's ideas permeated three of the documents upon which Panel F grounded its first discussions: his and Carroll's "Psychological Warfare in Germany"; Edmond Taylor's "Interim Plan for Intensified Psychological Warfare in Germany"; and State Department Airgram 1622. Nevertheless, Speier's most direct impact on Panel F, and hence PSB D-21, came as a result of the meetings he had with its members, particularly his good friend Henry Kellerman, the State Department official (and German exile) who, Allen reported, directed the "working party" responsible for "the major part of the actual drafting" of PSB D-21. Unfortunately, no records concerning Speier's advice about anti-GDR psychological warfare survive. Therefore, as with his influence on Project TROY, one is forced to base conclusions about Speier's influence on PSB D-21 upon a close reading of the document itself.[33]

PSB D-21 reveals that Speier's ideas shaped the strategy. Most important, the paper proclaimed, as Speier and Carroll did in "Psychological Warfare in Germany," that although East Germany was not yet a totalitarian state, it soon would be, and for this reason the United States needed to immediately undertake an anti-GDR psychological offensive that encouraged mass resistance. The notion that the United States had only a limited time to act before the GDR was firmly entrenched in the Soviet orbit—an idea at least partially traceable to Speier—was critical to legitimizing the aggressive East German rollback policy of 1952–1953. Additionally, PSB D-21's emphasis on both the importance of targeting key personnel and the value of the propaganda themes "European Unity" and "European Community"—which echoed "Return to Europe"—suggested that Panel F placed several of Speier's other ideas into the paper as well.[34]

Recently declassified documents reveal that PSB D-21 served as the lodestone for an anti-GDR psychological warfare offensive that lasted from February to June 1953. The strategic paper was released during a particularly tense period in U.S.-Soviet and U.S.–East German relations. In March 1952, seven months before the final version of PSB D-21 was approved, the United States and its allies rejected the so-called Stalin note, in which the Soviet dictator offered to negotiate German reunification and rearmament. After this rebuff, Stalin allowed the SED to socialize East Germany at a faster rate than previously and to "organize an independent state" with strict borders and an army. At the same time, the SED began to restrict travel between Berlin and West Germany, while Walter Ulbricht, the party's general secretary, started to openly threaten the West. These actions convinced U.S. policymakers that the Soviet Union was consolidating its hold on the GDR. To prevent this effort from succeeding, decision makers intensified the ongoing anti–East German psychological offensive and seized on PSB D-21's recommendations as they did so.[35]

To organize the offensive, in the winter of 1952–1953 the State Department established an interagency "field coordinating panel [in Germany] for operational planning under D-21" that was authorized to spend "some 8 million D[eutsch]-marks for 'special activities' under the plan." Despite the formation of this panel, however, the implementation of PSB D-21 got off to a slow start. HICOG lacked the personnel needed to execute the strategy, while the CIA, which was responsible for directing covert psychological activities in the GDR, refused to coordinate with other groups. It was only in February 1953 that the plan began to be enacted. By this point, members of HICOG had started to work more closely with local German officials who could aid them in their efforts, while the CIA had been persuaded to cooperate with HICOG and the State Department. With these conditions met, PSB D-21 became, as PSB member Mallory Browne asserted in June, "the real basis for [U.S.] psychological operations" in Germany.[36]

A newly declassified status report on PSB D-21's implementation reveals that during the first half of 1953, HICOG officials in Germany pursued a number of activities designed to subvert the SED and Soviet Union. First, HICOG aided an unnamed "West Berlin publishing house . . . in producing and distributing to youth outlets in the Soviet Zone . . . [P]archeesi-like games . . . which giv[e] young people a true picture of the history, economics, politics, arts and natural and industrial resources of the Free World and the Soviet orbit." Second, "the Association of German Students of the Federal Republic was enabled to continue circulation of its newspaper" in East Germany. Third, with U.S. support "a Cologne publishing house" produced "200,000 copies of a 48-page pamphlet [that] expos[ed] current Soviet policies to sabotage European integration," which HICOG hoped to distribute "to special target groups in East Berlin and the Soviet Zone." Fourth, HICOG supported "the development of a Youth Center in West Berlin" intended to facilitate East-West youth exchanges. Fifth, HICOG helped "provide air transportation to Berlin for 200 prominent West German Catholic leaders" to partake in a religious ceremony that brought them "into contact with their opposite numbers from East Germany, affording an opportunity . . . for buttressing the morale of Church leaders in the East." Sixth, for West Berlin's May Day celebrations, HIGOC assisted the Federation of German Trade Unions in initiating "a series of tag and leaflet actions" that "encourage[d] slow-downs in Soviet Zone production." Seventh, HICOG gave money to the German Red Cross's Berlin chapter, which enabled it "to undertake the task of registering and gathering information on former German soldiers—once residents of the Soviet Zone of Germany—who died during World War II or are still being detained by the Soviet Union" in order to heighten Soviet–East German antipathy and to focus attention on "Western humanitarian efforts." Eighth, HICOG helped "a West Berlin newspaper publisher . . . pu[t] out 50,000 fake copies of the official Soviet Zone labor organ, *Tribuene*," which encouraged "slowdowns in Soviet Zone production" and which "provid[ed] Soviet Zone resistance elements with ideological arguments in their efforts to convert fellow-workers to an anti-Communist point of view." Finally, HICOG ensured that "a liberal, pro-Western, political monthly" was distributed freely "to select residents of the Soviet Zone" "as a means of keeping alive the spark of democratic tradition, the will to resist totalitarianism, and the hope of eventual liberation, which exist among peoples of East Germany."[37]

When coupled with the popular anticommunist broadcasts of the Radio in the American Sector and the covert actions of the CIA (about which information remains classified), HICOG activities taken under PSB D-21 demonstrate that the United States prosecuted an aggressive psychological warfare offensive against East Germany in the winter and spring of 1953. The result of this offensive was the June 1953 uprising—an event U.S. policymakers did not anticipate, nor even, it turned out, desire. Though the rebellion had several other causes that cannot be traced to U.S. psychological operations—including the SED's implementation of widely detested socialization programs, production goals, and work quotas; a decline in East German living standards; and rapidly shifting policy changes that made the SED appear both fickle and sclerotic—U.S. efforts bolstered and gave voice to rising East German discontent. In so doing, the United States assisted in spurring the June 1953 uprising.[38]

To protest the unpopular policies of the SED, on June 15 workers in East Berlin went on strike; by June 16, anticommunist demonstrations started to engulf the entire GDR. According to Christian Ostermann, in the next five days "more than 500,000 people in over 560 East German cities and communities" participated in the uprising. Most worryingly for the SED, protesters did not merely call for changes to specific policies but rather demanded the transformation of East Germany's entire system. This ultimatum encouraged the SED and Soviet Union to quickly agree that the rebellion needed to be quashed, and to do so the Soviets deployed troops throughout the GDR.[39]

When the recently elected president Dwight D. Eisenhower learned about the uprising, he refused to support it. In a National Security Council meeting on June 18, the president declined to arm the rebels, announcing that "the revolts would have to be more serious and more widespread than at this moment before they promised real success and indicated the desirability of our intervening" with military assistance. Without U.S. military backing, the protesters had no hope of standing up to the Red Army, and the Soviet Union rapidly suppressed the insurrection. For the next forty-six years, the GDR remained under the Soviet yoke.[40]

Eisenhower's unwillingness to aid the uprising was the first step on a path that ended with his disavowal of the East German rollback policy. The rebellion's swift collapse suggested to the president that psychological warfare would be effective in the GDR only if it was augmented with U.S. military aid. In other words, U.S. weapons would have to be deployed for East German rollback to succeed. If this were true, Eisenhower concluded, then the logic for psychological warfare's use against the GDR—which was that it could push the Soviets out without risking a third world war—was spurious. Therefore, soon after the June 1953 uprising, Eisenhower rejected rollback and embraced the "magnet theory" of German integration. This theory, as the president described in a letter to Bernard Montgomery, claimed that West German integration into Western Europe was the key to "increas[ing] the pressure inside Eastern Germany for joining up with the other part of Germany." From the summer of 1953 onward, the Eisenhower administration refused to directly challenge the East German status quo.[41]

The uprising's failure also ended Speier's advocacy for psychological warfare campaigns designed to inspire mass revolution inside East Germany. Once the Soviets crushed the rebellion, Speier decided that, absent U.S. military assistance—which was not forthcoming—mass resistance to the SED and Soviet Union was pointless. Instead, he began to argue that the anti-GDR psychological warfare effort should focus solely on elites. As Speier avowed in a speech he delivered at the American Political Science Association's annual meeting in September 1953, the suppression of the June insurrection demonstrated that in Soviet satellites elite behavior mattered far "more than the dramatic fits and starts of the captive people, particularly if we are not in a position to follow up on such outbursts." Eisenhower's refusal to aid the protesting East Germans had dashed Speier's dream that mass rebellion could stimulate rollback in the GDR.[42]

After Eisenhower ended the East German rollback policy, Speier never again had as important an impact on U.S. foreign relations. On one hand, the termination of rollback made his particular expertise in anti-German psychological warfare less vital for policymakers. On the other hand, Speier's disinterest in studying economic development, a topic that increasingly occupied U.S. decision makers as the Cold War's center shifted from Europe to the Third World, marked him as a relic of the past. Nonetheless, Speier's long-term influence on the history of U.S. foreign relations is not to be found in his role as a policy adviser, a figure who inevitably concentrated on short-term problems. Rather, one must look to Speier's role as the builder of institutions that outlasted the early Cold War itself to find the source of his legacy.

Chapter 7

The Institution Builder

Speier's contributions to the institutional matrix of postwar American intellectual life extended beyond the RAND Corporation to encompass the Ford Foundation–funded Center for Advanced Study in the Behavioral Sciences (CASBS) and the Research Program in International Communication at the Massachusetts Institute of Technology's Center for International Studies (CIS).[1] Like many intellectuals in the postwar era, Speier believed in the "linear model of science," which, Hunter Crowther-Heyck elucidates, asserted that "'pure' research leads to 'applied research' leads to solutions to practical problems," and his support for CASBS and CIS's communications program emerged from this conviction.[2] Speier wanted CASBS, first, to advance the social sciences' long-term pragmatic utility by training promising young scholars in cutting-edge techniques of basic research and, second, to solidify the nascent elite of American social scientists by bringing the nation's top advanced and junior researchers together. For its part, Speier wanted CIS's communications program to encourage the scholars it employed to pursue basic research about elite communication and psychological warfare that think tanks like RAND and government groups like the Psychological Strategy Board largely ignored. Unlike Speier's consulting or RAND work, which were intended to have a short- or medium-term impact, he hoped CASBS and CIS's communications program would concentrate on more long-term concerns.

Though Speier was instrumental in persuading the Ford Foundation to fund CASBS and CIS's communications program, his vision for the two groups was only partially achieved. Owing to the opposition of university administrators, who were threatened by the potential advent of a new institutional model for social scientific education, CASBS operated as a scholarly retreat and not, as Speier intended, a training center. Meanwhile, within several years of the founding of CIS's communications program, some of the defense intellectuals who worked for it turned from basic to applied, immediately policy-relevant research and from psychological warfare to modernization theory. The failure of both CASBS and the communications program to take the forms Speier desired highlights the limits of foundations' influence on the projects they funded. As Bernard Berelson, who directed the Ford Foundation's program in the social sciences, stated, "when 'big ideas' are carried out, they [often] don't end up resembling the[ir] original blueprint."[3] In the 1950s, social scientists and administrators often had enormous latitude to use funds they received from foundations in the ways they saw fit, even if the directions in which they took their projects did not conform to their patrons' wishes.

In other ways, however, CASBS and CIS's communications program realized Speier's vision for them. Scholars and administrators alike quickly recognized CASBS as one of the most prestigious retreats for social scientists in the United States, and it rapidly became, in Crowther-Heyck's words, a "crucial node in the network of the postwar social and behavioral sciences," an important means through which a self-aware community of elite social scientists was constructed.[4] As Jamie Cohen-Cole has recently pointed out, an invitation to CASBS signified that an intellectual was "welcomed into the elite levels of the academy."[5] Influential scholars who spent time at CASBS in its first years included Kenneth Arrow, Daniel Bell, Milton Friedman, Seymour Martin Lipset, Talcott Parsons, Robert Solow, Fritz Stern, and Leo Strauss. As these names indicate, CASBS brought together scholars who would transform their disciplines, public discourse, and, in some instances, policy itself. Significantly, defense intellectuals formed a part of this cohort. In addition to Speier, Gabriel Almond, Alexander George, Herbert Goldhamer, Harold Lasswell, and Edward Shils accepted CASBS fellowships. By inviting defense intellectuals into its fold, CASBS increased these individuals' authority by signaling to the U.S. intellectual and policy elite that they were not only advisers but also respected scholars. Furthermore, spending time at

CASBS enabled defense intellectuals to think of themselves as true intellectuals, free thinkers who, at least sometimes, followed their scholarly interests as opposed to governmental dictates.

CIS's communications program also occupied a rarefied space in postwar U.S. intellectual life. Along with Paul Lazarsfeld's Bureau of Applied Social Research at Columbia and Carl Hovland's Communication and Attitude Change Program at Yale, it was one of the early Cold War's most academically and politically influential programs dedicated to communication studies. Academically, the program's staff, which included such leading figures as Daniel Lerner and Ithiel de Sola Pool, established and popularized the field of development communications. Politically, in the 1960s the program's conviction that mass media were a critical spur to modernization became a central element of U.S. policy toward the Third World. Thus, while the program ultimately did not, as Speier planned, focus on basic research or psychological warfare, it achieved his long-standing goal of bringing social science research to decision makers' attention.

Like RAND, CASBS and CIS were organizations of the rising American "meritocracy" and reflected an ongoing, albeit still quite limited and elitist, democratization of U.S. intellectual life. The primary idea animating both institutions was that they would support the "best" social scientists, regardless of class, ethnic, or religious background. Indeed, both CASBS and CIS's communications program were distinguished by their employment of Jews, members of the ethnic group that perhaps benefited most from the opening of American universities after World War II.[6] Lerner and Pool, who were two of the communications program's four initial senior staff members, were Jews, while dozens of Jews, including Almond, Arrow, Bell, Friedman, Shils, Stern, Strauss, and others, spent time at CASBS. With the financial assistance of the Ford Foundation, which was staffed primarily by white Anglo-Saxon Protestants, CASBS and CIS's communications program helped foster Jews' entrance into the U.S. intellectual and policy elite.

Speier's consulting work for the Ford Foundation embodied the elitist conception of society he had championed since the Soviet detonation of an atomic bomb in 1949. He had no qualms about using unaccountable private wealth for public ends. Speier expressed this opinion clearly in the midst of two congressional investigations that probed whether foundations used their funds for "un-American" purposes. In a memo to the Ford Foundation, Speier and a RAND colleague fully embraced the notion that private philanthropies had "an important," albeit undemocratic, "role [to play] in American scientific and cultural progress." According to Speier and his colleague,

Congress lacked the jurisdiction to question how foundations deployed their finances. "Private citizens," they asserted, had a right "to accumulate wealth and to develop their own conceptions of the public interest and welfare free from governmental supervision or coercive conformity." For this reason, they insisted that the decisions of "tax-exempt private [foundations]" must not be subject to "political inspection and supervision" and must not be "dependent on political approval."[7] To Speier, the congressional investigations into the foundations were just the latest demonstrations that the public will could not govern society justly or effectively.

Speier was one of the primary architects of the Ford Foundation's program in the social sciences. At first glance, his interest in an effort focused principally on academic affairs might seem strange. Speier, after all, had abandoned academia for a career in the interstices between private and government life and never displayed any desire to return to what he considered the isolated environment of the university. However, his willingness to spend the majority of 1951 shaping the foundation's social science program makes sense in light of the popularity of the linear model of science during the early Cold War. Molding the Ford Foundation's social science effort allowed Speier to channel an enormous amount of money toward basic research that, he was convinced, would eventually affect real-world decision making. Furthermore, Speier's work for the foundation provided him with the opportunity to create institutions that he believed would solidify the emergent elite of intellectuals that he hoped would take a robust interest in U.S. policymaking as the Cold War continued.[8]

The Ford Foundation was by far the richest philanthropy in the early Cold War United States. Founded by the automobile magnate Henry Ford in 1936 primarily to avoid estate taxes, upon Ford's death in 1947 his grandson, Henry Ford II, decided to transform the foundation into an international philanthropy dedicated to shoring up and exporting American values. The reinvigorated foundation quickly became the largest in the nation; by 1951, it controlled $417 million worth of stock, significantly more than the Carnegie Corporation's $170 million and the Rockefeller Foundation's $122 million. Nevertheless, though the younger Ford was dedicated to his project, he lacked a coherent plan of investment. To guide the foundation's efforts, in November 1948 Ford enlisted H. Rowan Gaither Jr.—the California lawyer who earlier that year had helped Frank Collbohm convert RAND into an independent nonprofit corporation—to chair a study committee that would, Ford declared, gather "the best thought available in the United States as to how th[e] Foundation can most effectively and intelligently put its resources to work for human welfare."[9]

Over the course of 1948–1949, Gaither and his staff interviewed dozens of influential Americans about their views of the world and its problems. After completing these interviews, the study committee produced a *Report of the Study for the Ford Foundation on Policy and Program*, which banally concluded "that today's most critical problems are . . . those which arise in man's relation to man," and which suggested that the foundation establish five interrelated programs to fund projects that would "eradicate the causes of [humankind's] suffering." The first four programs proposed by the study committee were "The Establishment of Peace" (Program Area I), "The Strengthening of Democracy" (Program Area II), "The Strengthening of the Economy" (Program Area III), and "Education in a Democratic Society" (Program Area IV). Though these four programs were devoted to supporting projects that were immediately implementable, Gaither and his staff also determined that the foundation's efforts would ultimately fail if elites did not achieve "a better understanding of man himself." They therefore recommended that the foundation create a final program on "Individual Behavior and Human Relations" (Program Area V), which would fund basic social science research. When they received the *Report*, the Ford Foundation's trustees unanimously endorsed it and established the five programs.[10]

Soon after submitting the study committee's report, Gaither accepted an offer to become an associate director at the Ford Foundation. In this position, he served as the foundation's strongest advocate for Program V, which was met with hostility or indifference from the majority of Gaither's colleagues, who considered a basic social science research program a waste of time. For example, Paul Hoffman, the president of the foundation between 1951 and 1953, once wryly noted that social science was a "good field to waste millions and get nothing." Gaither had gained his admiration for social science as a result of his experience with RAND, where he served as chairman of the Board of Trustees. He was particularly impressed with Speier, for whom he had "a very great respect," and with RAND's Social Science Division, which he considered "a strong expression of [the] hope" that social science could solve "the challenges of human affairs." (Indeed, Gaither considered asking Speier to become Program V's director.) By the time he arrived at the foundation, Gaither considered it his duty to act as "a layman who [provided] . . . scientists and scholars" with the unique opportunity to pursue research free from monetary pressures.[11]

Though excited to spearhead Program V, Gaither recognized that he required the help of bona fide social scientists able to translate his ideals into reality. Thus, in early 1951 he asked Speier and the psychologist Donald Marquis to plan the program. Speier and Marquis were obvious choices to aid Gaither. Alongside their personal history with him—Speier and Gaither knew each other from RAND, and Marquis had served on the 1948–1949 study committee—they were both intellectuals who had demonstrated their desire to have social science serve practical ends. Speier had extensive government experience and belonged to an organization that worked primarily on Air Force contracts. Marquis, who was then chair of the University of Michigan's Psychology Department, had worked for the government during World War II and was more recently a member of Project TROY and the head of the Research and Development Board's Committee on Human Resources. Gaither prudently concluded that his practical-minded colleagues at the foundation would respect Speier and Marquis's backgrounds. For their part, the two social scientists were eager to plan a program that would direct millions of dollars to their pet concerns and were therefore happy to accept Gaither's offer.

Speier and Marquis met for the first time on January 26, 1951, and convened regularly throughout the remainder of the year. The most important idea the two formulated was that Program V would make its greatest impact by funding centers that would gather talented social scientists to dedicate themselves to a particular task. Both Speier and Marquis had prior experience with centrally organized institutes of social science. Besides RAND, in Weimar Speier had been familiar with two Rockefeller Foundation–funded research centers—Alfred Weber's Institute for Social and Political Sciences and the Hochschule für Politik—that used social science to achieve practical ends. Marquis also had an interest in centers and was one of the authors of Project TROY's eleventh annex, which argued in favor of establishing an institute for psychological warfare research. Moreover, the two were well aware of the handful of influential research centers that already dotted the American intellectual landscape, including the Brookings Institution, Council on Foreign Relations, Foreign Policy Association, Hoover Institution, Institute of Pacific Relations, and National Bureau of Economic Research. For these reasons, from the beginning of their planning efforts Speier and Marquis discussed funding centers devoted to social science research and training.[12]

It was Speier, however, who advanced the idea that would eventually morph into the Center for Advanced Study in the Behavioral Sciences. At a

CENTER FOR ADVANCED STUDY IN THE BEHAVIORAL SCIENCES
Meeting of Directors and Fellows
January 4, 1957
Front row: Buck, Merton, Cook, Waterman, Stanton, Sears, L. Wilson, Tyler, Ballesteros.
Second row: Savage, Bridenbaugh, Craig, Rosenberg, Romney, Whiting, Morris, Popper, Knight, Speier, Weitzenhoffer, Singh, Fels.
Third row: Metzger, Evans-Pritchard, Guetzkow, Berlyne, Krieger, Wolpe, Kelley, Rothenberg, Madow, Caspari, Washburn, L. Davis, Hilgard.
Fourth row: Cutler, Agassi, Spindler, Deutsch, Schultz, White, Halsey, Lambert, Lewis, Dubin, Roberts
Wilensky, R. Wilson, Snyder, Attneave, Lane, Wallis, Opler, L. Davis, Newcomb, George, Hamburg.

Figure 9. Speier with his CASBS cohort and the CASBS board, January 4, 1957, *photo courtesy of the Ford Foundation Records—Photographs, Rockefeller Archive Center*

June 12 meeting with Marquis and others, Speier proposed establishing either "a conference of social scientists devoted to a particular problem in the field of behavioral science" or an Institute on the Study of Human Behavior that would do the same on a more permanent basis. Such a conference or institute, Speier affirmed, would have two major benefits: it would organize the best minds in the field to help solve pressing problems and, by doing so, would increase the prestige of Program V. Further implied in Speier's advocacy for a conference or center was the idea that he, or someone like him, could use these tools to establish or solidify elite networks that would improve the social sciences and, following the linear model of science, public policy.[13]

Indeed, Speier used his position as a consultant to Program V to invite many of his colleagues into the Ford Foundation's orbit. Intellectuals Speier brought to the foundation's attention included the political scientist Gabriel Almond, the psychologist Jerome Bruner, the newspaper editor Wallace Carroll, the sociologist Alex Inkeles, the anthropologist Clyde Kluckhohn, the political scientist Harold Lasswell, the émigré sociologist Paul Lazarsfeld, the sociologist Daniel Lerner, the Marxist émigré sociologist Leo Löwenthal, the sociologist Robert Merton, the economist Max Millikan, the political scientist Philip Mosely, the Marxist émigré political scientist Franz Neumann, the economist Waldemar Nielsen, the sociologist Talcott Parsons, the political scientist Ithiel de Sola Pool, the economic historian Walt Rostow, the communications specialist Wilbur Schramm, the sociologist Edward Shils, the sociologist Samuel Stouffer, the émigré political theorist Leo Strauss, the education specialist Ralph Tyler, the library scientist Douglas Waples, and Speier's RAND colleagues W. Phillips Davison, Herbert Goldhamer, Victor Hunt, and Nathan Leites. Over the course of the 1950s, several of Speier's associates received quite large grants from the foundation. For example, Lazarsfeld received $101,600 to fund "studies in methodology and in documentation for advanced training in social research"; Parsons received $36,000 for "support of work in social theory"; Shils received $30,000 to produce an "inventory of knowledge on social stratification"; Stouffer received $73,000 for self-study, institutional exchange, and a project that explored the "relation between pencil and paper tests, role playing, and actual behavior"; and Leo Strauss received $20,100 for "research on relations between political theory and empirical research." Additionally, Parsons and Stouffer received $475,250 for the "development and improvement of work in the behavioral sciences," while several of the scholars whom Speier recommended work with Program V, including Lasswell and Lazarsfeld, became consultants to the foundation and channeled its resources toward their own preferred projects.[14]

In terms of Program V, the most important individual whom Speier brought to the foundation was the library scientist Bernard Berelson, who in 1951 was dean of the University of Chicago's Graduate Library School. Speier had known Berelson since the early 1940s, when he had worked under Speier at the New School's Research Project on Totalitarian Communication in Wartime. After moving to Washington, Speier had employed Berelson at the Foreign Broadcast Intelligence Service, and furthermore, RAND had recently been in contact with Berelson to determine whether it should hire him as a consultant. When Gaither, Speier, and Marquis decided in February 1951 that Program V required a full-time staff person who was familiar with social science but who was not, in Marquis's phrasing, an "active research m[a]n," Speier suggested that Berelson serve in this position. Gaither and Marquis agreed with Speier's recommendation, and in June 1951 Berelson joined Program V as its chief staff officer.[15]

Owing to the influence of Paul Lazarsfeld, his collaborator and close colleague, Berelson was dedicated to establishing training centers that would improve the mathematical skills of young social scientists. As such, over the course of the late summer and early autumn of 1951, Berelson convinced Speier and Marquis that the proposed Institute on the Study of Human Behavior should become a training center for postdoctoral fellows. It was easy for Berelson to persuade Speier and Marquis of the wisdom of this approach, as in their very first meetings Speier, Marquis, and Gaither had discussed the "enrichment of research training opportunities in a selected number of universities by the establishment in each of a field training facility for community study." In October, Speier, Berelson, and Marquis informed Gaither that in their opinion the centerpiece of Program V should be a "training institute" funded at the amount of "at least" $500,000. In this way, the seeds that would bloom into the Center for Advanced Study in the Behavioral Sciences were planted.[16]

Speier, Berelson, and Marquis's call for a training institute was an implicit rebuke of universities, whose presumed inadequacies necessitated the establishment of such an organization. Indeed, the relationship between Program V and universities had been fraught since the former's inception. Before Speier and Marquis had even begun to consult for the foundation, Program V had distributed large grants to thirteen universities for, a foundation document explained, "the development of the personnel and the improvement of the conditions and facilities for effective research" in the social sciences. Though university administrators accepted the foundation's funds, they were nevertheless anxious, as Berelson reported in a letter to Speier, "that the Foundation was just going to . . . decide what everybody ought to do and then bribe them into doing it." In light of university officials' concerns, Speier, Berelson, and Marquis surmised that if their training institute—and Program V as a whole—was to succeed, they needed to build support for it among university-based social scientists, who would be the ones actually making use of the foundation's money. Therefore, in late November 1951, Berelson met with two groups of scholars, in Chicago and New York respectively, to receive their input on the draft plan for Program V that he had composed in discussion with Speier, Marquis, and Gaither.[17]

To Berelson's chagrin, those present at the Chicago meeting largely dismissed the training institute. In particular, the émigré economist Berthold Hoselitz and the political scientist Herbert Simon rejected the very notion of a training center, asserting that there were more effective ways to improve the social sciences. Things got off to a similarly rocky start at the New York meeting, where Talcott Parsons and Samuel Stouffer both worried that "the Institute would raid and ruin the universities," which would "degrade the level of graduate work at least temporarily." While Paul Lazarsfeld and Robert Merton endorsed the institute, Parsons and Stouffer's opposition led Berelson to conclude at the end of the New York meeting's morning session that, in his words, "the Center was dead."[18]

The training institute was saved only because Stouffer experienced a change of heart over his lunch break. In Berelson's telling, "Stouffer sort of caught fire" at the New York meeting's afternoon session: "Sam began to talk about [the training institute] and said he began to see that something like this was needed to get people out of the rat race of the university." "The universities," Berelson recalled Stouffer arguing, "now weren't what they were supposed to be" because scholars "were too busy" for "reflection and study and so on." Stouffer subsequently convinced his colleagues that the social sciences required an institute akin to the one recommended in Program V's draft plan. Over the next several hours, the attendees of the New York meeting started to elucidate a detailed vision for the center. They decided that it should be "an inter-university sponsored affair, with a core of three or four people who would be there to provide continuity for a period of, say, five years and with the others [i.e., other fellows] coming in at different points of time and for different periods of time from six months up to two or even three years." Though he was understandably glad to have won support for the institute, Berelson might have noticed that Stouffer defended the center without referencing postdoctoral training, its ostensible raison d'être. Instead, Stouffer embraced the institute because it provided time and space for research and individualized study. Even at this early moment in the center's planning process, then, a vocal advocate for it expressed little concern with pedagogy, which suggested that there was less general interest in a *training* institute than Speier, Berelson, and Marquis had supposed.[19]

Nevertheless, the training center became a pillar of the December 1951 *Proposed Plan for the Development of the Behavioral Sciences Program*, which Speier, Berelson, and Marquis co-authored with Gaither. The description of the center in the *Proposed Plan* differed from the one developed at the New York meeting in two crucial respects. First, the *Plan* made clear that "the actual control of the institute would not be vested in a single university or a group of universities"; rather, it would be governed independently. Second, the *Plan* distinguished between advanced and early career fellows. The center, the *Plan* declared, would support "ten or fifteen of the best behavioral scientists" in the world, with "a core of about four of them" remaining at the institute for five years. The rest of these advanced scholars would stay at the center "for varying periods of time ranging from . . . six months to two years." While these eminent social scientists "would be engaged on their own research programs," the *Plan* insisted that their primary duty would be to collectively educate "thirty to thirty-five [of the] best young people in the field" who were serving fellowship terms of two to three years. The *Plan* avowed that when their terms were completed, "the 'graduates' of the institute [having been trained in cutting-edge social science] would move back into the universities, where they could raise the level" of the disciplines in a relatively short period of time. Because the institute was to be Program V's flagship project, the *Plan* suggested that the foundation allocate a staggering $650,000 annually to it, by far the largest proportion of the program's recommended $3,000,000–$3,500,000 yearly budget. Though it did not state so explicitly, the *Plan*'s discussion of the training institute reflected a desire for elite rule, with the center's purpose being to identify, fund, and construct a nonpartisan social scientific elite whose research would, in the long run, make managing the nation's problems easier. Nonetheless, despite offering a plethora of details regarding the center's constituencies and goals, the *Plan* did not address the content of the training institute's program, an omission that would haunt the center's ensuing planning process.[20]

The Ford Foundation's officers endorsed the *Proposed Plan* on December 20, 1951, and on February 4, 1952, the foundation's trustees approved the establishment of a Behavioral Sciences Program (BSP) whose primary task was to fund basic social science research. With their duties completed, Speier and Marquis returned to RAND and Michigan full time, though each, particularly Speier, remained involved with the foundation for years, advising on projects, chairing fellowship committees, and winning grants. For his part, Berelson agreed to serve as the BSP's director. Over the course of the program's short existence—the foundation shuttered it in 1957—the BSP became one of the largest funders of social science research in the United States, if not the world. Moreover, as foreshadowed in the *Proposed Plan*, the center served as the BSP's flagship effort. However, to Berelson's disappointment, when the institute opened its doors in September 1954 as the Center for Advanced Study in the Behavioral Sciences, it had little to do with training postdoctoral fellows.[21]

Between 1952 and 1954, the raison d'être for the organization that became the Center for Advanced Study in the Behavioral Sciences transformed from training young social scientists to providing scholars with free time to research and write. Two factors engendered this shift. First, the social scientists charged with planning the center's program could not agree on its curriculum, which underscored the difficulty of creating a general pedagogy able to serve a group of scholars who hailed from diverse disciplines. Second, and more important, university administrators made a concerted effort to undermine the training institute's mission. Since the release of the study committee's *Report* in 1949, university officials were concerned—correctly—that the Ford Foundation intended to use its enormous wealth to shape the direction of social science, a task traditionally within universities' purview. The formation of a training institute for social scientists indicated to numerous university administrators that the foundation also planned to usurp, at least to some degree, universities' pedagogical function. To assuage these anxieties, the BSP invited administrators into the center's planning process, made university officials a plurality of the center's board of directors, and appointed Ralph Tyler, the dean of social sciences at the University of Chicago, the center's director. However, the BSP's attempts to harmonize the interests of the foundation with those of the universities failed. Instead of embracing the institute's training function, the academic administrators involved with the center subverted its mission and ensured that it became little more than a scholarly retreat.

The Ford Foundation's failure to establish a training institute for social scientists revealed the limits of philanthropic power in the early 1950s. When influential constituencies, such as university officials, concluded that a new organization threatened their own—and were given an opportunity to inform this organization's direction—they could mobilize and prevent the novel institution from coming into being with its original mission intact. Organizations like RAND and MIT's Center for International Studies could flourish in part because they were (relatively) sui generis in U.S. intellectual life and did not encroach on the functions of academic administrators. In contrast, a training institute, which potentially challenged universities directly, had a much harder time being accepted by academic officials.

Berelson, though, had no idea that his envisioned training center would be scuttled when he organized a meeting in New York on March 29–30, 1952, to begin its planning process. Berelson asked several of the usual suspects to attend, including Speier and Marquis, as well as Lazarsfeld, Merton, Shils, and Stouffer. But he also requested that university administrators participate in the gathering. Berelson was aware, as the notes of the meeting avowed, that to succeed "the center must rely upon the willing cooperation of the universities." It was administrators, after all, who would approve their faculties' requests for sabbaticals to spend time at the center, and administrative support would also lend the institute an aura of respectability. Therefore, to establish positive relations between the institute and universities, Berelson invited Thomas Carroll (dean of the School of Business Administration at the University of North Carolina), Ernest R. Hilgard (dean of Stanford's Graduate Division), F. F. Hill (provost of Cornell University), and Ralph Tyler to the meeting.[22]

The March 29–30 meeting provided the basic plan for the center upon which those who later designed its details elaborated. The meeting's attendees agreed with the *Proposed Plan* that the institute should have a central cohort of three to five distinguished fellows "who would serve for at least three years on staggered terms"; a cohort of seven to ten "senior fellows" who would stay at the center for six months to two years; and thirty to forty "junior fellows" who would study at the center for one to two years. Nevertheless, in a foreshadowing of future problems, the attendees could not reach a consensus regarding the center's actual training program. Rather, they discussed a hodgepodge of potential pedagogical models the institute could adopt, including an apprenticeship model, in which junior fellows would serve as research assistants to senior fellows; a problem-focused approach, in which junior fellows, overseen by senior fellows, would "work on a variety of basic problems in the field, such as the integration of theory and research"; and a traditional approach that mirrored graduate education, in which senior fellows would offer seminars on their areas of expertise. The attendees' inability to agree on a pedagogical program underlined the difficulties of creating a curriculum that could serve the needs of distinct disciplines with unique research methods and agendas.[23]

The March 29–30 meeting ended with the suggestion that a small committee be formed to develop a comprehensive plan for the center. Tyler became chair of this Planning Group, which included Berelson, Carroll, Lasswell, Marquis, Merton, Stouffer, David McClelland (a BSP staff member), and Douglas McGregor (president of Antioch College). Like the attendees at the March gathering, at their sole May 3–4 meeting the Planning Group's members were unable to settle on a general training program for the institute. Despite discussing this problem at length, the Planning Group's members did not offer any prescriptions about the center's possible content in their final *Report*. All they did was vaguely state that the center must guarantee that there was "intimate collaboration among the senior and junior fellows."[24]

The most consequential decision the Planning Group made concerned the name of the center, which was then called the Institute for Training of Behavioral Scientists. During the May 3–4 meeting, McClelland objected to "the word 'training'" in the institute's title because he believed the term implied that "the Center [would be] . . . a group of people to be fed a lot of information," when in actuality junior fellows were there to become better researchers through experience. McClelland's complaint resonated with the Planning Group's members, and at his suggestion they renamed the institute the Center for Advanced Study in the Behavioral Sciences. McClelland's objection pointed to a critical pedagogical question: In the social sciences, was it possible to distinguish simply between training and research, especially when learning occurred in the research process? The difficulty of answering this question opened an intellectual space for CASBS to transform into the scholarly retreat it eventually became, as supporters of a training institute could mollify doubts they had about the creation of a research-focused center by convincing themselves that learning necessarily occurred through research and writing, even absent a formal training program.[25]

The Ford Foundation's trustees received the Planning Group's report in June 1952 and in mid-July agreed to grant CASBS the enormous amount of $3,500,000 for one year of planning and five years of operation. To develop CASBS's nonexistent curriculum, Gaither organized an Informal Planning Group of social scientists that met for the first time in November. This group had a membership that contained several familiar names, including Lazarsfeld, Merton, Shils, Simon, and Tyler, as well as numerous scholars more recently invited into the BSP's orbit, such as the political theorist Robert Dahl and the historian Richard Hofstadter. Though a number of the sharpest minds of midcentury social science belonged to the Informal Planning Group, very quickly its members recognized that they were unable to agree on CASBS's pedagogical program. In an admission of defeat, the group's members declared that "a variety of training methods and approaches to behavioral science problems" would be employed at CASBS simultaneously and that, frustratingly, "sometimes one [had] to be satisfied with the conditions under which appropriate training is communicated [i.e., the pleasant and stimulating conditions they intended CASBS to have] without being able precisely to analyze the *how*." With this proclamation, CASBS's attempt to develop an interdisciplinary pedagogy was largely abandoned.[26]

Nonetheless, in late 1952 CASBS was still envisioned as a training institute, albeit one without a defined curriculum. This began to change only in early 1953, when CASBS's newly appointed board of directors, which, due to the BSP's continuing attempt to engender support for the institute among higher education officials, consisted of a plurality of university administrators, explicitly asserted that CASBS should be a research center. The board was chaired by Frank Stanton (president of CBS), and its members included Paul Buck (provost of Harvard), F. F. Hill (provost of Cornell), Clark Kerr (chancellor of the University of California), Robert Merton (sociologist at Columbia), Robert Sears (professor of education and child psychology at Harvard), Alan T. Waterman (chairman of the National Science Foundation), and Theodore Yntema (vice president of finance at the Ford Motor Company). At the board's very first meeting on January 22, Kerr insisted that "the Junior-Senior distinction" between fellows be eliminated, that CASBS "be conceived as a flexible Society of Fellows in which roles are worked out by the men themselves . . . rather than set for them in advance," and that the center abandon the goal of "improving disciplines as such." The other members of the board endorsed Kerr's recommendations, which eventually became CASBS policy. In one fell swoop, Kerr and the rest of the board erased two years of planning and started to transform CASBS into a research center. University administrators thus guaranteed that they would retain their monopoly over formal social science education and demonstrated to the Ford Foundation that they would not be pushed around.[27]

Several members of the Informal Planning Group were aghast at the board's decisions. Lazarsfeld, who had long advocated for advanced social science training centers, was particularly apoplectic, vowing at the group's January 31 meeting "that the Center is here to train Junior fellows" and that, if it abandoned this goal, it would become nothing more than "a 'gentleman's club for superannuated behavioral scientists.'" McClelland, Thomas Cochran (an economic historian at the University of Pennsylvania), and Joseph Spengler (an economist at Duke) seconded Lazarsfeld's opposition to the board's pronouncements. Nonetheless, for three reasons the Informal Planning Group was ultimately unable to assert itself over the board. First, the group's members remained incapable of agreeing on the center's pedagogical program, which provided them with little ammunition for an intellectual battle with Kerr and his colleagues. Second, Lazarsfeld and his allies lacked support from the larger scholarly community. In the course of planning CASBS, the Informal Planning Group had asked approximately fifteen social scientists to submit anonymously their visions for the center. Scholars' responses revealed that what they desired was *"a Guggenheim [fellowship] with feedback"*—that is to say, free time for research and writing with peer review—far more than they desired a training center. Finally, and most important, in June 1953 Ralph Tyler became CASBS's first director. Tyler, who had left his position as dean of the Social Sciences Division at the University of Chicago to join the center, concurred with his fellow administrators that the institute should focus on research, and his appointment ensured that CASBS would open as a scholarly retreat.[28]

From the beginning of his directorship, Tyler made clear that he wanted CASBS to emphasize research. In a board meeting that occurred shortly after he became director, Tyler referred to the center as a place where scholars "should be invited to push back the frontiers of knowledge" and made little mention of postdoctoral training. Berelson, who recognized in which direction the winds were blowing, expressed his disappointment with CASBS's new course in an October 1953 letter to Tyler, in which he pled with the director to "never forget" that the center "is *not* supposed to be a research center . . . [but] *is* supposed to be a training center." Tyler, though, ignored Berelson's entreaty, writing to Herbert Simon in December that under his leadership "the Center [would] certainly not be a coaching school or a place to make up deficiencies in previous background." When Tyler did discuss training, it was mostly in the abstract sense of fellows learning through "extended and intensive [informal] contact" with colleagues. As Berelson bitterly recalled years later, it was Tyler who "made [CASBS] into" "a kind of retreat" for social scientists.[29]

With the argument regarding CASBS's priorities essentially resolved in favor of research, those associated with the center turned toward deciding who, exactly, should be invited to it in its initial five years. One of Tyler's first acts was to dissolve the Informal Planning Group and replace it with an Advisory Committee of social scientists and administrators, which included Berelson, Buck, Lazarsfeld, Merton, Shils, Simon, and others. The Advisory Committee's primary task was to determine the meritocrats on whom the advancement of social science rested. Before it had even assembled, in August 1953 the committee received a list of twenty-one intellectuals already endorsed by CASBS's board of directors. Unsurprisingly, this list consisted of many of the nation's top social scientists—most of whom were already associated with CASBS or the Ford Foundation—such as Kluckhohn, Lasswell, Lazarsfeld, Parsons, Shils, Simon, and Stouffer. Over the next nine months, the Advisory Committee added more names to this list, including Speier and several of his associates, such as the social psychologist Raymond Bauer, the psychologist Alex Bavelas, the psychologist Jerome Bruner, the sociologist Alex Inkeles, the anthropologist Margaret Mead, the social psychologist Theodore Newcomb, and the sociologist Philip Selznick. CASBS was predictably an elite affair, with the majority of fellows whom the Advisory Committee and board approved hailing "from Yale, Harvard, Chicago, Columbia, and Stanford." The only non-academic organization to be well represented at CASBS in its first years was RAND, as Speier's Social Science Division—ever interested in being recognized as a place where the nation's best minds congregated, even if they worked on policy issues—sent Alexander George, Herbert Goldhamer, Nathan Leites, and John L. Kennedy to the center.[30]

When CASBS finally opened in Stanford, California, on September 20, 1954, it welcomed thirty-six fellows, including Lasswell and Lazarsfeld. With Tyler at the helm, CASBS quickly became the "Society of Fellows" for which Kerr had advocated. Early attempts at centralized programming, such as scheduled lectures, seminars, and courses, were rapidly replaced with ad hoc working groups that generally met infrequently. By the summer of 1955, CASBS was an institution that, Tyler avowed, "provides the scholar for one year both with free time to devote entirely to his own study and with access to colleagues of the same and related disciplines who are interested in some of the same problems." In other words, training had become part of CASBS's past.[31]

The fellows themselves were pleased with CASBS's decentralized, research-focused program. In evaluations written after the center's first year, the majority of fellows stressed that "their great satisfaction" with CASBS emerged from "the opportunity for free choice of study activities in an ideal physical setting." A 1957 remark from an unnamed RAND sociologist—most likely Speier—further affirmed that "the Center [was] one of the most imaginative, well conceived, and productive ventures of The Ford Foundation." CASBS's board of directors was equally satisfied with the center and in April 1957 asked the foundation for an additional $6,250,000 to fund it through 1964. Though Henry T. Heald, who in 1956 became president of the foundation, closed the BSP in May 1957, he nevertheless agreed to grant CASBS an extra $5,000,000. As these examples indicate, by the late 1950s social scientists, university officials, and foundation administrators embraced CASBS as a significant contribution to the U.S. intellectual landscape.[32]

In its first years, CASBS supported a number of the world's most prominent social scientists, including Kenneth Arrow, Daniel Bell, Kenneth Boulding, E. H. Carr, Ronald Coase, Gordon Craig, Merle Curti, Robert Dahl, Kingsley Davis, Karl Deutsch, Leon Festinger, Else Frenkel-Brunswick, Clifford Geertz, H. Stuart Hughes, Morris Janowitz, Frank Knight, Klaus Knorr, Milton Friedman, Roman Jakobson, Morton Kaplan, Leonard Krieger, Thomas Kuhn, Charles Lindblom, Seymour Martin Lipset, Leo Löwenthal, Jacob Marschak, Ernest Nagel, Talcott Parsons, Karl Popper, Howard Raiffa, Anatol Rapoport, Robert Solow, Carl Schorske, Fritz Stern, Leo Strauss, and

Ludwig von Bertalanffy. These and other scholars used their time at the center to develop, refine, and promote a number of influential methods and ideas, including game theory, systems theory, and the general application of formal approaches to the study of human behavior. In the words of the previously mentioned anonymous RAND sociologist, as early as 1957 CASBS "ha[d] become a major factor in American intellectual life."[33]

As Speier had hoped, the collections of elite social scientists that gathered at CASBS during the 1950s did not escape the attention of policymakers. In its first two months, Adlai Stevenson, who was planning his 1956 presidential campaign, traveled to the center in part to seek fellows' advice. Sometimes, government officials even visited the center to recruit scholars for specific projects, as happened in November 1956 when State Department officials and a congressional delegation traveled to CASBS to inquire whether its anthropologists would be interested in working on an unnamed assignment.[34]

Such encounters, though, do not suggest that CASBS was dedicated to policy research. It was, and remains, a place for social scientists to research, write, and (sometimes) collaborate with colleagues. Nevertheless, one should not overlook the fact that CASBS helped identify and solidify an emergent network of elite social scientists, many of whom were defense intellectuals. In addition to Speier, who accepted a CASBS fellowship in 1956–1957, CASBS fellows who worked or consulted for the government on national security issues included Gabriel Almond, Raymond Bauer, Alex Bavelas, Alexander George, Herbert Goldhamer, Alex Inkeles, John L. Kennedy, Clyde Kluckhohn, Nathan Leites, Ithiel de Sola Pool, Lucian Pye, and Edward Shils, among others. It was important to the identity of such defense intellectuals that they spend time at CASBS because it allowed them to maintain, to themselves and to others, that they were, in fact, free-thinking intellectuals able to pursue scholarly research without government interference. Though some of the research that defense intellectuals undertook at CASBS eventually shaped U.S. foreign policy, such as Almond's work on comparative politics, the center was a decidedly academic space where defense intellectuals could concentrate solely on scholarly interests (Speier, for example, spent his year at the center studying the writings of the seventeenth-century author Hans Jakob Christoffel von Grimmelshausen). In the final analysis, the presence of so many defense intellectuals at CASBS reveals that during the early Cold War the boundaries that had traditionally separated scholars from policy advisers were becoming increasingly permeable. Nowhere was this porousness more evident than at MIT's Center for International Studies, upon which Speier had a significant impact and to which we now turn.[35]

During his time as a Ford Foundation consultant, the project for which Speier advocated most fiercely was a university-based research center dedicated to producing basic knowledge about international communications generally and psychological warfare specifically. Speier aggressively promoted such a center because, after nine years of working for or with the government, he was convinced he had discovered two critical problems surrounding the relationship between social science and policymaking: on one hand, social scientists lacked basic knowledge about manifold topics, such as psychological warfare, which prevented them from providing policymakers with good advice; on the other hand, decision makers were so absorbed by short-term concerns that they did not support the basic research that, in the long run, would make U.S. foreign policy more effective. This situation made it impossible for defense intellectuals to serve as the clerisy Speier envisioned.

To rectify this problem, Speier insisted that the Ford Foundation finance university-based centers devoted to basic social science research. These centers formed part of a pyramidal vision for the military-intellectual complex that Speier believed would integrate the diverse research programs of universities, think tanks, and the government. At the bottom of Speier's pyramid, the base on which he averred wise policy must rest, stood university-based centers dedicated to long-range research. Speier wanted such organizations to ask basic research questions such as, How might psychological warfare increase paranoia? The middle layer of the pyramid was occupied by think tanks like RAND, which, though focused on applied research, were nonetheless able to explore mid-range problems not necessarily of immediate policy relevance. Speier imagined that a RAND-type organization would ask a question along the lines of, How might the United States use deception to induce paranoia in Soviet leaders? Finally, at the apex of Speier's pyramid were government agencies themselves, whose analysts, Speier assumed, would ask specific operational questions, such as, How can the United States use fake reports that describe a potential invasion of the Soviet Union to engender paranoia in Joseph Stalin next July? In Speier's vision for the military-intellectual complex, universities, think tanks, and the government would each have separate research tasks that, when integrated, would provide the basis for effective foreign policymaking.

In the end, Speier's effort to establish sharp boundaries between the different nodes of the military-intellectual complex failed, as the history of the program upon which he had the most direct impact, the Research Program in International Communication at MIT's Center for International Studies, demonstrated. By persuading the Ford Foundation to grant CIS $875,000 to found a communications program, Speier ensured that the center could at its outset allow this program's members to devote themselves to basic research projects not of immediate government interest. However, within several years of its founding, many of the program's staff began to undertake applied, explicitly policy-relevant research. This occurred most clearly in the realm of modernization theory, which by the mid-1950s emerged as CIS's primary focus. Furthermore, the staff of CIS's communications program became involved in short-term government operations, for instance producing materials used by Fulbright scholars traveling to India. As these examples indicate, Speier's scheme to have universities serve as the basic research units of the military-intellectual complex was unsuccessful. Speier's project failed because he did not anticipate the development of a prestige economy within CIS, where a defense intellectual's stature was premised on providing decision makers with immediately applicable knowledge. Even though they were based at a university—the traditional bastion of basic research—CIS's ambitious defense intellectuals, a group that included prominent figures such as Daniel Lerner, Ithiel de Sola Pool, and Walt Rostow, were always unlikely to adopt the long-term perspective Speier hoped they would because this would have attenuated their potential influence and thus stifled their career aspirations.

Speier first discussed the creation of a research center focused on psychological warfare in a memo he co-wrote with Donald Marquis on May 3, 1951, which recommended that the Ford Foundation support a "Center for Psychological Warfare and Peacefare." Within days, Speier rechristened the center the "Institute of International Communications"—"international communications" being an oft-used euphemism for psychological warfare during the early Cold War—and, in memos produced throughout 1951–1952, elucidated his vision for it. Speier asserted that the need for a communications research center emerged from the fact that "on the whole, the foreign information program of this country since World War II has been a failure": the United States was unable to persuade neutral nations to follow its lead, while the Soviet Union remained committed to the West's destruction. Speier placed intellectuals at the heart of this failure. In his telling, the lack of basic and "sound knowledge on which to base more enlightened [communications] programs" made it inevitable that the U.S. psychological warfare effort would disappoint. What was needed, Speier affirmed, was a financially independent research center whose members enjoyed the intellectual freedom to analyze the most fundamental issues of international communications. To guarantee that his proposed institute retained its autonomy from the government, Speier suggested that it be headquartered at a university. This did not imply, however, that Speier wanted his institute to produce knowledge for knowledge's sake. Rather, it was meant to discover information that would—following the linear model of science—ultimately shape U.S. psychological strategy and communications policy.[36]

Speier's Institute of International Communications easily won the support of Marquis and Bernard Berelson. Berelson had a personal interest in the subject; he had worked under Speier at the Foreign Broadcast Intelligence Service and in 1944 co-authored *The People's Choice* with Paul Lazarsfeld and Hazel Gaudet, an influential text in the emergent field of communications studies. For his part, Marquis had participated in Project TROY and also served as the chief of the Research and Development Board's Committee on Human Resources, which analyzed U.S. psychological warfare programs. Unsurprisingly given the three social scientists' connections to the subject, the communications institute became, along with the training center, one of the few concrete projects discussed in the December 1951 *Proposed Plan*.[37]

Foundation officials' initial responses to the communications institute were decidedly mixed. While Milton Katz enthusiastically declared that he believed the center could become "a sort of Rand organization to which contracts would later be given by a government agency," several of Katz's colleagues were worried that the institute's research would encroach on the government's territory, which could anger decision makers and limit the foundation's influence in Washington. Foundation officials therefore requested that the BSP ask policymakers, namely Edward Barrett, the assistant secretary of state for public affairs, and Gordon Gray, the director of the Psychological Strategy Board, whether they would make use of "such a center in view of the large governmental interest in international communications."[38]

Though Speier formally stopped working for the foundation after submitting the *Proposed Plan*, he continued to retain an active hand in the communication center's planning, and his connections to both Barrett and Gray made him the natural choice to pursue foundation officials' inquiry. In late December 1951, Speier met with Barrett and reported that the assistant secretary was "'quite enthusiastic'" about the institute and considered it "altogether possible for the Department of State to give research contracts to the Center." At the same time, Gray likewise informed Speier that he "was altogether in favor of such a Center." With these policymakers' blessings, in February 1952 the foundation's trustees agreed that planning for the communications institute could proceed.[39]

Ever since Speier first proffered the idea for a university-based communications research center, the question of its location had loomed large. Early on in the center's planning process, the Massachusetts Institute of Technology emerged as an ideal potential site. MIT had close connections to the national security establishment (it would soon be known as the "Pentagon on the Charles"); had hosted Project TROY, a progenitor of Speier's communications center; and most important, was linked to the foundation through H. Rowan Gaither Jr., who had worked at MIT during World War II as an administrator of its Radiation Laboratory, and through Richard Bissell, who was the head of Program Area III and a former MIT economist. However, to the disappointment of Speier and foundation officials, when TROY concluded in January 1951, MIT had begun to plan its own policy-focused Center for International Studies and evinced no desire to duplicate this effort. Moreover, Max Millikan, an MIT economist and CIS's director-designate, expressed little interest in exploring international communications. Nevertheless, in the autumn of 1951 an opportunity presented itself to Speier and foundation officials who hoped to place the communications center at MIT when James Killian, MIT's president, made clear to Speier that he wanted to ask the foundation for roughly $1,500,000 in funding for CIS. The institute's request provided Speier and foundation officials with leverage, which they quickly seized.[40]

In February and March 1952, Speier, Berelson, and Bissell met with Millikan to discuss the possibility of locating the communications center at CIS. While Millikan was at the time primarily absorbed by problems of economic development in the Third World, he was also an astute administrator who, sensing an opportunity, disingenuously informed Bissell that he was "very interested in th[e] proposal" for a communications center. On learning of Millikan's supposed interest, Gaither met with him and Julius Stratton, MIT's provost, in April to discuss the center, which, if it were headquartered in CIS, would become a dedicated research program. Soon thereafter, Gaither, Berelson, and Millikan agreed that as long as the foundation's trustees approved MIT's request for funding, CIS would host the foundation's communications program. The Research Program in International Communication thus became one of CIS's two founding efforts, the other being the Research Program in Economic Development and Political Stability.[41]

Speier was the communications program's driving intellectual force, and as its location was being decided he began to develop its content. In various memos, he explained that he wanted the primary focus of the program to be the study of elites, which, along with psychological warfare, remained his major long-term research interest. In general, Speier desired for the program to produce basic knowledge about elite governance. Specifically, he recommended that it explore, first, the ways in which "*governing elites*" and "*opinion leaders*" communicated with and affected the actions of various social groups and, second, the ways in which international communications, such as propaganda, informed these elites' attitudes and behaviors.[42]

In stark contrast to how it handled CASBS's planning process, the BSP, well aware that CIS required its money, ensured that Millikan adhered to Speier's vision by taking an active role in shaping the former's May 1952 request for foundation funding. Millikan's grant proposal directly echoed Speier, declaring that were it to receive foundation support, CIS's communications program would predominantly study political elites and opinion leaders. Speier was predictably pleased with Millikan's application. At his and Bissell's urging, in mid-July 1952 the foundation's trustees granted CIS $875,000 to fund the communications program for one year of planning and three years of operation. In contrast, the foundation provided Millikan's major interest, the economic development program, with only $125,000 for planning purposes.[43]

Throughout 1952–1953, Speier and foundation officials continued to direct the communications program's planning process. Millikan, who was not especially interested in the program, welcomed Speier's intervention. In August 1952, for example, Millikan informed Berelson that "I feel very strongly indeed that [Speier's] participation [in the program's planning] is absolutely essential" and that "if [Speier] should by any chance decide not to participate . . . I would feel very definitely sold down the river." Millikan need not have worried. Speier swiftly agreed to head the program's Planning Committee, which he staffed with his close colleagues Jerome Bruner, Wallace Carroll, Harold Lasswell, Paul Lazarsfeld, Ithiel de Sola Pool, and Edward Shils.[44]

Speier's Planning Committee met six times between September 1952 and February 1953 and enlisted the services of numerous consultants, including Gabriel Almond, McGeorge Bundy, Paul Kecskemeti, Nathan Leites, Daniel Lerner, Leo Löwenthal, Margaret Mead, and Walt Rostow. Predictably given that Speier had staffed the committee with scholars who shared his worldview, the *Advisory Report* it released in June 1953 repeated Speier's major recommendation that the communications program should study political elites and opinion leaders. Indeed, the *Advisory Report* said little that was new; the most consequential decision to emerge from the Planning Committee's sessions was the appointment of the political scientist Ithiel de Sola Pool as the communications program's director. Pool, who had served as the committee's secretary and who was then working at Stanford's Hoover Institution, had long-standing ties to Speier and his intellectual cohort. Pool had studied under Lasswell at the University of Chicago in the 1930s, where he was friends with Almond, Goldhamer, and Shils; had worked with Lasswell and Leites during World War II at the former's Experimental Division for the Study of Wartime Communications at the Library of Congress; and more recently was a consultant for RAND. In short, Speier trusted that Pool would take the communications program in the right direction.[45]

The Research Program in International Communication officially commenced in September 1953. In addition to Pool, who had assumed his directorship in June, the communications program's senior staff members included Raymond Bauer, a professor of social relations at Harvard and member of its Russian Research Center; Harold Isaacs, an MIT political scientist and former reporter at *Newsweek*; and Daniel Lerner, an MIT sociologist and specialist in psychological warfare. Millikan allowed Pool to direct the program as he saw fit, and in its first years he initiated three major projects: a study of international communications and their impact on French elites' attitudes and actions regarding European unity, which was overseen by Lerner; a study of international communications and their impact on Indian elites' attitudes and actions regarding a variety of domestic and international issues, which was overseen by Shils (who took a leave of absence from the University of Chicago to direct this project); and a study of international communications and their impact on U.S. businessmen's attitudes and actions regarding U.S. foreign relations and trade, which was overseen by Bauer. By the 1954–1955 academic year, several research themes had emerged to connect these otherwise disparate projects. As Pool stated, each project analyzed "the differences in reactions to international communications between persons with broader cosmopolitan experience and outlooks and persons with narrower or provincial frames of reference"; "the imaginary audiences of which a person is aware as he reacts" to communications; and "the relationship between communication and action." Per Speier's vision, the communications program's first projects examined basic issues surrounding elite governance and psychological warfare that think tanks and government agencies did not generally explore. Moreover, as Speier hoped, the projects all had explicit, long-term policy relevance.[46]

News about the communications program quickly spread throughout the military-intellectual complex and national security state. In its first three years, the program's staff spoke with or served as consultants to officials in the White House, Foreign Service Institute, Voice of America, United States Information Agency (USIA), Council on Foreign Relations, Committee for a Free Europe, Committee for a Free Asia, and Committee for Liberation from Bolshevism. Despite its members' many meetings with governmental and nongovernmental officials, however, in the program's first years its staff concentrated on publishing basic research in internal reports or scholarly journals. This changed at mid-decade when, in their search for influence, several of the program's members began to produce applied, immediately policy-relevant research.[47]

In early 1954, the Ford Foundation finally provided CIS with long-term funding for its economic development program, which had been Millikan's primary interest since the center's founding. This marked a turning point in CIS's history; thereafter, the development program was the center's primus inter pares. Pool recognized this transition and did what he could to accommodate the communications program to it. Most important, he encouraged the program's staff to collaborate with their colleagues in the development program. As a result of Pool's efforts, over the course of the mid to late 1950s members of the Research Program in International Communication became an important part of the center's collective project to understand and promote Third World development.[48]

The mid-1950s was also the moment when, as Millikan asserted in August 1956, "the advice and technical assistance of [CIS's] senior staff [were] requested with increasing frequency by . . . government officials." The defense intellectuals who comprised the center's communications program took full advantage of this development. Between 1956 and 1961, members of the communications program consulted or worked for the Department of Defense; Department of State; Army, Navy, and Air Force; USIA; Radio in the American Sector, Berlin; Radio Free Europe; Radio Liberation; Peace Corps; Special Operations Research Office; United Nations Educational, Scientific, and Cultural Organization; and Congress for Cultural Freedom, among other groups. Officials' interest encouraged the communications program's staff to refocus from long- to short-term projects, such as creating materials for Fulbright scholars traveling to India. Unsurprisingly, ambitious defense intellectuals like Pool and Lerner seized on the opportunity to inform U.S. foreign relations, even if doing so betrayed the communications program's supposed dedication to basic research.[49]

The communications program's most significant impact on U.S. thought and foreign policy emerged as a result of its members' contributions to modernization theory, an applied theory of development that sought to impel Third World societies to become "modern"—that is to say, to become like the United States. Indeed, it was Speier's old friend Daniel Lerner who produced the first major work of modernization theory, 1958's *The Passing of Traditional Society*. In this book, Lerner analyzed six Middle Eastern countries and drew the universal conclusion that throughout the Third World, ideas spread by the mass media stimulate "new desires" for modern life that "provide the dynamic power of modernization," the ideational base from which economic and political development arose. Specifically, Lerner argued that mass media forced "millions of people . . . who never left their native heath . . . to imagine how life is organized in different lands and under different codes than their own," which enabled them to recognize that there were better, more efficient, and more productive ways to live. If mass media technologies did not permeate the Third World, Lerner avowed, these nations might never modernize. As *The Passing of Traditional Society* demonstrated, by the late 1950s several members of CIS's communications program no longer focused primarily on studying elites; unlike Speier, as the Cold War's center shifted from Europe to the Third World, Lerner and his colleagues reoriented their research to focus on issue areas, such as development, which were of increasing concern to policymakers.[50]

According to a 1961 progress report that the communications program sent to the Ford Foundation, Lerner and his colleagues' efforts ensured that CIS's modernization theorists, a group that included Millikan, Pool, Everett Hagen, Lucian Pye, Paul Rosenstein-Rodan, and Walt Rostow, "carefully considered" "information and communication variables" in their work. For instance, in the CIS's collectively produced *The Emerging Nations*, the authors affirmed that "the mass media bring new aspirations and wider perspectives to developing countries," which "provide the psychic spark to modernization." Though a full analysis of the influence CIS's communications program had on development practice remains outside the scope of this book, suffice it to say that, partially due to the program's efforts, throughout the 1960s the U.S. government and associated institutions dedicated themselves to, first, using the mass media to encourage modernization and, second, building communications facilities in the Third World.[51]

As Speier intended, the Research Program in International Communication and the Center for International Studies of which it was a part served as important nodes in the emergent military-intellectual complex. In addition to acting as an intermediary institution that brought academic research to foreign policymakers' attention, CIS provided several of the early Cold War's most influential defense intellectuals with a base from which they moved into the government. Rostow, for example, used the center to begin a career that ultimately took him to the State Department and White House. Others, including Bauer, Hagen, Millikan, Lerner, Pool, Pye, and Rosenstein-Rodan, became government advisers who shaped manifold policies and programs. Furthermore, in terms of academic influence, the communications program essentially launched the field of development communications.

Yet the Research Program in International Communication's embrace of modernization theory also revealed that the sharp lines Speier hoped would separate the types of research undertaken by university centers, think tanks, and the government could not be maintained in practice. Surprisingly given his own career choices, Speier had not appreciated the degree to which defense intellectuals would want to influence policy, even when they were based at a university. However, while defense intellectuals were united in their desire to impact policy, they were nonetheless split by numerous internal disagreements. Perhaps no dispute was more contentious than the debate over whether qualitative or quantitative methods were most appropriate for policy research. This schism divided the RAND Corporation in its first twelve years and exposed the epistemological gaps that distinguished mathematically inclined defense intellectuals from those who, like Speier, refused to put their trust in numbers.

Chapter 8

Social Science and Its Discontents

When social scientists arrived in the military-intellectual complex, they brought with them methodological disputes that had permeated their disciplines since the latters' creation in the fin de siècle. In particular, there was a deep split between those who favored qualitative analysis and those who preferred quantitative and formal approaches. The fact that this disagreement was no longer confined to the academy, but instead had the potential to affect foreign policymaking, made the quarrel even more heated than it previously had been. Unsurprisingly given its employment of dozens of social scientists, the RAND Corporation emerged as a major site in the war between the quals and the quants. Under Speier's direction, RAND's Social Science Division became an outpost for qualitative research in an organization famous for its application of game theory, systems analysis, and other formal methods to the study of war and politics.[1] Partially in response to RAND's dominant formal, quantitative, and rational choice paradigms, the SSD created a "political-military game" that disregarded mathematics and had players simulate decision makers' activities. In contrast to formal and quantitative approaches, the SSD's political game emphasized the importance of judgment and wisdom to real-world decision making. The game eventually migrated from RAND to the Pentagon, where defense officials adopted it as a training exercise that is still used today.[2]

The story of the qualitative political game complicates the history of RAND and "Cold War social science"—social science that was geared toward, in Nils Gilman's words, "help[ing] the United States in its struggle against the communist challenge."[3] Many historians point to RAND as the paradigmatic representative of the postwar "behavioral revolution" that transformed the social sciences into disciplines that stressed systems, models, and the establishment of universally applicable theories.[4] Much of this is true when applied to RAND's Economics Division, which pioneered the use of formal approaches in the study of geopolitics. However, the political game reveals that the SSD differed: Speier and his colleagues were convinced that social knowledge was best accrued through nonformal methods and an engagement with concrete historical facts. They rejected the behavioral turn and promoted an analytical approach that marginalized systems and quantification. These convictions led the SSD to emerge as the most prominent organizational representative of the antiformal strand of international relations thinking in Cold War America.[5]

Speier and his colleagues' creation of the political-military game further highlights the importance of transatlantic and interwar encounters to U.S. social science after 1945.[6] To design the game, Speier and Herbert Goldhamer, a RAND co-worker, built on the pedagogy developed by Karl Mannheim, Speier's *Doktorvater*, in Weimar Germany. In Weimar, Mannheim faced the problem of teaching students how to navigate the political environment of a newly democratic society. He addressed this issue by creating a pedagogy of simulation that reproduced the "atmosphere"—that is to say, the structures of debate—of democratic politics. This simulacrum, Mannheim believed, imbued students with political empathy and the skills to act as effective political agents. Speier and Goldhamer's political game likewise sought to simulate the atmosphere of international relations and in so doing improve analysts' abilities, decision makers' talents, and the capacity for both groups to understand their enemies. In its methods and goals, Speier and Goldhamer's game mirrored Mannheim's pedagogy. The journey of the political simulation illuminates the peculiarity of mid-twentieth-century intellectual history, in which dramatic upheavals could thrust an idea from the seminar rooms of Heidelberg University to the conference halls of the RAND Corporation to the command center of the Pentagon.

In January 1989, Speier traveled to Santa Monica, California, to discuss RAND's history with five of his former colleagues: Bruno Augenstein, a physicist; Edward Barlow, an engineer; Burton Klein, an economist; Robert Specht, a mathematician; and Albert Wohlstetter, a mathematical logician. The subject of RAND's interdisciplinary culture repeatedly surfaced throughout the defense intellectuals' conversation. Most assessments of this culture were positive. Specht, for example, asserted that at RAND "the boundaries of the discipline[s] were unimportant" and that it "was rather uncommon and not typical" for people to "wor[k] [only] with their own discipline." Wohlstetter agreed that an "interdisciplinary character" defined RAND, which distinguished it from universities, where "there was really no genuine interdisciplinary work." For these intellectuals, one of RAND's remarkable features was its encouragement of cross-disciplinary collaboration.[7]

Yet in the midst of this discussion, Speier, who had mostly remained silent, interrupted. "I wanted to make a comment on Bob Specht's illuminating remarks," he declared, to "provide a grain of salt to [Specht's] wonderful sweet soup." In contrast to Specht, Speier averred that within RAND "there was . . . occasionally a tendency of snootiness, of disdain for people who were not, let's say, mathematicians." Moreover, he continued, there was often "open intrigue and criticism of people in . . . divisions [i.e., his Social Science Division] as being incompetent and so on." Although he believed members of RAND accomplished much that was notable, Speier wanted to ensure his erstwhile colleagues did "not gild the lily too much."[8]

Speier's observations called attention to a major rift that divided RAND from its incorporation of a Social Science Division in 1948 until the institution's restructuring in 1960. In an attempt to provide accurate recommendations to the military officers and policymakers who contracted with RAND, as well as to earn the respect of the technically oriented Air Force officials who deeply influenced the organization in its first fifteen years, the majority of RAND analysts endorsed quantified and formal methods of various stripes, including systems analysis, game theory, and computer simulations. These methods either ignored human behavior, culture, and politics or abstracted these factors into numerical values. Furthermore, RAND's quantifiers and formalizers frequently denigrated qualitative research, which relied on methods such as textual analysis and ethnography, and concepts such as judgment and insight, as unscientific.

The members of the SSD, however, argued that methods like systems analysis and game theory distorted the study of war and international relations because they either elided human considerations or relied on formal calculations that inaccurately reflected the real world. These convictions compelled the social scientists to maintain that their research, which examined issues like culture, psychology, and politics through qualitative approaches, provided a more effective, even a more scientific, basis for advice and action. The schism between the SSD and the rest of RAND revealed starkly different philosophical anthropologies. When quantifiers and formalizers incorporated human behavior into their work, they often assumed that individuals made rational choices based on utility calculations. For the social scientists, though, human beings were ultimately nonrational actors whose behavior was unpredictable and hence resistant to modeling. This fundamental philosophical difference was difficult to reconcile and pushed the social scientists to RAND's fringes.

But the SSD's peripheral position proved crucial to methodological innovation. It was the division's low status within RAND that encouraged the social scientists to create the political-military game, a heuristic that embraced everything—politics, culture, psychology, judgment, and intuition—that RAND's other analysts mostly ignored. Still, the SSD's adoption of a "gaming" method, which reflected the other types of war games played at RAND, indicated that the social scientists were at least somewhat influenced by their colleagues. Indeed, the development of the political game illustrates the complexities of cross-disciplinary engagements in early Cold War research organizations. On one hand, the antagonistic relationship between RAND's disciplinary communities encouraged the social scientists to create a heuristic they affirmed was based on their unique epistemological and philosophical convictions. On the other hand, the gaming form their heuristic assumed implied that the social scientists were influenced by RAND's other divisions, even if it was only to the extent that they hoped to reformulate a commonly used approach on their own terms. This suggests that the concept of interdisciplinarity should move beyond its implication of collaboration to incorporate instances in which research agendas were defined against, but also shaped by, colleagues in other disciplines. Such a rethinking of the term may make it possible to trace how varieties of interdisciplinary interaction historically contributed to methodological innovation and knowledge production.

The complexities of cross-disciplinary engagements at RAND further highlight the multitude of research cultures present in early Cold War policy research organizations. Recently, Jamie Cohen-Cole defined an interdisciplinary research culture as one that "emphasized the exchange of ideas and methods," and a multidisciplinary culture as one that "involved researchers working in parallel." At RAND in the 1950s, a number of cultures, both inter- and multidisciplinary, coexisted simultaneously. For example, Speier fostered an intradivisional interdisciplinary culture through public criticism and peer review. He was far less interested in encouraging cross-divisional collaboration, and thus a multidisciplinary culture separated the SSD from RAND's other divisions. This was complicated, however, by the fact that the social scientists created a game, which indicated that an interdisciplinary but antagonistic culture characterized the relationship between some of the SSD's members and the rest of RAND. The manifold inter- and multidisciplinary cultures that permeated RAND, and which operated at different moments and in different spaces, demonstrated that several research cultures may coexist in one institution, interact with one another, and have multiple and unpredictable effects.[9]

By the time he arrived at RAND, Speier had thought extensively about interdisciplinarity within, though not without, the social sciences. In 1947–1948, his colleagues at the New School had charged him with creating a Division for International Studies. In his prospective plan for the division, Speier cautiously endorsed intra–social science interdisciplinary study, asserting that to know anything about "international politics," one "must know a great deal in various disciplines." Yet he also warned that to "safeguard against amateurishness and superficiality," an intellectual concerned with international studies should also "be a specialist in one of the social sciences." To reconcile these two conflicting claims, Speier insisted that an analyst of international politics "must be a specialist with a non-specialist's state of mind," able "to bring knowledge from fields other than his own to bear upon the understanding of the international matter he studies." In short, Speier's model analyst had a total perspective that mirrored the one held by Karl Mannheim's free-floating intellectual. Both Speier and Mannheim's idealized intellectual was able to see the social totality and incorporate relative knowledge derived from various perspectives and disciplines into a synoptic—and thus more accurate—viewpoint. To encourage the development of such a total outlook, when Speier became chief of the SSD he stressed intra–social scientific teamwork. Nevertheless, his skepticism of quantified and formal methods led him to mostly discourage cross-disciplinary collaboration among the social, natural, and engineering sciences.[10]

The SSD began officially operating in July 1948. As discussed in chapter 5, Frank Collbohm, RAND's first director, let Speier staff the division as he saw fit. Speier made certain to recruit not only his colleagues and friends but also "traditionalist" social scientists trained in qualitative and historical methods who were experts in particular world regions. He further allowed his researchers to freely choose the methods they used to study a given problem. The most commonly utilized approach in the SSD was the analysis of primary and secondary texts, but researchers also employed anthropological methods, interview analysis, psychoanalysis, and psychological analysis. What united the majority of the SSD's research was its disregard for quantitative and formal approaches.[11]

Speier promoted interdisciplinary collaboration in his division through regular staff meetings and oral and written peer review. In a 1950 working paper, he reported that "in the Social Science Division very few studies require the exclusive skill of any particular discipline alone. Almost all are being worked on cooperatively by various specialists. The mixed-team [i.e., interdisciplinary] approach of RAND is thus repeated on the social science level." Although this was an exaggeration—individuals or small teams produced most of the division's research—it is fair to describe the institutional culture of the SSD as interdisciplinary. Members exchanged methods, concepts, and ideas and sometimes worked together on larger projects. The division's very name—that is to say, the fact that it used the singular "social science" instead of "social sciences"—underlined Speier's sincere conviction, derived from Mannheim, that there was a uniquely "intellectual" or "social scientific" way of viewing the world that transcended disciplinary boundaries.[12]

Throughout the 1950s, RAND's social scientists collectively endorsed a multifaceted epistemology. First, members of the SSD maintained that

Figure 10. Speier with Leon Gouré *(foreground)* at a RAND meeting, ca. 1960s, *published with the permission of the RAND Corporate Archives, RAND Corporation*

knowledge was best acquired through research into the concrete facts of a given historical situation. Once such social, economic, cultural, and political facts were known, an analyst could reach a *Verstehen* (understanding) of an object of study that enabled her or him to offer policy advice. Second, RAND's social scientists made use of generalized, even law-like, assumptions to study foreign nations. For example, the majority of the SSD maintained that totalitarian regimes were always governed primarily by political elites. Such assumptions, however, were not considered to be universally valid across time but were understood to be accurate only in the specific historical circumstances of the mid-twentieth century. Finally, RAND's social scientists stressed that judgment and intuition were important means to decide which factors were most relevant when explaining causal relationships.[13]

Most RAND analysts outside the SSD did not respect its epistemology. From RAND's beginnings, the majority of those associated with the organization betrayed a condescending attitude toward the social sciences. For example, John D. Williams, the head of RAND's Mathematics Division, affirmed in a 1962 interview that in terms of their sophistication the social sciences "were perhaps in the fourteenth century as compared with the physical sciences, with engineering, and so on." Even Charles Hitch, the director of RAND's Economics Division, derided the social sciences. In a series of essays written over the course of the 1950s, Hitch stressed the need to provide formal solutions to national security problems, declaring that his major goal was "to expand the area of 'rational' decisions and reduce the element of 'judgment' or hunch in the planning process." While Hitch admitted that some problems presented "uncertainties" that mathematics and modeling could not tame, he nonetheless argued that in their analyses RAND's economists must elide the "complex and uncertain political and strategic factors" that operated in the real world. Though formal approaches were imperfect, Hitch asserted that they were better than "alternatives"—for instance, social science—that relied on "unsystematic or piecemeal consideration of problems" or "intuition."[14]

One sees a quite serious degrading of the social sciences in a 1957 RAND report, *Game Theory*, written by Herman Kahn, a physicist, and Irwin Mann, a mathematician. According to Kahn and Mann, "the technical vocabulary" of formal analysis was "superior to the competing vocabulary of the Social Scientist" because "it is rich and suggestive without being ambiguous." "In the Social Sciences," Kahn and Mann continued, "partly because there is no mathematical discipline, and even more because no one *feels* compelled to use the results and terminology of anybody else's papers, the meaning of the terms is often not quite clear or generally accepted." Moreover, Kahn and Mann claimed that whereas "in the mathematics field one does not publish papers unless he has results (theorems) which he thinks are important and new," the opposite was true in the social sciences. Although Kahn in particular was a controversial and aggressive figure, his and Mann's assertions reflected a view held by many RAND analysts: the social sciences were not really sciences but rather were disciplines that offered inchoate and unproved opinions as facts. They were subsidiary fields of study that, at best, complemented the work of more developed research areas. For these reasons, most RAND analysts maintained that genuine collaboration between the social sciences and other disciplines was impossible.[15]

More quotidian realities further pushed the social scientists to RAND's (literal and figurative) fringes. Most important, half the SSD was based in Washington, D.C. The 2,700 miles that separated Washington from Santa Monica militated against the development of an interdisciplinary vocabulary and framework that could have perhaps brought RAND's social scientists closer to the organization's engineers, economists, and physical scientists. Speier, it should be stressed, did not find the distance between the SSD and RAND's headquarters particularly troubling. As he reported to Nathan Leites, the social scientists based in California regularly informed him "that the advantage of having less noise and more air [in RAND's Santa Monica office] is offset by the disadvantage of spending more time talking to others." On both sides of the divide between the quals and the quants, there was significant suspicion of interdisciplinary cooperation.[16]

The lack of interdisciplinary collaboration between the SSD and the rest of RAND made it difficult for the social scientists to contribute to "systems analysis," the method in which RAND's leaders placed particular faith during the organization's first years. As RAND's *Second Annual Report* explained, in a systems analysis "all factors in an operation [i.e., a military operation] are considered simultaneously and estimates of the possible effects of changes are worked out for the parts as well as for the whole of the operation." The *Report* further asserted that the use of quantified methods and computing techniques in a systems analysis allowed "objective analysis [to be] substituted for individual or group opinion," which enabled one to determine more accurately than previously how a proposed operation would proceed. Systems analyses, in short, attempted to rationalize war; in the process, they largely ignored the ways in which culture, psychology, and politics affected a military operation's course. In his influential systems analysis that examined where to place U.S. overseas bases, Albert Wohlstetter clearly expressed the

RAND interest in the quantifiable: "The principal factors considered [in the study] are the distances from bases to targets, to favorable entry points into enemy defenses, to the source of base supply, and to the points from which the enemy can attack these bases. . . . The analysis is concerned with the joint effects of these factors on the costs of extending bomber radius; on how the enemy may deploy his defenses, and the numbers of our bombers lost to enemy fighters; on logistics costs; and on base vulnerability and our probable loss of bombers on the ground." As Edward Barlow explicated, systems analysts purposefully did not go "deeply into the political issues" because they believed that "we don't know what the other guy's going to do, so what we want is a new min-max game solution . . . where even with the worst he can do, we're still okay."[17]

Systems analysis so dominated RAND in the late 1940s and early 1950s that the organization's social scientists felt compelled to present their work as a complement to it. For instance, in a 1950 working paper Speier declared that "sometimes Social Science research can heighten the plausibility of assumptions made in a given design for a systems analysis. Sometimes it can suggest the introduction of new variables into a new systems analysis." That same year, Herbert Goldhamer composed an entire report on the importance of human factors in systems analysis in order to encourage "closer cooperation between systems analysts and specialists in the human sciences." Goldhamer made the case that systems analysis required the social sciences because "any attempt to consider what is in fact likely to happen and how one can maximize what one wants to happen would be futile without consideration of human factors." For the SSD's members, the obvious importance of "human factors" to military operations—and hence systems analysis—appeared as a means through which they could integrate themselves into RAND.[18]

Yet skepticism of the mathematization and modelization of the study of war inherent in systems analysis permeated the SSD at the same time that its members sought to increase their organizational cachet by presenting themselves as crucial to cross-divisional projects. Goldhamer, for example, critiqued systems analysts for their "D" (degradation) variable, which he avowed unrealistically "includes just about everything humans might do in an operating system which you prefer that they would not do." Moreover, because this measurement considered "the tremendous host of human factors . . . [only] 'at the end'" of a study, they were "taken to be independent of several parameters where such independence can scarcely be credited." Goldhamer further argued that RAND's analysts needed to refine their understanding of human behavior and be more willing to make use of "judgment, sensitized by contact with operating personnel and by general professional knowledge," when determining how to incorporate human factors into a systems analysis.[19]

Systems analysis was not the only method RAND's researchers developed to formalize the study of war. Famously, RAND was one of the first organizations to use John von Neumann and Oskar Morgenstern's game theory to analyze military operations and strategy. As early as September 1948, RAND mathematicians avowed that "the competition of opposing forces [in war] is similar to a game of strategy between opposing players." For their part, RAND's leaders placed great hopes in game theory and continuously trumpeted its importance. Like systems analysis, game theory engendered and reflected tensions between the SSD and the rest of RAND.[20]

RAND's social scientists were quite wary of game theory. In July 1949, Bernard Brodie declared that "for various reasons I do not share [von Neumann and Morgenstern's] conviction that their theory could be directly and profitably applied to problems of military strategy." Even those in the SSD, such as John L. Kennedy, who believed analysts could use mathematical models to explain human behavior maintained that game theory was philosophically naive because it "suffers from having encompassed only part of the problem [of human interaction], namely, the rational competitive part." For RAND's social scientists, who insisted that a variety of nonrational and structural factors motivated human behavior, game theory was too abstract to be a useful method for studying war.[21]

In a 1952 report that reviewed Harold Lasswell and Daniel Lerner's collection *The Policy Sciences,* Paul Kecskemeti offered a programmatic statement of the SSD's traditionalist perspective. Kecskemeti explicitly rejected the notion that only by using "rigorously quantitative terms" and methods can one "ensur[e] objectivity and reliability of the findings" of the social and policy sciences. According to him, "in all social science, no matter how 'quantified' the correlations are that we establish among phenomena, the basic data themselves always involve interpretation and hence judgment." But Kecskemeti did not confine his critique to the increasing quantification of the social sciences; he lambasted systems analysis as well. Mocking the "D" variable, Kecskemeti asserted that relying solely on quantifiable information "introduce[s] a sizable 'degradation factor' into our theorizing" by making systems analysts "lose much of the insight that we need to grasp precisely the most important factors [i.e., human factors] on which fundamental social processes depend." For Kecskemeti and his colleagues, any analysis that ignored politics, culture, and psychology or attempted to elide judgment was, as Speier proclaimed in the 1980s, "*Unfug*" (nonsense).[22]

In the opinion of RAND's social scientists, the organization's emphasis on systems analysis, game theory, and formalization generally demonstrated that their knowledge and methods were little valued. Over the course of the 1950s, the SSD developed a unique identity defined by its dismissal of RAND's mathematized mainstream. At the same time, though, the rift between the social scientists and the rest of RAND played an important role in inspiring the former to develop their most influential innovation, the political-military game. In this instance, interdisciplinary antagonism engendered methodological creativity.[23]

The SSD's political-military game highlighted how RAND's social scientists occupied a liminal methodological and temporal position. On one hand, there were nineteenth-century intellectuals such as Jacob Burckhardt, who argued that only through analysis of a specific historical situation could one obtain knowledge in the social sciences. On the other hand, there were political scientists of the last quarter of the twentieth century, such as Bruce Bueno de Mesquita, who examined political phenomena beyond the cultural, social, and psychological contexts in which they occurred. The social scientists at RAND existed in the space between these two extremes. They used simulation as a rational technique to model concrete but irrational (in the sense of being unpredictable) historical situations. In doing so, they hoped to provide an alternative to the emerging methodological abstractions of the postwar period.[24]

While the political game incorporated issues mostly ignored in systems analysis and game theory, such as politics, culture, and psychology, it nonetheless underlined the social scientists' desire, in some sense, to integrate into RAND. Beginning in the late 1940s and continuing throughout the 1950s, the idea of gaming, or simulation, swept through the organization. Analysts from all of RAND's divisions played tactical and strategic war, political, and planning games using a variety of approaches, including Monte Carlo methods, game theory, and computer analysis. Though the SSD's political game rejected formalization, the very embrace of simulation revealed the division's interest in joining the RAND avant-garde.[25]

The political-military game first emerged in the mid-1950s. In 1954, Victor Hunt, the administrative head of the SSD's Santa Monica office, traveled to Washington, D.C., on RAND business. While there, Hunt, Speier, Goldhamer, and Joseph Goldsen discussed the creation of a nonformalized simulation that would move beyond the games then being played at RAND. Most infuriating for the social scientists, RAND analysts had recently designed a game that simulated international politics, which the social scientists considered their area of expertise. This game, dubbed COW for "Cold War game," was, as an army report later described, "an elaborate, multi-lateral cold-war game formulated by mathematicians, [which] employed players to represent about twenty countries in a two-week playthrough." The game was highly formalized and imposed significant strictures on its players. First, as Alexander Mood, who helped develop the game, explained, it had "a fixed set of rules so that experience gained in one play is valid in other plays." Second, the game provided "quantities that players can manipulate" to test certain strategies and tactics. In the case of a game in which a player assumed the identity of a nation's commander-in-chief, for instance, such quantified factors included military forces, economic resources, national priorities, and so on.[26]

The social scientists considered the COW's entire design ridiculous. Culture, psychology, politics, and emotions—all of which were unquantifiable, unformalizable, and unpredictable—were what mattered in international relations, yet these were precisely what the COW abstracted or ignored. For this reason, Speier, Goldhamer, Goldsen, and Hunt decided to create a simulation that would model geopolitics in an explicitly qualitative manner. Although a proximate response to the COW, the social scientists' proposed "Cold War game"—a linguistic nod to the COW that implied that the SSD's simulation would (or should) replace it—was in essence a reaction to RAND's general privileging of quantification and formalization. In contrast to most of the research undertaken by the rest of RAND, the SSD's game would rely on players' qualitative knowledge of a given nation's politics, culture, and society, that is, on history. It would further emphasize judgment and insight. Once Hunt returned to California, the social scientists continued to discuss their game, and Speier charged Goldhamer with elucidating their ideas in writing. In October, Goldhamer released *Toward a Cold War Game*, which expounded the purposes and goals of the SSD's simulation.[27]

How did Speier and Goldhamer, the two primary architects of the SSD's game, arrive at the idea that a qualitative simulation was a useful means to analyze international relations? To answer this question, one must look to the pedagogy developed in the Weimar Republic by Karl Mannheim, a scholar personally and professionally connected to both Speier and Goldhamer. In his 1929 *Ideology and Utopia*, Mannheim attempted to develop a "science of politics" that he hoped would stabilize the chaotic atmosphere of Weimar democracy. According to Mannheim, empirical investigation demonstrated that the major problem of democratic politics "consists essentially of the inescapable necessity of understanding both oneself and one's adversary in the matrix of the social process." Without mutual understanding and empathy, Mannheim maintained, a stable democratic politics would never be achieved. To engender empathy in his students, Mannheim taught them the sociology of knowledge, which he believed would allow them to recognize the interconnections between political ideology and social position. Mannheim anticipated that this would encourage sociopolitical integration and democratic stability by, in the words of David Kettler and Volker Meja, fostering "a synoptic perspective that will give [political] competitors an awareness of a common direction and some shared conception of meaning."[28]

But Mannheim identified significant obstacles that augured against the creation of a stability-promoting science of politics. Most important, he noted that politics was intrinsically "irrational" in the sense that it was dynamic and ever changing; for this reason, it could not be formalized. Mannheim thus needed to discover a way to "teach men, in action, to understand . . . their opponents in the light of their actual motives and their position in the historical-social situation." To do so, he developed a novel pedagogy, or what he termed "a new framework," of simulation. Politics, Mannheim insisted, was practice, and students could learn how to operate within the political realm as he hoped they would only through "actual conduct"—that is to say, simulation:

> It seems certain that the interrelations in the specifically political sphere can be understood only in the course of discussion, the parties to which represent real forces in social life. There is no doubt, for example, that in order to develop the capacity for active orientation [i.e., using the sociology of knowledge to understand one's political antagonists], the teaching procedure must concentrate on events that are immediate and actual, and in which the student has an opportunity to participate. There is no more favorable opportunity for gaining insight into the peculiar structure of the realm of politics than by grappling with one's opponents about the most vital and immediate issues because on such occasions contradictory forces and points of view existing in a given period find expression.

Mannheim averred that participating in simulations helped students learn political empathy, which attenuated partisan hatred. Simulation also had the practical benefit of teaching students "to reorient [themselves] anew to an ever newly forming constellation of factors," which transformed them into effective political actors. Mannheim therefore presented his pedagogy as having two main benefits: first, it inculcated in students a respect for their fellow citizens; second, it taught them how to be political operators.[29]

Mannheim made explicit methodological claims to justify his science of politics. In particular, he framed his pedagogy as a defense against the spread of quantitative and formal methods, declaring in no uncertain terms that he rejected the notion "that nothing is . . . 'true' or 'knowable' except what could be presented as universally valid and necessary." Foreshadowing the arguments of Speier, Goldhamer, and their colleagues in the SSD, Mannheim affirmed that formal approaches foolishly excluded "all knowledge which depended . . . upon certain historical-social characteristics of men in the concrete." Mannheim considered quantification and formalization to be "attempt[s] to eliminate the interests and values which constitute the human element in man," and it was against this eradication of the human that he posed his science of politics.[30]

Chapter 1 detailed how Mannheim influenced Speier, but the sociologist also had a profound impact on Goldhamer. Goldhamer met Mannheim in the early 1930s when he audited at least one course with him at the London School of Economics, where Mannheim had fled after his dismissal from the University of Frankfurt in 1933. Furthermore, as a doctoral student at the University of Chicago, Goldhamer retained a keen interest in German sociology and was a member of an intellectual circle that included European sociologists such as Alexander von Schelting, himself a prominent critic of Mannheim. It is therefore highly likely that Goldhamer and his associates discussed Mannheim's *Ideology and Utopia* when Edward Shils and Louis Wirth translated the book into English in 1936. Moreover, according to Shils, Goldhamer was the "protégé" of Wirth, who, as discussed in chapter 2, was quite attracted to the German sociology of knowledge. This is all to say that Mannheim was a significant part of not only Speier's but also Goldhamer's intellectual world. Although the two social scientists did not cite Mannheim in the course of their work on the political game, the similarities between the goals and methods of Speier and Goldhamer's simulation and those of Mannheim's pedagogy suggest that the ties that bound the three sociologists remained strong across oceans and decades.[31]

Goldhamer began his first working paper on the simulation, October 1954's *Toward a Cold War Game*, with a critique of RAND games that "introduce a variety of simplifying assumptions and special restrictions which

Figure 11. Herbert Goldhamer *(standing)* addressing a group of military officers, possibly RAND's Air Force Advisory Group, with Frank Collbohm *(far left in background)*, Herman Kahn, and Henry Rowen *(both to the left of Goldhamer)* looking on, ca. 1950s, *published with the permission of the RAND Corporate Archives, RAND Corporation*

have" the effect of making simulations of international politics and war unrealistic. The SSD's political game, he asserted, would avoid this problem by "encourag[ing] the introduction of many real life details" that other games "might not deal with." Goldhamer explained that in the SSD's proposed simulation players would assume the identities of members of the executive branches of the United States, Soviet Union, and countries in the communist bloc; unlike the other games played at RAND, then, the social scientists' game would locate decision-making authority in the individual person, as opposed to the model, equation, or computer simulation. The game would have no defined rules or limits on action, save for the fact that players would not be allowed to pursue strategies or make moves that the simulation's referees deemed outlandish because they either did not conform with a nation's cultural or political heritage or because they exceeded a nation's practical capabilities. The simulation would also incorporate a "committee on nature" "responsible for introducing into the game various events which are not introduced by the players," such as a drought. Goldhamer concluded that through its simulation of real-world decision making and real-world occurrences, the SSD's game would provide "a setting within which [players'] judgment and knowledge can be put to work in a fruitful manner."[32]

In 1955 and 1956, RAND analysts played four political-military games. Because the fourth game of April 1956 was the most developed and served as the model for later simulations, its mechanics are described in detail. This game was projected into the future and simulated American and Soviet actions in Western Europe starting on January 1, 1957. In the course of play, each team's moves were made via a short report in which a team's members stated "the motives of their moves and the expectations on which they were based." The game's referees could accept or reject a move based on their own knowledge and judgment, as well as background papers to which only they were privy. If referees rejected a move, a team could request that they explain the logic for rejection in writing. There were two classes of moves: they either were public and known to all players or were classified and known only to the referees. To replicate real-world intelligence leaks, however, referees could make certain secret information or moves publicly known. In the end, the game lasted three weeks, during which the players composed 150 papers and simulated approximately half a year's worth of events.[33]

In a post hoc working paper, Ewald Schnitzer remarked that the game's players found that "the necessity of weighing constantly the consequences of one's moves in . . . the political universe has a beneficial effect on [their] political judgment." Joseph Goldsen further testified in a different working paper that the game contributed to "a sharply heightened realization of the multivalence of political acts, that is, the multiple effects, in time and scope and the conflicting effects that have to be anticipated in sound policy planning." Additionally, numerous players asserted that the simulation was more valuable than the other games popular at RAND. For example, W. Phillips Davison avowed in yet another working paper that the game was a needed corrective to the "'cold war game' in which political dimensions were assigned quantitative values so that the relative worth of alternative strategies could be assessed mathematically." According to Davison, such simulations relied on an "oversimplification of the situation" that made them "of doubtful [scientific] value for the assessment of political strategies and tactics in the real world." In this way, RAND's social scientists affirmed that their game was more realistic, and hence more scientific, than the organization's other simulations.[34]

Speier and Goldhamer published the first public statement on the political game, "Some Observations on Political Gaming," in the October 1959 issue of *World Politics*, one of the nation's premier political science journals.

In this essay, Speier and Goldhamer emphasized the game's avoidance of "schematic simplifications of the international political situation," its desire "to simulate as faithfully as possible much of [geopolitics'] complexity," and its ability to improve players' judgment. Mannheim's influence emerged clearly in the *World Politics* piece. In an echo of *Ideology and Utopia*, Speier and Goldhamer argued that the game "performs an educational function" by giving "players a new insight into the pressures, the uncertainties, and the moral and intellectual difficulties under which foreign policy decisions are made." The authors further insisted, in language that mirrored Mannheim's, that the experience of simulation encouraged "participants to acquire an overview of a political situation" that allowed them to understand their opponents' motivations and to recognize the interconnectedness of the different spheres of international relations. Speier and Goldhamer professed that by viewing the realm of geopolitics in its totality—a framework that built on Mannheim's call for intellectuals and students to embrace a "total perspective"—players learned to operate more effectively within it.[35]

In its goals and methods, the SSD's political game reflected the influence of Mannheim's pedagogy. Both were simulations premised on the assumption that experiencing a simulacrum of an environment was the most efficacious means to teach people how to interact within it. Another major aim of both simulations was to tame a dynamic political atmosphere that, if allowed to descend into chaos, could have disastrous consequences. Mannheim, Speier, and Goldhamer also each subscribed to the notion that their simulations would enable those who participated in them to obtain a total view of the political process, which would increase their skills and engender understanding. Furthermore, the simulations were both responses to the rise of social science quantification and, as such, were minimally formalized. The striking similarities between Mannheim's pedagogy and Speier and Goldhamer's game, coupled with the personal and professional links that connected the three intellectuals, suggest that Speier and Goldhamer drew on Mannheim's work to develop their simulation.

The political game significantly differed from the other games played at RAND in the 1950s. In his August 1959 précis on war gaming, *An Introduction to War Games*, Milton Weiner divided RAND's other simulations into four categories: mathematical games, machine and man–machine games, board and bookkeeping games, and umpired games. Mathematical games used game theory to determine the utility of given military tactics or strategies. For example, if analysts wanted to establish the most effective way for a military unit to approach an enemy in a particular geographical environment, they would develop a model in which a Red Team attempted to attack a Blue Team. Each team would then be given a limited number of tactical choices. Thus, the Red Team had the option of traveling down either a covered mountain road that was difficult to traverse or an easily walked desert road that remained unconcealed, while the Blue Team—which knew the Red Team would attack but did not know where—had the ability either to deploy a large force of bombers against the mountain road and a small force against the desert road or vice versa. Analysts would then determine, based on strict rules and their knowledge of technical capabilities, how many Red units the Blue Team destroyed given various choices. In all mathematical games, analysts assumed they could determine the precise results of specific actions.[36]

Mathematical games incorporated no knowledge of a nontechnical kind. In these games, players ignored psychological factors (Were the soldiers or pilots anxious? Did they believe in their mission?), political factors (Was the described incident occurring during wartime or peacetime? If during the latter, was the Blue Team willing to wipe out all Red units, or did it just want to send a message to signal resolve?), and sociocultural factors (Did the Red Team believe attacking via concealment was cowardly, thus making it more likely Red units would perform poorly if they chose to attack via the mountain road?). In mathematical games, social scientific knowledge of the type privileged by the SSD was disregarded.

Computerized games were the second type of simulation Weiner identified. These simulations considered more variables than mathematical games, and indeed analyzed human factors, such as the probability of a pilot making navigational errors, in addition to technical and military factors. However, in these games human and nonhuman variables were assigned numerical values or probability distributions, which imbued them with a static quality. Besides pure computerized games, there were man–machine games that incorporated human participants who decided the order and types of attacks pursued in a given simulation. A computer then determined which combination of attacks was most effective given differently valued variables. Board and bookkeeping games were the third type of simulation Weiner discussed. The only major difference between these games and computerized games was that, in the former, human beings, instead of machines, calculated outcomes.

In computerized and board and bookkeeping games, social scientific, primarily psychological, knowledge was used only before a game began to help determine the various values of given variables. Once these static values were distributed, social science retreated from the scene. These games ignored the dynamism that characterized real-world interactions and reduced war to a mechanistic encounter devoid of political and cultural meaning. Even when human factors were included in these types of games, they were given a technical gloss that mirrored the "D" variable of systems analyses. These games thus reflected the subsidiary position that RAND's economists, mathematicians, engineers, and natural scientists assigned to social science.

The final type of war game Weiner examined were games managed by human umpires. Like the SSD's political-military simulation, an umpired game lacked definite rules; nevertheless, unlike the referees in the SSD's game, umpires used "standard, numerical, or mutually agreeable factors wherever possible" to determine a move's outcome and referred to "judgment or experience" only "when necessary." Though Weiner downplayed the importance of judgment in his discussion of umpired games, he admitted that in two cases judgment proved potentially critical to a game's result. The first occurred when a "judgment applies to a particular event or situation that is so important as to affect the entire outcome of the game," while the second arose when a "judgment applies to some set of effects or actions that occur with great frequency . . . such that over the entire game they can accumulate in a manner that affects the evaluation." In these cases, Weiner declared that "it may be necessary to review the game, taking several different values for the effect to determine how sensitive the evaluation [i.e., the game's outcome] is to the judgment." Once these values were taken, Weiner implied, the game could be made more accurate by recalibrating its result. Even in umpired games, whose benefit derived from the looseness of their structure, most RAND analysts hoped to create as rigid—and hence repeatable and testable—a simulation as possible.[37]

RAND's social scientists rejected Weiner's opinion that these types of war games could be employed "to obtain a more useful and general [quantified] model of military operations." Still, the SSD's members did not totally dismiss their RAND colleagues; indeed, the division's embrace of gaming may be read as a reflection of the social scientists' desire to integrate into RAND while maintaining their integrity in an environment where their methods, knowledge, and commitments were frequently scorned. Nonetheless, the epistemological gap between the SSD and RAND's other divisions proved too wide to bridge, and throughout the 1950s the social scientists remained on the organization's fringes. But the story of the political game was not one of failure. In fact, it proved to be the SSD's most lasting contribution to the theory and practice of international relations.[38]

As Joseph Goldsen reported in a working paper, Speier, Goldhamer, and others in the SSD considered the game "a uniquely valuable instrument for training and educational purposes" and heavily promoted it throughout the military-intellectual complex even as they determined that it was too expensive and time-consuming to play at RAND itself. In 1956, Speier presented on the game at a Social Science Research Council summer seminar; in 1957, he did the same at the Center for Advanced Study in the Behavioral Sciences; and in 1959, he discussed it at the U.S. Military Academy at West Point. For his part, Goldhamer gave lectures on the game at the Army War College and presented on it at the American Political Science Association's annual meeting, while Goldsen promoted the game at Yale and Princeton. Furthermore, as Speier and Goldhamer noted in "Some Observations on Political Gaming," members of the SSD held "informal discussions about political gaming . . . with personnel of the Department of State, the Center for International Affairs at Harvard, the Brookings Institution, Northwestern University, and the Massachusetts Institute of Technology." Through both formal and informal means, RAND's social scientists spread knowledge about the game among the United States' academic, think tank, and policy elite.[39]

MIT proved particularly crucial to the political game's academic dissemination. In 1956–1957, Ithiel de Sola Pool, a friend of Speier's who was chief of the Research Program in International Communication at MIT's Center for International Studies, led political games in his communications seminar. The following academic year, W. Phillips Davison took a leave of absence from RAND to become a visiting professor of political science at MIT. In Cambridge, Davison directed a political game that came to the attention of Lincoln Bloomfield, a professor of political science and former State Department official associated with CIS. In 1958–1959, Bloomfield, with the aid of RAND's Paul Kecskemeti, directed a game that, as he and a colleague recounted, "revolved around a hypothetical international crisis stemming from the demise of the head of the Polish government." This game was played by senior faculty from MIT, Harvard, Yale, and Columbia. Thereafter, the political-military game began to spread throughout the academy.[40]

In January 1961, John F. Kennedy became president of the United States. Academic expertise subsequently became a highly valued commodity in Washington, and manifold RAND analysts entered Robert McNamara's Department of Defense. Soon after Kennedy's inauguration, Henry Rowen, a former RAND economist cum deputy assistant secretary of defense for international security affairs, recommended that the newly established Joint War Games Control Group (JWGCG) organize political-military simulations modeled on the one developed by the SSD. The members of the JWGCG accepted Rowen's suggestion, and in September, Thomas Schelling, a RAND consultant and professor of economics at Harvard, directed a game at Camp David based on the Second Berlin Crisis, which began in 1958 when First Secretary of the Communist Party Nikita Khrushchev declared that the Western allies must leave West Berlin. Numerous high-level officials and consultants, including "DeWitt Armstrong, McGeorge Bundy, Alain Enthoven, Carl Kaysen, Henry Kissinger, Robert Komer, John McNaughton, Walt Rostow, . . . Rowen, and Seymour Weiss," participated in the game. Upon its completion, the game's players deemed the simulation a useful means through which one could practice international politics, and as a result the JWGCG—which became the Joint War Games Agency in 1963—organized at least four games a year throughout the remainder of the 1960s. Speier and Goldhamer's simulation thus became one of the methods decision makers utilized to help them develop foreign policy.[41]

Though the RAND Corporation is most famous for its analysts' use of formal methods, it was once an organization where traditionalist social scientists found a home, albeit a precarious one. The epistemological convictions of RAND's social scientists distanced them intellectually from the organization's other divisions. This rift prevented the social scientists from fully assimilating into RAND and engendered antagonistic exchanges that eventually prompted the SSD to create the political-military simulation. Unlike the rest of the games played at RAND, the SSD's simulation endorsed the idea that political life was, by definition, unquantifiable. RAND's social scientists, however, insisted that their game did not reject rationalism. Instead, they argued that by reproducing the irrational dynamism of international politics, the political simulation was a heuristic that was more scientific than RAND's other models and methods. For Speier and his colleagues, effective policy analysis required accepting—indeed embracing—the limits of knowledge.

Conclusion

Speier, Expertise, and Democracy after 1960

RAND reorganized in late 1960. As part of this restructuring, Speier, along with RAND's other division chiefs, vacated his position to join a Research Council that was intended to become an organization-wide advisory board. Though Speier served as head of the Research Council in 1961–1962, the new group did not have much influence. RAND was changing, but Speier failed to change with it. When the organization diversified into domestic research, Speier continued to write solely about foreign policy. His gaze remained fixed on Germany, and U.S.-German relations occupied him throughout the 1960s. But as the Cold War's center shifted from Europe to the Third World, Speier's Eurocentric focus became less vital to policymakers. Speier never became a development expert, did not write much about counterinsurgency, and though he spent a year at the Council on Foreign Relations and continued to consult for the government, his work on U.S.-German relations was never particularly influential. When the Kennedy administration called manifold RAND analysts to Washington, D.C., the best and the brightest ignored him. By the early 1960s, Speier's influence was at an end.[1]

With more free time, Speier returned to intellectual interests he had mostly ignored since the 1920s. He translated into English portions of the seventeenth-century author Hans Jakob Christoffel von Grimmelshausen's picaresque novel *Simplicissimus*, which told the story of Simplicius Simplicissimus, a rogue roaming through Europe during the Thirty Years War (1618–1648). Speier saw something of himself in Grimmelshausen. Both Speier and Grimmelshausen's lives were shaped by "total war"; both were "child[ren] of the lower middle class"; and both worked for elites from whom they "gained insight into the legal and economic affairs" of state. Most important, Speier identified Grimmelshausen as someone who understood "that man's nature makes the realization of the good order impossible." For Speier, the twentieth century had revealed time and again that evil can and will triumph. He concluded that life was tragic and was attracted to an author who felt the same way three hundred years before.[2]

The ghosts of Weimar haunted Speier throughout the 1960s. His anxieties regarding democracy's weakness emerged most clearly in his analysis of the anti–Vietnam War West German student protest movement. In Speier's opinion, the protests suggested that Weimar's last years were repeating themselves. He was apoplectic that at demonstrations, he witnessed students "bearing Viet Cong flags, waving them, wearing Viet Cong emblems, not calling for peace in Viet Nam but for more Viet Nams to defeat the United States, for the end of NATO, not for the end of the Warsaw Pact, . . . not a word about terror of the North Vietnamese but about germicide and immorality of the Americans in Vietnam and elsewhere." Speier insisted that the protesters' "extra-parliamentary opposition"—which mirrored the antidemocratic opposition of the Nazis and communists in Weimar—sought "to undermine the legitimate authority and subvert the political institutions of the German republic by provocation." While Speier did not believe the students had any real chance of taking over the government, he was deeply nervous that they would engender a "backlash . . . on the right," which might stimulate serious instability throughout West Germany. In the twilight of his career, Speier was convinced that "the terror, . . . the provocation, the violence, and the unmanageability of the people, and the undermining of authority" he observed throughout the Federal Republic pointed to another crisis of German democracy.[3]

Speier's diagnosis was wrong; West Germany was in no danger of falling prey to political extremism. He had been in the establishment for so long, and had worked so hard to defend democracy in ways he saw fit, that he could not countenance any resistance to the claims of the United States, a country that for him both saved and embodied Western civilization. Speier could not see that the students might be correct to protest the destructive U.S. war in Vietnam. Instead, he projected Weimar onto a situation that was

Figure 12. Speier at his retirement party, receiving a plaque from Henry Rowen, 1969, *published with the permission of the RAND Corporate Archives, RAND Corporation*

not analogous. The world had changed, but Speier did not, perhaps could not, change with it. Either way, RAND required its employees to retire at the age of sixty-five. In the autumn of 1969—one year short of his forced retirement—Speier left RAND to accept a position as the Robert M. MacIver Professor of Sociology and Government at the University of Massachusetts at Amherst.[4]

Speier spent the rest of his life disconnected from the power structures of Washington, D.C. He published a variety of essays on political humor, communication, and literature and co-edited, with his old colleagues Harold Lasswell and Daniel Lerner, the three-volume compendium *Propaganda and Communication in World History*, which remains the major reference work for the historical study of propaganda. Though many of these endeavors were thought-provoking, they nonetheless lacked the vitality of his earlier writings. Speier's interest in contemporary scholarship had waned, and in 1973, after only four short years, he retired from the University of Massachusetts—where he was honored in 1974 with a conference whose invitees included Daniel Bell, Reinhard Bendix, Lewis Coser, Herbert Goldhamer, Stanley Milgram, Robert Nisbet, Norman Podhoretz, Arthur Schlesinger Jr., Edward Shils, and James Q. Wilson—and settled into life in Hartsdale, New York.[5]

In his last seventeen years of life, Speier, as his friend Henry Kellerman recalled, "returned more and more to memories of the past." The past, in fact, refused to remain past. At the urging of the German historian Jürgen Kocka, in 1977 Speier finally published an edited version of his long-buried *Habilitationsschrift* on white-collar workers, which was released in English in 1986. He also produced a biographical essay on Emil Lederer, published portions of diaries he kept during visits to Germany between 1945 and 1955, wrote an autobiographical piece for the journal *Exilforschung*, and released an essay collection provocatively titled *The Truth in Hell*. Speier was further happy to sit for interviews regarding his experiences as an exile from Nazi Germany, and his interwar passport photo adorns the poster for the documentary film *The Exiles* (1989).[6]

The old émigré camaraderie from the 1930s returned in the 1970s when Speier reentered the New School's orbit. He became a visiting professor emeritus and taught some classes for the school's sociology department; received an honorary doctorate of humane letters from the school; participated in the fortieth and fiftieth anniversary celebrations for the University in Exile held in Bad Godesberg (June 1974), New York (April 1984), and West Berlin (December 1984); and connected Claus-Dieter Krohn, the author of a German-language book on the University in Exile, with the University of Massachusetts Press, which translated Krohn's book into English. When, months after the Cold War ended, Speier passed away on vacation in Sarasota, Florida—the last of the University in Exile's founding members to do so—the New School held a memorial service in his honor. At this event, the historian Ira Katznelson, then dean of the school, provided the most profound, and in my opinion accurate, summation of Speier's life. Speier, Katznelson remarked, was "a scholar who looked modernity in the eye and did not blink."[7]

The military-intellectual complex Speier helped create came under intense criticism in the 1960s. Even before then, some scholars had expressed discomfort with intellectuals' attachment to the emergent structures of the

Figure 13. Speier at the University in Exile's fiftieth anniversary celebration, standing in front of a photo of the university's founding members, April 1984, *photo courtesy of the New School*

national security state. In his 1956 *The Power Elite*, for example, C. Wright Mills—Speier's erstwhile epistolary partner and a scholar influenced by Karl Mannheim's writings on intellectuals—excoriated "men of knowledge" who worked with political and military elites. Mills averred that because defense intellectuals gained influence only when they endorsed ideas supported by their government patrons, they could not fulfill their primary social function of criticizing power. "Accordingly," Mills insisted, "in so far as intellectuals serve power directly . . . they often do so unfreely." Mills maintained that modern intellectuals needed to recognize that "only when mind has an autonomous basis, independent of power, but powerfully related to it, can mind exert its force in the shaping of human affairs."[8]

In the short term, Mills's critique largely fell on deaf ears; by 1968, as Joy Rohde has noted, "nearly 40 percent of all social science PhDs were employed full-time in [government-supported] research and development projects." Nonetheless, the intellectual consensus that undergirded scholars' work for the military-intellectual complex began to fray in the mid-1960s as a result of the United States' calamitous intervention in Vietnam. Noam Chomsky, an MIT linguist, gave voice to this transition in his biting 1967 essay "The Responsibility of Intellectuals." "It is the responsibility of intellectuals," Chomsky unambiguously proclaimed, "to speak the truth and to expose lies."

However, he lamented, American intellectuals consciously disregarded this duty. To prove his point, Chomsky highlighted multiple examples in which intellectuals aligned with power over truth, from Arthur Schlesinger Jr.'s lies about the Bay of Pigs invasion to Walt Rostow's false assertions about Soviet aggression. In language that harkened back to Mannheim's *Ideology and Utopia*, Chomsky bemoaned that in modern America "scholar-experts [were] replacing the free-floating intellectuals of the past" who used their detachment from the state to speak truth to power.[9]

Chomsky's blistering essay reflected a widespread disillusionment with defense intellectuals that spread among left-wing critics of U.S. foreign policy in the late 1960s and early 1970s. In that moment of left-wing ascendance, defense intellectuals were criticized as militaristic servants of power, destroyers of intellectual freedom, and a cause of the Vietnam War. These denunciations, which were bolstered by an anti-Vietnam student protest movement that took aim at institutions like RAND and CIS, eventually compelled the Department of Defense to significantly reduce its foreign area research budget. At the same time, several university-based organizations of the military-intellectual complex, including the Stanford Research Institute, American University's Center for Research on Social Systems, and George Washington University's Human Resources Research Institute, were forced off U.S. campuses. To contemporary observers, the left appeared to be on the verge of defeating the forces of intellectual militarism, and many looked forward to an era in which knowledge would be freed from power's perversions.[10]

The left-wing ascendance of the late 1960s and early 1970s, however, was short-lived; by the late 1970s, the military-intellectual complex had completely recovered. Since that moment, for instance, analysts working at RAND have influenced U.S. foreign policy on issues ranging from nation building to arms control, from NATO expansion to counterinsurgency. As these examples suggest, defense intellectuals, working for the military-intellectual complex Speier and his colleagues helped create at midcentury, have remained important actors in the formulation of U.S. foreign and national security policy.[11]

Nevertheless, the conditions, anxieties, and assumptions that shaped the military-intellectual complex and the national security state of which it formed a part are no longer relevant. The United States is the most powerful nation on earth, and, in my opinion, U.S. and Western democracy confront no external existential threats. Concerns about democracy's weakness, which are partially based in interwar Euro-American *Angst*, must therefore be rethought. In particular, it is worth considering whether Speier was wise to insist that the public have little influence on the careers of defense intellectuals. In the thousands of pages Speier wrote, he never once mentioned the notion of expert accountability. Like many in his generation, Speier assumed that defense intellectuals, or the decision makers to whom they reported, would naturally police themselves. But in the last seventy years, many experts whose policy advice contributed to disastrous decisions were never sanctioned for their recommendations. The career trajectory of Paul Wolfowitz—who received a PhD in political science from the University of Chicago, where he was advised by Speier's RAND colleague Albert Wohlstetter—is a case in point. As undersecretary of defense in the George W. Bush administration, Wolfowitz helped lead the United States into the ill-conceived Iraq War before moving from the Defense Department to the World Bank to the American Enterprise Institute to the foreign policy team of 2016 Republican presidential candidate Jeb Bush, with apparent lack of remorse or consequences.[12]

The public has a right to hold experts accountable for their advice. Indeed, this is the only way to ensure that expert governance functions effectively. A system that does not reprimand behavior that results in negative consequences is a system doomed to repeat its mistakes. Nonetheless, there is no simple way for a system of expert accountability to be established. Experts, for example, cannot, and should not, be held legally liable for sincere, if wrong (in hindsight), counsel. Still, at the very least it seems reasonable to work to create a moral norm that prevents experts who contributed to ruinous policies from remaining in or securing comfortable, and frequently lucrative, governmental, nongovernmental, or private positions. Moreover, when government officials purchase advice from institutions like RAND, the public should be able to view these recommendations. Currently, officials circumvent public disclosure of national security advice by classifying information they consider embarrassing or damaging. Though some national security information must of course be kept secret, democracy cannot function when too much of it is. It might therefore be wise for Congress to be more assertive in its oversight of the classification system or for there to be a group, responsible to Congress, tasked with guaranteeing that classification is not abused. If Americans were to develop means by which experts were morally and professionally sanctioned for poor advice, and if we were able to halt overclassification and promote transparency, we could help, in however small a way, bring certain practices of democracy back from the extended exile in which they have remained since the early Cold War.

Abbreviations

AAF	Army Air Forces
AD	Analysis Division
ADO	Area Division for Occupied Areas
BBC	British Broadcasting Corporation
BSP	Behavioral Sciences Program
CASBS	Center for Advanced Study in the Behavioral Sciences
CIA	Central Intelligence Agency
CIS	Center for International Studies
COI	Office of the Coordinator of Information
DDP	German Democratic Party
DVP	German People's Party
FBI	Federal Bureau of Investigation
FBIS	Foreign Broadcast Intelligence Service
FBMS	Foreign Broadcast Monitoring Service
FCC	Federal Communications Commission
FIS	Foreign Information Service

GDR	German Democratic Republic
HICOG	High Commission for Occupied Germany
ICD	Information Control Division
JWGCG	Joint War Games Control Group
KPD	Communist Party of Germany
MIT	Massachusetts Institute of Technology
OB	Overseas Branch
OIC	Office of International Information and Cultural Affairs
OMGUS	Office of Military Government, United States
OSS	Office of Strategic Services
OWI	Office of War Information
PEPCO	Political and Economic Projects Committee
PSB	Psychological Strategy Board
RIAS	Radio in the American Sector
SED	Socialist Unity Party of Germany
SPD	Social Democratic Party of Germany
SSD	Social Science Division
SSRC	Social Science Research Council
USIA	United States Information Agency

Archival and Source Abbreviations

AJP-N	Alvin Johnson Papers, Nebraska
DDEL	Dwight D. Eisenhower Presidential Library
FAD	*From the Ashes of Disgrace*
FFR	Ford Foundation Records
HSTL	Harry S. Truman Presidential Library
HUA	Heidelberg University Archives
MITASC	Massachusetts Institute of Technology Archives and Special Collections
NACP	National Archives at College Park
NSASC	New School Archives and Special Collections
PSBCFS	Psychological Strategy Board Central File Series
PSBF	Psychological Strategy Board Files
RAC	Rockefeller Archive Center
RCA	RAND Corporate Archives
RFR	Rockefeller Foundation Records
RG	Record Group

RHPI	RAND History Project Interviews
SP	Hans Speier Papers
UEG	*Uprising in East Germany*
USDDO	U.S. Declassified Documents Online
WPDG	Weekly Propaganda Directive, Germany

Notes

Introduction

1. Hans Speier, "Comment on the Research Project on Peace," October 26, 1939, 1, 3, Folder 79, Box 7, Hans Speier Papers, German and Jewish Intellectual Émigré Collection, M. E. Grenander Department of Special Collections and Archives, University Libraries, University at Albany, State University of New York, Albany, NY (hereafter SP).

2. Speier, "Comments on Current Policy Requirements," November 21, 1949, 4, Folder 32, Box 9, SP. For the prominence of the elite theory of democracy in the early Cold War, see Daniel Bessner, "The Night Watchman: Hans Speier and the Making of the American National Security State" (PhD diss., Duke University, 2013), 212–221; Nils Gilman, *Mandarins of the Future: Modernization Theory in Cold War America* (Baltimore: Johns Hopkins University Press, 2003), 47–56; Udi Greenberg, *The Weimar Century: German Émigrés and the Ideological Foundations of the Cold War* (Princeton: Princeton University Press, 2014); Andrew Jewett, *Science, Democracy, and the American University: From the Civil War to the Cold War* (New York: Cambridge University Press, 2012), 358–360; Peter Mandler, *Return from the Natives: How Margaret Mead Won the Second World War and Lost the Cold War* (New Haven: Yale University Press, 2013), 211; Joy Rohde, *Armed with Expertise: The Militarization of American Social Research during the Cold War* (Ithaca: Cornell University Press, 2013), 42–53; Jeremi Suri, *Henry Kissinger and the American Century* (Cambridge, MA: Harvard University Press, 2007), chapter 1; Robert B. Westbrook, *John Dewey and American Democracy* (Ithaca: Cornell University Press, 1991), 543–546.

3. For the notion that a "continuing crisis [that] generated perpetual fear," coupled with a "sense of permanent emergency," undergirded postwar thinking about national security, see Ira Katznelson, *Fear Itself: The New Deal and the Origins of Our Time* (New York: W. W. Norton, 2013), 481–482.

4. As far as I can tell, the term "defense intellectual" first became popular in the early 1960s, after the John F. Kennedy administration recruited manifold social scientists into its ranks. See, for example, Stewart Alsop, "Master of the Pentagon," *Saturday Evening Post*, August 5, 1961, 45. The term "military-intellectual complex" comes from Ron Theodore Robin, *The Making of the Cold War Enemy: Culture and Politics in the Military-Intellectual Complex* (Princeton: Princeton University Press, 2001), and was adapted from Stuart W. Leslie, *The Cold War and American Science: The Military-Industrial-Academic Complex at MIT and Stanford* (New York: Columbia University Press, 1993). Scholars who have explored social scientists who worked with the national security state include Michael A. Bernstein and Allen Hunter, eds., "The Cold War and Expert Knowledge: New Essays on the History of the National Security State," special issue, *Radical History Review* 63 (Fall 1995); Michael A. Bernstein, *A Perilous Progress: Economists and Public Purpose in Twentieth-Century America* (Princeton: Princeton University Press, 2001); Carol Cohn, "Sex and Death in the Rational World of Defense Intellectuals," *Signs* 12, no. 4 (Summer 1987), 687–718; David C. Engerman, *Know Your Enemy: The Rise and Fall of America's Soviet Experts* (New York: Oxford University Press, 2009); Matthew Farish, *The Contours of America's Cold War* (Minneapolis: University of Minnesota Press, 2010); Ellen Herman, *The Romance of American Psychology: Political Culture in the Age of Experts* (Berkeley: University of California Press, 1995); Daniel Immerwahr, *Thinking Small: The United States and the Lure of Community Development* (Cambridge, MA: Harvard University Press, 2015); Bruce Kuklick, *Blind Oracles: Intellectuals and War from Kennan to Kissinger* (Princeton: Princeton University Press, 2006); Michael E. Latham, *Modernization as Ideology: American Social Science and "Nation Building" in the Kennedy Era* (Chapel Hill: University of North Carolina Press, 2000); Michael E. Latham, *The Right Kind of Revolution: Modernization, Development, and U.S. Foreign Policy from the Cold War to the Present* (Ithaca: Cornell University Press, 2011); Mandler, *Return*; Gilman, *Mandarins*; Robin, *Making*; Rohde, *Armed*; Marc Trachtenberg, *History and Strategy* (Princeton: Princeton University Press, 1991). The literature that examines natural scientists' relationship with the national security state is similarly large, though it falls outside the scope of this book. For a recent example, see Sarah Bridger, *Scientists at War: The Ethics of Cold War Weapons Research* (Cambridge, MA: Harvard University Press, 2015), which contains an extensive bibliography of this field on 276–277n11.

5. Throughout the text, when I refer to someone as a defense intellectual, I do not mean to imply that this was necessarily his or her primary self-identification. Rather, it denotes that the individual being described belonged to a community of scholars who worked or consulted for the national security state, even if this was not his or her principal occupation.

6. RAND and similar institutions unquestionably had deep origins in U.S. culture that were unrelated to the midcentury desire to ensure that public opinion did not shape U.S. foreign relations. First, RAND represented the culmination of a seventy-year-old, transatlantic, and progressive project in which intellectuals attempted, in Daniel Rodgers's words, "to establish new forms of authority by colonizing the social space between university professorships and expert government service." Second, RAND belonged to the American tradition in which the state, as William Novak highlights, "distributed public goods and powers widely through the private sector." Third, RAND emerged from the fin de siècle American practice, adapted from Germany, of U.S. intellectuals working through intermediary institutions to inform policy. Daniel T. Rodgers, *Atlantic Crossings: Social Politics in a Progressive Age* (Cambridge, MA: Harvard University Press, 1998), 108, 94; William J. Novak, "The Myth of the 'Weak' American State," *American Historical Review* 113, no. 3 (June 2008), 769.

7. In the 1950s, Congress occasionally investigated research conducted by defense intellectuals. The most dramatic example occurred in 1958, when Paul Kecskemeti, Speier's employee in RAND's Social Science Division and a fellow European émigré, published a book

that analyzed when and if it would ever be prudent for the United States to make a "strategic surrender." Kecskemeti's book resulted in a firestorm of anger and condemnation, which eventually led Congress to pass a resolution that forbade the funding of any studies that could be considered defeatist. See Paul Kecskemeti, *Strategic Surrender: The Politics of Victory and Defeat* (Stanford: Stanford University Press, 1958); James E. King Jr., "Strategic Surrender: The Senate Debate and the Book," *World Politics* 11, no. 3 (April 1959), 418–429.

8. Speier, "Current Policy," 2, 6.

9. Michael J. Hogan, *A Cross of Iron: Harry S. Truman and the Origins of the National Security State, 1945–1954* (New York: Cambridge University Press, 1998); Douglas T. Stuart, *Creating the National Security State: A History of the Law That Transformed America* (Princeton: Princeton University Press, 2008).

10. Janet Farrell Brodie, "Learning Secrecy in the Early Cold War: The RAND Corporation," *Diplomatic History* 35, no. 4 (September 2011), 643–670; Robert D. Dean, "Introduction: Cultures of Secrecy in Postwar America," *Diplomatic History* 35, no. 4 (September 2011), 611–613; Mary Dudziak, *War-Time: An Idea, Its History, Its Consequences* (New York: Oxford University Press, 2012), chapter 3; Joan Hoff, *A Faustian Foreign Policy from Woodrow Wilson to George W. Bush: Dreams of Perfectibility* (New York: Cambridge University Press, 2008), chapter 5; Anna Kasten Nelson, "The Evolution of the National Security State: Ubiquitous and Endless," in *The Long War: A New History of U.S. National Security Policy since World War II*, ed. Andrew J. Bacevich (New York: Columbia University Press, 2007), 265–301; Shawn J. Parry-Giles, *The Rhetorical Presidency, Propaganda, and the Cold War, 1945–1955* (Westport, CT: Praeger, 2002), chapters 3, 5, and 6; Katznelson, *Fear*, chapters 11–12.

11. Hogan, *Cross of Iron*, 14, 16–17.

12. Dudziak, *War-Time*, 91.

13. Rüdiger Graf earlier made a similar point. See Rüdiger Graf, "Either-Or: The Narrative of 'Crisis' in Weimar Germany and in Historiography," *Central European History* 43, no. 4 (December 2010), 592–615.

14. Carl Schmitt, *Political Theology: Four Chapters on the Concept of Sovereignty*, trans. George Schwab (Chicago: University of Chicago Press, 2005 [1922]), 6.

15. The term "existential self-preservation" comes from Richard Wolin, "The Decline of the German Mandarins," *Modern Intellectual History* 10, no. 1 (April 2013), 255. I removed the emphasis that was in the original.

16. Carl Schmitt, *The Concept of the Political: Expanded Edition*, trans. George Schwab (Chicago: University of Chicago Press, 2007 [1932]), 26.

17. Daniel Wickberg, "Modernisms Endless: Ironies of the American Mid-Century," *Modern Intellectual History* 10, no. 1 (April 2013), 207–208.

18. This quotation comes from an essay Speier wrote about Emil Lederer, his professor when he was a doctoral student at the University of Heidelberg. Though Speier was here referencing Lederer's views, this summation nevertheless accurately described his own political perspective. Speier, "Emil Lederer (1882–1939): Life and Work," n.d. [late 1970s], 9, Folder 2, Box 7, SP.

19. Walter Lippmann, *Public Opinion* (Blacksburg, VA: Wilder Publications, 2010 [1922]); Walter Lippmann, *The Phantom Public* (New Brunswick, NJ: Transaction Publishers, 2011 [1925]).

20. The best description of the development of the global vision of U.S. power after World War II remains Melvyn P. Leffler, "The American Conception of National Security and the Beginnings of the Cold War, 1945–48," *American Historical Review* 89, no. 2 (April 1984), 346–381.

21. Jeremi Suri has charted how "the growth of American power meant the distribution of influence among a broader range of U.S. actors," such as Speier, who "did not draw on the

standard sinews of power in American society—electoral politics, business success, or elite-born families." Suri, *Kissinger*, 2. Many scholars have examined social scientists' entry into government service during World War II. Representative works on this subject include Peter Buck, "Adjusting to Military Life: The Social Sciences Go to War, 1941–1950," in *Military Enterprise and Technological Change: Perspectives on the American Experience*, ed. Merritt Roe Smith (Cambridge, MA: MIT Press, 1985), 203–252; James H. Capshew, *Psychologists on the March: Science, Practice, and Professional Identity in America, 1929–1969* (New York: Cambridge University Press, 1999); Herman, *Romance*, chapters 2–4; Barry M. Katz, *Foreign Intelligence: Research and Analysis in the Office of Strategic Services, 1942–1945* (Cambridge, MA: Harvard University Press, 1989); Mandler, *Return*, chapters 2–4; David H. Price, *Anthropological Intelligence: The Deployment and Neglect of American Anthropology in the Second World War* (Durham, NC: Duke University Press, 2008).

22. The best books on think tanks are Thomas Medvetz, *Think Tanks in America* (Chicago: University of Chicago Press, 2012); James Allen Smith, *The Idea Brokers: Think Tanks and the Rise of the New Policy Elite* (New York: Free Press, 1991).

23. For the pre–World War II relationship between intellectuals and U.S. foreign policymakers, see David Milne, *Worldmaking: The Art and Science of American Diplomacy* (New York: Farrar, Straus and Giroux, 2015), chapters 1–4; Joy Rohde, "Social Science and Foreign Affairs," in *Oxford Research Encyclopedia of American History*, ed. Jon Butler (New York: Oxford University Press, 2016), accessed November 16, 2016, http://americanhistory.oxfordre.com/view/10.1093/acrefore/9780199329175.001.0001/acrefore-9780199329175-e-154. The most important antecedent to RAND was the Council on Foreign Relations (1921), which emerged from the collection of scholars, dubbed "the Inquiry," that aided President Woodrow Wilson before and during the Paris Peace Conference of 1919. See Peter Grose, *Continuing the Inquiry: The Council on Foreign Relations from 1921 to 1996* (New York: Council on Foreign Relations, 1996); Inderjeet Parmar, *Think Tanks and Power in Foreign Policy: A Comparative Study of the Role and Influence of the Council on Foreign Relations and the Royal Institute of International Affairs, 1939–1945* (New York: Palgrave Macmillan, 2004); Robert D. Schulzinger, *The Wise Men of Foreign Affairs: The History of the Council on Foreign Relations* (New York: Columbia University Press, 1984).

24. Jan-Werner Müller, *Contesting Democracy: Political Ideas in Twentieth-Century Europe* (New Haven: Yale University Press, 2011), 68.

25. See chapter 6 in this book; Fred Kaplan, *The Wizards of Armageddon* (Stanford: Stanford University Press, 1991); Robin, *Making*, chapter 6.

26. Suri, *Kissinger*, 98.

27. For RAND as the prototypical Cold War think tank, see Kuklick, *Blind*, 79; Medvetz, *Think Tanks*, 26, 70–72.

28. Kuklick, *Blind*.

29. For the major scholarship on the intellectual migration from Europe to America in the 1930s, see Lewis A. Coser, *Refugee Scholars in America: Their Impact and Their Experiences* (New Haven: Yale University Press, 1984); Axel Fair-Schulz and Mario Kessler, eds., *German Scholars in Exile: New Studies in Intellectual History* (Lanham, MD: Lexington Books, 2011); Laura Fermi, *Illustrious Immigrants: The Intellectual Migration from Europe, 1930–41* (Chicago: University of Chicago Press, 1968); Donald Fleming and Bernard Bailyn, eds., *The Intellectual Migration: Europe and America, 1930–1960* (Cambridge, MA: Harvard University Press, 1969); Anthony Heilbut, *Exiled in Paradise: German Refugee Artists and Intellectuals in America, from the 1930s to the Present* (New York: Viking, 1983); H. Stuart Hughes, *The Sea Change: The Migration of Social Thought, 1930–1965* (New York: Harper and Row, 1975); Jarrell C. Jackman and Carla M. Borden, *The Muses Flee Hitler: Cultural Transfer and Adaptation, 1930–1945* (Washington, DC: Smithsonian Institution Press, 1983); David Kettler and Gerhard Lauer, eds., *Exile, Science, and Bildung: The Contested Legacies of German*

Émigré Intellectuals (New York: Palgrave Macmillan, 2005); Franz L. Neumann, Henri Peyre, Erwin Panofsky, Wolfgang Köhler, and Paul Tillich, *The Cultural Migration: The European Scholar in America* (Philadelphia: University of Pennsylvania Press, 1953); Jean-Michel Palmier, *Weimar in Exile: The Antifascist Emigration in Europe and America*, trans. David Fernbach (London: Verso, 2006). For scholarship that explores émigrés' influence on U.S. foreign relations and international thought, see Katz, *Foreign*, chapter 2; Tim B. Müller, *Krieger und Gelehrte: Herbert Marcuse und die Denksysteme im Kalten Krieg* (Hamburg: Hamburger Edition, 2010); Joachim Radkau, *Die deutsche Emigration in den USA: Ihr Einfluß auf die amerikanische Europapolitik, 1933–1945* (Düsseldorf: Bertelsmann Universitätsverlag, 1971); Alfons Söllner, ed., *Zur Archäologie der Demokratie in Deutschland, Band I: Analysen von politischen Emigranten im amerikanischen Geheimdienst, 1943–1945; Band 2: Analysen von politischen Emigranten im amerikanischen Außenministerium, 1946–1949* (Frankfurt a.M.: Fischer, 1986). The myriad biographies of Henry Kissinger also examine the ways in which his German experience did, or did not, inform his behavior. See especially Mario del Pero, *The Eccentric Realist: Henry Kissinger and the Shaping of American Foreign Policy* (Ithaca: Cornell University Press, 2006), 154n8; Niall Ferguson, *Kissinger, Volume I, 1923–1968: The Idealist* (New York: Penguin Press, 2015), chapters 1–2; Suri, *Kissinger*, chapter 1.

30. Greenberg, *Weimar*, chapter 4; Mark Greif, *The Age of the Crisis of Man: Thought and Fiction in America, 1933–1973* (Princeton: Princeton University Press, 2015), 46; Katznelson, *Fear*, 48–51; Suri, *Kissinger*, 7–10.

31. Volker R. Berghahn, *America and the Intellectual Cold Wars in Europe: Shepard Stone between Philanthropy, Academy, and Diplomacy* (Princeton: Princeton University Press, 2001), chapter 1; Greenberg, *Weimar*; William David Jones, *The Lost Debate: German Socialist Intellectuals and Totalitarianism* (Urbana: University of Illinois Press, 1999); Nicholas Rescher, "The Berlin Group and the USA: A Narrative of Personal Interactions," in *The Berlin Group and the Philosophy of Logical Empiricism*, ed. Nikolay Milkov and Volker Peckhaus (Dordrecht: Springer, 2013), 35–36.

32. James Sparrow makes a similar point when discussing the intellectual trajectory of the émigré international relations theorist Hans Morgenthau. James T. Sparrow, "Morgenthau's Dilemma: Rethinking the Democratic Leviathan in the Atomic Age," *The Tocqueville Review/La revue Tocqueville* 36, no. 1 (Summer 2015), 133n87.

33. James T. Kloppenberg, *Uncertain Victory: Social Democracy and Progressivism in European and American Thought, 1870–1920* (New York: Oxford University Press, 1986), 11.

34. For the literature that offers a generally negative appraisal of defense intellectuals, see Noam Chomsky et al., *The Cold War and the University: Toward an Intellectual History of the Postwar Years* (New York: New Press, 1997); Sigmund Diamond, *Compromised Campus: The Collaboration of Universities with the Intelligence Community, 1945–1955* (New York: Oxford University Press, 1992); Allan A. Needell, "'Truth Is Our Weapon': Project TROY, Political Warfare, and Government-Academic Relations in the National Security State," *Diplomatic History* 17, no. 3 (July 1993), 399–420; Christopher Simpson, *Science of Coercion: Communication Research and Psychological Warfare, 1945–1960* (New York: Oxford University Press, 1994); Christopher Simpson, ed., *Universities and Empire: Money and Politics in the Social Sciences during the Cold War* (New York: New Press, 1998), especially the introduction. For recent historiography that adopts a more sympathetic perspective on defense intellectuals, see David Ekbladh, *The Great American Mission: Modernization and the Construction of an American World Order* (Princeton: Princeton University Press, 2010); Engerman, *Know*; Gilman, *Mandarins*; Latham, *Modernization*; Latham, *Right*; Mandler, *Return*; David Milne, *America's Rasputin: Walt Rostow and the Vietnam War* (New York: Hill and Wang, 2008); Milne, *Worldmaking*; Rohde, *Armed*; Mark Solovey, *Shaky Foundations: The Politics-Patronage-Social Science Nexus in Cold War America* (New Brunswick, NJ: Rutgers University Press, 2013).

35. Kuklick, *Blind*, 16.

36. For the notion of exile as a state of suspension, see David Kettler, *The Liquidation of Exile: Studies in the Intellectual Emigration of the 1930s* (London: Anthem Press, 2011), 1.

1. Masses and Marxism in Weimar Germany

1. The scholarship on Weimar is voluminous. The two primary English-language starting points are Detlev J. K. Peukert, *The Weimar Republic: The Crisis of Classical Modernity*, trans. Richard Deveson (New York: Hill and Wang, 1992) and Eric D. Weitz, *Weimar Germany: Promise and Tragedy* (Princeton: Princeton University Press, 2007).

2. For the emergence of the "masses" as a political category, see Volker R. Berghahn, *America and the Intellectual Cold Wars in Europe: Shepard Stone between Philanthropy, Academy, and Diplomacy* (Princeton: Princeton University Press, 2001), 79–92; Stefan Jonsson, *Crowds and Democracy: The Idea and Image of the Masses from Revolution to Fascism* (New York: Columbia University Press, 2013).

3. I borrow the term "crisis of Marxism" from Douglas Kellner, *Critical Theory, Marxism, and Modernity* (Baltimore: Johns Hopkins University Press, 1989), 12; Rolf Wiggershaus, *The Frankfurt School: Its History, Theories, and Political Significance*, trans. Michael Robertson (Cambridge, MA: MIT Press, 1994), 40.

4. Unfortunately, the majority of Speier's correspondence from his youth in Germany has been lost. I have thus relied on oral histories, as well as other scattered published and unpublished reminiscences, for information about Speier's German period. In particular, this chapter makes use of the following materials: Speier to L. J. Henderson, "Myself," March 23, 1954, Folder 16, Box 2, Hans Speier Papers, German and Jewish Intellectual Émigré Collection, M. E. Grenander Department of Special Collections and Archives, University Libraries, University at Albany, State University of New York, Albany, NY (hereafter SP); "Hans Speier, Gesprächsweise Mitteilungen zu einer intellektuellen Autobiographie [I]," transcript of interview by Ursula Ludz, October 4, 5, 6, 1982, Folder 31, Box 2, SP; "Hans Speier, Gesprächsweise Mitteilungen zu einer intellektuellen Autobiographie [II]," transcript of interview by Ursula Ludz, October 8, 19, 20, 1982, Folder 32, Box 2, SP.

5. Klaus Tanner, "Protestant Revolt against Modernity," in *The Weimar Moment: Liberalism, Political Theology, and Law*, ed. Leonard V. Kaplan and Rudy Koshar (Lanham, MD: Lexington Books, 2012), 3–16; "An Interview with Hans Speier," conducted by Michael Prinz, trans. Winston Goodbody, n.d. [1970s–1980s], 5, Folder 30, Box 2, SP.

6. Speier, "Autobiographical Notes," early manuscript version of an English translation, n.d. [1980s], 8, Folder 4, Box 3, SP.

7. Rosanna M. Gatens, "Prelude to Gleichschaltung: The University of Heidelberg and the E. J. Gumbel Controversies, 1924 and 1932," *European History Quarterly* 31, no. 1 (Winter 2001), 67; Colin Loader, *Alfred Weber and the Crisis of Culture, 1890–1933* (New York: Palgrave Macmillan, 2012), 52.

8. Speier, "Emil Lederer (1882–1939): Life and Work," n.d. [late 1970s], 2, Folder 2, Box 7, SP; Paul Kecskemeti to Speier, April 11, 1977, 3, Folder 120, Box 3, SP; Paul Kecskemeti to Speier, March 20, 1977, 4, Folder 120, Box 3, SP.

9. Speier, untitled ["Mannheim began teaching . . ."], n.d. [1970s?], Folder 40, Box 3, SP; Speier, Interview, April 5, 1988, 2, Folder 14, Box 10, RAND History Project Interviews (Acc. 1999-0037), National Air and Space Museum, Smithsonian Institution, Washington, DC (hereafter RHPI); "Ergebnis der mündlichen Prüfung," May 24, 1928, H-IV 757/23, 376v, Heidelberg University

Archives, Heidelberg, Germany (hereafter HUA); "Zahlungsliste der Zuhörer des Herrn Professors-Privatdozent Dr. Mannheim für Winter Semester 1927/28," Rep 27/815, HUA; Speier, "Autobiographical Notes," III-2–III-3; Speier to L. Charles Cooper, April 27, 1973, 1, Folder 40, Box 3, SP; Speier, *The Truth in Hell and Other Essays on Politics and Culture, 1935–1987* (New York: Oxford University Press, 1989), 6. For a useful summary of the Weimar-era academic hierarchy, see Tracy B. Kittredge, "Social Sciences in Germany," August 9, 1932, Folder 186, Box 20, Subseries 717.S, Series 717, RG 1.1, Projects, FA386, Rockefeller Foundation Records (hereafter RFR), Rockefeller Archive Center, Sleepy Hollow, NY (hereafter RAC).

10. David Frisby, *The Alienated Mind: The Sociology of Knowledge in Germany, 1918–33* (London: Heinemann Educational Books, 1983), 2, 223, 227; David Kettler and Colin Loader, "Weimar Sociology," in *Weimar Thought: A Contested Legacy*, ed. Peter E. Gordon and John P. McCormick (Princeton: Princeton University Press, 2013), 15, 30; Loader, *Weber*, 101–102; David Kettler, Volker Meja, and Nico Stehr, "Rationalizing the Irrational: Karl Mannheim and the Besetting Sin of German Intellectuals," *American Journal of Sociology* 95, no. 6 (May 1990), 1454; Speier, "Lederer," 1.

11. Fritz Ringer, "Higher Education in Germany in the Nineteenth Century," *Journal of Contemporary History* 2, no. 3 (July 1967), 123.

12. Fritz Ringer, *The Decline of the German Mandarins: The German Academic Community, 1890–1933* (Cambridge, MA: Harvard University Press, 1969); Fritz Ringer, *Max Weber: An Intellectual Biography* (Chicago: University of Chicago Press, 2004), 9; Colin Loader, "Free Floating: The Intelligentsia in the Work of Alfred Weber and Karl Mannheim," *German Studies Review* 20, no. 2 (May 1997), 218; Colin Loader and David Kettler, *Karl Mannheim's Sociology as Political Education* (New Brunswick, NJ: Transaction Publishers, 2002).

13. Rüdiger vom Bruch, *Gelehrtenpolitik, Sozialwissenschaften und akademische Diskurse in Deutschland im 19. und 20. Jahrhundert* (Stuttgart: Franz Steiner, 2006); Britta Scheideler, "The Scientist as Moral Authority: Albert Einstein between Elitism and Democracy, 1914–1933," *Historical Studies in the Physical and Biological Sciences* 32, no. 2 (2002), 321; Peter Lassman, "Enlightenment, Cultural Crisis, and Politics: The Role of the Intellectuals from Kant to Habermas," *European Legacy: Toward New Paradigms* 5, no. 6 (2000), 821–822; Speier to Gerd Schroeter, June 10, 1971, 1, Folder 71, Box 4, SP.

14. David Kettler, "Political Education for a Polity of Dissensus: Karl Mannheim and the Legacy of Max Weber," *European Journal of Political Theory* 1, no. 1 (July 2002), 34; Max Weber, "Science as a Vocation," trans. H. H. Gerth and C. Wright Mills, in *From Max Weber: Essays in Sociology*, ed. H. H. Gerth and C. Wright Mills (New York: Oxford University Press, 1958 [original published in 1919]), 146, 150, 147, 152.

15. Karl Mannheim, *Ideology and Utopia: An Introduction to the Sociology of Knowledge*, trans. Louis Wirth and Edward Shils (San Diego: Harcourt, 1985 [1936; original published in 1929]), 155, 161, 158. My understanding of Karl Mannheim was profoundly shaped by the scholarship of David Kettler, Colin Loader, and Volker Meja, especially Loader and Kettler, *Mannheim's Sociology*; David Kettler and Volker Meja, *Karl Mannheim and the Crisis of Liberalism: The Secret of These New Times* (New Brunswick, NJ: Transaction Publishers, 1995); David Kettler, Colin Loader, and Volker Meja, *Karl Mannheim and the Legacy of Max Weber: Retrieving a Research Program* (Burlington, VT: Ashgate Press, 2008).

16. Loader and Kettler, *Mannheim's Sociology*.

17. Mannheim, *Ideology*, 162; David Kettler, "Self-Knowledge and Sociology: Nina Rubinstein's Studies in Exile," in *Intellectual Migration and Cultural Transformation: Refugees from National Socialism in the English-Speaking World*, ed. Edward Timms and Jon Hughes (Vienna: Springer, 2003), 199.

18. David F. Crew, "A Social Republic? Social Democrats, Communists, and the Weimar Welfare State, 1919–1933," in *Between Reform and Revolution: German Socialism and Communism from 1840 to 1990*, ed. David E. Barclay and Eric D. Weitz (New York: Berghahn Books, 1998), 223; Carl E. Schorske, *German Social Democracy, 1905–1917: The Development of the Great Schism* (New York: Harper Torchbooks, 1955), 18–19, 4–6.

19. My understanding of the Weimar-era SPD was deeply informed by Donna Harsch, *German Social Democracy and the Rise of Nazism* (Chapel Hill: University of North Carolina Press, 1993), whose influence shapes the remainder of this chapter.

20. Udi Greenberg, *The Weimar Century: German Émigrés and the Ideological Foundations of the Cold War* (Princeton: Princeton University Press, 2014), 79; William Smaldone, "Rudolf Hilferding and the Total State," *The Historian* 57, no. 1 (Autumn 1994), 102; Speier, "Alfred Weber," July 28, 1928, 1, Folder 50, Box 7, SP.

21. David E. Barclay and Eric D. Weitz, "Introduction," in *Between Reform and Revolution: German Socialism and Communism from 1840 to 1990*, ed. David E. Barclay and Eric D. Weitz (New York: Berghahn Books, 1998), 7; Donna Harsch, "The Iron Front: Weimar Social Democracy between Tradition and Modernity," in *Between Reform and Revolution: German Socialism and Communism from 1840 to 1990*, ed. David E. Barclay and Eric D. Weitz (New York: Berghahn Books, 1998), 252.

22. Speier to Henderson, "Myself," 9; Harsch, *Social*, 1.

23. Harsch, *Social*, 43.

24. Ibid., 24; Speier, "II. From Hegel to Marx: Lassalle's Philosophy of History," in *Social Order and the Risks of War: Papers in Political Sociology* (New York: George W. Stewart, 1952), 175–176. The original was Speier, "Die Geschichtsphilosophie Lassalles II," *Archiv für Sozialwissenschaft und Sozialpolitik* 61 (1929), 360–388.

25. Speier, "Zur Soziologie der Bürgerlichen Intelligenz in Deutschland," *Die Gesellschaft* 6, no. 7 (July 1929), 58; Speier, "Sociology or Ideology? Notes on the Sociology of the Intelligentsia," in *Knowledge and Politics: The Sociology of Knowledge Dispute*, ed. Volker Meja and Nico Stehr (London: Routledge, 1990), 213. The original was Speier, "Soziologie oder Ideologie? Bemerkungen zur Soziologie der Intelligenz," *Die Gesellschaft* 7, no. 4 (April 1930), 357–372.

26. Speier, "Zur Soziologie," 66–67; Speier, "Ideology?" 216, 213.

27. Speier, "Ideology?" 209, 215.

28. Ibid., 218.

29. Ibid., 214, 209.

30. Ibid., 214, 219.

31. Ibid., 220.

32. Harsch, *Social*, 86.

33. Speier, "Die Intellektuellen und Ihr sozialer Beruf," *Neue Blätter für den Sozialismus* 1, no. 12 (December 1930), 551, 557.

34. Ibid., 556; Speier to Ulf Matthiesen, November 15, 1983, Folder 33, Box 4, SP.

35. Speier, *German White-Collar Workers and the Rise of Hitler* (New Haven: Yale University Press, 1986), xix.

36. My information on the Hochschule für Politik comes primarily from Steven D. Korenblat, "A School for the Republic? Cosmopolitans and Their Enemies at the Deutsche Hochschule für Politik, 1920–1933," *Central European History* 39, no. 3 (September 2006), 394–430. This paragraph is also based on Wilhelm Bleek, *Geschichte der Politikwissenschaft in Deutschland* (Munich: C. H. Beck, 2001), 203–204; Peter Gay, *Weimar Culture: The Outsider as Insider* (New York: Harper and Row, 1968), 38–40; David F. Lindenfeld, *The Practical Imagination: The German Sciences of State in the Nineteenth Century* (Chicago: University of Chicago Press, 1997); Ernst Jäckh, ed., *Politik als Wissenschaft: Zehn Jahre Deutsche Hochschule für Politik* (Berlin: Hermann Reckendorf, 1931);

Jean-Michel Palmier, *Weimar in Exile: The Antifascist Emigration in Europe and America*, trans. David Fernbach (London: Verso, 2006), 483; Rainer Eisfeld, "Exile and Return: Political Science in the Context of (West-) German University Development from Weimar to Bonn," *History of Higher Education Annual* 8 (1988), 9–43; Christian Fleck, *A Transatlantic History of the Social Sciences: Robber Barons, the Third Reich and the Invention of Empirical Social Research*, trans. Hella Beister (London: Bloomsbury, 2011), 129.

37. Loader, *Weber*, 110; Sigmund Neumann, "Archiv," in *Politik als Wissenschaft: Zehn Jahre Deutsche Hochschule für Politik*, ed. Ernst Jäckh (Berlin: Hermann Reckendorf, 1931), 279; Korenblat, "School," 399–400.

38. Fleck, *Transatlantic*, 88; Gay, *Weimar*, 40; Korenblat, "School," 394–395, 403.

39. "Gesprächsweise [I]," 45.

40. Harsch, *Social*, 87–99, quotation from 89.

41. Speier, "Verbürgerlichung des Proletariats?" *Magazin der Wirtschaft* 7, no. 13 (March 27, 1931), 592, 591, 593.

42. Ibid., 594, 591.

43. I take Dehn's quotation from Speier's later condensed translation of "Verbürgerlichung des Proletariats?" See Speier, "The Worker Turning Bourgeois," in *Social Order and the Risks of War: Papers in Political Sociology* (New York: George W. Stewart, 1952), 59. The original German may be found in Speier, "Verbürgerlichung?" 596.

44. Speier, *Truth*, 9–10.

45. Speier, review of *Der Begriff des Politischen*, by Karl Schmitt, *Zeitschrift für Sozialforschung* 1, no. 1/2 (1932), 203–204.

46. "Interview [Prinz]," 12.

47. Speier, "Das Proletariat und Seine Kritiker," *Die neue Rundschau* 43, no. 9 (September 1932), 294, 298.

48. Ibid., 304.

49. Speier, *White-Collar*, xxi; Speier to Schroeter, June 10, 1971, 1; Speier, "Bemerkungen zur Erfassung der sozialen Struktur," *Archiv für Sozialwissenschaft und Sozialpolitik* 69 (1932), 724.

50. Speier, "The Salaried Employee in Modern Society," *Social Research* 1, no. 1 (February 1934), 125 (Speier was here referring explicitly to white-collar workers, but this statement reflected his opinion of both blue-collar and white-collar workers); Pamela E. Swett, *Neighbors and Enemies: The Culture of Radicalism in Berlin, 1929–1933* (New York: Cambridge University Press, 2004); Speier to Paul Kecskemeti, February 21, 1975, 1, Folder 120, Box 3, SP; "Interview [Prinz]," 14–15.

51. "Gesprächsweise [I]," 16.

52. Weitz, *Weimar*, 366; Theodor Geiger to Speier, September 27, 1933, Folder 73, Box 3, SP; Speier, untitled ["In 1932, while I was lecturer . . ."], n.d. [1970s], 1, Folder 11, Box 3, SP; Speier to Gabriel Almond, September 29, 1974, Folder 11, Box 3, SP.

53. Speier, *The Salaried Employee in German Society, Volume I* (New York: Works Progress Administration and Department of Social Science at Columbia University, 1939), 6, 8.

2. The Social Role of the Intellectual Exile

1. Thomas Bender, *New York Intellect: A History of Intellectual Life in New York City, from 1750 to the Beginnings of Our Own Time* (New York: Alfred A. Knopf, 1987), xiv.

2. Anthony Heilbut, *Exiled in Paradise: German Refugee Artists and Intellectuals in America, from the 1930s to the Present* (New York: Viking, 1983), 51–52.

3. Terry A. Cooney, *The Rise of the New York Intellectuals: Partisan Review and Its Circle* (Madison: University of Wisconsin Press, 1986), 7, 258–259, 261; David A. Hollinger, "Ethnic Diversity, Cosmopolitanism and the Emergence of the American Liberal Intelligentsia," *American Quarterly* 27, no. 2 (May 1975), 146–147.

4. Daniel Bessner, "'Rather More Than One-Third Had No Jewish Blood': American Progressivism and German-Jewish Cosmopolitanism at the New School for Social Research, 1933–1939," *Religions* 3, no. 1 (2012), 99–129.

5. Edward Said, "Reflections on Exile," in *Reflections on Exile and Other Essays* (Cambridge, MA: Harvard University Press, 2000), 173.

6. Alexander Bloom, *Prodigal Sons: The New York Intellectuals and Their World* (New York: Oxford University Press, 1986); Howard Brick, *Daniel Bell and the Decline of Intellectual Radicalism: Social Theory and Political Reconciliation in the 1940s* (Madison: University of Wisconsin Press, 1986); Cooney, *New York*; Harvey M. Teres, *Renewing the Left: Politics, Imagination, and the New York Intellectuals* (New York: Oxford University Press, 1996); Alan M. Wald, *The New York Intellectuals: The Rise and Decline of the Anti-Stalinist Left from the 1930s to the 1980s* (Chapel Hill: University of North Carolina Press, 1987); Hugh Wilford, *The New York Intellectuals: From Vanguard to Institution* (Manchester: Manchester University Press, 1995).

7. Speier's close relationship with these scholars clearly emerges in his early correspondence with Edward Shils. See Folder Speier, Hans Correspondence, Box 5, Series III, Edward A. Shils Papers, Special Collections Research Center, University of Chicago Library, Chicago, IL (hereafter Shils Papers).

8. Malachi Haim Hacohen, *Karl Popper—The Formative Years, 1902–1945: Politics and Philosophy in Interwar Vienna* (New York: Cambridge University Press, 2002).

9. David Milne, *Worldmaking: The Art and Science of American Diplomacy* (New York: Farrar, Straus and Giroux, 2015), 126–128; Leon Fink, *Progressive Intellectuals and the Dilemmas of Democratic Commitment* (Cambridge, MA: Harvard University Press, 1997), 43–44; Claus-Dieter Krohn, *Intellectuals in Exile: Refugee Scholars and the New School for Social Research*, trans. Rita and Robert Kimber (Amherst: University of Massachusetts Press, 1993), 60.

10. Thomas Bender, "E. R. A. Seligman and the Vocation of Social Science," in *Intellect and Public Life: Essays on the Social History of Academic Intellectuals in the United States* (Baltimore: Johns Hopkins University Press, 1993), 55.

11. Ibid., 56, 62–63; Thomas Bender, "Academic Knowledge and Political Democracy in the Age of the University," in *Intellect and Public Life: Essays on the Social History of Academic Intellectuals in the United States* (Baltimore: Johns Hopkins University Press, 1993), 133–134; Alvin Johnson, "The Intellectual in a Time of Crisis," *Social Research* 4, no. 3 (September 1937), 283.

12. Alvin Johnson, "The Soul of Capitalism," *Unpopular Review* 1, no. 2 (April–June 1914), 234; Alvin Johnson, *Pioneer's Progress: An Autobiography* (New York: Viking Press, 1952), 241.

13. Krohn, *Intellectuals*, 61. For more on the *Encyclopaedia*, see John M. Jordan, *Machine-Age Ideology: Social Engineering and American Liberalism, 1911–1939* (Chapel Hill: University of North Carolina Press, 1994), 165–179; Peter M. Rutkoff and William B. Scott, *New School: A History of the New School for Social Research* (New York: Free Press, 1986), chapter 4.

14. Alvin Johnson, quoted in an untitled and undated article ["country. I cabled . . ."], Folder Graduate Faculty–University in Exile, Box 47, Alvin Johnson, Economics Papers, 1898–1971, Archives and Special Collections, University of Nebraska–Lincoln Libraries, Lincoln, NE (hereafter AJP-N); Alvin Johnson, "Report to the Trustees of the Graduate Faculty of Political and Social Science in the New School for Social Research," February 1935, 2, Folder 38, Box GF Administrative Records, Folders 27–60 (barcode 3-1207-04002922-9) (currently contained in Graduate Faculty of

the New School for Social Research Collection, NS.02.02.01, unprocessed collection, New School Archives and Special Collections, New School, New York, NY [hereafter NSASC]).

15. Alvin Johnson to Agnes deLima, April 14, 1933, [back of page], Folder 27, Box 2, Alvin Saunders Johnson Papers (MS 615), Manuscripts and Archives, Yale University Library, New Haven, CT (thanks to Rutkoff and Scott, *New School*, 92, for pointing me to this letter); Speier, "Emil Lederer (1882–1939): Life and Work," n.d. [late 1970s], 27, Folder 2, Box 7, Hans Speier Papers, German and Jewish Intellectual Émigré Collection, M. E. Grenander Department of Special Collections and Archives, University Libraries, University at Albany, State University of New York, Albany, NY (hereafter SP).

16. "University in Exile," n.d., 1, Folder 3, Box 47, AJP-N; Krohn, *Intellectuals*, 63; Johnson, "Trustees," 4–5.

17. Rutkoff and Scott, *New School*, 93; Speier to R. D. Clark, July 26, 1940, 1, Folder 1, Box 2, SP.

18. Johnson, "Trustees," 8, 3, 3n; Rutkoff and Scott, *New School*, 101, 89.

19. "University in Exile," 3; Speier to Walter Sprondel, June 3, 1983, 2, Folder 82, Box 4, SP; Gabriel Almond to Edward Shils, August 19, 1977, Folder 11, Box 3, SP; Lewis Coser to Speier, December 20, 1977, Folder 41, Box 3, SP; Charles H. Page, *Fifty Years in the Sociological Enterprise: A Lucky Journey* (Amherst: University of Massachusetts Press, 1982), 34–36; Folder Correspondence, Class Notes, 1937–1940 (70–96), Box 4B352, Charles Wright Mills Papers, 1929–1975, 1997, 2000, Dolph Briscoe Center for American History, University of Texas at Austin, Austin, TX; Speier to Edward Shils, March 26, 1936, Folder Speier, Hans Correspondence, Box 5, Series III, Shils Papers. Unfortunately, the minutes from the General Seminars have been lost. Titles of the topics covered in the University in Exile's first years were "Methods and Objectives of the Social Sciences"; "The State and Economics in the Crisis"; "America and Europe"; "Political and Economic Democracy"; "Problems in the Social Sciences"; "The City"; "Contemporary Problems"; "Peace and War"; "The Role of Interests and Ideologies in Modern Politics"; "Labor in the United States and Abroad"; "Government and Business"; "The Future of Socialism"; "Public Opinion in the United States"; "Europe and World Trends"; "Liberalism Today"; "Private Business in Modern Society"; and "Power in the United States." Arthur J. Vidich, "Notes on the History of the General Seminar," 1991, 1–3, Arthur J. Vidich Papers, NA.0009.01, unprocessed collection, NSASC.

20. Krohn, *Intellectuals*, 60.

21. Hollinger, "Ethnic"; Thomas D. Fallace, *Dewey and the Dilemma of Race: An Intellectual History, 1895–1922* (New York: Teachers College Press, 2011), 119; Gary Gerstle, "The Protean Character of American Liberalism," *American Historical Review* 99, no. 4 (October 1994), 1051–1052; Rivka Shpak-Lisak, *Pluralism and Progressives: Hull House and the New Immigrants, 1890–1919* (Chicago: University of Chicago Press, 1989), 141–142; Robert B. Westbrook, *John Dewey and American Democracy* (Ithaca: Cornell University Press, 1991), 212–213; George L. Mosse, *German Jews beyond Judaism* (Bloomington: Indiana University Press, 1985).

22. Anonymous [Alvin Johnson], "Graduate Faculty of Political and Social Science ('The University in Exile'), 1933–1934," in *Graduate Faculty of the New School Catalogues, Fall 1933–Summer 1937* (barcode 3-1207-03980574-6) (currently contained in Course catalogs, NS.05.01.01, Folder 13, Box 1, NSASC); Johnson, "Intellectual," 285.

23. Speier, "The Social Conditions of the Intellectual Exile," *Social Research* 4, no. 3 (September 1937), 321, 328, 327.

24. Ibid., 321; Speier to Volker Meja, September 19, 1986, Folder 35, Box 4, SP; Speier to Alvin Johnson, n.d. [1934–1935], Folder 115, Box 3, SP; Speier to Sprondel, June 3, 1983, 2.

25. Untitled ["New York"], August 26, 1984, 7, Folder 42, Box 2, SP; "Hans Speier, Gesprächsweise Mitteilungen zu einer intellektuellen Autobiographie [II]," transcript of interview

by Ursula Ludz, October 8, 19, 20, 1982, 146, Folder 32, Box 2, SP; Daniel Geary, *Radical Ambition: C. Wright Mills, the Left, and American Social Thought* (Berkeley: University of California Press, 2009), 25–26; Charles Camic, "On Edge: Sociology during the Great Depression and the New Deal," in *Sociology in America: A History*, ed. Craig Calhoun (Chicago: University of Chicago Press, 2007), 225, 237–238, 241–242, 245–252.

26. Patricia Madoo Lengermann, "The Founding of the American Sociological Review: The Anatomy of a Rebellion," *American Sociological Review* 44, no. 2 (April 1979), 185–198; Elżbieta Hałas, "How Robert M. MacIver Was Forgotten: Columbia and American Sociology in a New Light, 1929–1950," *Journal of the History of the Behavioral Sciences* 37, no. 1 (Winter 2001), 27–43. The most well known instance of American sociologists building on the insights of European scholars is Talcott Parsons, *The Structure of Social Action: A Study in Social Theory with Special Reference to a Group of Recent European Writers* (New York: McGraw-Hill, 1937). Also see Theodore Abel, *Systematic Sociology in Germany: A Critical Analysis of Some Attempts to Establish Sociology as an Independent Science* (New York: Columbia University Press, 1929); Howard Becker, "Culture Case Study and Ideal-Typical Method: With Special Reference to Max Weber," *Social Forces* 12, no. 3 (March 1934), 399–405; L. L. and J. S. Bernard, "The European Viewpoint in Sociology," review of *Précis d'un système de sociologie*, by E. Chalupný et al., *Social Forces* 12, no. 2 (December 1933), 287–289; Eduard C. Lindeman, review of *Ideology and Utopia: An Introduction to the Sociology of Knowledge*, by Karl Mannheim, *Sociometry* 1, no. 1/2 (July–October 1937), 262–266; C. Wright Mills, "Language, Logic, and Culture," *American Sociological Review* 4, no. 5 (October 1939), 670–680; Alan Sica, "Merton, Mannheim, and the Sociology of Knowledge," in *Robert K. Merton: Sociology of Science and Sociology as Science*, ed. Craig Calhoun (New York: Columbia University Press, 2010), 164; Joseph Slabey Roucek and Charles Hodges, "Ideology as the Implement of Purposive Thinking in Social Sciences," *Social Science* 11, no. 1 (January 1936), 25–34. The term "epistemological heterogeneity" is adapted from George Steinmetz, "American Sociology before and after World War II: The (Temporary) Settling of a Disciplinary Field," in *Sociology in America: A History*, ed. Craig Calhoun (Chicago: University of Chicago Press, 2007), 314, 319.

27. Talcott Parsons, review of *Max Webers Wissenschaftslehre*, by Alexander von Schelting, *American Sociological Review* 1, no. 4 (August 1936), 680; Louis Wirth, preface to *Ideology and Utopia: An Introduction to the Sociology of Knowledge*, by Karl Mannheim (San Diego: Harcourt, 1985 [1936; original published in 1929]), xxvi.

28. Edward Shils, "Karl Mannheim," in *Portraits: A Gallery of Intellectuals*, ed. Joseph Epstein (Chicago: University of Chicago Press, 1997), 203–206; Speier to Louis Wirth, September 12, 1935, Folder 10, Box 11, Louis Wirth Papers, Special Collections Research Center, University of Chicago Library, Chicago, IL (hereafter Wirth Papers); Margaret Furez for Louis Wirth to E. T. Hiller, December 22, 1936, Folder 10, Box 11, Wirth Papers; Louis Wirth to R. C. Angell, February 19, 1938, Folder 10, Box 11, Wirth Papers.

29. Louis Wirth to Speier, September 18, 1935, Folder 10, Box 11, Wirth Papers; Louis Wirth to Speier, November 24, 1936, Folder 10, Box 11, Wirth Papers; Untitled ["Dr. Hans Speier of the Faculty . . ."], n.d. [1937], Folder 6, Box 2, Society for Social Research, Records, 1923–1956, Special Collections Research Center, University of Chicago Library, Chicago, IL; Speier, "Social Stratification in the Urban Community," *American Sociological Review* 1, no. 2 (April 1936), 193–202; Speier, "Freedom and Social Planning," *American Journal of Sociology* 42, no. 4 (January 1937), 463–483; Speier to Miss Zeller [first name unknown], February 23, 1939, Folder 109, Box 4, SP; Speier, review of *Ideology and Utopia*, by Karl Mannheim, *American Journal of Sociology* 43, no. 1 (July 1937), 155–166.

30. "Gesprächsweise [II]," 320; Speier to John Marshall, February 5, 1941, Folder 3099, Box 260, Subseries 200.R, Series 200, RG 1.1, Projects, FA386, Rockefeller Foundation Records (hereafter RFR), Rockefeller Archive Center, Sleepy Hollow, NY (hereafter RAC); Harold Lasswell to John Marshall, February 7, 1941, Folder 3099, Box 260, Subseries 200.R, Series 200, RG 1.1, Projects, FA386, RFR, RAC; Louis Wirth to John Marshall, February 19, 1941, 1, Folder 3099, Box 260, Subseries 200.R, Series 200, RG 1.1, Projects, FA386, RFR, RAC.

31. Speier to Louis Wirth, September 12, 1938, 1, Folder 11, Box 10, Wirth Papers; Gabriel A. Almond, *Ventures in Political Science: Narratives and Reflections* (Boulder, CO: Lynn Rienner, 2002), 5, 91; Shils, "Mannheim," 207, 205; Sica, "Merton," 164; Speier, review of *Ideology and Utopia*.

32. Speier to Edward Shils, November 17, 1938, 2 [back of page], Folder Speier, Hans Correspondence, Box 5, Series III, Shils Papers; Speier, "Germany in Danger: Concerning Oswald Spengler's Latest Book," review of *The Hour of Decision*, by Oswald Spengler, *Social Research* 1, no. 2 (May 1934), 240.

33. George Simpson, "Class Analysis: What Class Is Not," *American Sociological Review* 4, no. 6 (December 1939), 828–829.

34. Martin Jay, *The Dialectical Imagination: A History of the Frankfurt School and the Institute of Social Research, 1923–1950* (Berkeley: University of California Press, 1996), chapter 3; David Held, *Introduction to Critical Theory: Horkheimer to Habermas* (Berkeley: University of California Press, 1980), chapter 4; Martin Jay, "The Frankfurt School in Exile," in *Permanent Exiles: Essays on the Intellectual Migration from Germany to America* (New York: Columbia University Press, 1985), 46–47; Douglas Kellner, *Critical Theory, Marxism, and Modernity* (Baltimore: Johns Hopkins University Press, 1989), 35–43.

35. Speier, "Max Horkheimer and Frederick Pollock, Frankfurt am Main, June 7, 1952 and Wiesbaden, early June 1952," Folder 4, Box 9, SP; LLA A 826/1–10, Estate Leo Löwenthal, University Library Frankfurt a.M., Archives Center, Frankfurt a.M., Germany; E. Henne to Speier, November 7, 1957, III.12/1–174, Estate Max Horkheimer, University Library Frankfurt a.M., Archives Center, Frankfurt a.M., Germany (hereafter Estate Horkheimer); *Zeitschrift für Sozialforschung* to Speier, November 30, 1931, Folder 39, Box 5, SP; Speier to Gerd Schroeter, June 1, 1981, 2, Folder 71, Box 4, SP.

36. Speier, review of *Studien über Autorität und Familie*, ed. Max Horkheimer, *Social Research* 3, no. 4 (November 1936), 503, 501, 502.

37. Ibid., 504; Thomas Wheatland, *The Frankfurt School in Exile* (Minneapolis: University of Minnesota Press, 2009), 67; Jay, *Dialectical*, 133; Rolf Wiggershaus, *The Frankfurt School: Its History, Theories, and Political Significance*, trans. Michael Robertson (Cambridge, MA: MIT Press, 1994), 254.

38. Heilbut, *Exiled*, 89; Jay, *Dialectical*, 39–40, 114; Jay, "Exile," 40–41; Speier, June 7, 1952, in *From the Ashes of Disgrace: A Journal from Germany, 1945–1955* (Amherst: University of Massachusetts Press, 1981), 190; Wheatland, *Exile*, 65; Wiggershaus, *Frankfurt*, 253.

39. Wilfred M. McClay, *The Masterless: Self and Society in Modern America* (Chapel Hill: University of North Carolina Press, 1994), 195–196; Wheatland, *Exile*, 204, 141.

40. Speier, review of *Studien*, 503–504.

41. Ibid.; Speier, "Horkheimer," 1-b, 1-a. Thanks to Martin Jay for highlighting Horkheimer's sensitivity in a March 2015 telephone conversation.

42. Herbert Marcuse quotation, "was strictly forbidden . . . ," from Wheatland, *Exile*, 73; Wiggershaus, *Frankfurt*, 41–46, 123; Jay, *Dialectical*, 61–63, 53, 84; Jay, "Exiles," 47–48; John Abromeit, *Max Horkheimer and the Foundations of the Frankfurt School* (New York: Cambridge

University Press, 2011), 212; Held, *Critical*, 195; Speier, "Horkheimer," 1-a; Speier, "5 April 1954: Interview with Axel von dem Bussche-Streithorst, Bonn, Restaurant Kranzler—2½ Hours," Log Note No. 7, 3, Folder 5, Box 9, SP; Speier to Edward Shils, July 11, 1977, 1, Folder 75, Box 4, SP. Much of the secondary literature that examines the New School–Frankfurt School relationship reflects the tensions described in this paragraph. For example, Martin Jay refers to Speier's review as "extremely hostile" and reports that the New School was a "center of opposition" to the institute. Rolf Wiggershaus, for his part, claims that the New School spread rumors that the Frankfurt School was a group of communists either to discredit the institute among "American grant organizations" or "simply [to] give vent to [the New School faculty's] irritation with [the Frankfurt School]." Jay, *Dialectical*, 133; Jay, "Exiles," 62; Wiggershaus, *Frankfurt*, 255. This seems to me unnecessarily conspiratorial. Speier, at least, never once mentioned or discussed any anti–Frankfurt School conspiracy. Furthermore, Claus-Dieter Krohn points out the unfair nature of Jay's characterization of Speier's review in Krohn, *Intellectuals*, 192–193.

43. George Friedman, *The Political Philosophy of the Frankfurt School* (Ithaca: Cornell University Press, 1981), 18–19; Jay, *Dialectical*, 36–37, 80; Kellner, *Critical*, 16; McClay, *Masterless*, 204–205; Max Horkheimer, "Traditional and Critical Theory," in *Critical Theory: Selected Essays*, trans. Matthew J. O'Connell (New York: Continuum Publishing, 1992 [original published in 1937]), 207–208.

44. Jay, "Exile," 32; Kellner, *Critical*, 46; Horkheimer, "Critical," 242, 220, 233.

45. Max Horkheimer, "The Jews and Europe," trans. Mark Ritter, in *Critical Theory and Society: A Reader*, ed. Stephen Eric Bronner and Douglas MacKay Kellner (New York: Routledge, 1989 [original published in 1939]), 77–78.

46. A pre-circulated copy of Speier's talk may be found in Max Horkheimer's papers. Speier, "The Intellectual Immigrant," April 13, 1937 [intended date for the speech], I.19 / 103–296, Estate Horkheimer.

47. Ibid., 2, 5.

48. Ibid., 7, 12.

49. When Speier referred to "success or defeat in social conflict," he was clearly thinking about Marxism's Weimar failure. Ibid., 13–15; Speier, "Conditions," 326.

50. Speier, "Immigrant," 14.

51. Wheatland, *Exile*, 72, 13; Krohn, *Intellectuals*, 71–73, 191; "Hans Speier, Gesprächsweise Mitteilungen zu einer intellektuellen Autobiographie [I]," transcript of interview by Ursula Ludz, October 4, 5, 6, 1982, 129, Folder 31, Box 2, SP; Jay, *Dialectical*, 31, 34; Wiggershaus, *Frankfurt*, 4.

52. Franz Neumann to Max Horkheimer, July 20, 1940, 2, VI.30 / 111–112, Estate Horkheimer. Thanks to Krohn, *Intellectuals*, 194, for pointing me to this letter.

53. McClay, *Masterless*, 192–193.

54. Speier, "Danger," 242.

55. Speier, "Comment on the Research Project on Peace," October 26, 1939, 3, Folder 79, Box 7, SP; Max Weber, "Science as a Vocation," trans. H. H. Gerth and C. Wright Mills, in *From Max Weber: Essays in Sociology*, ed. H. H. Gerth and C. Wright Mills (New York: Oxford University Press, 1958 [original published in 1919]).

56. Colin Loader, "Free Floating: The Intelligentsia in the Work of Alfred Weber and Karl Mannheim," *German Studies Review* 20, no. 2 (May 1997), 218–219.

57. Speier to Edward Shils, n.d. [late 1930s, "Thank you for your note . . ."], 1 [back of page]–2, Folder Speier, Hans Correspondence, Box 5, Series III, Shils Papers. The quotation "the consciously subjective . . ." comes from a letter written by Hans Staudinger, a colleague of Speier's from the New School, and was referencing an opinion of Emil Lederer's. The translation

is Speier's. See Hans Staudinger to Speier, April 1, 1978, 2, for the original quotation, and Speier to Hans Staudinger, April 6, 1978, 2, Folder 84, Box 4, SP, for Speier's translation.

58. Speier and Alfred Kähler, "Introduction," in *War in Our Time*, ed. Speier and Alfred Kähler (New York: W. W. Norton, 1939), 13.

3. Public Opinion, Propaganda, and Democracy in Crisis

1. Speier, "Social Stratification," in *Political and Economic Democracy*, ed. Max Ascoli and Fritz Lehmann (New York: W. W. Norton, 1937), 255–270; Speier, "The Social Determination of Ideas," *Social Research* 5, no. 2 (May 1938), 182–205.

2. Speier, "Emil Lederer (1882–1939): Life and Work," n.d. [late 1970s], 8–9, Folder 2, Box 7, Hans Speier Papers, German and Jewish Intellectual Émigré Collection, M. E. Grenander Department of Special Collections and Archives, University Libraries, University at Albany, State University of New York, Albany, NY (hereafter SP).

3. Arthur J. Vidich, "Hans Speier, 1905–1990," n.d. [1990], 2, Folder Speier, Hans Memorial Circa 1990, Box 13 (barcode 3-1207-04002813-0) (currently contained in Arthur J. Vidich Papers, NA.0009.01, unprocessed collection, New School Archives and Special Collections, The New School, New York, NY [hereafter NSASC]).

4. Speier, "On Propaganda," *Social Research* 1, no. 3 (August 1934), 377.

5. This quotation comes from a propaganda directive written in August 1945 for which Speier was responsible. Weekly Propaganda Directive, Germany (hereafter WPDG), August 24, 1945, 2, Folder Record Regional Directives August 1945, Box 824, Director of Overseas Operations, Record Set of Policy Directives for Overseas Programs, 1942–1945, Entry 363, Records of the Office of War Information, Record Group (hereafter RG) 208, National Archives at College Park, College Park, MD (hereafter NACP).

6. This was a claim shared by several émigrés. It was, in fact, the exile Karl Loewenstein who gave this theory its name: militant democracy. See Udi Greenberg, *The Weimar Century: German Émigrés and the Ideological Foundations of the Cold War* (Princeton: Princeton University Press, 2014), chapter 4.

7. Ernst Kris and Speier, "Research Programme to be Undertaken under the Auspices of the Graduate Faculty of Political and Social Science at the New School for Social Research," n.d. [1940], 1, Folder 80, Box 7, SP.

8. There is an enormous amount of literature examining the Lippmann-Dewey debate. Because Speier entered into this debate vis-à-vis a discussion about propaganda, my reading of it is filtered through Brett Gary, *The Nervous Liberals: Propaganda Anxieties from World War I to the Cold War* (New York: Columbia University Press, 1999), 26–37. I do, however, rely on other works, particularly Robert B. Westbrook, *John Dewey and American Democracy* (Ithaca: Cornell University Press, 1991), chapter 9. Recent scholarship has questioned whether or not such a debate actually existed to the degree that scholars have assumed. See especially Sue Curry Jansen, "Phantom Conflict: Lippmann, Dewey, and the Fate of the Public in Modern Society," *Communication and Critical/Cultural Studies* 6, no. 3 (September 2009), 221–245; Michael Schudson, "The 'Lippmann-Dewey Debate' and the Invention of Walter Lippmann as an Anti-Democrat, 1986–1996," *International Journal of Communication* 2 (2008), 1031–1042; Tom Arnold-Forster, "Democracy and Expertise in the Lippmann-Terman Controversy," *Modern Intellectual History* (published online: September 4, 2017), 1–32. However, my reading of Speier's work leads me to conclude that he indeed thought there was a debate between "democratic realists" like Lippmann and "democratic

optimists" like Dewey, though he did not use these terms. The term "democratic realism" comes from Westbrook, *Dewey*, xvii, and I have adapted "democratic optimism" from the arguments in the same book.

9. Walter Lippmann, *Public Opinion* (Blacksburg, VA: Wilder Publications, 2010 [1922]), 20, 13, Part III, 21–22, 149–151.

10. Ibid., 22; Andrew Jewett, *Science, Democracy, and the American University: From the Civil War to the Cold War* (New York: Cambridge University Press, 2012), 173; Westbrook, *Dewey*, 299.

11. Walter Lippmann, *The Phantom Public* (New Brunswick, NJ: Transaction Publishers, 2011 [1925]), 179–180; Lippmann, *Opinion*, 171, 138 (Lippmann's specific phrase is "the manufacture of consent"); Westbrook, *Dewey*, 299–300.

12. John Dewey, "Public Opinion," review of *Public Opinion*, by Walter Lippmann, *New Republic* 30, no. 387 (May 3, 1922), 286–288; John Dewey, "Practical Democracy," review of *The Phantom Public*, by Walter Lippmann, *New Republic* 45, no. 574 (December 2, 1925), 52–54; John Dewey, *The Public and Its Problems* (Athens, GA: Swallow Press/Ohio University Press, 1954 [1927]), 206; Jewett, *Science*, 172–173; Gary, *Nervous*, 34; Westbrook, *Dewey*, 309.

13. Dewey, *Problems*, 208–209.

14. Gary, *Nervous*, 18–53.

15. Louis Wirth, preface to *Ideology and Utopia: An Introduction to the Sociology of Knowledge*, by Karl Mannheim (San Diego: Harcourt, 1985 [1936; original published in 1929]), xxix.

16. Corey Ross, *Media and the Making of Modern Germany: Mass Communications, Society, and Politics from the Empire to the Third Reich* (New York: Oxford University Press, 2008), 198–213; David Welch, *Germans, Propaganda and Total War, 1914–1918* (New Brunswick, NJ: Rutgers University Press, 2000).

17. The phrases "positive propaganda" and "to educate . . ." quoted in Ross, *Media*, 246; Donna Harsch, *German Social Democracy and the Rise of Nazism* (Chapel Hill: University of North Carolina Press, 1993), 79, 144; Rudy Koshar, "Introduction," in *The Weimar Moment: Liberalism, Political Theology, and Law*, ed. Leonard V. Kaplan and Rudy Koshar (Lanham, MD: Lexington Books, 2012), xiii–xiv; the phrase "to shift politics . . ." quoted in Ross, *Media*, 251.

18. Speier, "Nazi Propaganda and Its Decline," *Social Research* 10, no. 3 (September 1943), 366. Propaganda's importance to the Nazi victory explains why several of the most influential midcentury analysts of the mass media in the United States, including Speier, Theodor Adorno, Paul Lazarsfeld, and Leo Löwenthal, were Central European exiles.

19. Speier, "On Propaganda," 376–377. It is important to note that Speier never cited Lippmann or Dewey in his discussions of propaganda. There is, however, a salient historical reason for this: as a recent immigrant to the United States, Speier would not have wanted to be seen as taking sides in a potentially controversial debate between two prominent intellectuals associated with the New School.

20. Ibid., 377–378.

21. Ibid., 380.

22. Speier, review of *Die Macht des Charlatans*, by Grete de Francesco, *Social Research* 5, no. 1 (February 1938), 109–110; Speier, "Honor and Social Structure," *Social Research* 2, no. 1 (February 1935), 78; Benjamin L. Alpers, *Dictators, Democracy, and American Public Culture: Envisioning the Totalitarian Enemy, 1920s–1950s* (Chapel Hill: University of North Carolina Press, 2003), 12; Speier, "Ludendorff: The German Concept of Total War," in *Makers of Modern Strategy: Military Thought from Machiavelli to Hitler*, ed. Edward Mead Earle (Princeton: Princeton University Press, 1943), 307.

23. Speier, review of *Die Macht des Charlatans*, 111–112.

24. Speier, "Stratification," 255, 257–258.

25. U.S. Congress, House of Representatives, Select Committee to Investigate the Federal Communications Commission, *Hearings before the Select Committee to Investigate the Federal Communications Commission*, 78th Cong., 2nd sess., 1944, 3863.

26. Speier, "Class Structure and 'Total War,'" *American Sociological Review* 4, no. 3 (June 1939), 371; Speier, "Treachery in War," *Social Research* 7, no. 3 (September 1940), 258; Speier, "The Effect of War on the Social Order," *Annals of the American Academy of Political and Social Science* 218 (November 1941), 90; Speier and Alfred Kähler, "Introduction," in *War in Our Time*, ed. Speier and Alfred Kähler (New York: W. W. Norton, 1939), 13; Speier, "Social Order," 95; Speier, "The Social Types of War," *American Journal of Sociology* 46, no. 4 (January 1941), 447.

27. Speier, "Morale and Propaganda," in *War in Our Time*, ed. Speier and Alfred Kähler (New York: W. W. Norton, 1939), 324; Speier and Kähler, "Introduction," 13; Henry R. Luce, "The American Century," *Diplomatic History* 23, no. 2 (Spring 1999 [original published in February 1941]), 162.

28. Speier, "Morale and Propaganda," 302–303, 306.

29. Speier, "Treachery," 264–265, 275; Speier, "Morale Policy in Total War," n.d. [1941?], 1, 3–4, Folder 43, Box 7, SP; Speier, "Morale and Propaganda," 318.

30. Kris and Speier, "Programme," 1, 10; Speier, "Morale and Propaganda," 324; Ernst Kris and Speier to John Marshall, February 2, 1942, Folder 3102, Box 260, Subseries 200.R, Series 200, RG 1.1, Projects, FA386, Rockefeller Foundation Records (hereafter RFR), Rockefeller Archive Center, Sleepy Hollow, NY (hereafter RAC).

31. Ernst Kris to John Marshall, February 5, 1941, 1, Folder 3099, Box 260, Subseries 200.R, Series 200, RG 1.1, Projects, FA386, RFR, RAC. For Kris, see Louis Rose, *Psychology, Art, and Antifascism: Ernst Kris, E. H. Gombrich, and the Politics of Caricature* (New Haven: Yale University Press, 2016).

32. Gary, *Nervous*, chapter 3.

33. Kris and Speier, "Programme," 1, 8.

34. Harold Lasswell to John Marshall, December 15, 1940, Folder 3098, Box 260, Subseries 200.R, Series 200, RG 1.1, Projects, FA386, RFR, RAC; Louis Wirth to John Marshall, February 19, 1941, 1, Folder 3099, Box 260, Subseries 200.R, Series 200, RG 1.1, Projects, FA386, RFR, RAC.

35. Executive Committee Meeting Notes, March 21, 1941, 41057, 41055, Folder 3098, Box 260, Subseries 200.R, Series 200, RG 1.1, Projects, FA386, RFR, RAC; John Marshall, "Dr. Ernst Kris," March 3, 1942, Folder 3103, Box 260, Subseries 200.R, Series 200, RG 1.1, Projects, FA386, RFR, RAC; Alvin Johnson to Stephen Childs, February 3, 1941, Folder 3099, Box 260, Subseries 200.R, Series 200, RG 1.1, Projects, FA386, RFR, RAC.

36. Ernst Kris and Speier, "Report of the Research Project on Totalitarian Communication in War Time, About the Work Done in the First Year of Its Existence, and Proposals for Future Research," January 1942, 4, Folder 3102, Box 260, Subseries 200.R, Series 200, RG 1.1, Projects, FA386, RFR, RAC.

37. Gary, *Nervous*, 101; J. Michael Sproule, *Propaganda and Democracy: The American Experience of Media and Mass Persuasion* (New York: Cambridge University Press, 1997), 74–78; Anonymous [Ernst Kris and Speier], *Research Paper No. 1: German Radio News Bulletins and Problems and Methods of Analysis*, December 1941, 1, Box 1 (Totalitarianism Research Project, barcode 3-1207-04002918-7) (now contained in Institute of World Affairs records, NS.02.16.01, unprocessed collection, NSASC).

38. *Research Paper No. 1*, 14–16, 19.

39. Anonymous [Ernst Kris and Speier], *Research Paper No. 3: German Freedom Stations Broadcasting to Britain*, January 1942, 56–59, Box 1 (Totalitarianism Research Project, barcode 3-1207-04002918-7) (now contained in Institute of World Affairs records, NS.02.16.01, unprocessed collection, NSASC).

40. "Mailing List for Research Paper No. 1," n.d. [December 1941], Folder 3101, Box 260, Subseries 200.R, Series 200, RG 1.1, Projects, FA386, RFR, RAC; Harold Carlson to Ernst Kris, January 22, 1942, Folder 3102, Box 260, Subseries 200.R, Series 200, RG 1.1, Projects, FA386, RFR, RAC; E. Y. Hartshorne to Ernst Kris, December 31, 1941, 1, Folder 3101, Box 260, Subseries 200.R, Series 200, RG 1.1, Projects, FA386, RFR, RAC; Robert Tryon to John Marshall, March 6, 1942, 1, Folder 3103, Box 260, Subseries 200.R, Series 200, RG 1.1, Projects, FA386, RFR, RAC; Goodwin Watson to John Marshall, February 17, 1942, Folder 3102, Box 260, Subseries 200.R, Series 200, RG 1.1, Projects, FA386, RFR, RAC.

41. Hadley Cantril to Ernst Kris, February 24, 1942, Folder 3102, Box 260, Subseries 200.R, Series 200, RG 1.1, Projects, FA386, RFR, RAC; Harold Lasswell to John Marshall, "Research Project on *Totalitarian Communication*," February 13, 1942, Folder 3102, Box 260, Subseries 200.R, Series 200, RG 1.1, Projects, FA386, RFR, RAC; John Marshall, "Ernst Kris, Hans Speier," January 8, 1942, 2, Folder 3102, Box 260, Subseries 200.R, Series 200, RG 1.1, Projects, FA386, RFR, RAC; Executive Committee Meeting Notes, April 1, 1942, 42118, Folder 3098, Box 260, Subseries 200.R, Series 200, RG 1.1, Projects, FA386, RFR, RAC; Ernst Kris and Speier, in association with Sidney Axelrad, Hans Herma, Janice Loeb, Heinz Paechter, and Howard B. White, *German Radio Propaganda: Report on Home Broadcasts during the War* (New York: Oxford University Press, 1944). In addition to *German Radio Propaganda*, the project produced a glossary of National Socialist neologisms titled *Nazi-Deutsch*. Heinz Paechter, in association with Bertha Hellman, Hedwig Paechter, and Karl O. Paetel, *Nazi-Deutsch: A Glossary of Contemporary German Usage, with Appendices on Government, Military and Economic Institutions* (New York: Frederick Ungar, 1944). For the difficulties encountered in the run-up to *German Radio Propaganda*'s publication, see Folder 9, Box 13, Ernst Kris Papers, Manuscript Division, Library of Congress, Washington, DC.

42. Joseph E. Roop, *Foreign Broadcast Information Service: History, Part I, 1941–1947* (Washington, DC: CIA, April 1969), 6–9, accessed November 22, 2016, https://www.cia.gov/library/center-for-the-study-of-intelligence/csi-publications/books-and-monographs/foreign-broadcast-information-service/.

43. Harold Graves to Harwood Childs, July 24, 1941, Folder Letters Received and Copies of Letters Sent by Harold N. Graves, 1941–1944, Box 6, Records of the Office of the Director, Reading File of Harold N. Graves Jr., Apr. 1941 to Dec. 1943, Misc. Corres. of Harold N. Graves Jr., 1941–43, Entry 59 and 60, Records of the Foreign Broadcast Intelligence Service, RG 262, NACP; Roop, *Foreign Broadcast Information Service*, 9–11; Harold Graves to Ernst Kris and Speier, December 23, 1941, Folder n.d., Box 66, General Correspondence, Q–Z, Entry 2, RG 262, NACP; Sebastian de Grazia to Speier, November 10, 1941, Folder 3101, Box 260, Subseries 200.R, Series 200, RG 1.1, Projects, FA386, RFR, RAC; Speier to John Marshall, November 14, 1941, Folder 3101, Box 260, Subseries 200.R, Series 200, RG 1.1, Projects, FA386, RFR, RAC; Ernst Kris and Speier, "Statement," December 30, 1941, 1, Folder 3101, Box 260, Subseries 200.R, Series 200, RG 1.1, Projects, FA386, RFR, RAC; Ernst Kris and Speier, "Appendix I: Relations of the Research Project on Totalitarian Communication with United States Government Departments," in "Report of the Research Project on Totalitarian Communication in War Time"; Watson to Marshall, February 17, 1942; John Marshall, "Discussion of the Study of Totalitarian Communication Directed by Drs. Kris and Speier, at the New School for Social Research," February 19, 1942, 1, Folder 3102, Box 260, Subseries 200.R, Series 200, RG 1.1, Projects, FA386, RFR, RAC. Technically, until July 1942 the name of the FBIS group that analyzed foreign broadcasts was the Analysis Section. For simplicity's sake, I refer to it here as the Analysis Division. Goodwin Watson to Ernst Kris and Speier, December 26, 1941, Folder n.d., Box 66, General Correspondence, Q–Z, Entry 2, RG 262,

NACP; Lloyd Free to Speier, January 31, 1942, Folder n.d., Box 66, General Correspondence, Q–Z, Entry 2, RG 262, NACP.

44. Marshall, "Discussion of the Study of Totalitarian Communication," 1; Goodwin Watson to Harold Graves, February 20, 1942, 1, Folder Personnel—Back Records, Box 36, Records of the Analysis Division, General Records (Series II), 1941–44, Entry 74, RG 262, NACP; Goodwin Watson to Harold Graves, March 6, 1942, 2, Folder Personnel—Back Records, Box 36, Records of the Analysis Division, General Records (Series II), 1941–44, Entry 74, RG 262, NACP; U.S. Congress, House of Representatives, Select Committee to Investigate the Federal Communications Commission, *Hearings*, 3861–3862; John Marshall, "Dr. Hans Speier [I]," February 24, 1942, Folder 3102, Box 260, Subseries 200.R, Series 200, RG 1.1, Projects, FA386, RFR, RAC; Speier, Interview, April 5, 1988, 11, Folder 14, Box 10, RAND History Project Interviews (Acc. 1999-0037), National Air and Space Museum, Smithsonian Institution, Washington, DC (hereafter RHPI).

45. Marshall, "Dr. Hans Speier [I]"; John Marshall, "Dr. Hans Speier [II]," February 27, 1942, Folder 3102, Box 260, Subseries 200.R, Series 200, RG 1.1, Projects, FA386, RFR, RAC; Speier to Kurt Riezler, April 12, 1942, 1–2, Folder 57, Box 4, SP; Guy Hottel, "Hans Speier," July 20, 1949, 10, WFO 116–28395, FBI File on Hans Speier, Freedom of Information Act request by author.

46. Marjorie Lamberti, "The Reception of Refugee Scholars from Nazi Germany in America: Philanthropy and Social Change in Higher Education," *Jewish Social Studies* 12, no. 3 (Spring–Summer 2006), 179–181; H. Stuart Hughes, "Social Theory in a New Context," in *The Muses Flee Hitler: Cultural Transfer and Adaptation, 1930–1945*, ed. Jarrell C. Jackman and Carla M. Borden (Washington, DC: Smithsonian Institution Press, 1983), 113; Claus-Dieter Krohn, *Intellectuals in Exile: Refugee Scholars and the New School for Social Research*, trans. Rita and Robert Kimber (Amherst: University of Massachusetts Press, 1993), 165–166; Kris and Speier, "Statement," 1.

47. Goodwin Watson to Robert Leigh, May 12, 1943, Folder New Personnel—German, Box 49, Records of the Analysis Division, Records Relating to Personnel, 1942, Entry 75, RG 262, NACP; Robert Leigh to Goodwin Watson, May 14, 1943, Folder New Personnel—German, Box 49, Records of the Analysis Division, Records Relating to Personnel, 1942, Entry 75, RG 262, NACP; Goodwin Watson note on Robert Leigh to Goodwin Watson, May 14, 1943. A wariness of exiles permeated other organizations of the U.S. state. See Jessica C. E. Gienow-Hecht, *Transmission Impossible: American Journalism as Cultural Diplomacy in Postwar Germany, 1945–1955* (Baton Rouge: Louisiana State University Press, 1999), 18–20; Raffaele Laudani, introduction to *Secret Reports on Nazi Germany: The Frankfurt School Contribution to the War Effort*, by Franz Neumann, Herbert Marcuse, and Otto Kirchheimer, ed. Raffaele Laudani (Princeton: Princeton University Press, 2013), 7.

48. Roy F. Nichols, "War and Research in Social Science," *Proceedings of the American Philosophical Society* 87, no. 4 (January 29, 1944), 361; Alexander H. Leighton, *Human Relations in a Changing World: Observations on the Use of the Social Sciences* (New York: E. P. Dutton, 1949), 43.

49. Roop, *Foreign Broadcast Information Service*, 52–53, 57, 211, 45; Speier, Interview, RHPI, 9, 12.

50. Speier, Interview, RHPI, 8, 12; "Hans Speier, Gesprächsweise Mitteilungen zu einer intellektuellen Autobiographie [II]," transcript of interview by Ursula Ludz, October 8, 19, 20, 1982, 165, Folder 32, Box 2, SP.

51. Alexander George, *Propaganda Analysis: A Study of Inferences Made from Nazi Propaganda in World War II* (Evanston, IL: Row, Peterson, 1959), 83, 6, 40, 42.

52. Ibid., 253.

53. Speier, "What Hitler Might Say on November 8," n.d. [October 29, 1943], 1, Folder 6, Box 8, SP; George, *Analysis*, xi.

54. Speier, "What Hitler Might Say on November 8."

55. Goodwin Watson to Robert Leigh, November 10, 1943, Folder n.d., Box 32, Records of the Analysis Division, General Records (Series I), 1941–44, Entry 73, RG 262, NACP.

56. Goodwin Watson to Speier, November 13, 1943, 1, Folder Administrative Memorandums, Box 31, Records of the Analysis Division, General Records (Series I), 1941–44, Entry 73, RG 262, NACP; "Promotions in the Analysis Division," February 8, 1943, 1, Folder Personnel Memos, Box 36, Records of the Analysis Division, General Records (Series II), 1941–44, Entry 74, RG 262, NACP; Robert Leigh to Speier, July 30, 1943, Folder 5, Box 4, SP.

57. Much of the information in this final section comes from Susan L. Brinson, *The Red Scare, Politics, and the Federal Communications Commission, 1941–1960* (Westport, CT: Praeger, 2004), especially chapter 2; Roop, *Foreign Broadcast Information Service*, chapters 7–8.

58. Robert D. Leigh, "Politicians vs. Bureaucrats: The Case of FCC Chairman Fly and Congressman Cox," *Harper's Magazine* 190, no. 1136 (January 1945), 104–105.

59. Roop, *Foreign Broadcast Information Service*, 211; Theodore Newcomb to Robert Leigh, April 3, 1944, Folder n.d., Box 32, Records of the Analysis Division, General Records (Series I), 1941–44, Entry 73, RG 262, NACP.

4. Psychological Warfare in Theory and Practice

1. Speier to Robert Leigh, December 14, 1942, 1, Folder Memos to T. Newcomb, Box 38, Records of the Analysis Division, General Records (Series II), 1941–44, Entry 74, Records of the Foreign Broadcast Intelligence Service, Record Group (hereafter RG) 262, National Archives at College Park, College Park, MD (hereafter NACP).

2. Weekly Propaganda Directive, Germany (hereafter WPDG), May 11, 1945, 1, Folder Record Regional Directives May 1945, Box 824, Director of Overseas Operations, Record Set of Policy Directives for Overseas Programs, 1942–1945, Entry 363, Records of the Office of War Information, RG 208, NACP.

3. "Propaganda Policy Adviser (Germany) [Job Description]," n.d. [December 1944], 1, Folder 3, Box 2, Hans Speier Papers, German and Jewish Intellectual Émigré Collection, M. E. Grenander Department of Special Collections and Archives, University Libraries, University at Albany, State University of New York, Albany, NY (hereafter SP).

4. WPDG, December 21, 1944, 2, Folder Record Regional Directives December 1944, Box 823, Director of Overseas Operations, Record Set of Policy Directives for Overseas Programs, 1942–1945, Entry 363, RG 208, NACP.

5. Directive on Long Range Media for Germany, December 5, 1944, 5, Folder Basic Policy Directive for Information in Germany, April 26, 1945, Box 825, Director of Overseas Operations, Record Set of Policy Directives for Overseas Programs, 1942–1945, Entry 363, RG 208, NACP.

6. Harold D. Lasswell, "The Relation of Ideological Intelligence to Public Policy," *Ethics* 53, no. 1 (October 1942), 29.

7. The basic history of the Office of War Information, upon which this chapter draws, may be found in Clayton D. Laurie, *The Propaganda Warriors: America's Crusade against Nazi Germany* (Lawrence: University Press of Kansas, 1996); Holly Cowan Shulman, *The Voice of America: Propaganda and Democracy, 1941–1945* (Madison: University of Wisconsin Press, 1990);

Charles A. H. Thomson, *Overseas Information Service of the United States Government* (Washington, DC: Brookings Institution, 1948); Allan M. Winkler, *The Politics of Propaganda: The Office of War Information, 1942–1945* (New Haven: Yale University Press, 1978).

8. In addition to the FIS, the OWI incorporated the Office of Facts and Figures; the Office of Government Reports; the Outpost, Publications, and Pictorial Branches of the Office of the Coordinator of Information; and the elements of the Division of Information of the Office of Emergency Management that were concerned with disseminating public information. Bureau of the Budget, *The United States at War: Development and Administration of the War Program by the Federal Government* (Washington, DC: U.S. Government Printing Office, n.d. [June 1946]), 220–233; Franklin D. Roosevelt, "Executive Order 9182 Establishing the Office of War Information," June 13, 1942, accessed November 26, 2016, http://www.presidency.ucsb.edu/ws/?pid=16273.

9. This paragraph is based on Laurie, *Warriors*, chapter 6; Elmer Davis, "War Information," in *War Information and Censorship*, by Elmer Davis and Byron Price (Washington, DC: American Council on Public Affairs, 1943), 13, 10; Winkler, *Politics*, 112–113, 148; Shulman, *Voice of America*, 99, 152; J. Michael Sproule, *Propaganda and Democracy: The American Experience of Media and Mass Persuasion* (New York: Cambridge University Press, 1997), 192.

10. Edward Barrett to All Staff Members of the Overseas Branch, March 27, 1944, Folder Overseas Branch, Office of the Director, Box 6, Records of the Historian, Records of the Historian Relating to the Overseas Branch, 1942–45, Entry 6B, RG 208, NACP; Wallace Carroll, *Persuade or Perish* (Boston: Houghton Mifflin, 1948), 194, 202–203, 235–236.

11. Carroll, *Persuade*, 232–233, 201; Robert Lee Bishop, "The Overseas Branch of the Office of War Information" (PhD diss., University of Wisconsin, 1966), 102; Theodore Newcomb to Robert Leigh, March 23, 1944, Folder n.d., Box 32, Records of the Analysis Division, General Records (Series I), 1941–44, Entry 73, RG 262, NACP; "Propaganda Policy Adviser," 2.

12. Weekly Report—Foreign Broadcast Intelligence Service, May 14, 1943, Folder 5, Box 4, SP; Joseph E. Roop, *Foreign Broadcast Information Service: History, Part I, 1941–1947* (Washington, DC: CIA, April 1969), 120–122; Speier to Kurt Riezler, February 3, 1944, 2, Folder 57, Box 4, SP.

13. Carroll, *Persuade*, 232.

14. "Propaganda Policy Adviser," 1.

15. Speier and Margaret Otis, "German Radio Propaganda to France during the Battle of France," in *Propaganda in War and Crisis: Materials for American Policy*, ed. Daniel Lerner (New York: George W. Stewart, 1951 [original published in 1944]), 210.

16. Ibid., 212, 214.

17. Speier, "War Aims in Political Warfare," *Social Research* 12, no. 2 (May 1945), 157–158, 169.

18. Speier, "Morale and Propaganda," in *War in Our Time*, ed. Speier and Alfred Kähler (New York: W. W. Norton, 1939), 308; Speier, "Nazi Propaganda and Its Decline," *Social Research* 10, no. 3 (September 1943), 360; Speier, "War Aims," 157.

19. Morris Janowitz, "Written Directives," in *A Psychological Warfare Casebook*, ed. William E. Daugherty in collaboration with Morris Janowitz (Baltimore: Johns Hopkins University Press, 1958), 314–316; Thomson, *Overseas Information Service*, 48–49, 52n9.

20. Carroll, *Persuade*, 234–235; Shulman, *Voice of America*, 161–162; "an ace" and "the decisive man" quoted in Shulman, *Voice of America*, 161.

21. Carroll, *Persuade*, 234–235; Shulman, *Voice of America*, 161–162; Thomson, *Overseas Information Service*, 47–50.

22. Thomson, *Overseas Information Service*, 49.

23. Carroll, *Persuade*, 232–233.

24. Ibid., 235, 237.

25. WPDG, July 21, 1944, 1, Folder Record Regional Directives July 1944, Box 822, Director of Overseas Operations, Record Set of Policy Directives for Overseas Programs, 1942–1945, Entry 363, RG 208, NACP; Carroll, *Persuade*, 260; WPDG, June 23, 1944, 2, Folder Record Regional Directives June 1944, Box 822, Director of Overseas Operations, Record Set of Policy Directives for Overseas Programs, 1942–1945, Entry 363, RG 208, NACP.

26. WPDG, July 7, 1944, 1, Folder Record Regional Directives July 1944, Box 822, Director of Overseas Operations, Record Set of Policy Directives for Overseas Programs, 1942–1945, Entry 363, RG 208, NACP; Central Directive for week of June 20–27, 1944, 2, Folder Record Central Directives May thru June 1944, Box 818, Director of Overseas Operations, Record Set of Policy Directives for Overseas Programs, 1942–1945, Entry 363, RG 208, NACP.

27. Special Guidance on Germany, July 21, 1944, Folder Record Special Guidances June through September 1944, Box 826, Director of Overseas Operations, Record Set of Policy Directives for Overseas Programs, 1942–1945, Entry 363, RG 208, NACP; WPDG, July 28, 1944, 3, Folder Record Regional Directives July 1944, Box 822, Director of Overseas Operations, Record Set of Policy Directives for Overseas Programs, 1942–1945, Entry 363, RG 208, NACP; Special Guidance on Hitler's Speech, July 21, 1944, 1, Folder Record Special Guidances June through September 1944, Box 826, Director of Overseas Operations, Record Set of Policy Directives for Overseas Programs, 1942–1945, Entry 363, RG 208, NACP.

28. Special Guidance on Germany; WPDG, July 28, 1944, 1.

29. WPDG, August 11, 1944, 1, Folder Record Regional Directives August 1944, Box 822, Director of Overseas Operations, Record Set of Policy Directives for Overseas Programs, 1942–1945, Entry 363, RG 208, NACP; Special Guidance on Goebbels' Speech, July 26, 1944, 1, Folder Record Special Guidances June through September 1944, Box 826, Director of Overseas Operations, Record Set of Policy Directives for Overseas Programs, 1942–1945, Entry 363, RG 208, NACP; WPDG, August 4, 1944, 2, Folder Record Regional Directives August 1944, Box 822, Director of Overseas Operations, Record Set of Policy Directives for Overseas Programs, 1942–1945, Entry 363, RG 208, NACP.

30. Carroll, *Persuade*, 295, 290.

31. WPDG, December 21, 1944, 2, 1.

32. WPDG, September 21, 1944, 1, Folder Record Regional Directives September 1944, Box 822, Director of Overseas Operations, Record Set of Policy Directives for Overseas Programs, 1942–1945, Entry 363, RG 208, NACP; WPDG, October 5, 1944, 1, Folder Record Regional Directives October 1944, Box 822, Director of Overseas Operations, Record Set of Policy Directives for Overseas Programs, 1942–1945, Entry 363, RG 208, NACP.

33. Carroll, *Persuade*, 339; Interim Guidance on German Counter-Offensive, December 26, 1944, Folder Record Special Guidances October through December 1944, Box 826, Director of Overseas Operations, Record Set of Policy Directives for Overseas Programs, 1942–1945, Entry 363, RG 208, NACP; WPDG, January 12, 1945, 1, Folder Record Regional Directives January 1945, Box 823, Director of Overseas Operations, Record Set of Policy Directives for Overseas Programs, 1942–1945, Entry 363, RG 208, NACP; Interim Guidance on German Counter-Offensive, 1; WPDG, January 19, 1945, 1, Folder Record Regional Directives January 1945, Box 823, Director of Overseas Operations, Record Set of Policy Directives for Overseas Programs, 1942–1945, Entry 363, RG 208, NACP.

34. WPDG, February 16, 1945, 1, Folder Record Regional Directives February 1945, Box 823, Director of Overseas Operations, Record Set of Policy Directives for Overseas Programs, 1942–1945, Entry 363, RG 208, NACP.

35. Carroll, *Persuade*, 238; Laurie, *Warriors*, 180–181.

36. WPDG, April 20, 1945, 1, Folder Record Regional Directives April 1945, Box 823, Director of Overseas Operations, Record Set of Policy Directives for Overseas Programs, 1942–1945, Entry 363, RG 208, NACP; WPDG, April 27, 1945, 2–3, Folder Record Regional Directives April 1945, Box 823, Director of Overseas Operations, Record Set of Policy Directives for Overseas Programs, 1942–1945, Entry 363, RG 208, NACP; Special Guidance on Hitler's Death, May 1, 1945, 2, Folder Record Special Guidances May through Oct. 1945, Box 826, Director of Overseas Operations, Record Set of Policy Directives for Overseas Programs, 1942–1945, Entry 363, RG 208, NACP.

37. Special Guidance on Hitler's Death, 2; WPDG, May 4, 1945, 1, Folder Record Regional Directives May 1945, Box 824, Director of Overseas Operations, Record Set of Policy Directives for Overseas Programs, 1942–1945, Entry 363, RG 208, NACP.

38. WPDG, May 11, 1945, 1; Leonard W. Doob, "The Utilization of Social Scientists in the Overseas Branch of the Office of War Information," *American Political Science Review* 41, no. 4 (August 1947), 667, 664; Laurie, *Warriors*, 125; "Research Seminar in International Communication [Minutes]," November 29, 1956, 1–2, Folder M.I.T.-C.I.S., Research in International Communication, Box 74, Ithiel de Sola Pool Papers, MC 440, Massachusetts Institute of Technology, Institute Archives and Special Collections, Cambridge, MA; Thomson, *Overseas Information Service*, 89–90; Bishop, "Overseas," 28; Franklin D. Roosevelt, "Executive Order 9312 on the Office of War Information," March 9, 1943, accessed November 26, 2016, http://www.presidency.ucsb.edu/ws/?pid=16372.

39. M. I. Gurfein and Morris Janowitz, "Trends in Wehrmacht Morale," *Public Opinion Quarterly* 10, no. 1 (Spring 1946), 78–79; Edward A. Shils and Morris Janowitz, "Cohesion and Disintegration in the Wehrmacht in World War II," *Public Opinion Quarterly* 12, no. 2 (Summer 1948), 314; Winkler, *Politics*, 136; Laurie, *Warriors*, 230; Carroll, *Persuade*, 367.

40. WPDG, May 11, 1945, 1; Directive on Long Range Media for Germany, 5–6.

41. Directive on Basic Themes for Output to Germany: Theme #1: German War Guilt, May 29, 1945, 2, Folder Directive on Basic Themes for Output to Germany, May 29, 1945, Box 825, Director of Overseas Operations, Record Set of Policy Directives for Overseas Programs, 1942–1945, Entry 363, RG 208, NACP.

42. Speier, "Honor and Social Structure," *Social Research* 2, no. 1 (February 1935), 79; Konrad H. Jarausch, *After Hitler: Recivilizing Germans, 1945–1995*, trans. Brandon Hunziker (New York: Oxford University Press, 2006), 26; WPDG, May 11, 1945, 2; Special Guidance on German Military Exit Propaganda, May 11, 1945, 1, Folder Record Special Guidances May through Oct. 1945, Box 826, Director of Overseas Operations, Record Set of Policy Directives for Overseas Programs, 1942–1945, Entry 363, RG 208, NACP.

43. WPDG, August 24, 1945, 2, Folder Record Regional Directives August 1945, Box 824, Director of Overseas Operations, Record Set of Policy Directives for Overseas Programs, 1942–1945, Entry 363, RG 208, NACP.

44. Harry S. Truman, "Executive Order 9608—Providing for the Termination of the Office of War Information, and for the Disposition of Its Functions and of Certain Functions of the Office of Inter-American Affairs," August 31, 1945, accessed November 26, 2016, http://www.presidency.ucsb.edu/ws/?pid=60671; Ferdinand Kuhn Jr., to Speier, October 3, 1945, 1, Folder 5, Box 2, SP. For the importance of first letters home in the history of exile, see David Kettler, *The Liquidation of Exile: Studies in the Intellectual Emigration of the 1930s* (London: Anthem Press, 2011), chapter 6.

45. Speier, Bad Homburg, November 4, 1945, in Speier, *From the Ashes of Disgrace: A Journal from Germany, 1945–1955* (Amherst: University of Massachusetts Press, 1981) (hereafter *FAD*), 26.

46. Speier, Bad Homburg, November 14, 1945, in *FAD*, 33; Speier, Bad Homburg, October 28, 1945, in *FAD*, 21.

47. Karl Jaspers, *Die Schuldfrage* (Heidelberg: Lambert Schneider, 1946); Speier, November 18, 1945 [I], in *FAD*, 37–38.

48. Speier, November 18, 1945 [I], in *FAD*, 40.

49. Speier, November 18, 1945 [II], in *FAD*, 43. Emphasis added.

5. The Making of a Defense Intellectual

1. Odd Arne Westad, "Beginnings of the End: How the Cold War Crumbled," in *Reinterpreting the End of the Cold War: Issues, Interpretations, Periodizations*, ed. Silvio Pons and Federico Romero (London: Frank Cass, 2005), 68.

2. Janet Farrell Brodie, "Learning Secrecy in the Early Cold War: The RAND Corporation," *Diplomatic History* 35, no. 4 (September 2011), 647.

3. For the traditional U.S. foreign policy elite, see Robert D. Dean, *Imperial Brotherhood: Gender and the Making of Cold War Foreign Policy* (Amherst: University of Massachusetts Press, 2001).

4. Speier to Sigmund Neumann, September 8, 1945, 2, Folder 42, Box 4, Hans Speier Papers, German and Jewish Intellectual Émigré Collection, M. E. Grenander Department of Special Collections and Archives, University Libraries, University at Albany, State University of New York, Albany, NY (hereafter SP); Speier, Interview, RAND History Project Interviews (Acc. 1999-0037), National Air and Space Museum, Smithsonian Institution, Washington, DC (hereafter RHPI), 18. When World War II ended, there was a general "demobilization fever" among civilian officials. Earl F. Ziemke, *The U.S. Army in the Occupation of Germany, 1944–1946* (Washington, DC: Center of Military History, 1975), 448.

5. Frankfurt to William Stone and Ferdinand Kuhn Jr., November 20, 1945, 2, Folder Germany Cable, Box 108, Director of Overseas Operations, Area Policy Files, 1943–1946, Entry 358, Records of the Office of War Information, Record Group (hereafter RG) 208, National Archives at College Park, College Park, MD (hereafter NACP); Speier, November 23, 1945, in Speier, *From the Ashes of Disgrace: A Journal from Germany, 1945–1955* (Amherst: University of Massachusetts Press, 1981) (hereafter *FAD*), 45; Speier to Douglas Waples, October 7, 1946, 1, Folder 4, Box 2, SP; Speier to Leo Strauss, June 4, 1946, 1, Folder 12, Box 3, Leo Strauss Papers, Special Collections Research Center, University of Chicago Library, Chicago, IL (hereafter Strauss Papers); Speier to Henry Leverich, July 24, 1946, Folder 4, Box 2, SP; Speier, Interview, RHPI, 19.

6. Speier to Waples, October 7, 1946, 2; Jessica C. E. Gienow-Hecht, *Transmission Impossible: American Journalism as Cultural Diplomacy in Postwar Germany, 1945–1955* (Baton Rouge: Louisiana State University Press, 1999), 5, 181–182; Larry Hartenian, *Controlling Information in U.S. Occupied Germany: Media Manipulation and Propaganda* (Lewiston, NY: Edwin Mellen Press, 2003), 17; John H. Hilldring and Velma Hastings Cassidy, "Machinery for Making and Executing Policy in the Occupied Countries: Germany, Austria, Japan, and Korea," in *American Policy in Occupied Areas*, State Department Publication 2794 (Washington, DC: Government Printing Office, 1947), 7; Charles A. H. Thomson, *Overseas Information Service of the United States Government* (Washington, DC: Brookings Institution, 1948), 202; Edward N. Peterson, *The American Occupation of Germany: Retreat to Victory* (Detroit: Wayne State University Press, 1977), chapter 2; Speier to Bryn Hovde, June 3, 1947, 1, Folder 2, Box 2, SP. There is an enormous amount of literature written on the U.S. occupation of Germany. See Thomas W. Maulucci Jr., introduction to *GIs in Germany: The Social, Economic, Cultural, and Political History of the American Military Presence*, ed. Thomas W. Maulucci Jr.,

and Detlef Junker (Washington, DC: Cambridge University Press/German Historical Institute, 2013), 3n7. For the ADO's official responsibilities, see *Department of State Bulletin* XV, no. 377 (September 22, 1946), 557. For the OIC's official duties, see *Department of State Bulletin* XIV, no. 341 (January 6 and 13, 1946), 42–45.

7. Speier, introduction to *FAD*, 3; Henry Leverich and Speier to William Benton, "Possibilities for American Broadcasts to the Soviet Union in the Russian Language," April 12, 1946, 3, Folder 4, Box 2, SP.

8. Speier, Bad Homburg, March 20, 1946, in *FAD*, 63; Rebecca L. Boehling, *A Question of Priorities: Democratic Reform and Economic Recovery in Postwar Germany: Frankfurt, Munich, and Stuttgart under U.S. Occupation, 1945–1949* (New York: Berghahn Books, 1998), 2–3; James F. Tent, *Mission on the Rhine: Reeducation and Denazification in American-Occupied Germany* (Chicago: University of Chicago Press, 1982); Harold Zink, *American Military Government in Germany* (New York: Macmillan, 1947), 156–157.

9. Speier, "Immediate and Future Responsibilities of the Department of State for the Reeducation of Germany," May 28, 1946, 8, 3–5, Folder 11, Box 8, SP.

10. Ibid., 8.

11. Tony Judt, *Postwar: A History of Europe since 1945* (New York: Penguin, 2005), 86.

12. Thomson, *Overseas Information Service*, 259; Speier to William Stone, "SWNCC [State-War-Navy Coordinating Committee] Directive for Germany," January 3, 1947, Folder 4, Box 2, SP.

13. Speier, "History of and Draft Paper, 'Licensing of a Political Press in the US Zone of Germany,'" January 3, 1947, 1–2, Folder 4, Box 2, SP; Speier to Stone, "SWNCC Directive for Germany," January 3, 1947.

14. Speier to Alexander Gode-von Aesch, July 9, 1947, Folder 77, Box 3, SP; Douglas Waples to Speier, July 5, 1946, 1, Folder 4, Box 2, SP; Speier to Douglas Waples, July 17, 1946, 1, 3, Folder 4, Box 2, SP; Speier to Hans Wallenberg, October 7, 1946, Folder 110, Box 4, SP; Speier to Gode-von Aesch, July 9, 1947, 3; Speier to Douglas Waples, February 21, 1947, Folder 4, Box 2, SP; Speier to Fritz von Unruh, February 21, 1947, Folder 103, Box 4, SP.

15. Speier, "'Reeducation'—The U.S. Policy," in *Social Order and the Risks of War: Papers in Political Sociology* (New York: George W. Stewart, 1952 [original essay from 1947]), 404–405, 407, 410, 413.

16. Speier to Leo Strauss, September 16, 1946, Folder 12, Box 3, Strauss Papers; Speier to Arnold Brecht, August 8, 1947, Folder 3, Box 6, Arnold Brecht Papers, German and Jewish Intellectual Émigré Collection, M. E. Grenander Department of Special Collections and Archives, University Libraries, University at Albany, State University of New York, Albany, NY; "Hans Speier, Gesprächsweise Mitteilungen zu einer intellektuellen Autobiographie [II]," transcript of interview by Ursula Ludz, October 8, 19, 20, 1982, 229, Folder 32, Box 2, SP; Alexander George to Speier, November 8, 1946, 1, Folder 74, Box 3, SP.

17. Claus-Dieter Krohn, *Intellectuals in Exile: Refugee Scholars and the New School for Social Research*, trans. Rita and Robert Kimber (Amherst: University of Massachusetts Press, 1993), 139–149; Speier to Alvin Johnson, March 5, 1944, 1, Folder 115, Box 3, SP; Speier to Hans Staudinger, n.d. [early 1944?], 1, Folder 84, Box 4, SP; Speier to Hans Staudinger, March 13, 1943 [mislabeled, should be 1944], 2–3, Folder 84, Box 4, SP; Speier to Adolph Löwe, February 13, 1944, 2, Folder 14, Box 4, SP.

18. Adolph Löwe to Speier, February 23, 1944, Folder 14, Box 4, SP; Speier to Adolph Löwe, February 25, 1944, 1, Folder 14, Box 4, SP; Speier to Kurt Riezler, February 3, 1944, 1, Folder 57, Box 4, SP.

19. Speier to Staudinger, n.d. [early 1944?], 2; Speier to Hans Staudinger, March 3, 1944, 1, Folder 84, Box 4, SP; Hans Staudinger to Speier, February 28, 1944, 1, Folder 84, Box 4, SP; Speier

to Leo Strauss, May 15, 1946, 1, Folder 12, Box 3, Strauss Papers; *New School Bulletin: The Graduate Faculty of Political and Social Science, Courses of Study, 1946–1947* III, no. 37 (May 13, 1946), 29–30.

20. Speier to Albert Salomon, March 5, 1944, Folder 67, Box 4, SP.

21. Speier to Riezler, February 3, 1944, 1–2.

22. Speier, Interview, RHPI, 21, 19; *New School Bulletin* V, no. 4 (September 22, 1947), 2; *New School Bulletin: The Graduate Faculty of Political and Social Science, Announcement for the 1948 Spring Term* V, no. 19 (January 5, 1948), 5.

23. U.S. Congress, Senate, Committee on Military Affairs, *Hearings before the Committee on Military Affairs*, 79th Cong., 1st sess., 1945, 87; "Summary Notes on Telephone Discussion with Robert Lovett," October 29, 1958, 3, Folder 2, Box 4, Lawrence J. Henderson Papers (hereafter Henderson Papers), RAND Corporate Archives, RAND Corporation, Santa Monica, CA (hereafter RCA). The major works on RAND on which I have relied are Martin J. Collins, *Cold War Laboratory: RAND, the Air Force, and the American State, 1945–1950* (Washington, DC: Smithsonian Institution Press, 2002); David R. Jardini, "Out of the Blue Yonder: The RAND Corporation's Diversification into Social Welfare Research, 1946–1968" (PhD diss., Carnegie Mellon University, 1996); David R. Jardini, *Thinking through the Cold War: RAND, National Security, and Domestic Policy, 1945–1975* (self-published, September 2013), Kindle Edition; Fred Kaplan, *The Wizards of Armageddon* (Stanford: Stanford University Press, 1991); Andrew David May, "The RAND Corporation and the Dynamics of American Strategic Thought, 1946–1962" (PhD diss., Emory University, 1993); Bruce L. R. Smith, *The RAND Corporation: Case Study of a Nonprofit Advisory Corporation* (Cambridge, MA: Harvard University Press, 1966). The story told here is simplified, omitting characters, such as Edward Bowles, irrelevant to Speier.

24. Jardini, *Thinking*, chapter 2.

25. R. D. Specht, "RAND—A Personal View of Its History," *Operations Research* 8, no. 6 (November–December 1960), 825–827; Jardini, *Thinking*, chapter 3; "Chronology of Organization: The RAND Corporation," April 12, 1954, 1, Folder 2, Box 4, Henderson Papers, RCA; "Articles of Incorporation of the RAND Corporation," May 10, 1948 [endorsed May 14, 1948], Folder 11, Box 1-1, Brownlee Haydon Collection, RCA.

26. Arthur Raymond, "RAND (For Presentation at First Meeting of RAND Council)," D-74, December 12, 1946, 5, RCA; J. D. Williams to Frank Collbohm, "Project RAND," D-7, June 7, 1946, 3; J. D. Williams, "Summary of Conferences on Military Worth (July 25, 26, August 2)," D-17, August 6, 1946, 1, RCA.

27. J. D. Williams, "Subjective Account of the December Meetings among Olaf Helmer, Frederick Mosteller, S. S. Wilks, Warren Weaver, and JDW," RAD-79, January 28, 1947, RCA; Warren Weaver, "Appendix C: Proposed Program of the Military Worth Section of RAND," December 14, 1946, in "Subjective Account of the December Meetings among Olaf Helmer, Frederick Mosteller, S. S. Wilks, Warren Weaver, and JDW," by J. D. Williams, RAD-79, January 28, 1947, RCA; Olaf Helmer, "Recommendations Concerning the Participation of Social Scientists in RAND," December 10, 1946, 2, in "Subjective Account of the December Meetings among Olaf Helmer, Frederick Mosteller, S. S. Wilks, Warren Weaver, and JDW," by J. D. Williams, RAD-79, January 28, 1947, RCA.

28. Nicholas Rescher, "The Berlin Group and the USA: A Narrative of Personal Interactions," in *The Berlin Group and the Philosophy of Logical Empiricism*, ed. Nikolay Milkov and Volker Peckhaus (Dordrecht: Springer, 2013), 36.

29. Speier, Interview, RHPI, 29, 22.

30. U.S. Air Force Project RAND, *Conference of Social Scientists: September 14 to 19, 1947—New York* (Santa Monica, CA: RAND Corporation, R-106, June 9, 1948), 1.

31. Ibid., 5.

32. Ibid., 8; Speier, *The RAND Social Science Program* (Santa Monica, CA: RAND Corporation, D-717-PR, February 21, 1950), 4; Rescher, "Berlin," 35; Joy Rohde, *Armed with Expertise: The Militarization of American Social Research during the Cold War* (Ithaca: Cornell University Press, 2013), 31, 34–35, 54; Christopher Simpson, *Science of Coercion: Communication Research and Psychological Warfare, 1945–1960* (New York: Oxford University Press, 1994), 8.

33. "Gesprächsweise [II]," 209.

34. Brownlee Haydon, *Interview with Leo Rosten* (Santa Monica, CA: RAND Corporation, D-20037, August 11, 1969), 6–7.

35. "Report by the National Security Council on Coordination of Foreign Information Measures [NSC-4]," December 17, 1947, accessed November 29, 2016, http://fas.org/irp/offdocs/nsc-hst/nsc-4.htm; "National Security Council Directive to Director of Central Intelligence Hillenkoetter [NSC-4A]," December 17, 1947, Document 257, *Foreign Relations of the United States, 1945–1950: Emergence of the Intelligence Establishment*, ed. C. Thomas Thorne Jr., and Davis S. Patterson (Washington, DC: Government Printing Office, 2007), accessed November 29, 2016, https://history.state.gov/historicaldocuments/frus1945–50Intel/d257; "National Security Council Directive on Office of Special Projects [NSC-10/2]," June 18, 1948, Document 292, *Foreign Relations of the United States, 1945–1950: Emergence of the Intelligence Establishment*, ed. C. Thomas Thorne Jr., and Davis S. Patterson (Washington, DC: Government Printing Office, 2007), accessed November 29, 2016, https://history.state.gov/historicaldocuments/frus1945–50Intel/d292; "Report by the National Security Council on U.S. Objectives with Respect to the USSR to Counter Soviet Threats to U.S. Security [NSC-20/4]," November 23, 1948, Document 61, *Foreign Relations of the United States, 1948, General: The United Nations*, Volume I, Part 2, ed. Neal H. Petersen, Ralph R. Goodwin, Marvin W. Kranz, and William Z. Slany (Washington, DC: Government Printing Office, 1976), accessed November 29, 2016, https://history.state.gov/historicaldocuments/frus1948v01p2/d61; Speier, *RAND Social Science Program*, 1.

36. Speier, Interview, RHPI, 26, 30.

37. Frank Collbohm to Karl Compton, L-736, January 22, 1951, 3–4, Reel 1046, Series Ford Foundation Grants—O to R, FA732F, Ford Foundation Records, Rockefeller Archive Center, Sleepy Hollow, NY. Speier had gained an admiration for the intelligence of military officers after working with them during and after World War II, which probably also increased his interest in RAND. Speier to Bernard Brodie, November 30, 1954, Folder The Washington Office, Box 4, Bernard Brodie Papers (Collection 1223), UCLA Library Special Collections, Charles E. Young Research Library, Los Angeles, CA.

38. Speier, Interview, RHPI, 48, 51; "Individuals Rendering Consulting or Part-Time Professional Services to the Economics and Social Science Divisions of the RAND Corporation," ca. 1954, Folder 4, Box 2, J. Richard Goldstein Papers, RCA; Speier to Harold Hurwitz, April 23, 1979, Folder 107, Box 3, SP; Edward Shils to Speier, August 9, 1948, 1, Folder Correspondence 1948, Box 1, Series III, Edward A. Shils Papers, Special Collections Research Center, University of Chicago Library, Chicago, IL (hereafter Shils Papers). For Frank Collbohm's management style, also see Charles Hitch, Interview, February 9, 1988, 15–16, Folder 4, Box 9, RHPI.

39. Karl Mannheim, *Ideology and Utopia: An Introduction to the Sociology of Knowledge*, trans. Louis Wirth and Edward Shils (San Diego: Harcourt, 1985 [1936; original published in 1929]), 160; Speier, Interview, RHPI, 56; Speier, *RAND Social Science Program*, 2. The quotations "a specialist . . ." and "to bring knowledge . . ." come from Speier's prospectus for a Division for International Studies he intended to found at the New School in 1947–1948, though they describe well what he sought in those he hired to RAND. Speier, "A Prospective Division for International Studies," February 12, 1948, 5, Folder 2, Box 9, SP.

40. "Conference on Elite Studies, December 22–24, 1948, Washington Office: Summary," January 3, 1949, Folder 1095, Box 89, Harold Dwight Lasswell Papers (MS 1043), Manuscripts and Archives, Yale University Library, New Haven, CT (hereafter Lasswell Papers); Alexander George, *Propaganda Analysis: A Study of Inferences Made from Nazi Propaganda in World War II* (Evanston, IL: Row, Peterson, 1959); U.S. Air Force Project RAND, *Conference on Methods for Studying the Psychological Effects of Unconventional Weapons* (Santa Monica, CA: RAND Corporation, RM-120, January 26–28, 1949); Speier to Margaret Mead, May 18, 1949, 1, Folder 1, Box G77, Margaret Mead Papers and South Pacific Ethnographic Archives, Manuscript Division, Library of Congress, Washington, DC (hereafter Mead Papers); Nathan Leites, *The Operational Code of the Politburo* (New York: McGraw-Hill, 1951); Folder Rand Corp., 1947–48, Box G76, Mead Papers; Folders 1 and 2, Box G77, Mead Papers; Speier, *Psychological Warfare Reconsidered* (Santa Monica, CA: RAND Corporation, P-196, February 5, 1951); Paul Lazarsfeld to Speier, June 23, 1949, 1, Folder Project RAND, Box 7, Papers of Samuel Andrew Stouffer, HUGFP 31.6, Harvard University Archives, Cambridge, MA.

41. Speier to Edward Shils, December 14, 1953, 1, Folder Speier, Hans Correspondence, Box 5, Series III, Shils Papers.

42. Brodie, "Secrecy."

43. Hans [last name unknown] to Herbert Marcuse and Otto Kirchheimer [misidentified as a letter from Hans Speier], September 16, 1948, 1, Folder 22, Box 2, Otto Kirchheimer Papers, German and Jewish Intellectual Émigré Collection, M. E. Grenander Department of Special Collections and Archives, University Libraries, University at Albany, State University of New York, Albany, NY; Brodie, "Secrecy," 653; Speier to Philip Mosely, WL-242, April 19, 1950, 1, Folder RAND Corporation, 1950–54, Box 19, Philip E. Mosely Collection (Record Series 15/35/51), University of Illinois at Urbana-Champaign Archives, Urbana, IL; Paul Lazarsfeld, July 1950, 1, Folder Round Letters I, Box 3A, Paul Felix Lazarsfeld Papers, Rare Book and Manuscript Library, Columbia University Library, New York, NY; Folder 74, Box 3, SP; Folder 78, Box 3, SP; Folder 79, Box 3, SP; Frank Collbohm, Interview, July 28, 1987, 28, Folder 13, Box 8, RHPI.

44. Brodie, "Secrecy," 652–653; "Gesprächsweise [II]," 217.

45. Emil Lederer, "The Search for Truth," *Social Research* 4, no. 3 (September 1937), 278–279.

46. Speier, "War Aims in Political Warfare," *Social Research* 12, no. 2 (May 1945), 160; Speier, "The Future of German Nationalism," *Social Research* 14, no. 4 (December 1947), 425, 445.

47. Speier to Richard Martin, June 24, 1978, 2, Folder 32, Box 5, SP.

48. Speier, "Soviet View of Diplomacy," March 1, 1949, 2, 1, Folder 28, Box 9, SP; Speier to Paul Kecskemeti, "Your Memorandum on PW Strategy of March 31, 1949," April 11, 1949, 2, Folder 120, Box 3, SP.

49. Arnold A. Offner, "Liberation or Dominance? The Ideology of U.S. National Security Policy," in *The Long War: A New History of U.S. National Security Policy since World War II*, ed. Andrew J. Bacevich (New York: Columbia University Press, 2007), 6–8; Speier, "Comments on Current Policy Requirements," 2, 4, November 21, 1949, Folder 32, Box 9, SP; Speier, "Foreign Policy and International Communication: A Case Study of German Rearmament," September 10–12, 1953, 16, Folder 61, Box 9, SP; Speier, "Comments on Harold D. Lasswell's 'The Prospects of Cooperation in a Bipolar World,'" April 11, 1949, 3, Folder 1095, Box 89, Lasswell Papers.

50. Speier, "Current Policy," 5–6; [Redacted sender] to the Executive Director, "Panel on Human Relations and Morale," April 9, 1948, 2, CIA-RDP80R01731R003500200050–1, CIA Records Search Tool, https://www.cia.gov/library/readingroom/collection/crest-25-year-program-archive; Speier, "Social Consequences of the Use of Atomic Energy for Peaceful Purposes," n.d. [Summer 1946], 1, Folder 75, Box 4, SP.

51. Speier, "Historical Development of Public Opinion," *American Journal of Sociology* 55, no. 4 (January 1950), 387. The phrase "those who carry . . ." comes from Speier's description of a former Wehrmacht officer's perspective, though it accurately describes his own opinion as well. Speier, "5 April 1954: Interview with Axel von dem Bussche-Streithorst, Bonn, Restaurant Kranzler—2 ½ Hours," Log Note No. 7, 14, Folder 5, Box 9, SP. According to Markman Ellis, Speier's argument, which he offered in "Historical Development of Public Opinion," that eighteenth-century coffeehouses and salons were critical, in Ellis's words, to encouraging "the development of public opinion," influenced the work of Jürgen Habermas, Terry Eagleton, and others. Markman Ellis, *The Coffee House: A Cultural History* (London: Weidenfeld and Nicolson, 2004), 223.

52. For propaganda in the 1950s, see Kenneth Osgood, *Total Cold War: Eisenhower's Secret Propaganda Battle at Home and Abroad* (Lawrence: University Press of Kansas, 2006).

53. Speier, *Soviet Atomic Blackmail and the North Atlantic Alliance* (Santa Monica, CA: RAND Corporation, RM-1837, December 10, 1956); Speier, *Divided Berlin: The Anatomy of Soviet Political Blackmail* (New York: Frederick A. Praeger, 1960); Nathan Leites and Speier, *Possibilities of Research on the Subject Soviet Behavior in the Case of an Increase in Soviet Military Capability* (Santa Monica, CA: RAND Corporation, D-514, June 8, 1949), 11.

6. The Adviser

1. The books I have relied on in this chapter are Laura A. Belmonte, *Selling the American Way: U.S. Propaganda and the Cold War* (Philadelphia: University of Pennsylvania Press, 2008); Nicholas J. Cull, *The Cold War and the United States Information Agency: American Propaganda and Public Diplomacy, 1945–1989* (New York: Cambridge University Press, 2008); Peter Grose, *Operation Rollback: America's Secret War behind the Iron Curtain* (Boston: Houghton Mifflin, 2000); Justin Hart, *Empire of Ideas: The Origins of Public Diplomacy and the Transformation of U.S. Foreign Policy* (New York: Oxford University Press, 2013); Walter L. Hixson, *Parting the Curtain: Propaganda, Culture, and the Cold War, 1945–1961* (New York: St. Martin's Press, 1997); Scott Lucas, *Freedom's War: The American Crusade against the Soviet Union* (New York: New York University Press, 1999); Kaeten Mistry, *The United States, Italy and the Origins of the Cold War: Waging Political Warfare, 1945–1950* (Cambridge: Cambridge University Press, 2014); Gregory Mitrovich, *Undermining the Kremlin: America's Strategy to Subvert the Soviet Bloc, 1947–1956* (Ithaca: Cornell University Press, 2000); Kenneth Osgood, *Total Cold War: Eisenhower's Secret Propaganda Battle at Home and Abroad* (Lawrence: University Press of Kansas, 2006); Shawn J. Parry-Giles, *The Rhetorical Presidency, Propaganda, and the Cold War, 1945–1955* (Westport, CT: Praeger, 2002); Giles Scott-Smith, *Networks of Empire: The US State Department's Foreign Leader Program in the Netherlands, France, and Britain, 1950–1970* (Brussels: Peter Lang, 2008).

2. Assessing Speier's precise impact on U.S. foreign policy is a difficult task. Only rarely can one trace Speier's ideas from a report he wrote or a meeting he had through the government bureaucracy and into a policy paper. The best a historian can generally do is examine the similarities between Speier's language and arguments and those that appear in government documents that he had a reasonable chance of influencing; stated simply, one can establish only correlations between his ideas and policy.

3. Kevin M. Schultz, *Tri-Faith America: How Catholics and Jews Held Postwar America to Its Protestant Promise* (New York: Oxford University Press, 2011).

4. Hart, *Empire*, 78–79, 82–83, 130–133, 152, 158; Hixson, *Parting*, chapter 1; Parry-Giles, *Rhetorical*, 19–22. The classic statements on the strategy of truth are Elmer Davis, "OWI Has

a Job," *Public Opinion Quarterly* 7, no. 1 (Spring 1943), 8; Archibald MacLeish, "The Strategy of Truth," in *A Time to Act: Selected Addresses* (Boston: Houghton Mifflin, 1943), 19–31.

5. William Benton, "The Struggle for the Minds and Loyalties of Mankind—Proposing a Marshall Plan of Ideas," 96 *Cong. Rec.* 3763 (1950), 3763–3764; Belmonte, *Selling*, 39–43; Cull, *United States Information Agency*, 51–67; Hixson, *Parting*, 14–16; Parry-Giles, *Rhetorical*, 57–65, 76–78; Harry S. Truman, "Address on Foreign Policy at a Luncheon of the American Society of Newspaper Editors," April 20, 1950, accessed November 30, 2016, http://www.presidency.ucsb.edu/ws/?pid=13768.

6. Christopher Simpson, *Science of Coercion: Communication Research and Psychological Warfare, 1945–1960* (New York: Oxford University Press, 1994), chapter 4; Speier, "The Future of Psychological Warfare," *Public Opinion Quarterly* 12, no. 1 (Spring 1948), 9; Speier, "Historical Development of Public Opinion," *American Journal of Sociology* 55, no. 4 (January 1950), 387.

7. Franz Borkenau, *Pareto* (New York: John Wiley, 1936); William David Jones, *The Lost Debate: German Socialist Intellectuals and Totalitarianism* (Urbana: University of Illinois Press, 1999); Frederick Pollock, "State Capitalism: Its Possibilities and Limitations," in *Critical Theory and Society: A Reader*, ed. Stephen Eric Bronner and Douglas MacKay Kellner (New York: Routledge, 1989 [original published in 1941]), 95–118; Speier, *The RAND Social Science Program* (Santa Monica, CA: RAND Corporation, D-717-PR, February 21, 1950), 11–12; "Conference on Elite Studies, December 22–24, 1948, Washington Office: Summary," January 3, 1949, 6, Folder 1095, Box 89, Harold Dwight Lasswell Papers (MS 1043), Manuscripts and Archives, Yale University Library, New Haven, CT.

8. Speier, *Psychological Warfare Reconsidered* (Santa Monica, CA: RAND Corporation, P-196, February 5, 1951), 7, 9.

9. Speier, "Political and Psychological Strategy," February 11, 1952, 12, U.S. Declassified Documents Online (hereafter USDDO), accessed November 30, 2016, http://tinyurl.galegroup.com/tinyurl/45SLR0.

10. Speier, *Reconsidered*, 30–38, 9; Speier, "Political and Psychological Strategy," 19–20; Speier, "Psychological and Political Strategy: Notes on a Talk Given at the National War College," February 11, 1952, 14–15, Folder 47, Box 9, Hans Speier Papers, German and Jewish Intellectual Émigré Collection, M. E. Grenander Department of Special Collections and Archives, University Libraries, University at Albany, State University of New York, Albany, NY (hereafter SP).

11. Mitrovich, *Undermining*, 7–8; Scott-Smith, *Networks*, 257–265; Speier, "Political and Psychological Strategy," 1.

12. Edward W. Barrett, *Truth Is Our Weapon* (New York: Funk and Wagnalls, 1953), 75–78. The major works on TROY, on which this section draws, are Allan A. Needell, "'Truth Is Our Weapon': Project TROY, Political Warfare, and Government-Academic Relations in the National Security State," *Diplomatic History* 17, no. 3 (July 1993), 399–420; Allan A. Needell, "Project TROY and the Cold War Annexation of the Social Sciences," in *Universities and Empire: Money and Politics in the Social Sciences during the Cold War*, ed. Christopher Simpson (New York: New Press, 1998), 3–38.

13. Deborah Douglas, "MIT and War," in *Becoming MIT: Moments of Decision*, ed. David Kaiser (Cambridge, MA: MIT Press, 2010), 81–102; James R. Killian Jr., *The Education of a College President: A Memoir* (Cambridge, MA: MIT Press, 1985), 63–65; Needell, "Truth," 400n5.

14. John Burchard to Edward Purcell, August 14, 1950, 1, Folder 7, Box 220, Office of the President, Records of Karl Taylor Compton and James Rhyne Killian, AC 4, Massachusetts Institute of Technology, Institute Archives and Special Collections, Cambridge, MA; "Annex 16: Biography of Team," in *Project TROY: Report to the Secretary of State, Volume III*, February 1, 1951,

Folder Records Relating to Project TROY, 1950–1951, Box 1, International Information Agency, Office of Policy and Plans, Records Relating to Project TROY, 1950–1951, Lot File 52–283, General Records of the Department of State, Record Group (hereafter RG) 59, National Archives at College Park, College Park, MD (hereafter NACP).

15. "Annex 18: Project TROY Briefing," in *Project TROY, Vol. III*; *Project TROY: Report to the Secretary of State, Volume I*, February 1, 1951, viii, Folder Records Relating to Project TROY, 1950–1951, Box 1, International Information Agency, Office of Policy and Plans, Records Relating to Project TROY, 1950–1951, Lot File 52–283, RG 59, NACP.

16. *Project TROY, Vol. I*, 41, 45.

17. Howland Sargeant to [William?] McWilliams, "What We Have Learned from Project Troy Bearing on Other Departmental Problems," December 27, 1950, 1, Folder n.d., Box 1, International Information Agency, Office of Policy and Plans, Records Relating to Project TROY, 1950–1951, Lot File 52–283, RG 59, NACP; James Webb to John Burchard, March 9, 1951, File 611.00/2–1951, Central Decimal Files, 1950–1954, RG 59, NACP; "blazed important . . ." quoted in Needell, "Truth," 413–414; W. Park Armstrong Jr., to Edward Barrett, "Project Troy," March 26, 1951, 1, Folder RAND Corporation Study, Box 1, Psychological Strategy Board Files, Staff Member and Office Files, Harry S. Truman Papers (hereafter PSBF), Harry S. Truman Presidential Library, Independence, MO (hereafter HSTL); "really quite an . . ." and "one of the most . . ." quoted in Needell, "Truth," 414; Robert Hooker to Paul Nitze, March 26, 1951, Document 59, *Foreign Relations of the United States, 1950–1955: The Intelligence Community, 1950–1955*, ed. Douglas Keane and Michael Warner (Washington, DC: Government Printing Office, 2007), accessed November 30, 2016, https://history.state.gov/historicaldocuments/frus1950–55Intel/d59.

18. Quotation "principal research undertaken . . ." from Needell, "Truth," 415; "An Analysis of the Principal Psychological Vulnerabilities in the USSR and of the Principal Assets Available to the US for Their Exploitation," n.d. [April 1951], 17, CIA-RDP80R01731R003500180030–6, CIA Records Search Tool, https://www.cia.gov/library/readingroom/collection/crest-25-year-program-archive.

19. Charles Bohlen, "The Bases of Soviet Action (The General Nature of Future Soviet Actions)," March 27, 1952, Document 5, *Foreign Relations of the United States, 1952–1954: National Security Affairs, Volume II, Part 1*, ed. Lisle A. Rose and Neal H. Petersen (Washington, DC: Government Printing Office, 1984), accessed November 30, 2016, https://history.state.gov/historicaldocuments/frus1952–54v02p1/d5; Barrett, *Truth*, 278.

20. Hart, *Empire*, 154–170; Hixson, *Parting*, 17–19; Lucas, *Freedom's War*, chapter 9; Needell, "Truth," 414–415; "A Strategic Concept for a National Psychological Program with Particular Reference to Cold War Operations under NSC 10/5 [PSB D-31]," November 26, 1952, 7, Folder PSB D-31, Box 5, Executive Secretariat, Psychological Strategy Board Working File, 1951–1953, Lot File 62 D 333, RG 59, NACP; Mitrovich, *Undermining*, 109–114.

21. Gregory Mitrovich has traced at least one psychological operation—Operation Overload and Delay—to Project TROY. Mitrovich, *Undermining*, 75–77.

22. Speier, introduction to *From the Ashes of Disgrace: A Journal from Germany, 1945–1955* (Amherst: University of Massachusetts Press, 1981) (hereafter *FAD*), 8 (Stone was familiar with Speier's work on psychological warfare and kept a copy of "The Future of Psychological Warfare" in his archives—see Folder 36, Box 20, Shepard Stone Papers, Rauner Library, Dartmouth College, Hanover, NH); Christian Ostermann, "Cold War in Germany: The United States and East Germany, 1945–1953" (PhD diss., University of Cologne, 2008), 148–149, 180.

23. Speier, "Report of Visit in 1950," December 7, 1950, in *FAD*, 93, 102–103.

24. Ibid., 94, 105.

25. Wallace Carroll and Speier, "Psychological Warfare in Germany: A Report to the United States High Commissioner for Germany and the Department of State," Frankfurt a.M., December 1, 1950, 3–5, 18, Folder Psychological Warfare in Germany (Carroll-Speier Report), Box 62, Bureau of Public Affairs, Subject Files of the Policy Plans and Guidance Staff, 1946–1962, Dept. Circ Tel#168 (9/5/1956) Summaries/Replies to EUR/P-Miscellaneous, Entry A1 1587-M, Lot File 60D605, RG 59, NACP.

26. Ibid., 20, 24.

27. Ostermann, "Cold War," 184; "Minutes of the Thirty-Eighth Meeting of Pepco," Frankfurt, December 27, 1950, 1, Tab 38, Box 3, U.S. High Commission for Germany, Berlin Element, Political Affairs Division, Security Segregated General Records, 1949–53, Entry 174, Records of the U.S. High Commissioner for Germany, RG 466, NACP; Shepard Stone to Speier, January 19, 1951, Folder 5, Box 2, SP; "PEPCO Position on Carroll-Speier Paper ('Psychological Warfare in Germany', dated December 1, 1950)," January 26, 1951, 1, File 511.62A/1–2651, Central Decimal Files, 1950–1954, RG 59, NACP.

28. "The Concept of Europe," Special Guidance No. 86, May 8, 1951, 1–2, USDDO, accessed December 1, 2016, http://tinyurl.galegroup.com/tinyurl/45t4a4.

29. Henry Ramsey, "Exploitation of the Return to Europe Concept," July 24, 1951, 1, 4, 6, Tab 53, Box 3, U.S. High Commission for Germany, Berlin Element, Political Affairs Division, Security Segregated General Records, 1949–53, Entry 174, RG 466, NACP.

30. Edmond Taylor, "Interim Plan for Intensified Psychological Warfare in Germany," n.d. [September 1951], 10, Folder Secret Copies of Enclosures to HICOG Frankfurt Despatch 724, Box 5, U.S. High Commission for Germany, Berlin Element, Political Affairs Division, Security Segregated General Records, 1949–53, Entry 174, RG 466, NACP; James Webb to HICOG, A-1622 [Airgram-1622], November 23, 1951, 8, File 511.62A/9–2851, Central Decimal Files, 1950–1954, RG 59, NACP.

31. "Actions Taken by the National Security Council on Scope and Pace of Covert Operations [NSC-10/5]," Document 90, *Foreign Relations of the United States, 1950–1955: The Intelligence Community, 1950–1955*, ed. Douglas Keane and Michael Warner (Washington, DC: Government Printing Office, 2007), accessed December 2, 2016, https://history.state.gov/historicaldocuments/frus1950–55Intel/d90.

32. Raymond Allen to David K. E. Bruce et al. [transmittal letter of PSB D-21], July 29, 1952, 3–4, Folder Germany—File 2 [1 of 3], Box 6, PSBF, HSTL. The information about the creation of PSD D-21 contained in this chapter comes from Folder PSB D-21, Box 2, Executive Secretariat, Psychological Strategy Board Working File, 1951–1953, Lot File 62 D 333, RG 59, NACP; Folder Germany—File #1 [1 of 3], Box 5, PSBF, HSTL; Folder Germany—File #1 [2 of 3], Box 5, PSBF, HSTL; Folder Germany—File #1 [3 of 3], Box 5, PSBF, HSTL; Folder Germany—File 2 [1 of 3], Box 6, PSBF, HSTL; Folder Germany—File #2 [2 of 3], Box 6, PSBF, HSTL; Folder Germany—File #2 [3 of 3], Box 6, PSBF, HSTL. For a helpful timeline of PSB D-21's development, see "Journal for Germany Plan," n.d. [late 1952–early 1953], USDDO, accessed December 2, 2016, http://tinyurl.galegroup.com/tinyurl/4647k9.

33. Paul Davis to Tracy Barnes, "Your Memorandum Dated 11 December 1951 to PSB Staff," December 14, 1951, n.d. [3], USDDO, accessed December 2, 2016, http://tinyurl.galegroup.com/tinyurl/463x30; Paul Davis to Raymond Allen and George Morgan, "Planning for Psychological Operations (Hans Speier Article)," January 25, 1952, Folder Spier [*sic*], Hans, Box 14, PSBF, HSTL; Henry Byroade to James Webb, "Psychological Warfare Plan for Germany: New Project Suggested by General Walter B. Smith," December 19, 1951, Folder PSB D-21, Box 2, Executive Secretariat, Psychological Strategy Board Working File, 1951–1953, Lot File 62 D 333, RG 59, NACP; Allen to Bruce et al., July 29, 1952, 4.

34. "A National Psychological Strategy with Respect to Germany [PSB D-21]," October 9, 1952, 5, 9–11, Folder PSB D-21, Box 2, Executive Secretariat, Psychological Strategy Board Working File, 1951–1953, Lot File 62 D 333, RG 59, NACP.

35. The information in this paragraph comes from Ostermann, "Cold War," 208–215, Stalin quotation from 212.

36. John Anspacher to Edmond Taylor, "German Plan Implementation," October 15, 1952, Folder Germany—File #2 [2 of 3], Box 6, PSBF, HSTL; Charles Norberg to Edmond Taylor, "Progress Report on PSB D-21 'National Psychological Strategy with Respect to Germany,'" January 13, 1953, Folder Germany (1), Box 12, Psychological Strategy Board (PSB) Central File Series, National Security Council Staff: Papers, 1953–61, White House Office (hereafter PSBCFS), Dwight D. Eisenhower Presidential Library, Abilene, KS (hereafter DDEL); John Anspacher to Edmond Taylor et al., "Conversations with Henry Kellerman," January 15, 1953, 1, Folder Germany (1), Box 12, PSBCFS, DDEL; John Anspacher to Charles Norberg, "Conversations with Mr. Lewis and Mr. Kellerman, Department of State GER," January 22, 1953, 1, Folder Germany (1), Box 12, PSBCFS, DDEL; John Anspacher to Mallory Browne, "Progress Report—D-21 and D-21/2—February 16–February 29, 1953," February 27, 1953, 1, Folder Germany (2), Box 12, PSBCFS, DDEL; Mallory Browne to George Morgan, "Attached notes on meeting with A. V. Boerner, HICOG Public Affairs Officer (CN-804)," June 16, 1953, Folder Germany (6), Box 12, PSBCFS, DDEL.

37. "Report on Implementation of PSB D-21, Psychological Warfare Program," n.d. [June 1953], 1, 3–4, 6–7, Folder Germany (6), Box 12, PSBCFS, DDEL.

38. Burton Lifschultz to Allen Dulles, "RIAS," July 10, 1953, Folder RFE [Radio Free Europe], Box 5, C. D. Jackson Papers, 1931–1967, DDEL; Nicholas J. Schlosser, *Cold War on the Airwaves: The Radio Propaganda War against East Germany* (Urbana: University of Illinois Press, 2015), chapters 3–4; Ostermann, "Cold War," 215; Christian Ostermann, introduction and acknowledgments to *Uprising in East Germany 1953: The Cold War, the German Question, and the First Major Upheaval behind the Iron Curtain*, ed. Christian Ostermann (Budapest: Central European University Press, 2001) (hereafter *UEG*), xxii; "Chronology of Events," in *UEG*, xxxi–xxxvii; Eleanor Lansing Dulles to James Riddleberger, July 9, 1953, File 962A.40/7–953, Central Decimal Files, 1950–1954, RG 59, NACP.

39. This paragraph relies on Ostermann, "Cold War," chapter 5, quotation from 312; *UEG*; Schlosser, *Airwaves*, chapter 4.

40. "Minutes of Discussion at the 150th Meeting of the National Security Council," June 18, 1953, in *UEG*, 228.

41. Dwight Eisenhower to Bernard Montgomery, July 14, 1953, in *UEG*, 353; Lucas, *Freedom's War*, 182–184; Ostermann, "Cold War," 358–359. The phrase "magnet theory" comes from Ostermann, editor's note [top of page], in *UEG*, 353.

42. Speier, "Some Cases of Successful Political Warfare," September 23, 1953, 21, Folder 62, Box 9, SP.

7. The Institution Builder

1. Throughout this chapter, I use the term "social science" instead of "behavioral science" unless I am quoting documents. This is because, as Jefferson Pooley recently highlighted, within the Ford Foundation—the subject of this chapter—"the 'behavioral sciences' term was never coherently defined. . . . From the beginning the term had no stable referent, and was often used

generically as a substitute for the more common 'social sciences' designation." Jefferson D. Pooley, "A 'Not Particularly Felicitous' Phrase: A History of the 'Behavioral Sciences' Label," *Serendipities* 1, no. 1 (2016), 39.

2. Hunter Crowther-Heyck, "Herbert Simon and the GSIA: Building an Interdisciplinary Community," *Journal of the History of the Behavioral Sciences* 42, no. 4 (Autumn 2006), 314.

3. Bernard Berelson, *Five Year Report on Program V*, August 1956, 5, Folder 010420, Box 422, Catalogued Reports, Reports 9287–11774, FA739D, Ford Foundation Records (hereafter FFR), Rockefeller Archive Center, Sleepy Hollow, NY (hereafter RAC).

4. Hunter Crowther-Heyck, "Patrons of the Revolution: Ideals and Institutions in Postwar Behavioral Science," *Isis* 97, no. 3 (September 2006), 440–441.

5. Jamie Cohen-Cole, *The Open Mind: Cold War Politics and the Sciences of Human Nature* (Chicago: University of Chicago Press, 2014), 125.

6. Andrew Jewett, *Science, Democracy, and the American University: From the Civil War to the Cold War* (New York: Cambridge University Press, 2012), 344–348; Jeremi Suri, *Henry Kissinger and the American Century* (Cambridge, MA: Harvard University Press, 2007), chapter 3.

7. Speier and Joseph Goldsen to Rowan Gaither, *Comments on the Activities of the Ford Foundation*, November 5, 1953, 17, 2, Folder 010637, Box 429, Catalogued Reports, Reports 9287–11774, FA739D, FFR, RAC.

8. The works on which I have relied to understand the Ford Foundation and its social sciences program are Emily Hauptmann, "The Ford Foundation and the Rise of Behavioralism in Political Science," *Journal of the History of the Behavioral Sciences* 48, no. 2 (Spring 2012), 154–173; Inderjeet Parmar, *Foundations of the American Century: The Ford, Carnegie, and Rockefeller Foundations in the Rise of American Power* (New York: Columbia University Press, 2012); Pooley, "Phrase"; Peter J. Seybold, "The Ford Foundation and the Triumph of Behavioralism in American Political Science," in *Philanthropy and Cultural Imperialism: The Foundations at Home and Abroad*, ed. Robert F. Arnove (Boston: G. K. Hall, 1980), 269–303; Mark Solovey, *Shaky Foundations: The Politics-Patronage-Social Science Nexus in Cold War America* (New Brunswick, NJ: Rutgers University Press, 2013), chapter 3; Francis X. Sutton, "The Ford Foundation: The Early Years," *Daedalus* 116, no. 1 (Winter 1987), 41–91.

9. Rebecca S. Lowen, *Creating the Cold War University: The Transformation of Stanford* (Berkeley: University of California Press, 1997), 194–195; Solovey, *Shaky*, 112; Henry Ford II, preface to *Report of the Study for the Ford Foundation on Policy and Program* (Detroit: Ford Foundation, November 1949 [preface from October 1950]), 10.

10. *Report of the Study for the Ford Foundation on Policy and Program* (Detroit: Ford Foundation, November 1949), 14, 22, 52–89, 51, 90–99.

11. Sutton, "Ford Foundation" ("a strong expression of hope" and "the challenges of human affairs"), 71–72, 46; Bernard Berelson, Interview, July 7, 1972 ("a very great respect" and "a layman who . . ."), 5–10, 3–4, Folder 152, Box 32, Subseries Access Copies, Series IV Transcripts, Oral History Project, FFR, RAC; Dwight Macdonald, *The Ford Foundation: The Men and the Millions* (New York: Reynal, 1956), 98; Parmar, *Foundations*, 54; Solovey, *Shaky*, 116, 119–120; "Excerpt From: Minutes of Staff Meeting," January 5, 1951, Reel C-1139, Series 1951 General Correspondence, FA735 (hereafter Reel C-1139), FFR, RAC; Donald Marquis, Interview, October 27, 1972, 12, Folder 207, Box 38, Subseries Access Copies, Series IV Transcripts, Oral History Project, FFR, RAC; Speier to Lisa Speier, 1950, 1 [back of page], Folder 6, Box 1, Hans Speier Papers, German and Jewish Intellectual Émigré Collection, M. E. Grenander Department of Special Collections and Archives, University Libraries, University at Albany, State University of New York, Albany, NY (hereafter SP).

12. See chapter 1; Jerome Bruner, Francis L. Friedman, Donald G. Marquis, Robert S. Morison, and Robert Wolff, "Annex 11: Research in Support of Political Warfare," in *Project TROY: Report to the Secretary of State, Volume III*, February 1, 1951, Folder Records Relating to Project TROY, 1950–1951, Box 1, International Information Agency, Office of Policy and Plans, Records Relating to Project TROY, 1950–1951, Lot File 52–283, General Records of the Department of State, Record Group (hereafter RG) 59, National Archives at College Park, College Park, MD (hereafter NACP); Donald Marquis to Rowan Gaither and Speier, "Topics for Discussion During the San Francisco Meeting April 30," April 24, 1951, 2, Folder 74, Box 7, Series V Area Five Individual Behavior and Human Relations, Office of the President, Office Files of H. Rowan Gaither, FA621 (hereafter Gaither Files), FFR, RAC.

13. Speier to Rowan Gaither, "Project: Conference on (Annual) Institute on the Study of Human Behavior," June 12, 1951, 1, Reel C-1139, FFR, RAC; Leo Doyle to Rowan Gaither, "Conference Meeting with Dr. Speier, Dr. Marquis, and Dr. Herring, June 11 and 12 in San Francisco," June 20, 1951, 1–2, Reel C-1139, FFR, RAC; Speier to Gaither, "Project: Conference on (Annual) Institute on the Study of Human Behavior."

14. "Total List of Grants," n.d. [May 1957], A-1-A-2, A-4-A-5, A-7, Folder 243, Box 9, Series III Program Area V Individual Behavior and Human Relations, Associate Director and Vice President, Office Files of William McPeak, FA704 (hereafter McPeak Files), FFR, RAC.

15. Ernst Kris and Speier, "Statement," December 30, 1941, 1, Folder 3101, Box 260, Subseries 200.R, Series 200, RG 1.1, Projects, FA386, Rockefeller Foundation Records, RAC; Oral History interview with Bernard Berelson, 1967, 8–13, *Carnegie Corporation Oral History Project*, Columbia Center for Oral History Archives, Rare Book and Manuscript Library, Columbia University in the City of New York; Donald Marquis to Rowan Gaither, "Staff and Consultants," February 23, 1951, 1, Reel C-1139, FFR, RAC; Untitled [Press release: "Three prominent social scientists . . ."], June 27, 1951, 1, Reel C-1139, FFR, RAC.

16. Arnold Thackray, "CASBS: Notes toward a History," in *Center for Advanced Study in the Behavioral Sciences: Annual Report 1984*, 65–66; Paul F. Lazarsfeld, Bernard Berelson, and Hazel Gaudet, *The People's Choice: How the Voter Makes Up His Mind in a Presidential Campaign* (New York: Columbia University Press, 1948); Marquis to Gaither and Speier, "Topics for Discussion During the San Francisco Meeting April 30," 2; Speier, Donald Marquis, and Bernard Berelson to Rowan Gaither, October 15, 1951, 2, Folder 75, Box 7, Gaither Files, FFR, RAC.

17. "Individual Behavior and Human Relations," August 2, 1950, 3, Reel C-1139, FFR, RAC; Bernard Berelson to Speier, December 3, 1951, 1, Folder 75, Box 7, Gaither Files, FFR, RAC.

18. Berelson to Speier, December 3, 1951, 2, 4; "Rough Notes Taken by T.H.C. at After Dinner Conference on 29 November 1951 in NYC," 2, Folder 75, Box 7, Gaither Files, FFR, RAC; Berelson, Interview, July 7, 1972, 51.

19. Berelson, Interview, July 7, 1972, 51–52; Berelson to Speier, December 3, 1951, 4.

20. *The Ford Foundation Behavioral Sciences Program: Proposed Plan for the Development of the Behavioral Sciences Program*, December 1951, 42–44, 59, Reel C-1139, FFR, RAC; Thackray, "Notes," 67.

21. Rowan Gaither to Joseph McDaniel Jr., "Program Five: Action of Officers on December 20, 1951," December 28, 1951, Folder 75, Box 7, Gaither Files, FFR, RAC; "Excerpt from Minutes of Special Meeting of Board of Trustees," July 15–16, 1952, Folder 238, Box 9, McPeak Files, FFR, RAC; Speier and Goldsen to Gaither, *Comments on the Activities of the Ford Foundation*; Speier to William McPeak, WL-1576, November 18, 1953, Folder 261, Box 9, McPeak Files, FFR, RAC; *The Ford Foundation Annual Report: October 1, 1955 to September 30, 1956*, 53, Foundation Center Historical Foundation Collection, Ruth Lilly Special Collections and Archives, IUPUI University

Library, Indiana University–Purdue University, Indianapolis, IN; Roger L. Geiger, *Research and Relevant Knowledge: American Research Universities since World War II* (New York: Oxford University Press, 1993), 99–105; Hauptmann, "Rise," 154–173; Heyck, "Patrons," 437–440; Seybold, "Triumph," 269–303; Solovey, *Shaky*, chapter 3.

22. Bernard Berelson, "Summary of Discussions on Advanced Training Center," April 1952, 3, Folder 15, Box 10, Center for Advanced Study in the Behavioral Sciences Records (SC1055), Department of Special Collections and University Archives, Stanford University Libraries, Stanford, CA (hereafter CASBS Records); Bernard Berelson to Bernard Gladieux, March 21, 1952, 1, Reel C-1147, Series 1952 General Correspondence, FA735 (hereafter Reel C-1147), FFR, RAC.

23. Berelson, "Summary," 7, 10.

24. "Notes of the Discussion of the Planning Group for the Center for Advanced Study of the Behavioral Sciences, New York City, May 3–4, 1952," May 1952, Folder 15, Box 10, CASBS Records; *The Center for Advanced Study in the Behavioral Sciences: Report of the Planning Group*, June 1952, 13, Folder 15, Box 10, CASBS Records.

25. "Notes of the Discussion," 2, 8.

26. "Excerpt from Minutes of Special Meeting of Board of Trustees," July 15–16, 1952; "Informal Planning Group on Center for Advanced Study, Third Meeting," December 6–7, 1952, 9, accessed December 6, 2016, http://doi.library.cmu.edu/10.1184/pmc/simon/box00042/fld03362/bdl0008/doc0001, Herbert Simon Collection, Carnegie Mellon University Archives, Pittsburgh, PA (hereafter Simon Collection); "Informal Planning Group on Center for Advanced Study, First Meeting," November 19, 1952, 3, accessed December 3, 2016, http://doi.library.cmu.edu/10.1184/pmc/simon/box00042/fld03362/bdl0004/doc0001, Simon Collection.

27. Untitled [Press release: "Mr. Paul G. Hoffman . . ."], February 1, 1953, Folder 12, Box 10, CASBS Records; "Minutes of First Meeting, Board-Designate, Center for Advanced Study in the Behavioral Sciences," January 22, 1953, 6–7, Folder 41, Box 11, CASBS Records.

28. "Informal Planning Group on Center for Advanced Study, Sixth Meeting," January 31, 1953, 6–8, 3–4, Folder 12, Box 10, CASBS Records; Folder 5, Box 11, CASBS Records; Anonymous, "Statement No. 1," n.d. [1953], 1, Folder 5, Box 11, CASBS Records; "Minutes of the Third Meeting, Board-Designate, Center for Advanced Study in the Behavioral Sciences," June 30, 1953, 1, Folder 43, Box 11, CASBS Records.

29. "Minutes of the Third Meeting, Board-Designate, Center for Advanced Study in the Behavioral Sciences," 4; Bernard Berelson to Ralph Tyler [Draft], October 27, 1953, 1, Folder 11, Box 11, CASBS Records; Ralph Tyler to Herbert Simon, December 31, 1953, 1, accessed December 3, 2016, http://doi.library.cmu.edu/10.1184/pmc/simon/box00042/fld03357/bdl0002/doc0001, Simon Collection; Ralph Tyler, "Center for Advanced Study in the Behavioral Sciences," January 1954, 1, Folder 14, Box 21, CASBS Records; Berelson, Interview, July 7, 1972, 57.

30. "Notes on Meeting of Advisory Committee: Center for Advanced Study in the Behavioral Sciences," August 22, 1953, 3, Folder 14, Box 11, CASBS Records; "Master List for May 16, 1954, Meeting," n.d. [May 1954], Folder 18, Box 11, CASBS Records; "Minutes of the Fifth Meeting, Board-Designate, Center for Advanced Study in the Behavioral Sciences," January 2, 1954, 3, Folder 1, Box 12, CASBS Records.

31. Arnold Thackray, "A Site for CASBS: East or West?" in *Center for Advanced Study in the Behavioral Sciences: Annual Report 1987*, 63–71; Ralph Tyler, Untitled ["Within the past year . . ."], December 1954, 1, 3, Folder 14, Box 21, CASBS Records; Ralph Tyler, "The Center for Advanced Study in the Behavioral Sciences: A Report of Its First Year of Operation, 1954–55," n.d. [Summer 1955], 11–13, 2, Folder 14, Box 21, CASBS Records.

32. Tyler, "First Year," 17; "Center for Advanced Study in the Behavioral Sciences: General Support [Docket Excerpt]," September 27–28, 1957, 3, Reel 1322, Series Ford Foundation

Grants—C to D, FA732B (hereafter Reel 1322), FFR, RAC; *The Ford Foundation Annual Report: October 1, 1955 to September 30, 1956*, 55; Board of Directors to Henry Heald, April 20, 1957, 1, Folder 7, Box 14, CASBS Records; Berelson, Interview, July 7, 1972, 40–43; Henry Heald to Staff, May 15, 1957, Folder 243, Box 9, McPeak Files, FFR, RAC; Solovey, *Shaky*, 142–145; F. F. Hill to Ralph Tyler, October 4, 1957, Folder 7, Box 14, CASBS Records; "Plans for Continuation of the Center," October 1959, 1, Reel 1323, Series Ford Foundation Grants—C to D, FA732B, FFR, RAC.

33. Solovey, *Shaky*, 130–131; "General Support," 4.

34. Ralph Tyler to Board of Directors and the Advisory Committee, October 30, 1954, 3, Folder 15, Box 11, CASBS Records; Francis X. Sutton to Files, November 27, 1956, 1, Reel 1322, FFR, RAC.

35. Nils Gilman, *Mandarins of the Future: Modernization Theory in Cold War America* (Baltimore: Johns Hopkins University Press, 2003), 149.

36. Speier and Donald Marquis to Rowan Gaither, "Further Discussion and Recommendations Pertaining to Program One," May 3, 1951, 4, Folder 4, Box 1, Gaither Files, FFR, RAC (though this memo was officially co-written, later events and oral histories suggest that Speier was the prime mover behind the communications institute); Donald Marquis and Speier, "Institute of International Communications," May 5[?], 1951, 1–2, Reel 1194, Series Ford Foundation Grants—L to N, FA732E (hereafter Reel 1194), FFR, RAC; Speier, "Research Center on International Communication," March 10, 1952, 1, Reel 1194, FFR, RAC.

37. Lazarsfeld, Berelson, and Gaudet, *People's Choice*; *Proposed Plan*, 52–53, 59.

38. Speier, Donald Marquis, and Bernard Berelson to Rowan Gaither, December 20, 1951, 2, Folder 75, Box 2, Gaither Files, FFR, RAC; Gaither to McDaniel Jr., "Program Five: Action of Officers on December 20, 1951," 2.

39. Speier to Rowan Gaither and Bernard Berelson, "Conversation with Ed Barrett," December 28, 1951, Reel 1194, FFR, RAC; Speier to Rowan Gaither and Bernard Berelson, "Conversation with Gordon Gray," December 28, 1951, Reel 1194, FFR, RAC; "Draft of Report on Program Five to Be Included in President's Report to Trustees," January 9, 1952, 9, Folder 76, Box 7, Gaither Files, FFR, RAC.

40. Rowan Gaither note on Speier to Rowan Gaither, "MIT Center of International Studies," September 18, 1951, 7, Reel 1194, FFR, RAC; David Kaiser, "Elephant on the Charles: Postwar Growing Pains," in *Becoming MIT: Moments of Decision*, ed. David Kaiser (Cambridge, MA: MIT Press, 2010), 104; Stuart W. Leslie, *The Cold War and American Science: The Military-Industrial-Academic Complex at MIT and Stanford* (New York: Columbia University Press, 1993), 235; "Appendix: Origins and Objectives of the Center for International Studies," April 1952, in *Center for International Studies: Past, Present, and Future, Volume II* (Cambridge, MA: Center for International Studies, March 1954), 1–2; Lloyd Berkner to Dean Acheson, "Formulation of Analyses to Support Political Warfare," December 27, 1950, 4–5, Folder n.d., Box 1, International Information Agency, Office of Policy and Plans, Records Relating to Project TROY, 1950–1951, Lot File 52-283, RG 59, NACP; Donald L. M. Blackmer, *The MIT Center for International Studies: The Founding Years, 1951–1969* (Cambridge, MA: MIT Center for International Studies, 2002), chapter 1; James R. Killian Jr., *The Education of a College President: A Memoir* (Cambridge, MA: MIT Press, 1985), 67–68; Allan A. Needell, "'Truth Is Our Weapon': Project TROY, Political Warfare, and Government-Academic Relations in the National Security State," *Diplomatic History* 17, no. 3 (July 1993), 415–417; Untitled [Press release: "The appointment of . . ."], March 2, 1952, Folder News Office Announcement: Max Millikan Founding CIS 1952, Box 14, Massachusetts Institute of Technology, Center for International Studies Records, AC 236 (hereafter CIS Records), Massachusetts Institute of Technology, Institute Archives and Special Collections, Cambridge,

MA (hereafter MITASC); Speier to Rowan Gaither, "Conversation with Jerry Wiesner," October 4, 1951, Reel 1194, FFR, RAC; Speier to Gaither, "MIT Center of International Studies," 6.

41. Bernard Berelson to William McPeak, "International Communication Program at MIT," November 16, 1955, 1, Reel 1194, FFR, RAC; Richard Bissell Jr., to Rowan Gaither, February 26, 1952, 1–2, Reel C-1148, Series 1952 General Correspondence, FA735 (hereafter Reel C-1148), FFR, RAC; Berelson, Interview, July 7, 1972, 67–69; Blackmer, *MIT Center*, 39; Richard Bissell Jr., to the Officers of the Ford Foundation, "Progress Report," April 9, 1952, 1, Reel 1194, FFR, RAC; Max Millikan to Paul Buck, May 20, 1952, 1, Folder Center for International Studies, Advisory Board, 1951–55, Box 13, Max F. Millikan Papers, MC 188, MITASC.

42. Anonymous [Speier], "Appendix 'A': What Is Meant by International Communication?" in "Research Center on International Communication," by Speier, March 10, 1952, 1–2, Reel 1194, FFR, RAC.

43. Millikan to Buck, May 20, 1952, 1; Berelson to McPeak, "International Communication Program at MIT," 1; Center for International Studies, "Proposal for a Research Program in International Communication," [May] 1952, 2–3, 7, Reel 1194, FFR, RAC; Blackmer, *MIT Center*, 43–44; "Research Program on International Communication (A-835)," October 6, 1952, 6, Reel 1194, FFR, RAC; "Excerpt from the Docket for the Board of Trustees Meeting: Research Program on International Communication," July 15–16, 1952, 1, Reel 1194, FFR, RAC; Rowan Gaither to Paul Hoffman, "Grants to MIT Center for International Studies," August 6, 1952, Reel 1194, FFR, RAC; Paul Hoffman to James Killian, August 7, 1952, Reel 1194, FFR, RAC.

44. Max Millikan to Bernard Berelson, August 7, 1952, Reel 1194, FFR, RAC.

45. Folder International Communications Research Program, 1953 (2/2), Box 88, Ithiel de Sola Pool Papers, MC 440 (hereafter Pool Papers), MITASC; Speier, Jerome Bruner, Wallace Carroll, Harold D. Lasswell, Paul Lazarsfeld, Edward Shils, and Ithiel de Sola Pool, *Research in International Communication: An Advisory Report of the Planning Committee* (Cambridge, MA: MIT Center for International Studies, June 1953); Max Millikan to Rowan Gaither, February 6, 1953, 1, Reel 1194, FFR, RAC; "Ithiel de Sola Pool," December 24, 1952, Reel 1194, FFR, RAC.

46. Anonymous [Ithiel de Sola Pool], *Progress Report: Research Program in International Communication* (Cambridge, MA: Center for International Studies, B/54–15, October 1954), 2, 10–15, 5–6; "Center for International Studies: Massachusetts Institute of Technology [Staff List]," in *Center for International Studies: Past, Present, and Future, Volume II* (Cambridge, MA: Center for International Studies, March 1954); *The Center for International Studies, 1952–1953* [Annual Report], n.d. [August 1953], 7–9, Folder Annual Report, 1952–1953, Box 14, CIS Records, MITASC; Anonymous [Ithiel de Sola Pool], *Research Program in International Communication: Second Progress Report* (Cambridge, MA: Center for International Studies, B/55–9, October 1955), 3–9; Ithiel de Sola Pool to Communications Staff, n.d. [Summer 1955], 2, Folder International Communications Research Program, 1953 (1/2), Box 88, Pool Papers, MITASC.

47. William Morgan to Assistant Director of the PSB, "Comments on CENIS Communications Research Projects," December 5, 1952, Folder Comments on CENIS—Communications Research Projects, Box 9, Psychological Strategy Board Files, Staff Member and Office Files, Harry S. Truman Papers, Harry S. Truman Presidential Library, Independence, MO; Pool, *Progress Report*, 20–21; Pool, *Second Progress Report*, 12–13; *The Center for International Studies: A Description* (Cambridge, MA: Massachusetts Institute of Technology, July 1955), 41–44.

48. Blackmer, *MIT Center*; David C. Engerman, "The Center for International Studies and Indian Economic Development," in *Staging Growth: Modernization, Development, and the Global Cold War*, ed. David C. Engerman, Nils Gilman, Mark H. Haefele, and Michael E. Latham (Amherst: University of Massachusetts Press, 2003), 199–223; Gilman, *Mandarins*, chapter 5; Michael E. Latham, *Modernization as Ideology: American Social Science and "Nation Building" in the Kennedy Era* (Chapel Hill: University of North Carolina Press, 2000), 54–57.

49. Max Millikan, *Fifth Annual Report, July 1, 1955–June 30, 1956* (Cambridge, MA: Center for International Studies, August 1956), 1; Ithiel de Sola Pool to Robert Chandler, "Summary of Accomplishments of Research Program in International Communication, Center for International Studies, Massachusetts Institute of Technology," April 8, 1959, 3, Reel 1194, FFR, RAC; Ithiel de Sola Pool, *Report to the Ford Foundation from the International Communication Program*, December 1961, 38, Folder Pool, Report to the Ford Foundation from the Int'l Communication Program 1961, Box 134, Pool Papers, MITASC.

50. Gilman, *Mandarins*, chapter 5; Walt Whitman Rostow, "Development: The Political Economy of the Marshallian Long Period," in *Pioneers in Development*, ed. Gerald M. Meier and Dudley Seers (New York: Oxford University Press, 1984), 229–261; Walt Whitman Rostow, *Eisenhower, Kennedy, and Foreign Aid* (Austin: University of Texas Press, 1985), chapter 3; Daniel Lerner, *The Passing of Traditional Society: Modernizing the Middle East* (Glencoe, IL: Free Press, 1958), 46, 54.

51. Pool, *Report to the Ford Foundation*, 16; Max Millikan and Donald L.M. Blackmer, ed., *The Emerging Nations: Their Growth and United States Policy* (Boston: Little, Brown, 1961), 109; "National Film Laboratory, Kabul, Afghanistan," June–July 1961, Folder National Film Laboratory Specifications, Box 1, USAID Mission to Afghanistan/Assistant Director for Development, Records Relating to the Construction of the Afghan National Film Laboratory, 1961–1968, Entry P178, Records of the Agency for International Development, RG 286, NACP (thanks to Molly Geidel for sending me this document); Nicholas J. Cull, *The Cold War and the United States Information Agency: American Propaganda and Public Diplomacy, 1945–1989* (New York: Cambridge University Press, 2008), passim; Nick Cullather, *The Hungry World: America's Cold War Battle against Poverty in Asia* (Cambridge, MA: Harvard University Press, 2010), 165–166; Héctor Lindo-Fuentes and Erik Ching, *Modernizing Minds in El Salvador: Education Reform and the Cold War, 1960–1980* (Albuquerque: University of New Mexico Press, 2012), 117–118; Emile G. McAnany, *Saving the World: A Brief History of Communication for Development and Social Change* (Urbana: University of Illinois Press, 2012), chapters 1–3; Jeffrey F. Taffet, *Foreign Aid as Foreign Policy: The Alliance for Progress in Latin America* (London: Routledge, 2007), 43–44.

8. Social Science and Its Discontents

1. Nicolas Guilhot, "Cyborg Pantocrator: International Relations Theory from Decisionism to Rational Choice," *Journal of the History of the Behavioral Sciences* 47, no. 2 (Summer 2011), 287; Gregg Herken, *Counsels of War*, rev. ed. (New York: Oxford University Press, 1987), 75–76, 100–101; David R. Jardini, "Out of the Blue Yonder: The RAND Corporation's Diversification into Social Welfare Research, 1946–1968" (PhD diss., Carnegie Mellon University, 1996), 101; Fred Kaplan, *The Wizards of Armageddon* (Stanford: Stanford University Press, 1991), 121, 201–202, 228–229, 243; Robert Leonard, *Von Neumann, Morgenstern, and the Creation of Game Theory: From Chess to Social Science, 1900–1960* (New York: Cambridge University Press, 2010), 297n6; Ron Theodore Robin, *The Making of the Cold War Enemy: Culture and Politics in the Military-Intellectual Complex* (Princeton: Princeton University Press, 2001), 8.

2. For the purposes of this chapter, "social science" generally refers to the disciplines whose members belonged to RAND's Social Science Division, which included sociology, political science, psychology, anthropology, philosophy, and history. It does not refer to economics, the representatives of which had their own Economics Division, a fact that reflected economics' privileged disciplinary position at midcentury. For the midcentury notion that economics was more sophisticated than the other social sciences, see Roger E. Backhouse and Philippe Fontaine, "Toward a History of the Social Sciences," in *The History of the Social Sciences since 1945*, ed.

Roger E. Backhouse and Philippe Fontaine (New York: Cambridge University Press, 2010), 216–221; Robert Leonard, "War as a 'Simple Economic Problem': The Rise of an Economics of Defense," in *Economics and National Security: A History of Their Interaction, Annual Supplement to Volume 23, History of Political Economy*, ed. Crauford D. Goodwin (Durham, NC: Duke University Press, 1991), 261–283; Jefferson Pooley and Mark Solovey, "Marginal to the Revolution: The Curious Relationship between Economics and the Behavioral Sciences Movement in Mid-Twentieth-Century America," *History of Political Economy* 42, supplement 1 (2010), 199–233.

3. Nils Gilman, "The Cold War as Intellectual Force Field," *Modern Intellectual History* 13, no. 2 (August 2016), 514. In this context, Gilman is referring to what he labels "first-order Cold War social science." Also see David C. Engerman, "Social Science in the Cold War," *Isis* 101, no. 2 (June 2010), 393–400; Lawrence Freedman, "Social Science and the Cold War," review of *How Reason Almost Lost Its Mind: The Strange Career of Cold War Rationality*, by Paul Erickson, Judy L. Klein, Lorraine Daston, Rebecca Lemov, Thomas Sturm, and Michael D. Gordin, *Journal of Strategic Studies* 38, no. 4 (2015), 554–574; Joel Isaac, "The Human Sciences in Cold War America," *Historical Journal* 50, no. 3 (September 2007), 725–746; Joel Isaac, "Introduction: The Human Sciences and Cold War America," *Journal of the History of the Behavioral Sciences* 47, no. 3 (Summer 2011), 225–231; Mark Solovey, "Cold War Social Science: Specter, Reality, or Useful Concept?" in *Cold War Social Science: Knowledge Production, Liberal Democracy, and Human Nature*, ed. Mark Solovey and Hamilton Cravens (New York: Palgrave Macmillan, 2012), 1–22.

4. For the behavioral revolution, see Robert Adcock and Mark Bevir, "Political Science," in *The History of the Social Sciences since 1945*, ed. Roger E. Backhouse and Philippe Fontaine (New York: Cambridge University Press, 2010), 71–101; Hunter Crowther-Heyck, *Herbert A. Simon: The Bounds of Reason in Modern America* (Baltimore: Johns Hopkins University Press, 2005), 170–179; Emily Hauptmann, "The Ford Foundation and the Rise of Behavioralism in Political Science," *Journal of the History of the Behavioral Sciences* 48, no. 2 (Spring 2012), 154–173; Robin, *Making*, 6–8, 24–27. For the behavioral revolution and RAND, see S. M. Amadae, *Rationalizing Capitalist Democracy: The Cold War Origins of Rational Choice Liberalism* (Chicago: University of Chicago Press, 2003), passim; Martin J. Collins, *Cold War Laboratory: RAND, the Air Force, and the American State, 1945–1950* (Washington, DC: Smithsonian Institution Press, 2002); Hunter Crowther-Heyck, "Herbert Simon and the GSIA: Building an Interdisciplinary Community," *Journal of the History of the Behavioral Sciences* 42, no. 4 (Autumn 2006), 313; Paul Erickson, Judy L. Klein, Lorraine Daston, Rebecca Lemov, Thomas Sturm, and Michael D. Gordin, *How Reason Almost Lost Its Mind: The Strange Career of Cold War Rationality* (Chicago: University of Chicago Press, 2013), 14; Sharon Ghamari-Tabrizi, *The Worlds of Herman Kahn: The Intuitive Science of Thermonuclear War* (Cambridge, MA: Harvard University Press, 2005), 47–49; David Hounshell, "The Cold War, RAND, and the Generation of Knowledge, 1946–1962," *Historical Studies in the Physical and Biological Sciences* 27, no. 2 (1997), 265; Andrew Jewett, *Science, Democracy, and the American University: From the Civil War to the Cold War* (New York: Cambridge University Press, 2012), 354–355; Bruce Kuklick, *Blind Oracles: Intellectuals and War from Kennan to Kissinger* (Princeton: Princeton University Press, 2006), 23–29, 34–36, 54–55; Jennifer S. Light, *From Warfare to Welfare: Defense Intellectuals and Urban Problems in Cold War America* (Baltimore: Johns Hopkins University Press, 2003), 37–41; Peter Mandler, *Return from the Natives: How Margaret Mead Won the Second World War and Lost the Cold War* (New Haven: Yale University Press, 2013), 238; Philip Mirowski, *Machine Dreams: Economics Becomes a Cyborg Science* (New York: Cambridge University Press, 2002), chapter 6.

5. For more on this strand of thinking, see Nicolas Guilhot, *After the Enlightenment: Political Realism and International Relations in the Mid-Twentieth Century* (New York: Cambridge University Press, 2017).

6. Andrew Abbott and James T. Sparrow, "Hot War, Cold War: The Structures of Sociological Action," in *Sociology in America: A History*, ed. Craig Calhoun (Chicago: University of Chicago Press, 2007), 281–314; David C. Engerman, "Bernath Lecture: American Knowledge and Global Power," *Diplomatic History* 31, no. 4 (September 2007), 603–607; Christian Fleck, *A Transatlantic History of the Social Sciences: Robber Barons, the Third Reich and the Invention of Empirical Social Research*, trans. Hella Beister (London: Bloomsbury, 2011); Daniel Geary, *Radical Ambition: C. Wright Mills, the Left, and American Social Thought* (Berkeley: University of California Press, 2009), chapters 1–2; Nils Gilman, *Mandarins of the Future: Modernization Theory in Cold War America* (Baltimore: Johns Hopkins University Press, 2003), chapter 2; Gilman, "Force Field," 508, 518–519; Joel Isaac, *Working Knowledge: Making the Human Sciences from Parsons to Kuhn* (Cambridge, MA: Harvard University Press, 2012), chapter 5; Solovey, "Cold War Social Science," 15–16.

7. Interview Four, January 27, 1989, 49, 51, 58–59, Record Unit 9536, The Research and Development (RAND) Corporation Interviews, Smithsonian Institution Archives, Washington, DC.

8. Ibid., 56–57.

9. Jamie Cohen-Cole, "Instituting the Sciences of Mind: Intellectual Economies and Disciplinary Exchange at Harvard's Center for Cognitive Studies," *British Journal for the History of Science* 40, no. 4 (December 2007), 567; Speier to Harold Lasswell, August 6, 1951, Folder 1096, Box 89, Harold Dwight Lasswell Papers (MS 1043), Manuscripts and Archives, Yale University Library, New Haven, CT; Speier to Hans Staudinger, April 6, 1978, Folder 84, Box 4, Hans Speier Papers, German and Jewish Intellectual Émigré Collection, M. E. Grenander Department of Special Collections and Archives, University Libraries, University at Albany, State University of New York, Albany, NY (hereafter SP).

10. Speier, "A Prospective Division for International Studies," February 12, 1948, 2, 4–5, Folder 2, Box 9, SP; chapter 1.

11. Guilhot, "Cyborg"; Speier and W. Phillips Davison, *Psychological Aspects of Foreign Policy* (Santa Monica, CA: RAND Corporation, P-615, December 15, 1954), 36–40. For SSD studies based on textual research, see Jean M. Hungerford, *The Exploitation of Superstitions for Purposes of Psychological Warfare* (Santa Monica, CA: RAND Corporation, RM-365, April 14, 1950); Irving L. Janis, *Are the Cominform Countries Using Hypnotic Techniques to Elicit Confessions in Public Trials?* (Santa Monica, CA: RAND Corporation, RM-161, April 25, 1949); Nathan Leites, *The Operational Code of the Politburo* (New York: McGraw-Hill, 1951); Nathan Leites, *Some Useful Passages from Lenin and Stalin* (Santa Monica, CA: RAND Corporation, RM-569, March 20, 1951); Nathan Leites and Elsa Bernaut, *Ritual of Liquidation: The Case of the Moscow Trials* (Glencoe, IL: Free Press, 1954); Margaret Mead, *Soviet Attitudes toward Authority: An Interdisciplinary Approach to Problems of Soviet Character* (New York: McGraw-Hill, 1951); Leon Gouré and Herbert S. Dinerstein, *Political Vulnerability of Moscow: A Case Study of the October 1941 Attack* (Santa Monica, CA: RAND Corporation, RM-788, April 25, 1952); Raymond L. Garthoff, *Soviet Military Doctrine* (Glencoe, IL: Free Press, 1953); Herbert Goldhamer and Andrew W. Marshall, *Psychosis and Civilization: Two Studies in the Frequency of Mental Disease* (Glencoe, IL: Free Press, 1953). For a study based on anthropological methods, see Mead, *Authority*. For a study based on interviews, see Gouré and Dinerstein, *Moscow*. For studies that used psychoanalytic methods, see Leites, *Code*; Leites and Bernaut, *Ritual*. For studies based on psychological analysis, see Hungerford, *Exploitation*; Janis, *Cominform*.

12. Speier, *The RAND Social Science Program* (Santa Monica, CA: RAND Corporation, D-717-PR, February 21, 1950), 2; RAND Corporation Social Science Division, *The Warning of Target Populations in Air War* (Santa Monica, CA: RAND Corporation, RM-275-PR, November 1, 1949).

13. Leites, *Code*; Speier, *Psychological Warfare Reconsidered* (Santa Monica, CA: RAND Corporation, P-196, February 5, 1951).

14. Vaughn D. Bornet, *John Williams: A Personal Reminiscence (August, 1962)* (Santa Monica, CA: RAND Corporation, D-19036, August 12, 1969), 22; Mark Solovey, *Shaky Foundations: The Politics-Patronage-Social Science Nexus in Cold War America* (New Brunswick, NJ: Rutgers University Press, 2013), 9–10, 15, 62, 68; Charles Hitch, "Planning Defense Production," *American Economic Review* 40, no. 2 (May 1950), 193; Charles Hitch, "An Appreciation of Systems Analysis," *Journal of the Operations Research Society of America* 3, no. 4 (November 1955), 474, 476.

15. Herman Kahn and Irwin Mann, *Game Theory* (Santa Monica, CA: RAND Corporation, P-1166, July 30, 1957), 2, 2n3; Ghamari-Tabrizi, *Kahn*.

16. Speier to Nathan Leites, March 6, 1953, 5, Folder 57, Box 9, SP.

17. U.S. Air Force Project RAND, *Second Annual Report* (Santa Monica, CA: RAND Corporation, RA-15075, March 1, 1948), 25; U.S. Air Force Project RAND, *Special Staff Report: The Selection of Strategic Air Bases* (Santa Monica, CA: RAND Corporation, R-244-S, March 1, 1953), 1; Edward Barlow, Interview, February 10, 1988, October 11, 1989, November 10, 1990, 98, Folder 5, Box 8, RAND History Project Interviews (Acc. 1999-0037), National Air and Space Museum, Smithsonian Institution, Washington, DC.

18. Speier, *RAND Social Science Program*, 6; Herbert Goldhamer, *Human Factors in Systems Analysis* (Santa Monica, CA: RAND Corporation, RM-388, April 15, 1950), prefatory note, 22.

19. Goldhamer, *Human Factors*, 6, 9, 7–8, 24.

20. H. Bohnenblust, M. Dresher, M. A. Girshick, T. E. Harris, Olaf Helmer, J. C. C. McKinsey, L. S. Shapley, R. N. Snow, *Mathematical Theory of Zero-Sum Two-Person Games with a Finite Number or a Continuum of Strategies* (Santa Monica, CA: RAND Corporation, R-115, September 3, 1948), 1; U.S. Air Force Project RAND, *Third Annual Report* (Santa Monica, CA: RAND Corporation, R-134, March 1, 1949), 19; J. D. Williams, *The Compleat Strategyst* (New York: McGraw-Hill, 1954). For game theory at RAND, see Amadae, *Rationalizing*, 6–7, 76, 103; Paul Erickson, *The World the Game Theorists Made* (Chicago: University of Chicago Press, 2015); Hounshell, "RAND," 253–254; Leonard, *Von Neumann*, chapter 13; Mirowski, *Dreams*, 319–369.

21. Bernard Brodie, "Strategy as a Science," *World Politics* 1, no. 4 (July 1949), 479n13; John L. Kennedy, *The Uses and Limitations of Mathematical Models, Game Theory and Systems Analysis in Planning and Problem Solution* (Santa Monica, CA: RAND Corporation, P-266, February 11, 1952), 14.

22. Paul Kecskemeti, *The "Policy Sciences": Aspiration and Outlook* (Santa Monica, CA: RAND Corporation, P-287, April 1, 1952), 8, 15, 18; "Hans Speier, Gesprächsweise Mitteilungen zu einer intellektuellen Autobiographie [II]," transcript of interview by Ursula Ludz, October 8, 19, 20, 1982, 269, Folder 32, Box 2, SP.

23. Fred Kaplan highlights that "the issue of political games and their relevance was one that symbolized and further sharpened the rift between the social science division and the rest of RAND." Kaplan, *Wizards*, 202.

24. Jacob Burckhardt, *Die Kultur der Renaissance in Italien* (Berlin: Th. Knaur Nachf., 1928 [1860]); Bruce Bueno de Mesquita, *The War Trap* (New Haven: Yale University Press, 1981).

25. Sharon Ghamari-Tabrizi, "Simulating the Unthinkable: Gaming Future War in the 1950s and 1960s," *Social Studies of Science* 30, no. 2 (April 2000), 170–173.

26. United States Army, Strategy and Tactics Analysis Group (STAG), *Directory of Organizations and Activities Engaged or Interested in War Gaming* (Alexandria, VA: Defense Documentation Center for Scientific and Technical Information, Cameron Station, n.d. [1962]), 86; Alexander M. Mood, *War Gaming as a Technique of Analysis* (Santa Monica, CA: RAND Corporation, P-899, September 3, 1954), 4, 8. Some information in this and the subsequent paragraph comes from a RAND working

paper: Herbert Goldhamer, *Summary of Cold-War Game Activities in the Social Science Division* (Santa Monica, CA: RAND Corporation, D-2850, April 12, 1955), 1–2.

27. Sharon Ghamari-Tabrizi notes that the political game was a response to quantified and formal war games but emphasizes this immediate impetus as opposed to the larger culture within which the SSD operated. See Ghamari-Tabrizi, "Simulating," 173–174.

28. Chapter 1; Karl Mannheim, *Ideology and Utopia: An Introduction to the Sociology of Knowledge*, trans. Louis Wirth and Edward Shils (San Diego: Harcourt, 1985 [1936; original published in 1929]), 171–172; David Kettler and Volker Meja, *Karl Mannheim and the Crisis of Liberalism: The Secret of These New Times* (New Brunswick, NJ: Transaction Publishers, 1995), 69.

29. Mannheim, *Ideology*, 163–164, 171, 184, 172, 176.

30. Ibid., 167–168.

31. Christian Dayé, "In fremden Territorien: Delphi, Political Gaming und die subkutane Bedeutung tribaler Wissenskulturen," *Österreichische Zeitschrift für Geschichtswissenschaften* 25, no. 3 (2014), 101; Herbert Goldhamer, *The 1951 Korean Armistice Conference: A Personal Memoir* (Santa Monica, CA: RAND Corporation, P-7869, 1994), xi; Edward Shils, *A Fragment of a Sociological Autobiography: The History of My Pursuit of a Few Ideas*, ed. Steven Grosby (New Brunswick, NJ: Transaction Publishers, 2006), 33; Herbert Goldhamer to Speier, January 7, 1975, Folder 78, Box 3, SP; Shils, *Fragment*, 45. Christian Dayé has compellingly suggested that Speier and Goldhamer's unwillingness to cite Mannheim may be connected to Americans' reception of Mannheim's later writings on social planning. Specifically, Dayé argues that Speier and Goldhamer may have been reticent to cite Mannheim for fear of being designated socialist sympathizers. Christian Dayé, "Methods of Cold War Social Science: The Development of Political Gaming and Delphi as Means of Investigating Futures" (paper submitted to the 2012 Young Scholar Prize of the ISA Research Committee on the History of Sociology, awarded on the occasion of the Interim Conference "Changing Universities: Changing Sociology," University College Dublin, Ireland, June 27–30, 2012), 3n1.

32. Herbert Goldhamer, *Toward a Cold War Game* (Santa Monica, CA: RAND Corporation, D(L)-2603, October 22, 1954), 1, 4, 9.

33. Herbert Goldhamer and Speier, "Some Observations on Political Gaming," *World Politics* 12, no. 1 (October 1959), 71–83, quotation from 74–75.

34. Paul Kecskemeti, *Summary of Cold War Game Activities in the Social Science Division—May Experiment* (Santa Monica, CA: RAND Corporation, D-2975-RC, June 20, 1955), 59; Joseph M. Goldsen, *The Political Exercise: An Assessment of the Fourth Round* (Santa Monica, CA: RAND Corporation, D-3640-RC, May 30, 1956), 40; W. Phillips Davison, *A Summary of Experimental Research on "Political Gaming"* (Santa Monica, CA: RAND Corporation, D-5695-RC, October 1, 1958), 1.

35. Goldhamer and Speier, "Gaming," 73, 79.

36. This section is based on Milton G. Weiner, *An Introduction to War Games* (Santa Monica, CA: RAND Corporation, P-1773, August 1959).

37. Ibid., 23, 35.

38. Ibid., 28.

39. Goldsen, *Exercise*, 37; Davison, *Summary*, 9–10; Ghamari-Tabrizi, "Simulating," 176–177; Goldhamer and Speier, "Gaming," 80.

40. "Research Seminar in International Communication [Minutes]," October 25, 1956, Folder M.I.T.-C.I.S., Research in International Communication, Box 74, Ithiel de Sola Pool Papers, MC 440 (hereafter Pool Papers), Massachusetts Institute of Technology, Institute Archives and Special Collections, Cambridge, MA (hereafter MITASC); "Research Seminar in International Communication [Minutes]," December 13, 1956, Folder M.I.T.-C.I.S., Research in

International Communication, Box 74, Pool Papers, MITASC; "Research Seminar in International Communication [Minutes]," January 10, 1957, Folder M.I.T.-C.I.S., Research in International Communication, Box 74, Pool Papers, MITASC; Lincoln P. Bloomfield and Norman J. Padelford, "Teaching Note: Three Experiments in Political Gaming," *American Political Science Review* 53, no. 4 (December 1959), 1105. This and the following paragraph are based on Thomas B. Allen, *War Games: The Secret History of the Creators, Players, and Policy Makers Rehearsing World War III Today* (New York: McGraw-Hill, 1987), 148–160; Ghamari-Tabrizi, "Simulating," 176–179; Ghamari-Tabrizi, *Kahn*, 157–159.

41. Kaplan, *Wizards*, chapter 16; Francis J. McHugh, *Fundamentals of War Gaming*, 3rd ed. (Newport, RI: Naval War College, March 1966), 2–40; "Major DoD Efforts to Evaluate the Relative Strategic Strength of the United States and USSR," Enclosure, Clark Clifford to Maxwell Taylor, September 20, 1968, Document 215, *Foreign Relations of the United States, 1964–1968: Volume X, National Security Policy*, ed. David S. Patterson (Washington, DC: Government Printing Office, 2001), accessed December 7, 2016, https://history.state.gov/historicaldocuments/frus1964-68v10/d215#fn1. The list of participants in Schelling's game comes from Ghamari-Tabrizi, "Simulating," 213n52.

Conclusion

1. Daniel Bessner, "The Night Watchman: Hans Speier and the Making of the American National Security State" (PhD diss., Duke University, 2013), epilogue.

2. Hans Jakob Christoffel von Grimmelshausen, *Courage, The Adventuress and the False Messiah*, trans. Speier (Princeton: Princeton University Press, 1964); Speier, "A Woman Named Courage," in *The Arts in Society*, ed. Robert N. Wilson (Englewood Cliffs, NJ: Prentice-Hall, 1964), 197, 202, 209–210, 245.

3. Speier, "Trip Report," March 5, 1968, 20–21, 26, Folder 16, Box 9, Hans Speier Papers, German and Jewish Intellectual Émigré Collection, M. E. Grenander Department of Special Collections and Archives, University Libraries, University at Albany, State University of New York, Albany, NY (hereafter SP); Speier, Untitled ["As was to be expected . . ."], n.d. [1968], 2, Folder 46, Box 10, SP.

4. Untitled [Press release: "Dr. Hans Speier . . ."], August 14, 1969, University of Massachusetts at Amherst Records, Faculty and Staff (RG40/11), Special Collections and University Archives, University of Massachusetts at Amherst Libraries, Amherst, MA (hereafter Speier-Amherst Papers).

5. Speier, "Über den politischen Witz," *Freiburger Universitätsblätter* 11, no. 36 (June 1972), 13–26; Speier, *Witz und Politik: Essay über die Macht und das Lachen* (Zürich: Edition Interfrom AG, 1975); Speier, "The Truth in Hell: Maurice Joly on Modern Despotism," *Polity* 10, no. 1 (Autumn 1977), 18–32; Speier, "The Communication of Hidden Meaning," *Social Research* 44, no. 3 (Autumn 1977), 471–501; Harold D. Lasswell, Daniel Lerner, and Speier, *Propaganda and Communication in World History, Volume I: The Symbolic Instrument in Early Times; Volume II: Emergence of Public Opinion in the West; Volume III: A Pluralizing World in Formation* (Honolulu: University Press of Hawaii, 1979–1980); "Intellectuals, Knowledge, and the Public Arena," n.d. [1973], Folder 10, Box 4, SP; "Announcing a Conference on Intellectuals, Knowledge, and the Public Arena, May 10th–11th, University of Massachusetts, Amherst, Honoring the Work of Hans Speier, emeritus Robert M. MacIver, Professor of Sociology and Political Science," n.d. [Spring 1974], Speier-Amherst Papers.

6. Henry Kellerman, remarks in "A Memorial: Hans Speier, 1905–1990," April 1, 1990, Folder 14, Box 2, New School for Social Research Office of the Dean Records, NS.02.02.03, New School Archives and Special Collections, The New School, New York, NY (hereafter NSASC); Speier, *Die Angestellten vor dem Nationalsozialismus: Ein Beitrag zum Verständnis der deutschen Sozialstruktur, 1918–1933* (Göttingen: Vandenhoeck and Ruprecht, 1977); Speier, *German White-Collar Workers and the Rise of Hitler* (New Haven: Yale University Press, 1986); Folder 125, Box 3, SP; Speier, "Emil Lederer: Leben und Werk," in *Kapitalismus, Klassenstruktur und Probleme der Demokratie in Deutschland, 1910–1940*, by Emil Lederer (Göttingen: Vandenhoeck and Ruprecht, 1979), 253–272; Speier, *From the Ashes of Disgrace: A Journal from Germany, 1945–1955* (Amherst: University of Massachusetts Press, 1981); Speier, "Nicht die Auswanderung, sondern der Triumph Hitlers war die wichtige Erfahrung: Autobiographische Notizen eines Soziologen," *Exilforschung* 6 (1988), 152–173; Speier, *The Truth in Hell and Other Essays on Politics and Culture, 1935–1987* (New York: Oxford University Press, 1989); *The Exiles*, directed by Richard Kaplan (1989; New York: Exiles Project, 1989), videocassette.

7. Speier to Harry Gideonse, February 23, 1974, Folder 76, Box 3, SP; Joseph Greenbaum to Speier, June 7, 1974, Folder 2, Box 2, SP; 40th Anniversary (Graduate Faculty), 1973, [and] 50th Anniversary (Graduate Faculty), 1984, New School Publicity Office Records, NS.03.01.05, unprocessed collection, NSASC; Jonathan Fanton to Speier, October 29, 1984, Folder 2, Box 2, SP; Folder 135, Box 3, SP; Ira Katznelson, remarks in "A Memorial: Hans Speier, 1905–1990."

8. C. Wright Mills, *The Power Elite* (New York: Oxford University Press, 1959 [1956]), 353.

9. Joy Rohde, *Armed with Expertise: The Militarization of American Social Research during the Cold War* (Ithaca: Cornell University Press, 2013), 96; Noam Chomsky, "The Responsibility of Intellectuals," *New York Review of Books* 8, no. 3 (February 23, 1967), accessed December 9, 2016, http://www.nybooks.com/articles/1967/02/23/a-special-supplement-the-responsibility-of-intelle/.

10. Much of the information in this and the following paragraph comes from Rohde, *Armed*, chapters 4–5.

11. For RAND's influence, see RAND Corporation, *Sixty Ways RAND Has Made a Difference* (Santa Monica, CA: RAND Corporation, CP-526, 2008), accessed December 9, 2016, http://www.rand.org/about/history/60ways.html.

12. James Mann, *Rise of the Vulcans: The History of Bush's War Cabinet* (New York: Viking, 2004); David Milne, *Worldmaking: The Art and Science of American Diplomacy* (New York: Farrar, Straus and Giroux, 2015), chapter 8.

Archives Cited

CIA Records Search Tool (CREST)
Carnegie Mellon University Archives, Pittsburgh, PA
—Herbert Simon Collection
Columbia University Library, Rare Book and Manuscript Library, New York, NY
—Carnegie Corporation Oral History Project
—Paul Felix Lazarsfeld Papers
Dartmouth College, Rauner Library, Hanover, NH
—Shepard Stone Papers
Dwight D. Eisenhower Presidential Library, Abilene, KS
—C. D. Jackson Papers
—Psychological Strategy Board Central File Series
Federal Bureau of Investigation
Harvard University Archives, Cambridge, MA
—Papers of Samuel Andrew Stouffer
Harry S. Truman Presidential Library, Independence, MO
—Psychological Strategy Board Files
Heidelberg University Archives, Heidelberg, Germany

Indiana University–Purdue University Library, Ruth Lilly Special Collections and Archives, Indianapolis, IN
—Foundation Center Historical Foundation Collection
Library of Congress, Manuscript Division, Washington, DC
—Ernst Kris Papers
—Margaret Mead Papers and South Pacific Ethnographic Archives
Massachusetts Institute of Technology Archives and Special Collections, Cambridge, MA
—Ithiel de Sola Pool Papers
—Massachusetts Institute of Technology, Center for International Studies Records
—Max F. Millikan Papers
—Office of the President, Records of Karl Taylor Compton and James Rhyne Killian
National Air and Space Museum, Smithsonian Institution, Washington, DC
—RAND History Project Interviews
National Archives at College Park, College Park, MD
—Record Group 59, General Records of the Department of State
—Record Group 208, Records of the Office of War Information
—Record Group 262, Records of the Foreign Broadcast Intelligence Service
—Record Group 286, Records of the Agency for International Development
—Record Group 466, Records of the U.S. High Commissioner for Germany
The New School Archives and Special Collections, New York, NY
—Arthur J. Vidich Papers
—Graduate Faculty of the New School for Social Research Collection, 1933–2011
—Institute of World Affairs Records
—New School Course Catalogues, 1919–2011
—New School for Social Research Office of the Dean Records
—New School Publicity Office Records
RAND Corporation, RAND Corporate Archives, Santa Monica, CA
—Brownlee Haydon Collection
—J. Richard Goldstein Papers
—Lawrence J. Henderson Papers
Rockefeller Archive Center, Sleepy Hollow, NY
—Ford Foundation Records
—Rockefeller Foundation Records

Smithsonian Institution Archives, Washington, DC
—The Research and Development (RAND) Corporation Interviews
Stanford University Libraries, Department of Special Collections and University Archives, Stanford, CA
—Center for Advanced Study in the Behavioral Sciences Records
State University at Albany, M. E. Grenander Department of Special Collections and Archives, University Libraries, German and Jewish Intellectual Émigré Collection, Albany, NY
—Arnold Brecht Papers
—Hans Speier Papers
—Otto Kirchheimer Papers
University of California–Los Angeles, UCLA Library Special Collections, Charles E. Young Research Library, Los Angeles, California
—Bernard Brodie Papers
University of Chicago Library, Special Collections Research Center, Chicago, IL
—Edward A. Shils Papers
—Leo Strauss Papers
—Louis Wirth Papers
—Society for Social Research, Records, 1923–1956
University of Illinois at Urbana-Champaign Archives, Urbana, IL
—Philip E. Mosely Collection
University of Massachusetts at Amherst Records, Special Collections and University Archives, Amherst, MA
University of Nebraska–Lincoln, Archives and Special Collections, Lincoln, NE
—Alvin Johnson, Economics Papers
University of Texas at Austin, Dolph Briscoe Center for American History, Austin, TX
—Charles Wright Mills Papers
University Library Frankfurt a.M., Archives Center, Germany
—Estate Leo Löwenthal
—Estate Max Horkheimer
U.S. Declassified Documents Online
Yale University Library, Manuscripts and Archives, New Haven, CT
—Alvin Saunders Johnson Papers
—Harold Dwight Lasswell Papers

Index

Note: page numbers followed by "f" and "n" refer to figures and endnotes.